Contents

Part Three: The Peace Process

The New Israel

The New Israel

Peacemaking and Liberalization

Edited by
Gershon Shafir
Yoav Peled

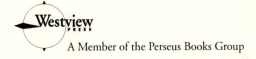

A Member of the Perseus Books Group

Copyright © 2000 by Westview Press, A Member of the Perseus Books Group

Published in 2000 in the United States of America by Westview Press, 5500 Central Avenue, Boulder, Colorado 80301–2877, and in the United Kingdom by Westview Press, 12 Hid's Copse Road, Cumnor Hill, Oxford OX2 9JJ

Find us on the World Wide Web at www.westviewpress.com

The new Israel: peacemaking and liberalization / [edited by] Gershon Shafir, Yoav Peled.
    p. cm.
Includes bibliographical references and index.
ISBN 0-8133-3567-1 (hc) —ISBN 0-8133-3873-5 (pb)
    1. Israel—Economic conditions.   2. Israel—Economic policy.
3. Peace.   I. Shafir, Gershon.   II. Peled, Yoav.
HC415.25.N485 1999
338.95694—dc21   99-41453
                                                                        CIP

The paper used in this publication meets the requirements of the American National Standard for Permanence of Paper for Printed Library Materials Z39.48–1984.

PERSEUS
POD
ON DEMAND   10   9   8   7   6   5   4   3   2   1

To Neeva Shafir with love
To the memory of Matti Peled

Acronyms

BOI	Bank of Israel
CCITT	International Consultative Committee for Telephones and Telegraph
CZA	Central Zionist Archive
DOP	Declaration of Principles
EESP	Emergency Economic Stabilization Plan
EU	European Union
FDI	Foreign direct investment
GATS	General Agreement on Trade in Services
GATT	General Agreement on Tariffs and Trade
GDP	Gross Domestic Product
GZ	General Zionists
HE	Histadrut Executive
HLC	Haifa Labor Council
IDF	Israel Defense Forces
IMF	International Monetary Fund
ISA	Israel State Archive
ISI	"import substitution industrialization"
ITU	International Telecom Union
JNF	Jewish National Fund
LA	Labor Archive
LSM	Labor Settlement Movement
MAI	Manufacturers' Association of Israel
MENA	Middle East/North Africa
MIL	Israel Management Center
NAT	National Telecommunication Authority
NIS	New Israel Shekel
NOC	national oil companies
OPEC	Organization of Petroleum Exporting Countries
PAWS	Palestine Arab Workers' Society
PEC	Palestine Economic Corporation
PJCA	Palestine Jewish Colonization Association
PLL	Palestine Labor League
PPL	Palestine Potash, Ltd.
PTTs	Post, Telegraph, and Telephone administrations

QIZ   Qualifying Industrial Zone
REDWG   Regional Economic Development Working Group
TASE   Tel Aviv Stock Exchange
WEF   World Economic Forum
WTO   World Trade Organization
WZO   World Zionist Organization
ZOA   Zionist Organization of America

1

Introduction:
The Socioeconomic Liberalization of Israel

GERSHON SHAFIR AND YOAV PELED

In September 1993 Israel and the Palestine Liberation Organization stunned the world by signing the Oslo Accords that stipulated mutual recognition between the two contracting parties and the beginning of Israeli withdrawal from Palestinian territories that had been occupied since 1967. Thus, the Israeli-Palestinian conflict, which had been on everyone's short list of the world's most intransigent international feuds, took a decisive step toward peaceful resolution.

On the Israeli side, the Oslo Accords signaled the maturation of a long and painful process of political change. Parallel to this political change, an equally profound, though less well-known economic transformation was also taking place. Between 1975 and 1995 Israel's GDP grew sevenfold and its "dollar product" increased by about 600 percent. At the end of 1996 this growth rate placed the per capita income of Israelis at $16,690 and in the twenty-first place internationally, ahead of some member countries of the European Union, such as Spain. In April 1997, in recognition of its rapid growth, Israel was added by the IMF, together with the East Asian "tigers"—Singapore, South Korea, Hong Kong, and Taiwan—to its list of developed countries.

The thesis we wish to advance in this volume is that the two processes—peacemaking and economic growth—are closely related. For this purpose, the various chapters in the volume examine the forces that have shaped the Israeli economy and society in the past 100 years, since the onset of Zionist settlement in Palestine, and try to account for their contemporary transformation and decipher their relation to the peace process. Our claim, it should be emphasized at the outset, is *not* that the growth and liberalization of the Israeli economy can, by themselves, account for Israel's decision to explore the option of peace. Other factors, such as the collapse of the Soviet Union and the 1991 Gulf War, have played their part in this decision, as has, most importantly, the *intifada*, the national uprising of the Palestinians living in the West Bank and the Gaza Strip.

The six-year *intifada* (1987–1993) shook the confidence of Israeli decision makers in their ability to control the Palestinians in the occupied territories; it also sharply reduced the economic benefits accruing to Israel from the continued occupation. (Lustick, 1993, 1996) In itself, however, the *intifada* did not defeat Israel militarily nor did it cripple its economy. It merely spurred Israel's leaders in new directions already made attractive to the country's political and economic elites by ongoing social changes. By the same token, these very social changes limited the ability of Israel's security forces to use excessively repressive measures in their efforts to quell the uprising.

Since the mid-1980s Israel's economic elites had benefited from a profound multi-step process which recast the Israeli economy from its protectionist and state-centered origins into a more internationally-oriented, neo-liberal economy. Thus began the transformation of Israel's social structure, a process that, as this volume shows, while still partial and riled with contradictions and occasional setbacks, has already revolutionized Israeli society beyond recognition and has made a decisive contribution to the moderation of Israeli attitudes toward the Palestinian people and Palestinian nationalism.

The Israeli-Palestinian conflict had remained at an impasse so long as it was viewed solely in security terms, as an ethnic or national confrontation. The conflict became "solvable" when it was reconceptualized as the main obstacle to the full participation of Israeli businesses in the international economy, at a time when the economic stakes in the global race between "winning" and "losing" countries became enormously high. In the new global economy, favorite countries have become not the biggest ones, but rather the "fastest integrators." Under this new thinking, territorial, economic, and power redistribution were subjected to the primacy of economic growth. Thus the potential was created for replacing a zero-sum game, in which one side's gain is the other side's loss, with an open-ended approach, in which opposing sides might both come out ahead by compromising.

Part One: A State-Centered Economy

Zionist attempts to colonize the economically unattractive Palestine through private initiative only inevitably ended in failure. Capitalist profit calculations, which mandated the employment of low-paid Arab workers on Jewish-owned land, were at odds with the nationalist goal of creating a Jewish majority. The demographic needs of Zionism favored the socialist approach and co-operative institutions of the Labor Settlement Movement (LSM), because these were conducive to massive Jewish immigration as well as to the disciplining of the immigrants themselves in the service of national goals. The predominant Zionist method of colonization—evolved by the LSM—was based on the imposition of non-market mechanisms on land allocation and labor relations. This method was intended not only to close off

Jewish agricultural and industrial enterprises to Arab workers, but also to subsidize the wages of Jewish workers, who otherwise might have emigrated to more attractive locations.

The LSM's colonization method rested on two exclusivist pillars: the World Zionist Organization's Jewish National Fund (JNF) and the LSM's own umbrella labor organization—the Histadrut. The aims of the JNF and the Histadrut were the removal of land and labor, respectively, from the market, closing them off to Palestinian Arabs. Thus, the Histadrut, incongruously for a labor union, became the owner of many large economic enterprises which employed (and subsidized) solely Jewish workers. These enterprises were centralized under the umbrella of Hevrat Ha'ovdim (The Workers' Society) holding company, formally owned by the Histadrut membership.

On land purchased and owned by the JNF, cooperative settlements of only Jewish members—kibbutzim and moshavim—were established. Within this separate, co-operative Jewish economic sector, Jewish immigrants were able to settle the land and attain a subsidized European standard of living, giving Zionist colonization its particular cast. This colonization method attracted Jewish immigrants to Palestine by providing them with a relatively high living standard not through high productivity but rather by means of subsidizing the economy by foreign aid, fund-raising among diaspora Jews and international loans.

Two of the three chapters of Part One illustrate some consequences of this colonization method by examining not the standard cases of cooperative Histadrut enterprises but rather a few of the major privately-owned industrial concerns that operated in pre–1948 Palestine. Michal Frenkel and her co-authors discuss Palestine Potash Ltd., the largest Jewish-owned private company in the Mandatory period. The company, established in order to extract potash from the Dead Sea, was owned by private British and American shareholders and employed both organized and non-organized Jewish and Arab workers. The authors discuss the ways in which the aura of pioneering (*chalutziyut*) was extended from cooperative agricultural settlement to privately-owned industry that was also deemed helpful to Zionist colonization. This clearly indicated that the Zionists' preference for collective economic ventures resulted from the expediencies of the colonization process itself rather than from principled opposition to private enterprise.

The price private enterprise had to pay for being defined as a national project was to adopt the dominant nation-building discourse of the LSM. By adopting this discourse the owners of private enterprises could legitimate their own particular concerns, such as productivity and profit, gain access on favorable terms to the resources of the Zionist movement, and discipline their Jewish workers. Ironically, then, the colonization method of the LSM, adopted in consequence of the failure of private-enterprise colonization, provided the conditions for the success of Jewish private capital in Palestine.

Deborah Bernstein focuses on labor relations in three Jewish-owned industrial companies that employed both Jewish and Arab workers. She is particularly concerned with the failed efforts of Jewish and Arab workers to cooperate in struggling for better wages and working conditions. These efforts failed because Jewish and Arab workers occupied different niches within the labor market, even when working for the same firm, and because the Histadrut was more interested in banishing Arab workers from Jewish-owned enterprises altogether, than in improving the lot of Jewish workers. Thus, just like Frenkel et. al., Bernstein also shows how the priority of the national dictum subverted whatever genuine socialist strivings there were in the project of Zionist colonization. (Sternhell, 1998)

The dual goals of immigration and colonization led to the identification of state-building with economic development in the Yishuv (Jewish community in pre-1948 Palestine). This institution-building aspect of its settlement project accounts for the frequent description of Zionism as revolutionary, a designation that bestowed on Zionist institutions, and later on the Israeli state as well, the legitimation they needed for imposing a tutelary regime on society.

Israel was not "exceptional" in approaching the task of economic development with statist tools. It shared this approach with many of the new states formed after World War II and, indeed, with all late developers that fashioned themselves into self-conscious "developmentalist states." But Israel already was, on its foundation, a "strong state" in Joel Migdal's terms (1988), with a long and, in contrast to many other new states, successful practice of developmentalism. The opposition of the Palestinian population to Zionist colonization in general, and to its separatist and exclusionary methods in particular, accounts for the Yishuv's and Israel's investment in powerful war-making capacities which further contributed to the construction of a powerful state. The confluence of nationalist and colonial goals and the disciplinary means of socialist and military practices endowed the institutions of the Israeli state-in-the-making with a generous measure of autonomy. This developmental model continued to work relatively successfully for about two and half decades after Israel's establishment as a sovereign state. (Levy, 1997)

With sovereignty, the goal of providing employment for new immigrants became even more pressing. Priority was therefore assigned to labor-intensive economic sectors, most prominently agriculture. Only in 1952, with the exhaustion of untapped agricultural assets, was the first industrial policy adopted, aiming, as in so many other new industrializing states, at import substitution, in order to ease foreign currency shortages. The main tools of the new industrial policy were exchange-rate controls, multiple exchange rates, direct administrative allocation of foreign currency, investment subsidies, and tariff barriers to protect infant industries.

In order to incorporate the new immigrants without harming the interests of veteran Jewish workers, the state, led by the major political party of the LSM, Mapai, created a multi-tiered split labor market. In this market Palestinian Arabs were excluded from the Jewish economy altogether (a long-sought after goal of the LSM), while new immigrants, mostly mizrachim (Jews hailing from Muslim countries) were confined to its secondary sector. As Dov Khenin argues, this was a crucial decision both for the future development of Israeli society and for Mapai itself.

By splitting the Jewish labor market along ethnic lines, Mapai gave up the option of forging a political alliance between veteran and newcomer workers and chose, instead, to ally its traditional power base—veteran ashkenazi (Jews hailing from Western, mostly Eastern European countries) workers and the LSM bureaucracy—with the established middle classes. This was the source of Mapai's future alienation from the Jewish working class and led to its loss of control of the government in 1977.

Khenin's argument is based on a discourse analysis of the changing rhetoric of Mapai's election campaigns of the 1950s. He argues that Mapai's definition of its own constituency—the "us" versus its political rivals the "them"—shifted during the 1950s from a one-way upwards demarcation, distinguishing Mapai's constituency from the middle classes represented by the General Zionists, to a two-way demarcation, distinguishing its constituency *both* from the middle classes above it and from the mizrachi proletariat below it. This shift paralleled the change that occurred in Mapai's socio-economic platform, from mild criticism of the existing capitalist social order to its defense. In policy terms, in addition to the construction of a split labor market, Mapai's change of heart was reflected in discarding the policy of economic austerity and rationing *(tsena),* adopted in 1949, and blaming its adoption in the first place on the General Zionists. (Levy, 1999)

Mapai's alliance with the middle classes was cemented in the early 1960s, as new efforts were undertaken to enhance exports, alongside import substitution. The new industrial policy consisted in subsidizing exporting companies and selectively encouraging industries, such as textiles, that were expected to perform in the international market. The 1955–1965 decade indeed witnessed rapid growth of the economy: a 12 percent per annum growth of industrial production, accompanied by an 5.5 percent growth in employment, 10 percent in capital reserves, and 20 percent of exports. (Bar, 1990, p.29) With the exception of the 1965–1967 recession, state-centered development was a success until 1974.

The creation of a government-owned military industrial complex began as yet another facet of the policy of "import substitution industrialization" (ISI); its extension, as it were, to a new sphere. The impetus was an embargo on military sales to Israel imposed by the French government in the wake of the 1967 war, and the ensuing resolve of the Israeli government to develop the production capacity in Israel for supplying the Israeli military with its main weapons systems. Military production then became the engine of growth and the focus of knowledge dissemination for advanced high technology industries, and the primary influence in the modernization of industry and of large segments of the economy in general. The new industries trained and recruited technological and managerial personnel, a portion of which subsequently moved to private and/or civilian industry as employees and entrepreneurs. Military production generated spin-offs of civilian uses, and at the end of the 1970s high-tech civilian companies began to expand rapidly. Since their major client was the Israeli military, however, the new companies remained tied to the state and failed to develop an entrepreneurial approach.

Starting in the late 1970s, the complex of military industries became the main source of growth for exports, moving Israeli industry from ISI to genuine export orientation. Defense corporations, that included three of Israel's top five corporations, had become major earners of foreign currency. Not only did military production generate relatively high added-value, it also helped pry open doors for Israeli civilian products. By the mid-1980s, however, as Israel's military budgets were beginning to decline in the wake of the peace agreement with Egypt, and in the context of the general downturn experienced by the Israeli economy since 1974, the military industrial complex was also plunged into a veritable crisis.

Israel's state-building era left a legacy of four distinct characteristics in the area of economic development and social organization: (1) a state-driven, or dirigiste, economic growth, typical of "developmentalist states," and (2) unparalleled financial dependence on non-investment type foreign capital, mostly in the form of unilateral transfers (hence better described as foreign subsidies). The Zionist movement and the Yishuv were in this sense rentier bodies, just as Israel would become a rentier state. This massive foreign aid, higher per capita than for any other country, has traditionally been used to help governments achieve a budgetary balance without a substantial reduction in the size of the public sector. Features (1) and (2) became interconnected after the gaining of sovereignty in 1948, when the state became the main conduit of capital influx and, consequently, maintained and enhanced its control, conjointly with the Histadrut, over the economy. In the 1960–1968 period, Histadrut-owned enterprises employed an average of 24 percent of the labor force, and produced 22 percent of the domestic product, with the state producing 25 percent. (3) The building of quasi-state institutions provided the LSM with its elan and subsequent political hegemony. Membership in its institutions provided a set of social citizenship rights which cemented the loyalty of the LSM's members and encouraged the self-organization of other social groups, mostly Orthodox Jews, as recipients of state largesse. The dependence of the citizens on state institutions and their resources was largely responsible for ensuring their support for the leadership of Mapai and for keeping it in power continuously for a generation-and-a-half (1936–1977). (4) The predominance of the state and its virtually exclusive control over imported capital prevented the emergence of an autonomous entrepreneurial stratum. All of these characteristics were to be drastically transformed in the subsequent period, the period of liberalization.

Part Two: Liberalization

Part Two presents the transformation of the Israeli economy and society since 1974. Among the topics discussed are the successful Emergency Economic Stabilization Plan (EESP) undertaken by Shimon Peres's government of national unity in 1985, which drastically reduced monetary inflation that had reached an annual rate of 466 percent; the shrinking of state control over the capital markets; the opening of the Israeli economy to the world; the decline and collapse of the Histadrut's economic and social welfare enterprises; and the "constitutional revolution" of the 1990s. The partial, uneven and sometimes contradictory character of the new, neo-liberal social order is also highlighted, particularly by Michael Shalev and David Levi-Faur, while Uri Ram emphasizes, among other things, the localistic reaction to globalization by some of the groups that have been harmed by the transformation of the Israeli economy and society.

As shown most comprehensively by Michael Shalev, the policy of accelerated economic growth through inflows of unilateral capital transfers and immigration, insulated from market forces, worked remarkably well, with some interruptions, from the 1920s until the war and energy crisis of 1973. For the fifteen years between 1974 and 1989, Israel's GDP remained relatively stagnant, while the first half of the 1980s was, according to Economic Models, an economic forecasting firm, "the worst period in the history of the Israeli economy [as] both inflation and the foreign debt seemed to spiral out of control." (1993, p.31) The annual growth of industrial production fell from an average of 12 percent in the 1960s and early 1970s to 3.8 percent in the 1973–1987 period, accompanied by falling productivity. According to economists Assaf Razin and Efraim Sadka, "the period which started with the [1973] Yom Kippur War and lasted until the . . . wave of immigration [from the ex-Soviet Union] which began in 1990 is known as the 'lost years.'" (Razin and Sadka, 1993, p.16)

Not until 1985 was a new model of development adopted, based primarily on the reduction of state-intervention, the liberalization of the capital markets, and significant opening of the economy to the world. The transformation of the Israeli economy has had some parallels with the liberalization of the British and American economies under Margaret Thatcher and Ronald Reagan. But whereas the British and American experiences were presented as revival movements—returning to a period prior to massive state intervention—in Israel there never was a period approximating free enterprise. Thus, the change in Israel, even if it has not gone as far as it has in Great Britain or the United States, is far more radical, because it has shallower roots and the opposition to it is more potent. As amply demonstrated in the chapters of Part Two, in Israel the transformation was, indeed, revolutionary; it combined interlocking changes in economic organization, labor relations, social welfare and constitutional law. But, as these chapters also show, the shape Israeli society is assuming in the wake of these changes is still not entirely clear and is open to varying interpretations.

Attempts to integrate Israel into the world economy had commenced already in the 1970s, and took the form of partial free trade agreements with the European Community (since 1992, the European Union) in 1975 and with the United States in 1985. A significant area in which Israel remained insulated, however, was international finance. Capital flows to Israel were by and large not market-driven but unilateral. Israel received only a very small share of foreign investment and even that was frequently "Jewish" capital. The capital that did arrive made Israel into a relatively high-wage economy, effectively blocking its use for offshore production. For-

eign capital has generally bypassed Israel because of its relatively high wage structure, comparatively low domestic demand, interstate conflict, and the Arab boycott.
(Barnett, 1996)

Fearful of the secondary Arab boycott, that severed economic relations with companies doing business with Israel, multinational companies were unwilling to invest
in Israel and, as a result, Israel ranked second from the bottom, even when compared with all Third World states, in its share of firms fully owned by foreigners. No
more than 5 percent of all investment in Israel until the late 1970s was undertaken
by multinational corporations. In short, though seeking to create an open economy,
as long as the Arab boycott, especially the secondary boycott, was in effect, Israel
was able to take only partial advantage of its willingness to partake in the process of
economic globalization.

As emphasized particularly by Grinberg and Shafir, capital formation in Israel was
traditionally a circular affair: the Histadrut's pension and provident funds were
made available to the government to finance public and private investments it approved. In addition, in Efraim Kleiman's calculation, approximately three-quarters
of all capital imports were received by the public sector, which, in turn, financed
nearly two-thirds of all capital formation. (Kleiman, 1967, p.233) The economy's
chief source of investment credit remained under effective government control, regardless of whether the investment was effected in the public, Histadrut, or private
sector. As long as the private sector remained dependent on government-allocated
credit, it remained for all practical purposes another branch of government and
could not attain autonomy. What seemed like a private sector was, in fact, tied to
the state's apron strings. No autonomous business sector could emerge, and business
decisions were made in response to, or as part of, political decisions.

The 1985 Stabilization Plan led to the liberalization of the capital market by
gradually abolishing its most thoroughly interventionist, and inflationary, instrument: the fixed interest non-tradable public bonds issued to pension funds. An even
more important role in liberating the capital markets was the relaxation of the rules
governing the borrowing of foreign capital. Accompanying reforms, mentioned by
Shalev in this volume, included substantial privatization, the institution of a stable
exchange rate, reduced capital subsidies and increasing governmental resistance to
bailouts of individual firms (but not necessarily of whole economic sectors) and cuts
in the defense budget and budget deficit. These economic reforms have enabled the
Israeli economy to take advantage of globalization processes and have thus affected
Israel's social structure. If the second generation of the LSM elite (such as Yitzhak
Rabin and Shimon Peres) made their careers in the various public bureaucracies, the
third generation, those who have come of age after 1967, were drawn to the private
sector. At the same time, increased economic opportunities opened up new venues
of mobility for individuals from social strata outside the LSM.

In this new environment, business executives, even of government- or Histadrut-owned corporations, could make themselves autonomous by raising equity
through the newly opened private venues. They have been the principal champions

of economic liberalization and of the integration of Israel's economy with the world market through the reduction of tariff and administrative barriers. (Note, however, the dissenting view of David Levi-Faur, who argues that in Israel even the liberalization drive has been led by the state.) As shown by Shalev, by Ram, and by Grinberg and Shafir, the growth in the influence of capital was accompanied by the weakening of labor unions. This was signaled, for example, by the demise, especially in the private sector, of the economy-wide "framework agreements," the biannual collective wage agreements that had served as the basis for industrial, professional, and enterprise-level negotiations. Most dramatically, the Labor movement lost control of its formative institution—the Histadrut—which had been fatally weakened by the rapid inflation of the early 1980s and by the economic changes introduced since 1985. The final coup de grace came with the passage in 1994 of the State Health Insurance Law that nationalized Israel's HMOs, including the Histadrut's all-important Kupat Holim, that had served as the Histadrut's main vehicle of recruitment and revenues. This process is carefully portrayed in Grinberg and Shafir's chapter.

David Levi-Faur's chapter focuses on the liberalization of two key sectors of the Israeli economy, telecommunications and energy, and uses it to illustrate his argument that liberalization, in Israel as elsewhere, is a much more complex and complicated process than simply the retreat of the state and the expansion of the market. Judged by the standard ideological claim that privatization is meant to increase competition and thus benefit consumers, the privatization of the telecommunications sector in Israel must be judged a relative success, while that of the energy sector must be judged a relative failure. In the former sector partial privatization has resulted in greater competition and price reductions (although the final outcome is still far from being clear), while in the latter it has not. These sectoral differences have to do with the different kinds of economic activities that take place in these two sectors, with the power regimes that have prevailed in them, both globally and locally, and with their particular histories in Israel. Generally, Levi-Faur argues, characterizing liberalization as a transition from a "developmental state" to a "competition state" is an over-simplification. In Israel, as elsewhere, the state continues to play a crucial, if different, role in the economy even after liberalization, and competition is not necessarily enhanced by the transfer of public resources to private hands.

The cultural and legal aspects of liberalization are emphasized in the chapters by Uri Ram and Ran Hirschl, respectively. Drawing on Benjamin Barber's famous distinction between Jihad and McWorld, (Barber, 1996) Ram argues that the two should be seen as two sides of the same coin: Jihad is a reaction to McWorld by the economic, political and cultural losers of globalization. (Beyer, 1994) In Israeli Jewish political culture these two phenomena appear as neo-liberal post-Zionism (that is not always conscious of its latter quality) and as nationalist and religious neo-Zionism. In political behavior this division is expressed as voting for the Left and Right, respectively. Judging by the results of the 1996 general elections, neo-

Zionists outnumber post-Zionists among Israeli Jews by a ratio of 55:45. While the neo-Zionist camp is not uniformly opposed to the peace process (which since 1993 has always enjoyed the support of the majority of Israelis), it is from within this camp that the opposition to the peace process comes.

Ran Hirschl analyzes the "constitutional revolution" that took place in Israel in 1992, with the passage of two constitutional "basic laws" protecting human rights, and places it in the context of the general neo-liberal transformation of the society. Instead of the conventional view that lauds these laws, and subsequent adjudication, as affirming Israel's commitment to human rights, Hirschl emphasizes their limited effect in many areas of civil rights and their great effect in weakening traditional defenses of social and workers' rights. Thus, the "constitutional revolution" should be seen, Hirschl argues, primarily as establishing the legal nexus necessary for the transition to a free-enterprise economy.

Taken together, the essays of Part Two problematize the meaning of social and economic liberalization on at least three levels: the very nature of the process of liberalization, in any society; its particular manifestation in Israel; and its political consequences. On the most general level, none of the major phenomena commonly associated with liberalization—privatization, deregulation, state contraction, economic globalization, decline of the welfare state—turn out to appear in an unproblematic manner. What does appear is a major change in the distribution of power and wealth in the society, in a way that benefits the owners of private capital at the expense of non-owners.

In Israel, where historically the public sector, much of it owned by the Histadrut, had played a major role in the economy, the transformation has been particularly acute and particularly riddled with contradictions. The Histadrut's power stemmed in large measure from the fact that it combined within itself union representation, capital ownership and social citizenship. Liberalization, therefore, could not proceed without its agreement or destruction. Yet, the multifaceted character of the Histadrut made it vulnerable to pressure from the state that controlled the flow of subsidies on which all sectors of the economy were dependent. It is mainly for this reason that in Israel the state has been leading the move toward liberalization, and that a crucially important measure of liberalization has been the *nationalization* of the healthcare system.

Lastly, liberalization has generated its own opposition in the form of anti-liberal political movements, many of them religiously fundamentalist. This phenomenon is not unique to Israel, of course, but it has taken on a particularly acute form there because of the salience of Jewish religion in Israeli politics and because of the protracted conflict between Arabs and Jews. The advocates of liberalization have also advocated reconciliation with the Arabs and, perforce, a diminution of the role of Jewish religion in public life. This has resulted in the crystallization of a political camp that opposes all three elements of the liberal program, although not necessarily with the same intensity. The fact that membership in each of these two political camps correlates very highly with (Jewish) ethnic origin, also contributes to the fe-

Ashkenazi v. Mizrahi

rocity of the debate between them. The implications of this complex situation on the prospects for peace will be discussed in the remaining chapters of this volume.

Part Three: The Peace Process

Part Three examines directly the interaction between economic transformation and the peace process. Shafir and Peled analyze the relationships between economic and social liberalization in Israel and the breakthrough achieved by the Oslo Accords, emphasizing the interest of the new Israeli economic elites in joining the process of economic globalization. Jonathan Paris describes the international economic bodies, primarily the Middle East/North Africa (MENA) economic summits, that were designed to translate political progress in the peace process to economic cooperation between Israel and its neighbors.

The structural transformation of the Israeli economy that began in the mid-1980s was motivated, at least in part, by the growing confidence of the Israeli economic elites that they could compete in the open market, both domestically and internationally, and that they no longer needed to be protected by the institutions of the state-centered economy. However, as long as the Arab boycott remained in force, and the Israeli-Arab conflict threatened to destabilize the region at any moment, Israel was ignored by multinational companies and remained outside the international investment circuit. Not surprisingly, therefore, prominent Israeli business leaders, as well as academic economists, played a prominent role, alongside traditionally "dovish" politicians, in the effort to reconceptualize the Israeli-Palestinian conflict in economic, rather than strictly geo-strategic terms.

As Shafir and Peled relate in their chapter, in the Jerusalem Business Conference held one week before the crucial 1992 Israeli national elections, Dov Lautman, President of the Israeli Manufacturers' Association, issued his first open statement linking the then deadlocked Madrid peace talks to economic issues. In his words, the major obstacle to foreign investment in the Israeli economy was regional instability, and only a combination of an appropriate economic policy and progress in the peace talks could make Israel attractive to foreign investors. In January 1993, Lautman promised that a breakthrough in the peace talks in the coming year would constitute an important turning point in the fortunes of the Israeli economy in general and of Israeli industry in particular. Eli Hurvitz, a past President of the same body, and Danny Gillerman, Chairman of the Association of Chambers of Commerce, were among the other vocal business supporters of the peace process. Benny Gaon, CEO of Koor, the largest Israeli conglomerate, was among the first to seek business relations with the Arab world in general and with the Palestinians in particular. In addition, the hotel industry that had known ups and downs due to the instability of the region, was clearly thrilled with the prospects of peace. With the backing of these business leaders, the Rabin government could "sell" its peace efforts to the public not only by promising an end to the *intifada* and greater personal security, but also by presenting peace as the key to economic prosperity and well-being.

The broad framework for global involvement, economic as well as political, in the Middle East peace process was laid out in the novel approach taken by the Bush administration after the Gulf War of 1991: the simultaneous conduct of bilateral and multilateral talks. The bilateral talks took place between Israel and each of its Arabs interlocutors—the Palestinians, Syria, and Jordan—separately, and covered political issues such as borders, sovereignty, and recognition. The multilateral talks included international, as well as additional regional participants, and focused on economic and security issues: water resources, refugees, arms control and regional security, environment, and regional economic development. The combination of bilateral and multilateral talks, taking place simultaneously, highlighted the global dimension of Middle Eastern peace and the assumption that a measure of economic cooperation could spur the peace process along.

As related by Jonathan Paris, a participant-observer of the process, the first Middle East/North Africa (MENA) Economic Summit in Casablanca, convened by the Council on Foreign Relations and the Davos-based World Economic Forum in the fall of 1994, was motivated by the desire to reinforce the political track of normalizing Arab-Israeli relations by generating economic incentives to peace. Given the reluctance of Arabs and Israelis to meet in political and cultural forums, the idea was to bring together Arab and Israeli business people in a large conference in an Arab country that might result in joint ventures and other investments, with positive spillover effects onto the political track.

Out of the 1994 Casablanca Economic Summit came the MENA Executive Secretariat, plans for a Middle East Bank for Development and Cooperation, a blue ribbon panel of the Council on Foreign Relations' Middle East Economic Strategy Group chaired by Paul Volcker, former Chairman of the Federal Reserve Board, and a regional tourism board and business council. Working groups from the core peace parties were formed to identify fast track cross-border infrastructure and transportation projects that could be presented to the next MENA Summits. The MENA Economic Summits themselves were to have become institutionalized as annual events in the region.

Israel's economic transformation was mirrored by similar transformations in the Arab countries. The Egyptian private sector, for example, had prodded the Egyptian government into undertaking deep economic reforms, legislative changes, privatization measures and the like, spurred by the international focus on Egypt. The Israeli business community was quick to note these developments in the Arab countries and formed joint business councils, first with Jordan and then with Egypt. It was hoped that these informal business councils, as well as the MENA summits, would help keep their respective governments on the track of peace by linking each country's economic growth and prosperity to continuation of the peace process.

The results of 1996 elections in Israel, and the obstacles put in the path of the peace process by the Netanyahu government, resulted in the suspension of most Israeli-Arab economic relations as well, including the MENA summits themselves. But the peace/prosperity link is hard to sever, as evidenced by the decline experienced by the Israeli economy since 1997. Prime Minister Netanyahu, like many other leaders of the Israeli Right, though very reluctant to accommodate Palestinian national aspirations, is committed to the continuation of economic liberalization. Since liberalization requires extensive economic relations with the outside world, and these are not likely to develop in a warlike atmosphere, the Netanyahu government had no choice but to accept the agreement negotiated at Wye Plantation in 1998. This agreement resulted in the desertion of the most right-wing members of Netanyahu's governing coalition and brought about the fall of his government.

We concluded the preparation of this volume on the eve of the May 1999 national elections in Israel. It is our hope, and undoubtedly the hope of all the contributors to this volume, that, whatever their results, after the elections we will see the vigorous resumption of the peace process, the development of multi-faceted, including economic, relations between Israel and its Arab neighbors. The analyses presented in this volume make us optimistic that this, indeed, will be the case.

References

Bar, Aryeh. 1990. "Industry and Industrial Policy in Israel: Landmarks," in David Brodet et. al., eds. *Industrial-technological Policy for Israel.* Jerusalem: Institute for Israel Studies, pp. 22–46. (Hebrew).

Barber, Benjamin R. 1996. *Jihad vs. McWorld: How Globalism and Tribalism Are Reshaping the World.* New York: Ballantine Books.

Barnett, Michal N. 1996. "Israel in the World Economy: Israel as an East Asian State?" in his *Israel in Comparative Perspective.* Albany, N.Y.: State University of New York Press, pp. 107–140.

Beyer, Peter. 1994. *Religion and Globalization.* London: Sage.

Economic Models (Modelim kalkaliyim). 1993. *The Israeli Economy: Outlook.* Ramat Gan. (Hebrew).

Kleiman, Efraim. 1967. "The Place of Manufacturing in the Growth of the Israeli Economy," *Journal of Development Studies* 3, pp. 226–248.

Levy, Yagil. 1997. *Trial and Error: Israel's Route from War to De-Escalation.* Albany, NY: State University of New York Press.

_____. 1999. "The Austerity and Rationing Regime," in Adi Ophir, ed. *50 to 48: Critical Moments in the History of the State of Israel.* Jerusalem: The Van Leer Jerusalem Institute and Tel Aviv: Hakibbutz Hameuchad (special issue of *Teorya uvikoret*, 12–13). (Hebrew).

Lustick, Ian S. 1993. "Writing the *Intifada*: Collective Action in the Occupied Territories," *World Politics* 45, pp. 560–594.

_____. 1996. "To Build and to Be Built By: Israel and the Hidden Logic of the Iron Wall," *Israel Studies* 1, pp. 196–223.

Migdal, Joel S. 1988. *Strong Societies and Weak States: State-Society Relations and State Capabilities in the Third World.* Princeton, N.J. : Princeton University Press.

Razin, Assaf and Efraim Sadka. 1993. *The Economy of Modern Israel: Malaise and Promise.* Chicago: University of Chicago Press.

Sternhell, Zeev. 1998. *The Founding Myths of Israel : Nationalism, Socialism, and the Making of the Jewish State.* Princeton, N.J.: Princeton University Press.

PART ONE

A State-Centered Economy

2

Challenges to Separatism: Joint Action by Jewish and Arab Workers in Jewish-Owned Industry in Mandatory Palestine

DEBORAH S. BERNSTEIN

Separation and Contact

The goal of Zionist settlement in Palestine was the establishment of a Jewish community which aimed at becoming an autonomous, national entity, the future dominant force in the land. It was to be a clearly distinguished community, separate from the Arab majority of the population of Palestine and from the governing power, first Ottoman and later British. The Jewish community, composed largely of immigrants from Europe, under the auspices of the World Zionist Organization, grew rapidly. From 85,000 people prior to World War 1, the Jewish population doubled by 1931. It then tripled by 1945, growing from 176,000 in 1931 to 554,000 in 1945. (Gertz, 1947, p. 47) The Arab population of Palestine increased as well, doubling its number from 600,00 prior to the War, to 1,250,000 by 1945. Nevertheless, the massive immigration of Jews to Palestine increased their relative share from 1 percent in 1922 to 33 percent in 1947, and shrunk the Arab majority from 89 percent to approximately 67 percent respectively. (Gertz, 1947, p.47; Klinov-Malul and Halevi, p.11) As the Jewish community grew, it defined its boundaries and consolidated its separateness. It established a wide network of institutions; these included "national institutions," affiliated with the World Zionist Organization, and communal institutions of the Jewish community in Palestine—the Yishuv. After the First World War, with the commitment of the British government to the establishment of a Jewish National Home, the Zionist institutions expanded and served as the main executive bodies in the development of the Jewish community. These institutions were responsible for mediating relations between the Jewish settlement in Palestine and Zionist institutions and funds abroad, between the Yishuv and the Palestine government and administration, and between the Yishuv and the British government in London. There were additional representative bodies, elected by the Jewish population of Palestine, the Elected Assembly *(Asefat Ha-niv'harim)* and its executive body, the National Council *(Hava'ad Hale'umi)*.

The Yishuv developed its economic sector, a Jewish owned economy financed by private capital which was brought by the newly arrived immigrants, and by national capital of the Zionist funds. It was one of a number of economic sectors in Palestine, to be discussed later on. The Jewish community, under its Zionist leadership, established numerous Jewish settlements, rural and urban, and new neighborhoods within mixed Arab and Jewish towns. Many political parties developed, among which the workers' parties, and especially the largest party Mapai *(Mifleget Po'alei Eretz Israel—*the Party of the Eretz Israeli Workers), played a leading role. There were also parties which represented the middle classes (most important, the General Zionists), religious parties, and the right wing Revisionist party. A large and influential labor movement was established, The General Federation of Jewish Labor—*Hahistadrut Haklalit shel Ha'ovdim Ha'ivrim Be'eretz Yisrael.* The Histadrut considered class formation and nation building to be closely linked. It strove to help create a Jewish working class, organize it and obtain a monopoly over the Jewish labor market, so as to advance the interests of the class which it considered to be the vanguard of national development. Thus the Histadrut organized Jewish workers only, excluding any Arab workers, and became a nationally defined labor movement, strongly committed to the separation of the Jewish community as a self-contained social, political and economic entity. The Yishuv developed its cultural life in complete separation from the Arab majority. Its newly revived Hebrew language, new musical works, dances, literary publications and periodicals, all reinforced the boundaries and helped create a new Jewish community, a pervasive national ideology and identity.

And yet, the Jewish community, despite the boundaries it created, did not exist in a vacuum. The Yishuv consolidated its separate institutions and developed its national identity, while interacting, inevitably, with other, at times competing and hostile, forces. It developed within an Arab majority, even if a shrinking one, and was governed by British colonial rule. The Government of Palestine was committed to advancing the Jewish National Home and accordingly accepted the Yishuv's autonomy. Nevertheless, it was not an unconditional acceptance, but rather a continuously negotiated, at time tenuous, relationship.

More crucial for the future development of the Yishuv, the Arab population was also consolidating its national identity, national aspirations and national movement. (Kimmerling and Migdal, 1993; Porath, 1976, 1978*)* It entered into an encompassing clash of interests with the Zionist settlement—clash over control of land, demographic composition of the population, establishment of representative institutions, government economic policy and cultural identity of Palestine. The centrality of the national conflict between the Jewish settlers and the Palestinian Arab majority subordinated most other factors—or rather, interrelated with them in ways which gave national considerations a powerful impact. Economic class interests within each national collective, and across national boundaries, were often subsumed under, or shaped by, national goals, as defined by the dominant forces in the respective national movements.

The separation between the Jewish Yishuv and the Palestinian Arab population has been well recognized by all who studied the Jewish settlement in Palestine. For many, the distinctiveness of the new community was taken for granted, and no other possibility was even conceived. They could thus proceed to discuss the Yishuv in relation to its own internal dynamics, unrelated to its immediate surrounding. Other students of Israeli society, most notably the leading sociologists of the Yishuv, Dan Horowitz and Moshe Lissak, portrayed the Jewish community as existing "side by side" with the Palestinian Arab population. Side by side, meaning autonomous and separate, a situation attributed, above all, to the far reaching social differences between the Jewish community and its population, and the Arab population. (Horowitz and Lissak, 1977) But having established the separation between the two communities as unproblematic, they continued to focus on the Jewish community alone and on its internal, primarily political, developments. (Horowitz and Lissak, 1977, Chapter 2) Over recent years a new perspective has developed in Israeli historiography which, rather than taking the separateness of the Jewish community for granted, sees it as the focus of their concern. Its proponents argued that the separateness itself had to be explained, that it had to be studied as a social process involving conflicts of interest, competing perspectives, and legitimizing rhetoric. Some, such as Shafir and Shalev, emphasized the economic factors that caused the Jewish community to separate itself from the Palestinian Arab population, led by organized Jewish labor which attempted to protect itself from substitution by much cheaper Arab labor. (Shafir, 1989; Shalev, 1992) Others, such as Kimmerling, point to a wider range of factors, political, social, symbolic, as well as economic. (Kimmerling, 1983a, 1983b)

In the following chapter I hope to contribute to the understanding of the separation between the communities by studying situations that appear to challenge it. Situations in which Jews and Palestinian Arabs, specifically Jewish and Arab workers, did come in close daily contact, did embark on joint action, despite the overall context of separation in which they were engulfed. The pervasive separation discussed above never achieved total closure, despite the efforts which were invested by Jewish labor and settlement institutions, despite the major social and political campaigns, despite the institutions which were devised and the economic barriers which were constructed. Far from it. The territory was too small, the Palestinian Arab population too numerous, the British rule too inclusive, for such a closure to be feasible. In fact, it is precisely because hermetic closure was impossible, because points of contact were abundant, that so much effort, and such diverse means, were applied by the Jewish elites, primarily the Histadrut and the Jewish National Fund. This article will deal with points of contact in the economic sphere and in the labor market; therefore, a somewhat more detailed discussion of the economic structure of Palestine is called for.

The economy of Palestine was made up of two major economic sectors, the Jewish and the Arab sectors, which were supplemented by the government sector. The Palestinian Arab sector was still largely agrarian, in transition from a semi-subsistence economy to a market oriented, capital-based economy. Agriculture dominated the Arab economy while capitalist oriented manufacture and construction played a much larger role in the Jewish economy. This was due to the large one-directional import of capital by individual Jewish immigrants and Zionist institutions. The previous experience of most of the immigrants in their countries of origin provided the resources essential for economic development: experience in wage labor, skills acquired by workers, entrepreneurs and managers, international connections, as well as patterns of consumption which created a market for new local products. The political framework in which immigration took place facilitated the efficient exploitation of these resources of manpower and capital. The rate of economic growth was exceptionally high, reaching an average annual growth rate of 21.7 percent between 1922 and 1935. (Metzer and Kaplan, 1985, p.329)

The Arab sector was also undergoing rapid growth and had become, to a large extent, market oriented. (Metzer and Kaplan, 1985, p.343) The average annual growth rate of the Arab sector was 7 percent, with a lower growth rate in agriculture and a significantly higher growth rate in manufacture and construction. (Metzer and Kaplan, 1985, p.329)

The third sector of Palestine's economy was the mandatory government. It included the government department of agriculture, education, justice, police and finance, as well as infrastructural services such as public works, railways, ports and the postal service. The government sector was smaller and less varied than the two national sectors, yet it was the single largest employer in Palestine.

The three economic sectors functioned separately, with clear boundaries between them, yet they were interrelated in a complex combination of exchange, competition and attempts at disengagement. The interrelations between the sectors included the mobility of labor between sectors, the movement of capital, the reciprocal impact on products, services, employment and on the extent of industrialization.

The majority of the Jewish workers were from eastern and central Europe. They were a newly proletarianized and newly arrived labor force. They immigrated under the auspices of the World Zionist Organization, with no private means of their own, from industrialized or industrializing countries, and were familiar with political and labor organizations. Their previous experience helps explain much of the strength of Jewish labor and its ability to obtain higher compensation for its labor than would be expected in a country with an abundant supply of cheap, local labor and in an economy that was only beginning to industrialize.

The organization of Jewish labor, the Histadrut, was established in 1920. It fulfilled a wide range of functions, the protection of workers' rights and wages via their trade unions, the allocation of work via the Histadrut controlled Labor Exchange, the creation of employment via the Histadrut owned contracting company—Solel Boneh— and the provision of essential service. (Tzahor, 1979; Grinberg, 1993;

Shalev, 1992). Histadrut institutions were composed of representatives of the major workers' parties. Mapai was the dominant party in the Histadrut, both at the top level of the Histadrut Executive and at the level of the local Labor Councils. To the left of Mapai were the Hashomer Hatza'ir, the left wing of Po'alei Tzion, and the Palestine Communist Party. Although it is beyond the scope of this brief presentation to discuss these latter movements, suffice it to say that all three strove to establish greater solidarity between Jewish and Arab workers. The Hashomer Hatza' ir, on the left of Mapai, fully supported Zionist settlement and the separatist orientation of the Histadrut, while the Palestine Communist Party, on the other hand, was vehemently opposed to it. The Histadrut, which was composed of Jewish workers only, nevertheless attempted, from time to time, to attract Arab workers as well. For this purpose the Histadrut decided, in its Third Convention, 1927, to form the Palestine Labor League. Theoretically this was to be a bi-national organization of Jewish and Arab workers, divided into two national units. In practice, the Palestine Labor League came to refer only to the adjunct organization for Arab workers, through which the Histadrut hoped to bring Arab workers under its auspices, to diminish their opposition to Zionist settlement, and yet to avoid incorporating them as full members in the Histadrut. (Bernstein,1998)

The Arab labor force was made up largely of peasants who were in the process of proletarianization. Land was becoming scarce due to heritage laws, transfer of land to Jewish owners. and debts of small land owners, thus many of the villagers, the *falahin,* were potential migrants into the urban centers. The combination of the supply of peasants-cum-workers and the casual nature of much of the work, led to a high labor turnover. As many of the workers migrated into town on a temporary basis, labor organization was extremely difficult.[1] Arab labor began to organize in the mid–1920s. Skilled and semi-skilled workers from among the railways workers established the Palestine Arab Workers' Society in 1925. It held its first convention in 1930 and became an active force in the early and mid-1930s until it, like much else in the Palestinian society, came to a stand still during the Arab Rebellion of 1936–1939. (Aboud, 1988; Budeiri, 1979)

Thus, despite attempts to organize, the Arab wage earners in Palestine earned much lower wages than the Jewish wage earners. The ratio of wages between Jewish and Arab unskilled workers varied between 1:2 to 1:3, and taking into account the much longer hours of work, at times even 1:4. Wage differential was much smaller among skilled workers, though in most cases it did not completely disappear.[2]

The striking wage differentials between the higher priced Jewish workers and the much cheaper Arab workers, created a situation of a *split labor market.* As a result, Jewish workers felt threatened by the abundant supply of cheap Arab workers and feared substitution and displacement. Their response was to tighten their organization and strive for a closure of the Jewish sector of the economy, so as to gain full monopoly over that sector. This strategy, typical, according to Bonacich, of conditions of split labor markets, (Bonacich, 1979) was reinforced by the overall "closure" of the Jewish Yishuv, discussed earlier on. Such closure policy, which called for

"Jewish labor" *(Avoda Ivrit),* became the dominant policy and rallying cry of Jewish labor, embodied in its ideological discourse and its institutional structure.

And yet, despite a high degree of closure obtained by Jewish labor, there were occasions where Jews and Arabs did work together, in the same work place, under the same employer. This occurred in two circumstances. Firstly, in the government sector, where Jewish labor could not get the employer, the government, to close the market, or any part of it, to cheap Arab labor. Secondly, in the Jewish sector, where despite the very strong pressure applied on Jewish employers to refrain from employing Arab workers, some employers did not comply and did employ a mixed labor force. That is where our discussion will begin.

I will be focusing on mixed workplaces within the Jewish sector, rather than in the government sector, as these directly challenge the dominant forms of organization of the Jewish community. Thus they sharpen the contradiction between the experience of joint employment and joint action on the one hand, and the separatist context of the Jewish sector, on the other. I shall attempt to examine whether such a meeting ground, in contradiction to all the "rules of the game" of the Jewish Yishuv, led to the development of new relations between Jews and Arabs, that is, whether daily contact, in the same work place, served to mitigate the separatism of the Yishuv, and whether it created cooperation and solidarity between Arab and Jewish workers, reflecting their work place experience, which would be strong enough to withstand the overall discourse and practice of separation and hostility. Furthermore, whether those cases where Jewish and Arab workers joined forces in a struggle against their employer, served as a starting point for relations which transcended national confrontation, or, to the contrary, whether national separatism limited the potential for cooperation.

Having set the stage, it is time to move into the arena, or in this case, into the three industrial enterprises to be examined in some detail. The three enterprises, owned by Jewish entrepreneurs, where both Jewish and Arab workers were employed over an extended period, were Nur, the match factory, Nesher, the cement factory and Mosaica, the tile factory. The three enterprises were located in Haifa and the surrounding area. Haifa, both town and district, was characterized by a mixed Arab and Jewish population, and an industrial economy. It was the center of industrial development for the Jewish sector, the Arab sector, and the large enterprises of the Palestine Government and international firms. It is not a coincidence that Haifa played an important role in the development of both Jewish and Arab labor movements. The founding assembly of the Histadrut (1920) and of the Palestine Arab Workers' Society (1930) both took place in Haifa.[3] The Haifa Labor Council, the strongest local council, was the first to organize Arab workers under its affiliation in the 1920s, and it continued to be more closely involved with the Palestine Labor League than was any other local council.

In these three enterprises, Nur, Nesher and Mosaica, workers of both nationalities not only worked in the same place, but joined forces to carry out a strike, thus showing, at least for the duration of the strike, a high level of solidarity. At the same time, in each of these three enterprises, Jewish and Arab workers were separated to some extent and in some manner. In Nur and in Mosaica, the level of separation was low. In both places the workers worked in the same location, with at least some of them carrying out the same jobs. Nevertheless, there was also some gendered and national segregation. In Nur, the Arab and Jewish women worked in the labor intensive "female" work of packaging the matches, while the Arab and Jewish male workers were separated according to level of skill. In Mosaica, Jewish women were concentrated in specific jobs which they did not share either with Arab women, who were not employed in Mosaica, or with the men, while Jewish and Arab men were employed, on the whole, in similar positions. At Nesher, the separation was most clearly structured, with the Jewish workers working in the production of cement, while the Arab workers excavated the raw material from the nearby quarries.

The following discussion will examine the complex combination of separation and solidarity, both within each enterprise, and as affected by the overall political, social and economic context. In Nur, the strike took place in the winter and Spring of 1927, a year of deep depression, while in Nesher and in Mosaica, the strikes were held in the 1930s, a period of economic growth and prosperity. By the 1930s, both national and labor movements had consolidated, and thus we shall see a far more intricate inter-play between the economic and the political, as well as a greater range of parties involved, in the strikes of that decade.

Three Strikes—Three Attempts at Joint Action

The Nur Match Factory

In 1925, Gershon and Meir Weitzman[4] established the Nur match factory in the northern town of Acre. They had owned a match factory in Lithuania and brought with them to Palestine their machinery and some of their skilled and experienced workers. The factory was located in the town of Acre at the northern tip of the Haifa Bay. It was an Arab town with a very small Jewish community, some sephardi families and a small number of European Jewish workers of the Zionist labor immigration. The decision of the Weizmann brothers to establish their factory in an Arab town, rather than in Haifa with its concentration of Jewish owned industry and its strong organization of Jewish labor, attracted immediate attention. Concern was expressed by the representatives of labor in the National Council and by some non-labor representatives, lest the owners by-pass the self imposed control of the Jewish national institutions and avoid the employment of Jewish workers. (Tishby to Col. Kish, May 15, 1925. CZA S9/1842) Indeed, despite promises to the contrary, given by the Weizmann brothers to the representatives of the national institutions, they employed a mixed and diverse labor force. By the beginning of 1927, approximately one and a half years after production began, 102 workers were employed. Of these, 57 were Jewish workers and 45 Arab. The majority of the Jewish workers, 35 of them, were women and four more were children, ages 6, 12, 13 and 14. Approximately half of the women came from Haifa where many pioneering immigrants were concentrated, in need of work. The rest were young women from the Sephardic Jewish families of Acre. Of the 45 Arab workers, 13 were children, mostly under the age of twelve. The number of Arab women was not stated, but they were most probably the majority of the adults, employed in the "female" occupation of packaging. (*Davar,* March 23 and 24, 1927)

The labor conditions were extremely poor. Wages were very low. We know more about the wages of the Jewish than the Arab workers. The wages of both Jewish men and women were well below the customary wages in the Jewish sector. While Jewish women workers in industrial enterprises earned, in most cases, between 120–150 mils, unskilled male workers, approximately 250–300 piasters, and skilled male workers from 400 piasters and upwards, the wages at Nur were 50–100 mils, 200, and 250 respectively the currency in Palestine was the sterling). It was the Egyptian sterling until 1927, and the Palestine sterling after that year. The pound sterling, the *lira,* was composed of 100 piasters, *grush* in Arabic, or 1,000 mils. The Arab women earned still less, 30–50 mils per day, though I don't know how this wage compares to the wage of Arab women in general. Workers were not paid extra for night shifts or for over time. (*Davar,* March 22, 1927) Sanitation and hygiene were poor, and the work with flammable material and poisonous gas fumes was carried out under hazardous conditions. No less oppressive to the workers was the domineering and callous manner of the management.

The employment of Arab workers was a major source of contention between the Jewish workers and management. Depression had set in by the end of 1925 and Jewish workers were in dire need of employment. They protested against the manner in which the employers made use of the Arab workers to denigrate the Jewish workers and block their demands. The Weizmann brothers avoided paying the Jewish women workers for the first 18 days of their employment, and then paid them only 5 piasters, as that was what they paid the Arab women. Furthermore, they put pressure on the skilled Jewish workers to train Arab workers who would then be able to fill similar positions.[5]

From the summer of 1926 tensions mounted. Most of the workers of Nur were employed only three or four days a week. Wages dropped and Gershon Weizmann attempted to transfer the women packaging workers from daily wages to piece rates. The workers began to organize. A workers' committee was chosen, composed of Jewish workers, members of the Histadrut. A number of Arab workers made contact with the workers' committee and expressed their support. In January of 1927 a delegation met with Gershon Weizmann and put forward their demands for improved sanitary and health conditions, raise of wages, a full week's work, decent treatment and an end to capricious firing. (Nekritz to HE, January 18, 1927, LA, IV 208–1–58) None of these demands referred to the employment of Jewish, as opposed to Arab, workers. Weizmann refused to make any concessions. (Nekritz to HE, late January, 1927) Within a few days, management announced a lock out and the workers announced their strike. The following day a leaflet, in Arabic, addressed to "The Workers of Acre," was distributed calling upon the Arab workers to join the struggle, to avoid any work in the factory, and to bring it to a complete stoppage. (Leaflet signed by the workers' committee of Nur, February 19, 1927. LA, IV 511–3)

Both parties, workers and management, prepared for a long and difficult struggle. The strike was organized largely by the Jewish workers who were recent immigrants from eastern Europe and politically involved in the Jewish Labor Movement. The men led the strike and represented the workers in negotiations while the women played a major role in the strikers' picketing. (*Davar,* March 7, 1927) Other workers, the sephardi Jewish workers and the Arab workers, gave their support, but there are few indications of active involvement. Picketers prevented all attempts to introduce strike breakers or to remove merchandise from the warehouses. The police, called in daily by the owners, clashed with the picketers, many of whom were arrested and brought to trial. (*Davar,* February 23, March 11, 13, 24, April 6, May 13, 1927) The Histadrut Executive took the strike under its auspices and organized contributions from places of work all over the country. The strikers' committee organized the distribution of aid, which was shared equally by all the workers, Jews and Arabs alike.

The Arab workers supported the strike as did the Arab community. Four of the Arab workers of Nur were actively involved in the strike and in the picketing, and the rest showed their support passively. Philip Hasoun and Avraham Khalfon of Haifa, active on behalf of the Haifa Labor Council among Arab workers,[6] visited Sheikh As'ad Shukeiri, the leader of the Arab community of Acre, and obtained his support for the strike. (*Davar,* March 8, 1927,) There are no Arab sources concerning the strike and no reference was made to it in the Arab press. Thus, I can only suggest possible grounds for the support shown by the Arab community and Arab workers. The community leaders in Acre, as in most of the north of Palestine, were in opposition to the national leadership headed by the Mufti of Jerusalem, Haj' Amin al-Husseini. Sheikh As'ad Shukeiri was one of the active members of this political alignment which was generally more moderate in its opposition to Zionist settlement. Furthermore, in 1927 the Jewish community was hit by a severe depression. It was not a period of salient national strife, but rather one of economic hardship. In this context, the solidarity shown by the Jewish leadership of the strike, and their concern to share all contributions obtained from other Jewish work places with the Arab workers of Nur, may indeed have had a profound impression on Sheikh Shukeiri, as *Davar* (March 8, 1927), the Labor Movement daily newspaper, reported.

The Weizmann brothers tried to create a split among the workers. A day before the lockout, they announced that the European workers, the "ashkenazi" workers, were fired, while the Sephardi and the Arab workers could continue as before. (*Davar,* February 16, 1927,) They tried to spread suspicion and discontent among the Arab workers. They claimed that the cause of the strike was the demand of the Jewish workers for the dismissal of all Arab workers employed at Nur. They offered one of the Arab workers, who actively supported the strike, an increase of forty mils a day which he rejected, declaring, according to *Davar,* that ". . . one worker would not betray another. We shall retain our solidarity to the end." (*Davar,* March 7, 1927)

Months passed. The aid organized by the Histadrut petered out. Unemployment was at its peek, a bad time to sustain so long and drawn out a strike. At the end of April, two and one half months after the strike had started, negotiations began once again. The workers had to acknowledge their weakness, and they realized that they would have to accept far less than their initial demands. (Meeting of Histadrut Executive, May 11, 1927. Minutes of Histadrut Executive, LA Library) The Weizmann brothers attempted once again to bring about a split between the Jewish and Arab workers. They refused to negotiate with the Jewish workers over the Arab workers' work conditions. All concessions, they argued, would be granted to the Jewish workers only. (*Davar,* May 17, 1927) When the workers' delegates refused, the owners agreed to extend the wage increase to all workers, Jewish and Arab, but only to those working on a daily basis, thus excluding the piece rate workers. The Jewish workers were strongly opposed to this restriction. They feared that it would enable the owners to employ new workers, mainly Arab workers, on a piece rate basis. They could then establish two levels of pay, and eventually push out the higher paid workers.

Nevertheless, there appeared to be little choice. The Histadrut Executive pressured the workers to end the strike and gave little support. The Arab workers, who had received no aid for some weeks, were losing their patience, and rumors were spread, possibly on behalf of the owners, against the Jewish workers. The workers were split. Some of the members argued that they had no choice but to accept the conditions put forward by management. Others objected. (May 19, 1927. LA, IV 208–1–58)

The Histadrut Executive made the final decision to end the strike. The agreement between the workers and Gershon and Meir Weizmann was signed. (Agreement between Meir and Gershon Weizmann and H. Apter, on behalf of the workers. LA, IV 208-I-58. n. d.) The workers did gain some of their demands, though many fewer than were victoriously reported in *Davar* (June 28, 1927). The strike had lasted close to five months, and, all in all, Jewish and Arab workers had retained their solidarity. The strike created its own dynamics. The success of the operation necessitated full cooperation of all workers, and this, in turn, created mutual commitment and responsibility which had not existed previously. And yet the basic conditions had not changed. The Arab residents of Acre and of the nearby villages were still a reserve of cheap labor. The Jewish workers were still threatened by substitution and by the manipulative ability of the employer to take advantage of the situation. Only one month after the end of the strike, Gershon Weizmann tried to undermine the agreement by reducing wages for all the workers, by excluding the Arab workers from the agreed benefits and by substituting Arab for Jewish workers. (Letter of Acre Committee to HE, July 12, 1927. LA, IV 208–1–58) This led some of the Jewish workers to leave the firm, and their place was taken by Arab workers. There was little cooperation between the Arab and Jewish workers. To the contrary, the Jewish workers appear to have been extremely worried by the increase in the number of Arab workers. By 1929, one of the Jewish workers reported, approximately 60 percent of the labor force was composed of Arab workers, some of whom worked on the machines of the box-making and packaging departments, where only Jewish workers had been employed before. (*Davar,* July 18, 1929)

In August of 1929 relations between Jews and Arabs deteriorated throughout Palestine, as a result of the clashes which began near the Wailing Wall in Jerusalem, and tension increased in Acre as well. The management of Nur, quick to take advantage of the situation, further reduced the number of Jewish workers, driving still others to leave. (Acre Workers' Committee to HE, 15 and 30 October, 1930, IV 208–1–191) In 1932, Jewish workers composed slightly less than one-third of the labor force, 29 out of 98 workers,[7] and by 1938 the Jewish workers were down to less than 10 percent of the work force, 18 out of 200 workers. (Report on strike of Arab Nur workers, 1938, LA, IV 104–22)

After World War 11, in February 1945, the workers of Nur went out on strike again, but this time the strikers were all Arab workers, and the strike was led by the Palestine Arab Workers' Society. The Jewish workers remained a small group of skilled, clerical and managerial workers, with little to do with the Arab employees. The conflict over the future of Palestine was escalating, and the tension between Arabs and Jews in the Nur factory increased. The Jewish workers called on the owners to move their factory to a Jewish locality as they had called on them before, and, as before, the Weizmann brothers promised they were seriously considering to do so. (Report from the Nur factory by Abu Yosseph, Hagana Archive, 105/106)

To conclude, the success of the joint strike of Jewish and Arab workers was indeed short-lived. At the time of the strike, it could be seen as a significant achievement of class solidarity. A strike was declared by the workers, led by their committee, despite little initial support by the labor establishment. Once the strike began it was given ample support, and contributions from other workers were generous. But, given the depression and increasing unemployment, support declined and pressure by the labor establishment forced the workers to compromise and conclude the strike. All along solidarity had been maintained, and the Jewish workers insisted on sharing all contributions, and more important, all achievements, with the Arab workers. Yet, they were also greatly aware of the employers' interest in splitting the workers among themselves and in establishing two levels of pay within the factory. Their solidarity was fueled by their conviction that different levels of pay would undermine any of their gains within a very short period of time. Under these circumstances, the issues of the labor conflict at Nur were primarily those of economic competition between higher priced and lower priced labor, and the manipulation of this competition by the employers. Nevertheless, the strike and its aftermath were embedded in the large national conflict. This was keenly felt two years after the strike, when the outburst of national strife led to the displacement of many of the Jewish workers and their substitution by Arabs, as shown above.

Employment in the same workplace had led to joint action. But the overall context of national conflict, and the abundance of cheap Arab labor, enabled management to split the two groups of workers and abort their cooperative efforts. The cooperation that developed during the strike had not become the starting point for new relations. Before long it gave way to renewed competition.

Nesher Cement Factory

The Nesher Cement Factory, a shareholding company under the ownership of Michael Pollak, was the largest privately owned enterprise in Palestine. It was a far more advanced industrial enterprise than the match factory at Nur. Nesher was one of the early heavy industries, which made use of local raw material (lime stone), to manufacture a product, cement, important for the future development of the Jewish settlement and of Palestine's economy. Michael Pollak, the major stockholder and manager of Nesher, intended it to serve both the growing Jewish Zionist economy and to become part of the economy of the Middle East. The Zionist establishment was extremely interested in the success of Nesher, as a leading venture of Jewish private capital, and gave political support to the demands put forward by Nesher for protective taxation. The Palestine government, in turn, responded positively to most of these demands, even though this was contrary to imperial taxation policy and raised strong opposition among the leaders of the Arab community who claimed that they would be the ones to carry the burden of the added taxes. The Histadrut was also concerned with the success of Nesher, as a proof of the viability of Jewish private capital, but only on condition that it would employ Jewish labor.

Nesher was established in 1923, and production began two years later, in 1925. Pollak insisted on employing Arab workers as well Jewish ones, as part of the incorporation of Nesher in the Middle Eastern economy. Part of the work was subcontracted to an Arab contractor, and, as a result, Arab and Jewish workers were employed under distinctly different conditions.

The Jewish workers were employed by Nesher and worked in the location of the factory in the manufacture of cement, while the Arab workers were employed by the sub-contractor Musbah Shkiffi in the nearby quarries, excavating the raw material from which the cement was produced. The Jewish workers were employed at the starting rate of 300 mils (30 grush) per day,[8] which increased to 312 mils, and later to as much as 480 mils, for an eight hour day. The workers were organized in the Histadrut, and their representatives negotiated with management over labor conditions. The workers enjoyed an annual paid leave and numerous additional social benefits. (See HLC leaflet March 25, 1930, p.4, LA Library; Labor Council of Nesher-Yagur, Report on the actions of the Labor Council of Nesher-Yagur, April-

May 1932, pp. 6–7: LA IV 208–1–894; Labor Council of Nesher-Yagur to HE, October 30, 1935, LA IV 208–1–1150)

The conditions of the Arab workers were totally different. They worked 11 to 12 hours a day, under the strict control of their contractor. They were brought into town by him and were dependent on him for work and for accommodations. He frequently dismissed many of the workers and exchanged them for others from the villages in the district of Nablus and Jenin. Their wage was very low, varying between 100 and 125 mils, and on the rare occasion 140 mils, for a very long day of work. (HLC leaflet, March 25, 1930, probably written by Zvi Grinberg, the chair of the Nesher workers' committee.)

The Jewish workers at Nesher enjoyed good work conditions and were not under threat of displacement by the much cheaper Arab workers. Pollak, unlike the Weizmann brothers, was a supporter of the employment of Jewish labor, and his commitment exceeded his immediate economic interests. The Arab workers, on the other hand, were, or could be, aware of the much improved conditions enjoyed by the Jewish workers. Thus, it is far more likely that the Arab workers would be the ones to protest and turn to the Jewish workers for help, in contrast to the course of events examined above in Nur.

Indeed, Nesher quarry was one of the few arenas of recurring strikes by Arab workers. The first strike took place in 1930, and this was followed by strikes in September 1932, April 1933, and January through to March of 1936. In the case of Nesher it was the Arab workers who went on strike and who needed the support and solidarity of the Jewish workers. They needed the benefit of their experience in organization and class struggle, and sought their advice and guidance. But they also needed their support in refusing to work with raw material excavated and supplied by strike breakers brought in by the contractor. Considering the dilemma of the Jewish workers, who opposed the employment of Arab labor on the one hand, but identified with their hard plight on the other, the outcome of such potential cooperation was highly tenuous.

The first strike broke out in July 1930, caused by the mass dismissal of all the quarry workers. For the first time, the workers organized and turned to the Jewish workers' committee of Nesher for help. They protested against the arbitrary dismissals and against their low rates, and as much against the contractor Shkiffi's demand that they buy their food from his shop at unprecedented prices. We have no documentation of the reasons for their turning to the Jewish workers, but it can be assumed that they were well aware of the Jewish workers' relatively superior work conditions and of their organization. Zvi Grinberg, the secretary of the Jewish workers' committee, appealed to the Haifa Labor Council to intervene. The contractor seemed to concede. He agreed to take all workers back, and to continue to employ both old and new workers at the previous rate of 120 mils per day. He furthermore agreed to let them buy their food wherever they chose. (Aba Houshi to HE, 14 July, 1930. LA IV 208–1–186)

By 1932 Shkiffi had lowered wages and tightened control, despite the expansion of construction and excavation. Once again the workers went out on strike, turning again to the well-organized Jewish workers. (Grinberg to HE, September 28, 1932. LA IV 208–1–321) Zvi Grinberg took it upon himself to come to their aid. He turned to the Haifa Labor Council, which in turn activated the Palestine Labor League and appealed for support to the Histadrut Executive. The rank and file workers of Nesher were far more ambivalent than their secretary. They were less committed to help workers whose employment they opposed in the first place. Furthermore, they were unsure to what extent their support, if given, should be made public, lest that it be seen as an acceptance of the employment of Arab workers in a Jewish-owned enterprise. The dilemma of the Jewish workers focused on their response to the employment of strikebreakers. Would they risk appearing to legitimize the employment of Arab workers, by supporting their struggle, or would they turn a blind eye to the introduction of strike breakers, an anathema to all class-conscious workers? In practice, the workers did not have to make this decision. The factory was about to close for an extended break over the Jewish new year holiday, and thus there was no urgent need for the supply of additional raw material.

The strike of the Arab quarry workers received much publicity in both the Jewish and Arab press. The cooperation which evolved between the Arab strikers and the Histadrut establishment aroused criticism from a number of circles. On the left of the Jewish labor movement, from the left wing of Po álei Tzion, which was within the Zionist consensus, and from the Palestine Communist Party, which was strongly anti-Zionist, demands were raised for an all-out strike of the Jewish workers of Nesher, for the equalization of wages and for the substitution of Histadrut involvement by grass root solidarity. (Leaflet of Po álei Tzion, September 28, 1932. LA IV 407–981; Leaflet of Palestine Communist Party, October 10, 1932. LA IV 208–1–321) At the same time, criticism was leveled at the Arab workers, from within the Arab community of Haifa, for turning to the Zionist Histadrut for help. (Undated leaflet, LA IV 208–1–321; *al-Karmil*, October 8, 1932)

Surrounded by ambivalence and criticism, negotiations continued. The strike lasted for close to three weeks. Finally, shortly after the factory re-opened after its holiday break, an agreement was signed by Musbah Shkiffi, the employer, and by the Nesher labor council and the committee of the Arab quarry workers, as the representatives of the workers.[9] Many of the demands of the workers had been accepted. Their representatives were recognized, and they would henceforth be employed nine hours a day, for 125 mils, with the prospect of a raise to 150 mils within three months. Once again Shkiffi acknowledged the right of the workers to purchase their food wherever they chose.

The success of the negotiations under the auspices of the Histadrut led the Arab workers to join the Palestine Labor League. Nevertheless, before long it became clear that little had changed. Within a few months the contractor Shkiffi brought in new workers to whom he owed nothing. In April 1933, he sent the workers on leave for the Passover and the Muslim holidays. On their return they found that he had retained the new workers only and would not take back any of the "veterans." A strike was declared once again. For the first time, 80 Jewish workers, those who received the raw material directly from the quarry, stopped their work. Nesher, the largest Jewish-owned private industry, was at the risk of a total shutdown in support of the Arab quarry workers. The Haifa Labor Council and the Histadrut Executive were quick to intervene. They put pressure on the contractor to accept arbitration and to continue to employ the previous workers. Six weeks later the arbitrator, Baruch Binah, a Jewish district officer of the government administration, announced his decision. He rejected some of the most important demands put forward by the workers, though he did accept some of the others. The contractor, in turn, totally ignored the decisions which had been in their favor. Instead, he "argued, cursed, pressured, incited the police and unchecked, chased away the workers." (Agassi, "Action among Arab workers in Haifa 1932–1933." LA IV 208–1–435)

Thus the struggle of the Arab workers, which began in September 1932 and lasted intermittently until the summer of 1933, ended in failure. There was not enough Histadrut support for a renewed struggle, and the Palestine Labor League appeared helpless. Under threat of dismissal by the contractor, the Arab workers left the Palestine Labor League and severed their connection with the Histadrut. There is no indication of any further contact between the Arab workers and the Jewish workers or their committee. Aba Houshi, of the Haifa Labor Council, wrote in his final report to the Histadrut Executive: "The failure is attributable in large measure to the stance of the Jewish workers of Nesher, but even more so to the indifference of the Histadrut Executive and its lack of help." (Zvi Grinberg and Aba Houshi to HE, August 1933. LA IV 208–1–894)

For a number of years work continued undisturbed in both factory and quarry. At the beginning of 1936, the workers went out on strike once again. Little seemed to have changed, despite the prosperity of the mid-1930s. This time, a new demand was added to the previous ones. The workers, all villagers from the hilly district of Jenin and Nablus, wanted to bring their families with them, to reside together on the outskirts of Haifa. It may well be that, due to the years of prosperity, urban employment became more steady and a more permanent option to village life. This demand, like the freedom to purchase food, met with the opposition of the employer, fearing, in all likelihood, to loosen his control over his workers. (Agassi's report, February 6, 1936. LA IV 250–27–2–199)

After 1933, the Arab workers retained little contact with the Jewish workers of Nesher. Despite the help that had been extended, and despite the solidarity, limited though it was, which had been shown by the Jewish workers during the Arab workers' strike, the latter felt badly let down. The Histadrut, able to ensure highly satisfactory conditions for its own Jewish members, had not been able, or willing, to bring the Arab workers' strike to a successful end, even though they were members of the Palestine Labor League. Furthermore, conditions had changed. The Palestine Arab Workers' Society had become an active force on the Haifa labor scene. The Palestine Arab Workers' Society was established in 1925 but took its first steps only in 1930 when it held its first convention in Haifa. (Aboud Nadir) Over the years of prosperity, with the growth of the Palestinian Arab urban working class and more frequent labor conflicts, the Palestine Arab Workers' Society had slowly established itself as the spokesman and the representative of the workers. It was closely affiliated with the Arab national movement, and vehemently opposed to any organizational steps taken by the Histadrut, especially via the Palestine Labor League, among Arab workers. (Bernstein, 1995) Thus, the workers of the Nesher quarry, neither needed, nor—it would seem—wanted, to turn to the Jewish workers of Nesher or to the Histadrut establishment. They received help from the Palestine Arab Workers' Society,[10] though the renewal of the strikes over the first three months of 1936 indicates that the Palestine Arab Workers' Society was no more successful than the Histadrut had been in getting Shkiffi to honor the contracts he signed. At the same time, the Jewish workers were no longer an active party to the conflict. This time the strikes were seen as an opportunity to exclude Arab labor, rather than as an occasion for workers' solidarity over basic working class issues.

On April 20, 1936, the general strike of Arabs in Palestine was declared, and the Arab Rebellion had begun, to last, intermittently, through 1939. Work had stopped in most places, and the quarry workers, like most Arab wage earners, returned to their villages. But only for a few days. In an exceptional step, Solel Boneh, the Histadrut contracting company, subcontracted the quarry work from Nesher and, with the consent of the Palestine Arab Workers' Society, employed both Arab and Jewish workers.[11] For the first time, in Nesher, Jewish and Arab workers worked in the same location, doing the same work. Nevertheless, the separation between the workers had not broken down. The Jewish workers were members of the Histadrut, the Arab workers were not. They worked under different conditions of pay. The Jewish workers received a relatively high daily wage, while the Arab workers received much lower pay and worked on a piece rate basis.[12] Depression had set in. Unemployment among Jewish workers was increasing. Workers of Nesher were being dismissed, and others worked two to three days a week, to enable as many workers as possible to obtain at least a minimal income. Under those conditions, the continued employment of Arab workers in the quarry, and especially by the Histadrut contracting company, was a source of severe contention. The very proximity and visibility of the Arab workers only aggravated matters. This lasted until the summer of 1938. The Arab Rebellion had escalated and strong pressure was put on the Arab workers to join the general strike. In August they left the quarry, putting an end to many years of employment of Arab labor in the Nesher cement enterprise.

To conclude, for thirteen years Jews and Arabs worked in the Nesher cement factory and quarry. The separation between them, within the same enterprise, reflected the overall separation between Jewish and Arab labor—different locations, different skills, different wages, different labor organizations, and differential success in their struggles with their employer. Nevertheless, at specific moments, the essential identification of workers with the plight of other workers bridged their conflicting class and national interests. But even those moments could not transcend the context in which they took place.

Mosaica: Wolfman's Tile Factory

The Mosaica tile factory was established in Haifa, in 1923, by A. Wolfman. It began as a small workshop, employing a number of Arab workers. Over the years, with the rapid expansion of construction work, the workshop grew into a factory which employed approximately 100 workers. By the early 1930s, Jewish workers had entered the factory. The labor force was composed of approximately half Arab and half Jewish workers, many of whom were young women, the first to enter the tile industry. All workers were initially paid on a piece rate basis, as was the custom in the tile industry in general. But, after much pressure by the workers, Wolfman agreed to pay both Jewish and Arab workers on a daily basis, though only for a trial period. The Jewish male workers were paid between 400 and 500 mils per day in 1933 and up to 550–650 mils in 1935. The Jewish women were paid between 250 and 330 mils in 1933 and up to 360 mils in 1935. The Arab workers, all men, migrants from the villages surrounding Jenin and Nablus, earned between 120 and 250 mils (or 12–25 grush) per day. (See undated, unsigned report, Giv'at Haviva Archive, 217.90(3), probably from 1933; wage rates for 1935, February 1, 1935. LA IV 250–27–2–256)

The Jewish workers, who belonged to the left wing labor party Hashomer Hatza'ir, upon beginning their work at Wolfman's, found the Arab workers already there. Unlike other such cases, they did not call for the exclusion of Arab workers, but rather, persuaded them to organize and join the Palestine Labor League. Thus the relations in Wolfman's Mosaica were quite different from those in either Nur or Nesher. And yet, the future held an inevitable challenge to the existing relations between the Jewish and Arab workers of Wolfman's. The enterprise was to move, by the end of 1935, to a new industrial zone developed on the outskirts of Haifa. The land was bought by the Jewish National Fund and leased to individual Jewish industrialists on condition that no Arab worker would be employed in any enterprise established on Jewish National Fund land. The transfer of Mosaica, and the resulting dismissal of the Arab workers, was strongly supported by the Haifa Labor Council and the Construction Workers' Union.

The Jewish workers of Mosaica, and especially their militant workers' committee, were far from accepting the Histadrut's policy. They felt personally committed to the well-being of the Arab workers. Having convinced them to join the Palestine Labor League, they considered their Arab co-workers to be genuine members of the Histadrut—even if their membership was channeled via a separate body. At the same time, the Jewish workers were well aware that there was little they could do. They could hardly declare a strike over the continued employment of Arab workers, knowing that the Haifa Labor Council would strongly oppose such a step, and so would many of the members of their own political movement.

Unhappily, they withdrew the demand to enable some of the Arab workers to remain and focused on two alternative courses—the payment of compensation by the
employer, as he was obligated to pay any worker whom he dismissed after a year's
work or more, or, much better, the provision of alternative work by the Haifa Labor
Council, via the Palestine Labor League. (Hashomer Hatza'ir Haifa branch. October 29, 1935, Givat Haviva Archive 17.90 A (4)) Only a provision of a new place of
work, they argued, could prove that the Histadrut was as concerned for the Arab
workers as it was for Jewish workers who were dismissed or unemployed. And yet,
such an undertaking was extremely difficult. The Histadrut was able, most often, to
provide employment for Jewish workers because of its monopoly over the Jewish
labor market and its insistence on Jewish labor only. It could not, and would not,
use that monopoly to provide employment for Arab workers, even for members of
the Palestine Labor League. (Report sent by the workers' committee of Mosaica to
the Arab Department of the HE, with copies to the HLC and the PLL. October 9,
1935, Giv'at Haviva archive, 17.90 B (3)) Thus, the only course of action agreed
upon by both the Mosaica's workers' committee and the Haifa Labor Council, was
the demand for compensation. All parties concerned were, at the same time, well
aware that the dismissals were brought about by the transition to "Hebrew Labor"
as required by the Jewish National Fund and by the Histadrut and the Haifa Labor
Council.

Aba Houshi turned the demand for compensation into a major issue, a genuine
struggle of the Haifa Labor Council on behalf of the rights of the Arab workers. (Aba
Houshi to HE, October 22, 1935. LA IV 208–1–781 A) Wolfman, in reply, was
quite adamant in rejecting any such demand, coming from the Histadrut which had
always strongly objected to his employing Arab labor. (Wolfman to HLC, October
23, 1935. LA IV 250–27–2–256) He was not the only one to object. The Arab
workers showed little interest in receiving compensation and in supporting Aba
Houshl's efforts "on their behalf". On the contrary, they expected to be able to continue working at the factory where they had been employed, in most cases, for a
number of years. They were deeply disillusioned by Aba Houshi's position in support
of their dismissal. Compensation was hardly the point, as far as they were concerned.
As members of the Palestine Labor League, they expected the Haifa Labor Council
to support their right to continue working, despite the opposition of the Jewish National Fund, and to put up the same struggle on their behalf as they would on behalf
of the Jewish workers. (Agassi's diary, November 28, 1935. LA IV 205–4)

Indeed, the Jewish workers of Mosaica were also in conflict with Wolfman. By
the middle of October, 1935, the tile factory was experiencing severe difficulties.
Depression had set in, as a result of the Italian invasion of Ethiopia, and production
contracted. Wolfman refused to continue paying his workers on a daily basis, nor
could he promise to pay their wages regularly for the months to come. Towards the
end of October, not having received their wages, the Jewish workers' committee declared a general strike, and called on all workers, Jewish and Arab, to join.

As far as the Haifa Labor Council and the Jewish workers of Mosaica were concerned, the strike centered on two distinct issues: the demand for the payment of compensation to the Arab workers, about to be dismissed by the end of the month with the transition of the factory to land leased from the Jewish National Fund, and the demand for immediate payment of the wages due to the workers and commitment to pay their wages, in the future, on a regular basis. (Letter of HLC to Wolfman, October 21 1935. LA IV 250–27–2–256; Minutes of secretariat of HLC, November 29, 1925. LA IV 250–27–1–625) The Arab workers, themselves, were bitterly disillusioned, and most wanted nothing to do with the strike and the workers' struggle with Wolfman. After all, the Haifa Labor Council did not commit itself to pay them compensation regardless of the outcome of the negotiations, and thus most preferred to continue working, despite the strike, until the end of the month, receive the wage due to them and return to their village. (Agassi's diary. LA IV 205–4)

The strike continued. It lasted close to a month before the major economic institutions of the Jewish community—the Department of Commerce and Industry of the Jewish Agency, the Industrialists' Association, and the Histadrut Executive intervened and put pressure on both parties to accept arbitration. The arbitrators, Abraham Krinitzi, an industrialist and public figure, and P. Gorokhovski of the Histadrut Executive in charge of its cooperative movement, obtained the commitment of Wolfman to pay his workers regularly, but avoided a clear decision concerning the payment of compensation to the dismissed Arab workers. Both Wolfman and the Haifa Labor Council, eager to bring the strike to an end, agreed to by-pass the issue. They decided to negotiate over each individual Arab worker, thus postponing any decision on the matter to an unspecified future date. The agreement was thus concluded, without either the Jewish or Arab workers of Mosaica being directly involved. (Conclusion of arbitrators, Item E., CZA, S9/1261, no date, probably middle of December 1935.)

Work was resumed. By the end of 1935, the tile factory located in the town of Haifa was closed and re-opened in the Haifa Bay industrial area, employing Jewish workers only. We can only assume that most of the Arab workers returned to their villages, as few new employment opportunities opened during the deepening depression of 1936.

A few months had passed since the Jewish workers returned to work. Construction work had dropped sharply and so did the work in Mosaica. The workers had returned, but there was not enough work to go around, and many, especially the women workers, worked only a few days a week. To the workers it seemed that little had been gained by their long strike. As in the two previous cases, the agreement which ended the strike held far more promise than the following weeks seemed to justify. Three months after the end of the strike the members of the workers' committee analyzed their struggle and its outcome. In theory, they wrote, two achievements had been won: compensation for the Arab workers and a commitment of the factory owner to pay wages on a regular basis. In fact, none of the Arab workers had received any compensation. As in many other cases, they concluded, the Histadrut began the struggle far better than it ended it.[13] The report went on to specify the infringement of promises made to the Jewish workers as well, the reduction in days of work, the attempts of the employer to lower wages, his efforts to get rid of the women workers and to challenge the authority of the workers' committees.

In the three cases discussed, the rank and file felt badly let down by the Histadrut. In all cases they claimed that the support given them was intermittent, piecemeal, and could not be counted on. Even so, the case of the Mosaica tile factory was somewhat exceptional. The disparity between the position of the workers' committee and that of the Histadrut, was striking. At no point did the Jewish workers ask for the exclusion of the Arab workers, and yet, the Arabs were excluded and work was resumed with Jewish labor only. The stringent "Jewish labor only" policy of the Haifa Labor Council and of the Construction Workers' Union, together with the separatist formal policy of the Jewish National Fund, left little room for the commitment expressed by the workers, the members of the Hashomer Hatza'ir, to their comrades. By the time the Arab general strike and rebellion broke out in April 1936, only a few months later, little was left of the pre-strike relations of cooperation.[14]

New Beginnings?

This article focused on case and event analysis; case studies of three workplaces where both Jewish and Arab workers were employed; and event analysis of a major strike which took place in each of these places and involved both the Arab and the Jewish workers. A work place, where workers come daily over an extended period of time, provides a meeting ground. Workers may interact directly or they may not; they may cooperate with each other, or compete, yet they are mutually visible and accessible to a far greater extent than elsewhere. Working in the same place, under the same employer, creates at least the potential for the emergence of common interests. Thus, a common work place provides an opportunity for the development of a new kind of identity and solidarity—as workers, a class solidarity—instead of, or more likely, supplementary to, national identity and solidarity. The event of a strike calls for the actual practice of solidarity. A strike creates a front of workers in opposition to their employer; their unity, the cooperation among them, is crucial for their success. Thus industrial enterprises where workers of both nationalities were employed, on more than a short, casual, basis, could be a good testing ground for the emergence of such an alternative identity. The conclusion at which I arrived was that in no case did such an alternative appear. In no case did the common experience transcend the national and economic dividing lines beyond a short period of time in which joint action, joint conflict, gave an impetus to cooperation and necessitated solidarity.

The three work places and work forces were clearly embedded in the dynamics of separatism before they entered upon a period of common struggle, though the specific expressions were somewhat different in each case. In no case was the employment of Arab workers by a Jewish private employer a simple neutral fact, accepted as a logical economic imperative. On the contrary, in each case opposition was expressed, and pressure was applied to reverse the situation. In the case of Nesher and Nur, the Jewish workers strongly objected to the employment of Arab workers, and considered such employment to be a displacement of Jewish workers who were far more entitled to such employment due to the presumed role of Jewish ownership in the development of a Jewish national community. This position was reinforced by both labor and national institutions. In the case of Mosaica, the Jewish workers did not oppose the continued employment of Arab workers. Yet the local labor institutions, the Haifa Labor Council and the Construction Workers' Union, and the national institutions in the form of the Jewish National Fund, were as stringent as ever in applying pressure for the implementation of the "Jewish only" labor policy.

Furthermore, despite the common denominator of working in the same enterprise, there were various differentiating factors within the work place. This was least evident in Nur, where the Jewish and Arab workers seem to have done approximately the same work, though differences according to gender and level of skill, did exist. In Nesher, the differentiation was the most obvious in location of work, type of work, conditions of labor and form of organization. Finally, in the case of Mosaica, there seems to have been greater cooperation than elsewhere, though even there the workers' organization did not avoid the impact of labor's separatist orientation. The Jewish and the Arab workers had different workers' committees, though the committees worked in close cooperation with each other. Furthermore, although both were organized under the auspices of the Histadrut, they belonged to different organizations—the Jewish workers belonged to the overall framework of the Histadrut with its local institutions and trade unions, while the Arab workers belonged to "their" special organization—the Palestine Labor League.

The struggle itself, the point at which national barriers were transcended and a new sense of class solidarity emerged, was not totally divorced from the national, i.e. separatist, impact. In the three cases, the broader political and economic context intruded again and again. In the case of Nur, the employers tried to manipulate the dividing lines between the Jewish and Arab workers to break down their newly achieved common front. They spread rumors concerning the intentions of the Jewish workers to expel their Arab co-workers, and attempted to create a clash of interests by offering the Jewish workers benefits to be denied to the Arab workers. The Jewish workers did not succumb to such divisive temptations, but it would appear that they were guided more by an awareness of the loss they would incur by accepting such offers than by a newly felt solidarity. In the case of the strike of the workers in the Nesher quarry, the Jewish workers were quite explicit about their ambivalence, which stemmed from the clash between their identification with workers who were so blatantly exploited by their employer on the one hand and, on the other, their opposition to those workers being employed at all. Their support was extended, but it was never divorced from the larger struggle for Jewish labor only in the Nesher cement company and quarry. Finally, in Mosaica, the overall political context was no less intrusive. The Arab and Jewish workers faced different as an outcome of their strike, even though the grass roots workers would have preferred it otherwise.

The overall impact of the political-ideological context for both Jewish and Palestinian Arab workers is evident in the wide range of parties which intervened at various points—the Haifa Labor Council, the Histadrut Executive, the Palestine Labor League, the Jewish Agency, the Industrialists' Association, the National Council, and later, the Palestine Arab Workers' Society—all of these parties were directly involved in determining the relations of separation on the Jewish side, and of rejection, on the Palestinian side, which shaped Arab-Jewish relations. It should be noted that as time passed there were more parties involved. In the 1920s, in the case of Nur, the Haifa Labor Council and the Histadrut Executive were involved in the strike but in nothing else. In the 1930s, in the cases of both Nesher and Mosaica, two additional parties were involved, the Palestine Labor League on the one hand and, on the other, the Palestine Arab Workers' Society. These two parties were in direct opposition to each other. Their appearance on the scene further complicated the ability of the workers to shape their relations, unaffected by the national conflict surrounding them.

The success of the struggle was limited. Only some of the goals were won, and these were eroded before long. In the case of Nur, the workers had to give up many of their demands and accept two levels of wages in the factory, very much against their better judgment. In the case of Nesher, the Arab workers had to accept the arbitrator's decisions, even though he refused to call off the dismissal of the leaders of the strike. Finally, in the case of Mosaica, the workers returned after the demands of the Jewish workers had been met, while those of the Arab workers had been pushed aside. The Histadrut was unable to provide sufficient help for the striking Arab workers of Nesher or Mosaica, nor could it provide them with alternative employment. Thus, even as the strikes ended, doubts existed as to the potential of joint action.

Little changed in each case as a result of the strikes. They did not bring about any significant change in the conditions of Jewish and Arab labor and in the institutional, economic and political relations between them. The Arab workers still earned much lower wages than the Jewish workers. Even if the particular workers who participated in the strike, as in the case of Nur, were to earn the same wages, there was still a large supply of much cheaper workers near by. Arab workers were still much less effectively organized than the Jewish workers, and there was little tendency for organizational cooperation, even in the 1930s when new organizations appeared on the scene. Thus it is not surprising that within a short period of time the few achievements which had been attained, or had appeared to be attained, were lost. Furthermore, there was neither the individual or organizational strength to embark on an additional strike, once the few achievements were eroded.

As the attempt to improve the conditions of labor, which culminated in the unsuccessful strikes, could not be repeated, before long relations at the work place between the three parties—Jewish workers, Arab workers and management—deteriorated. Management increased its exploitation, well aware of the workers' fatigue. The relations between the workers themselves were somewhat more complex. The solidarity gave way to latent or manifest competition, which had characterized relations (at least in Nur and Nesher) prior to the joint strike. In the absence of any significant improvement, relations continued to deteriorate, and, before too long, the labor force in each of the three workplaces was no longer mixed. Within a year or two Nur employed almost only Arab workers, while in Mosaica and in Nesher only Jewish workers were employed.

The discussion so far has focused on workplaces in the Jewish sector of the economy in which both Jewish and Palestinian Arab workers were employed. Such joint employment characterized the government sector of the economy as well. Separatist principles were not adopted in the government sector, and thus greater cooperation could be expected. Nevertheless, this usually was not the case. The issue is beyond the scope of this article. Suffice to note that the government sector was not removed from the national conflict and was affected by it in numerous ways. The national and labor spokesmen of the conflicting parties were divided concerning the employment and wage policies of the government sector, and the workers remained affiliated with their respective nationally oriented labor organizations. The Palestine Railways, the one work place where cooperation continued on a long-term basis, even though intermittently, hesitantly and not always successfully, can serve primarily as the exception which reinforces the rule. The Jewish and Arab workers who led the Joint ventures in the Palestine Railways were, unlike the cases discussed above, all skilled workers, who worked, over many years, in the same place, within the same workshops, doing the same work. They were employed directly by the Railway management, which meant, in the case of the Jewish workers, that they were not recruited via the labor exchange of the Histadrut. Furthermore, their organization— the Railway, Post and Telegraph Workers' Organization—while affiliated with the Histadrut, retained some autonomy in relation to the Histadrut Executive. Nevertheless, even under these conditions, the national conflict kept intruding and was not significantly transcended by class solidarity for more than the duration of the common struggles.

To return to the cases discussed in this article, I have argued that the employment of both Jewish and Arab workers in Jewish owned factories, which, it was hypothesized, might have led to a new solidarity between the workers, was unable to do so. These workplaces were not able to transcend either the split labor market or the political-ideological setting in which they existed and on which they were, to a major extent, dependent. Regrettably, but not surprisingly, the split labor market was too blatant, and the national conflict too encompassing, for a contrasting, or even an autonomous, identity to emerge, or for cooperation to significantly moderate both separatism and rejection.

To conclude, I have argued that the employment of both Jewish and Arab workers in Jewish-owned factories, which, it was hypothesized, might have led to a new solidarity between the workers, was unable to do so. These workplaces were not able to transcend either the split labor market or the political-ideological setting in which they existed, and on which they were, to a major extent, dependent. Regrettably, but not surprisingly, the split labor market was too blatant, and the national conflict too encompassing, for a contrasting, or even an autonomous, identity to emerge, or for cooperation to significantly moderate both separatism and rejection.

References

Aboud, Nader. 1988. The Palestinian Arab Labor Movement Association, 1925–1947. Masters thesis, University of Haifa, Haifa. (Hebrew).

Bernstein, Deborah. 1995. "From Split Labor Market Strategy to Political Co-optation: The Palestine Labor League." *Middle Eastern Studies* 31: 755–771.

_____. 1996. "Expanding the Split Labor Market Theory: Between and Within Sectors of the Split Labor Market of Mandatory Palestine." *Comparative Studies of Society and History* 38, pp. 243–266.

_____. 1998. "Strategies of Equalization: Jews and Arabs in the Split Labor Market of Mandatory Palestine." *Ethnic and Racial Studies* 21, pp. 449–475.

Bonacich, Edna. 1979. "The Past, Present and Future of Split Labor Market Theory." *Research in Race and Ethnic Relations* 1, pp. 17–64.

Budeiri, Musa. 1979. *The Development of the Workers' Movement in Palestine, 1919–1948.* Jerusalem: Dar al-Kitab. (Arabic).

Gertz, A. 1947. *Statistical Handbook of Palestine—1947.* Jerusalem: Department of Statistics of the Jewish Agency.

Grinberg, Lev Luis. 1993. *The Histadrut Above All.* Jerusalem: Nevo. (Hebrew).

Horowitz, Dan and Moshe Lissak. 1977. *The Origins of the Israeli Polity.* Tel Aviv: Am Oved. (Hebrew).

Kimmerling, Baruch. 1983a. *Zionism and Territory: The Socioterritorial Dimensions of Zionist Politics.* Berkeley: Institute of International Studies, University of California.

_____. 1983b. *Zionism and Economy.* Cambridge: Schenkman.

Kimmerling, Baruch and Joel S. Migdal. 1993. *Palestinians, The Making of a People.* New York: Free Press.

Klinov-Malul, Ruth and Nadav Halevi. 1968. *The Economic Development of Israel.* Jerusalem: Academon. (Hebrew).

Metzer, Jacob and Oded Kaplan. 1985. "Jointly but Severally: Arab-Israel Dualism and Economic Growth in Mandatory Palestine." *The Journal of Economic History* 45.

Porath Y. *1976. The Emergence of the Palestinian-Arab National Movement, 1918–1929.* Tel Aviv: Am Oved. (Hebrew).

_____. 1978. *From Riots to Rebellion, The Palestinian-Arab, National Movement, 1929–1939.* Tel Aviv: Am Oved. (Hebrew).

Shafir, Gershon. 1989. *Land and Labor and the Origins of the Israeli Palestinian Conflict, 1882–1914.* Cambridge: Cambridge University Press.

Shalev, Michael. 1992. *Labor and the Political Economy in Israel.* Oxford: Oxford University Press.

Tzahor, Ze'ev. 1979. *The Histadrut—the Formative Period* (no place, no publisher). (Hebrew).

Notes

1. Report of R. Graves, formerly an official of the British Administration in Egypt, presented the Palestine Government with a detailed report of Arab labor in Palestine and the difficulties facing the consolidation of labor organization, June 19, 1941. ISA, CO, 733/441, Tape 75430/2.

2. There are numerous sources documenting wages of Arab and Jewish workers; suffice it to point to two government reports: Report of the Wage Commission1928, ISA, CO,733/152; Labor Legislation Report, 6 October1932, ISA, CO, 733/220, Tape 97130/1; and to Gertz, *Statistical Handbook*, p.300

3. The Palestine Arab Workers' Society was founded, in Haifa, in 1925 but held its first large conference only in January 1930.

4. The Weizmann brothers were not related to the leader of the Zionist movement, Chaim Weizmann.

5. This is taken from an unsigned and undated hand-written report. The content indicates that it was written in the summer of 1926, about half a year before the outbreak of the strike. The workers' committee was composed of Jewish men, and most probably one of them wrote this report.

6. Philip Hassoun was a Christian Arab who attempted to recruit support for the Histadrut among Arab workers in Haifa and ran the Workers' Club established by the Haifa Labor Council for Arab workers. Avraham Khalfon, a member of a distinguished Sephardi family in Haifa, served as a translator in joint meetings of Arab and Jewish workers and later became the secretary of the Haifa Municipal Council.

7. Of the Jewish workers, 21 were men and 8 women, and among the Arab workers, 51 were men and 12 were women. March 3, 1932, *Davar*.

8. They had earned only 250 mil per day during the construction of the plant, but they went out on strike, together with the workers of two other large, Jewish, privately-owned enterprises, and won a raise to 300 mils as a starting wage.

9. It was signed by Zvi Grinberg on behalf of the workers and by Musbah Shkiffi, the contractor, and by an additional eight witnesses, six Arab quarry workers, a member of the Nesher workers' committee and Aba Houshi of the HLC, October 16, 1932. LA IV208–1–615.

10. The PAWS issued a number of leaflets in support of the quarry workers. March 2, 13, 1936. LA IV 104–49–73.

11. David Hacohen of Solel Boneh and his negotiating partner Hana Asfour, of the Palestine Arab Workers' Society, were both members of the Haifa Municipal Council, and thus had both formal and informal relations.

12. For further details of the different wage systems see Bernstein, Deborah. 1995. "'Jews and Arabs in the Nesher Cement Company," *Cathedra* 78, p.103 (Hebrew)

13. Undated report of workers' committee of Mosaica, Giv'at Haviva 17.90 B (3), mentions being written three months after end of strike.

14. In an interview with one of the Jewish workers, conducted in his kibbutz in 1994, all he could recall was the defense of the factory from Arab attacks during the height of the Arab Rebellion. Little was left in his memory concerning the earlier period of cooperation, though he claimed that, given the dates I gave, he was sure to have been employed at the time.

3

The Ideological Wellspring of Zionist Capitalism: The Impact of Private Capital and Industry on the Shaping of the Dominant Zionist Ideology

MICHAL FRENKEL, YEHOUDA SHENHAV,
AND HANNA HERZOG

Despite deep paradigmatic differences, most researchers of Israeli society agree that from its beginnings to the present day it has undergone a political, economic, and cultural revolution. The core of that revolution was the transition from a socialist to a capitalist orientation, from a centralist, planned economy controlled by the labor movement and the Histadrut (General Federation of Labor) to a semi-competitive economy in which the owners of private capital play a central role and decisions are affected by a liberal-economic ideology. An additional assumption shared by most students of Israeli society is that the political institutions—the labor parties, the Histadrut, and the state—are dominant factors in engineering the structural shift. The principal benefactors of the transformation—the capitalists, the industrialists, and the merchants—are omitted from the explanation.

Researchers date the rupture—the turnabout from a socialist to a capitalist orientation—differently. Some place it approximately contiguous with the state's establishment, others suggest a much later period, such as 1977 (Ram, 1992) or 1985 (Shalev, 1997). According to the advocates of the early date, who take a functional approach, the absorption of the vast numbers of immigrants who inundated the

The authors thank the Sapir Center at Tel Aviv University, Faculty of the social sciences, for partial funding of this study. The assistance and services received from the dedicated workers of the Central Zionist Archive, The Israel State Archive and the Pinchas Lavon Archive are highly appreciated.

nascent state, accompanied by inexorable modernization processes and a metamor-
phosis of values that was integral to these processes, were the main driving forces of
the change (Eisenstadt, 1967; Horowitz and Lissak, 1989). Neomarxist perspectives attribute the shift to modifications in the attitude of Mapai (Rosenfeld and
Carmi, 1976); almost overnight, this view maintains, the party discarded its traditional national socialist ideology and espoused a statist, capitalist oriented ideology.
As a result, the public means of production could be appropriated into private
hands and a middle class could emerge, to become the foundation for the relentless
rise of capitalism and mounting allocative inequality in Israel. Amir Ben-Porat
(1993), too, emphasizes the importance of the state in the germination and efflo-
rescence of capitalism in Israel. The incubation period of Israeli capitalism, he argues, began with the state's establishment, and its rapid development was influenced
by the penetration of Western ideas into the country and by the state's operation as
an independent agent.[1]

These writers, along with many others, ascribe exclusivity to the project of the
labor movement in shaping the dominant discourse during the period of the Yishuv,
the pre–1948 Jewish community in Palestine (see, for example, Shapiro, 1977;
Sternhell, 1995). The industrialists and the bourgeoisie are considered a passive factor. They cooperate with the agenda-setters in the understanding that nothing on
the agenda will damage their interests directly, and they play no role in shaping the
dominant discourse of Israeli society.

In this essay we wish to challenge the two conventional approaches outlined
above: the ascription of exclusivity to the political institutions in shaping the dominant discourse, and the assumption of a dramatic turnabout proximate to the historic milestone of 1948. We describe the involvement of the industrialists and the
owners of capital in configuring the dominant Zionist ideology already in the pre-
state years. Our contention is that the capitalist discourse and practices that were
applied ever more intensively immediately after the genesis of the state were preceded by an extensive ideological phase. Since cultural transformations do not occur
overnight, and since practices that lack an ideological infrastructure may be considered illegitimate in the public discourse, it is important to trace the way in which industry was integrated into the dominant Zionist discourse.

The article describes how the industrialists sought, for their own reasons, to expand the boundaries of the basic conceptions in the Zionist-socialist discourse to incorporate—and legitimate—their project. These basic concepts, such as "private
capital" and "national capital," "pioneering" (*chalutziyut*), "conquest of the wilderness," and the "conquest of labor," which are usually attributed to the ideological
lexicon of the labor movement, underwent a process of expanded meaning in order
to make possible the participation of ostensibly antagonistic groups, such as the industrialists and the owners of capital, in the legitimate discourse. It is important to
emphasize that we do not claim that the industrialists and capitalists managed their
project from the outset with the intention of expanding the dominant discourse or
entering it. The industrialists were motivated by a specific interest, which was

bound up with the needs of the enterprises they controlled. Their impact on the public discourse was a by-product of the gains they achieved for their enterprises by extending the dominant ideology. Those gains will be closely analyzed in the article.

We will argue that the extension of the legitimate discourse, as described above, enabled the labor movements themselves to promote pro-capitalist practices. Under the sheltering wings of the Histadrut, for example, the Work Productivity Institute was established in 1949, with the aim of increasing industrial productivity in private and Histadrut factories alike. That and other projects were perceived by the labor leadership of the 1930s as conflicting with labor's interests; but after the symbols of the dominant discourse were extended and industrial productivity became a legitimate Zionist goal, the Histadrut's institute was accepted as the natural continuation of its other actions. A view of these practices as normal development and not as a sharp deviation or ideological upheaval enabled the labor parties to advance a pro-capitalist policy without undermining their dominant position.

The article's empirical aspect is based on a close perusal of one case, which encapsulates private industry in Palestine—Palestine Potash, Ltd. This case is instructive about attributes of private industry during the period of the British Mandate, and those attributes, moreover, have left their imprint on contemporary Israeli industry.

Palestine Potash, Ltd. (PPL), our research case, was the largest Jewish-owned private company during most of the Mandate period. PPL was registered in Britain, established by Jews with British, American and Jewish shareholders, and employed Arabs and Jews—union-organized and otherwise. A survey of the history of PPL uncovers the ideological struggles waged by the industrialists within the framework of the socialist-Zionist-discourse and outside it to further their interests. We argue that these ideological struggles spawned a different, expanded, dominant ideology, which afterward enabled the rise of a capitalist ideology without acute opposition.

This study, then, seeks to add another significant layer in order to complete the picture painted by Israeli historiography, which until now has focused on the role of the politicians, their movements, and their institutions in the shaping of the dominant discourse in Israel. Yet the reasons for this sweeping disregard by Israeli historiography and sociology of the contribution made by the owners of capital and the industrialists to forging the Zionist ideology and shaping the country's economic institutions themselves merit a thorough sociological analysis.

The heated debate being conducted in Israel nowadays between the so-called "old" and "new" historians does little to shed light on the role of industrialists (or managers) in shaping the dominant Israeli ideology. The "old" historians are blamed for adhering to the political elite's socialist-Zionist ideology, which exalted the principles of nation-building by organized workers rather than industrialists and managers, and by means of national rather than private capital. Hence, it is argued, the inability of these scholars to uncover the part played by moneyed and other groups in setting the national agenda (Giladi, 1969). The "old" historians, who are really a key element in the ruling elite, reproduce the dominant political and cultural discourse and accept the basic tenets of Zionist ideology as the foundation of their ostensibly "objective" studies (Kimmerling, 1992; Ram, 1989; Herzog, 1985). This, as well as the division of labor in academia, which placed industry and management in the fields of economics and business studies, rather than in sociology, discouraged research into the role of the industrialists in shaping Israeli society.

The "new" historians, on the other hand, set themselves up as an opposition to the Zionist elite and its historiography. Most of their work addresses the 1948 War and the Palestinian-Zionist conflict. While rejecting many of the "old" historians' underlying assumptions, the "new" school uncritically adopt their focus on the organized workers and the political leadership as the main (albeit not the only) protagonists on the Zionist side (Shafir, 1989; Shalev, 1992; Grinberg, 1993). To the extent that narratives of capitalists are related, they are treated as an alternative pole to the leadership's policy—an alternative which was completely rejected (in this sense they continue the tradition of the "old" critical historians, such as Shapiro, 1977; and Sternhell, 1995).

Infused with the postmodernist spirit, other "new" as well as "old" historians have recently begun to give voice to traditionally weak or marginal groups, such as women, oriental Jews, Palestinians with Israeli citizenship, homosexuals, and others. Paradoxically, industrialists and managers remain excluded from the narrative. Indeed, industrialists and managers, despite their organizational weakness, were never truly marginal and, as we show, their world-view was ultimately accepted.

This paper then, deals with a neglected story in both the "old" and the "new" historiography. From a critical point of view, it promulgates unheard, though not necessarily weak, voices, and our hope is to contribute to a better understanding of present-day Israeli society.

Industry and the
Socialist-Zionist Discourse

Most scholars characterize the Zionist discourse conducted in the Yishuv during the Mandate period as basically socialist, resting on four main organizing principles: national rather than private capital, collectivism not individualism, commitment to equality, and a preference for agriculture as a way of life and livelihood (Beilin, 1978, p.55; Shapiro, 1977). These principles conflict with Western concepts, which were the bedrock on which modern industry evolved. The principles espoused by private industrialists traditionally uphold private capital, individualism, and of course industry over agriculture. The private industrialists in Mandate Palestine were no exception, but their situation became more complicated as the political carriers of the socialist-Zionist discourse accumulated power.

The amplification of the nationalist-socialist discourse, particularly at the beginning of the 1930s, signifies the triumph of the orientation advocated by one of the numerous groups that placed on the Zionist agenda complex and mutually contradictory issues arising from the political and economic conditions in Palestine. That this particular discourse assumed hegemony was due to the political victory of the Palestine Zionists (also known as the "Europeans") headed by Chaim Weizmann, over the American Zionists led by Louis Brandeis. Until 1921, the two groups fought each other in Zionist institutions over a central principle in the shaping of the Yishuv economy: the sources of capital and its mode of investment. At the ideological level, the debate involved the character of the country's development. The Brandeis group, impressed by the intensive industrialization in the United States, put their trust in market forces and "unadulterated" economic interests.[2] Weizmann's followers were influenced by the land-settlement political movements and sought to strengthen the control of the World Zionist Organization (WZO) over the Jewish institutions and politics by concentrating capital and allocating resources on the basis of "national needs" to be determined by the Zionist institutions.

The struggle ended with Weizmann's victory at the 1921 conference of American Zionists held in Cleveland (Shapiro, 1971), at which Brandeis's followers were effectively removed from their key positions in the Zionist Organization of America. One result was the establishment of the "Keren Hayesod" fund as an institutional expression of the decision to build Palestine utilizing national capital to be raised from world Jewry. Distribution of the funds would be on national rather than economic grounds, with the emphasis on a centralized structure. The Brandeis group reacted by setting up the Palestine Economic Corporation (PEC) to raise and invest funds based both on national and economic considerations. PEC competed with Keren Hayesod both in fundraising and in capital investment in Palestine. Their rivalry had far-reaching consequences for the attitude of the dominant Zionist discourse toward private capital and industry. Zionism held the view that private capital was the antithesis of national capital, a view based on the identification of the nation, in this context, with the institutions of the WZO (Metzer, 1979). Private capital was perceived to jeopardize national goals (and also, in practice, the WZO's control). Weizmann's victory, then, went a long way toward determining the political and ideological conditions in which the industrialists and capitalists had to operate—conditions which differed substantively from those in which industry developed in the Anglo-Saxon world.

In 1920s' Palestine—as in Western Europe at the launch of industrialization[3]— even before the emergence of the labor-oriented ideology, the industrialists faced sharp opposition: they had to contend with an agrarian aristocracy and with workers who feared for their future. Their problem was compounded by the victory of socialist-Zionism. They now had to operate within the framework of a Zionist ideology which was all but openly hostile to their endeavors and to deal with laborers who besides being well-organized were part of the ruling political elite.

To cut through this tangle, we will employ the terms "legitimation" and "ideology." The legitimation accorded to the ideology of a particular group within the wider social discourse enables it to employ practices which serve its interests unopposed. The term ideology, in this context, is derived from Stuart Hall (1982), who draws a connection between the Geertzian perception of ideology as a system of meanings and the theme of power, which is absent from Geertz but is pronounced in neo-Marxist discourse and especially in Gramsci's analysis of hegemony. Following Hall, ideology will be defined as a system of meanings which is created and attributed in the course of a forceful political struggle: different forces, in different historical periods, compete for the use of symbols and ideas drawn from the society's dominant symbolic system in order to further their interests. By successfully identifying itself with symbols or signs, a group can render its interpretation dominant—that is, define how other groups, too, are expected to perceive reality. Ideology, then, is the symbolic system of a group, which controls the ability to frame reality for itself and for other groups. Hall emphasizes that ideology is conceptualized in terms of articulation of elements. The ideological sign is always equivocal and ambivalent, and generally is not part of a rigid hierarchy of signs. The adversarial groups try to reshape it and endow it with new meanings which will serve their interests, and to associate it with various social carriers. By constructing meanings for the signs, they seek to posit social subjects in a different manner.

Using a slightly different concept of the term ideology, Reinhard Bendix (1974) discusses the strategies that served industrialists, entrepreneurs, and managers as they endeavored to legitimate industry: "Wherever enterprises are set up," he writes, "a few command and many obey. The few, however, have seldom been satisfied to command without a higher justification even when they abjured all interest in ideas, and the many have seldom been docile enough not to provoke such justifications." (1974 [1956], p. 1).

Bendix depicts two central ideologies which industrialists in different societies drew on to justify industrialization and their control of the workers. In the West these were rational, scientific ideologies, directly associated with the managerial sphere, which portrayed industrialization as a way of life expressing progress and rationality. The distinction between managers and laborers was emphasized, and the former's control of the latter was justified by their alleged possession of relevant, rational, scientific knowledge. "Rationality," a cardinal tenet of the modern society, legitimates the operations of industrialists and managers. This was the underlying idea for the development of the "scientific management" by Frederick Taylor and his disciples.

Ideology of an entirely different stripe emerged in Eastern Europe: collectivist, royalist, or socialist. The core difference between the two types of ideology is the question of legitimation, and especially legitimation for controlling the fate of others. Whereas in the West this legitimation derives from recognition of the right of those who have "made it" to manage their property as they wish (i.e., legitimation deriving initially from ownership and afterward from a monopoly on specific scientific knowledge which is, ostensibly, in the possession of the salaried managers), in Russia the justification for the rule of the few over the many lay in the subordination of controllers and controlled alike to one supreme body—the autocratic ruler and then the ruling party. Tsar and Communist Party alike were perceived to embody the common interests of employers and employed, of the dominant and the dominated.

Palestine might have been expected to accommodate elements from the two types of ideologies which Bendix located in the West and the East. Most of the country's industrialists and owners of private capital were originally from Russia or Germany, where they had also engaged in industry and engineering. The laborers, and especially their leaders, were also educated in Russia and Poland, and might have been thought to accept, at least in part, the "eastern-European" system of justifications. Moreover, the British administration in Palestine, which controlled some of the resources needed by industry, was part of the Western industrial discourse. Nevertheless, the industrialization ideologies, whether their sources lay in the West or the East, are not entirely germane to the Palestine context, which accepted neither scientific management nor industrial engineering as legitimate doctrines. True, Louis Brandeis, the leader of the American Zionists, was a keen advocate of Taylor's ideas and actively promoted rational management doctrines; however, like Brandeis's other suggestions, his ideas on management were spurned by the dominant Zionist discourse. Kahane (1968) maintains that the Yishuv thought that professionalism conflicted with its central ethos, and therefore theories of scientific management which emphasized professional elements could not guarantee legitimation for the industrialists' demands in this context.

Nor could royalist or communist ideologies accord legitimation in the absence of both a monarch and a monolithic political ideology. Effective coercion was impossible without a binding political entity that could arouse identification. Still, the collectivist ideologies bore priority in the Zionist context, which held up collectivism as a central value. Furthermore, the "body" which was exalted, to which both employers and employed paid obeisance, was the nation.[4]

The sections that follow, then, deal with the political and historical conditions that characterized the Israeli case with respect to industry and with the "system of justifications" that developed in Yishuv industry as a result of those conditions. We will try to uncover the ideologies that underlay the industrialists' financial investments and the methods by which they ensured their control of both production and labor. We will argue that in a period of nation building, in which nationalist ideology in a socialist version served as a central mobilizing mechanism, the industrialists and capitalists also sought to incorporate their interests within the framework of that discourse, which they the proceeded to utilize and expand.

Because few secondary sources exist about the industrialists in the Yishuv period, we have chosen, as mentioned above, to try and extrapolate their practices through one case study, Palestine Potash, Ltd. The analysis is based on primary archival sources, memoirs, biographies and autobiographies, and books of documentation.

Palestine Potash, Ltd.:
Industrial Organization in a Political Context

PPL, the subject of our cases study, was the largest private industrial enterprise in Palestine during most of the period under discussion. An attempt is made to trace the practices and ideologies through which the company and its founder-manager, Moshe Novomeysky, sought legitimation, primarily in the form of obtaining funding and gaining control over the workers in straitened political and economic conditions.

The company's existence, from the beginning of the effort to acquire the potash charter in 1920 until its shutdown in 1948, corresponds with the time frame which is defined as the formative period of the Israeli society's institutional and ideological patterns. PPL was established concurrent with the consolidation of the British Mandate government in Palestine. Upon Israel's creation the enterprise was shut down in its original format, to be reopened in 1954, this time under state ownership. PPL was in a sense a crossroads at which nearly all the factors that were involved in shaping Yishuv's image converged at some point. The company was registered in Britain. The Dead Sea Charter to extract potash was granted by His Majesty's Government only after a lengthy contest in which the paths of diverse interests intersected: the British Empire, which needed potash to manufacture explosives; Zionism in all its branches, which saw in the exploitation of the Dead Sea's resources the realization of Herzl's vision in *Altneuland* and the repulsion of interests harbored by the Trans-Jordan authorities, who considered themselves sovereign over half of the Dead Sea; and the Palestine faction in the WZO. The latter invested part of the "national capital" with which it aspired to build the Yishuv in PPL, intending for it to be managed in line with the WZO's principles, contrary to the interests of the American Zionists led by Brandeis, who had lost the battle to build the Yishuv on capitalist principles but still invested their private capital as well as PEC funds in PPL and sat on its board of directors. Another group with vested interests was Jewish labor, which was organized in various forms. Some of the Jewish laborers were organized in the Histadrut, which on the one hand controlled part of the resources needed by PPL and on the other hand sought to protect its political interests in the company. Another group of organized workers was the "Labor Battalion" of Ramat Rachel, a kibbutz near Jerusalem who later on settled in Beit Ha'aravah by the Dead Sea. Their leader, Yehouda Kopolovich, later became the most prominent spokesperson of the organized Jewish workers in the site. He was able to convince the leading political figures of the labor parties of the firm's importance.

Other Jewish workers, particularly the clerks, joined PPL for other reasons entirely; they were also organized in a completely different manner from the manual laborers, and their life style was very unlike that of the kibbutz members. Arab workers (mostly Bedouin) were also employed in the plants, mainly in simple manual labor.

The groups with which the company had to interact in order to obtain legitimation—i.e., get the charter, receive economic and political support, and mobilize and control workers—were also institutionally and ideologically diverse. Within this complex historical context, we shall examine the ideologies that served the industrialization process, and particularly the nationalist ideology in its "laborite" version, expanded to incorporate the industrialists' interests.

The foundation for considering the working of the Zionist praxis at the Dead Sea was laid in the movement's early literature. In 1882, E.L. Levinsky published his utopian novel *A Journey to the Land of Israel in the [Jewish] Year 5800* (i.e., the year 2040), which described an industrialized city of salt by the Dead Sea. (Almog and Eshel, 1956, p.129) Herzl, visiting Palestine in 1898, also heard about the possibility of exploiting the Dead Sea, and devoted much of the chapter in *Altneuland* about the flourishing industry to be established in the "old-new" land to the subject. (Herzl, 1903, p.168) In 1904, probably under the influence of Herzl's ideas, the Zionist Executive organized a research mission to Palestine headed by M. Blanckenhorn (a world-renowned European geologist) to collect concrete information, which the Zionist movement needed in order to purchase the salt charter from the government of Turkey.[5] However, at this stage the entrepreneurs were not awarded the charter. This and other attempts by the Zionist institutions to obtain a foothold in the Dead Sea area, mainly by trying to purchase nearby land for settlement, failed.[6]

Moshe Novomeysky, the eventual initiator and founder of PPL, was a mining engineer who had gained experience in extracting salts at Lake Baykal, in Siberia. Novomeysky cites personal and national reasons as his motivation for establishing the company. In his book, *My Siberian Life* (1956), he explains that nationalist feelings drew him to the area. Herzl's writings, he says, inspired him to develop the Dead Sea region and further the Zionist cause. (Novomeysky, 1958, p.238) "I thought that my professional qualifications and practical experience of industrial and mining development in an underdeveloped country (Siberia) would be of value in the land in which was now to be established that 'Jewish national home' by which I was already inspired. Material advantage was far from my thoughts. At the time, Palestine was as devoid of industry as had been a great portion of Siberia in the days when I started my industrial career there, and the prospect of being one of those to develop it excited me greatly." (Novomeyski, p. 335) Elsewhere, he likens his activities and rationale to the motivations of the Zionist leaders: "The present writer came to Israel exactly thirty years ago. He did not come seeking lucre. He came for the same reason that brought many others at that time or earlier, among them today's leaders. " (1951).

Patently, the effort to frame industry as part of the "national project" developed on fertile ground; but the fact that a private firm worked the only natural resource in the "Land of Israel" was not necessarily legitimate in the Jewish public discourse, least of all in view of the rise of the socialist aspect of Zionism to dominance. The following section will describe PPL's ideological struggle to win legitimation for its operations as a capitalist enterprise within the framework of that discourse. We argue that industrialists' success in this struggle set the stage for the subsequent rise of capitalistic policy.

Ideological Work,
the Struggle to Reframe the
Basic Concepts of Socialist Zionism

Private Capital, National Capital, and the Fight for Control of PPL

Was PPL a private firm or a national enterprise? This question, which has never been satisfactorily answered and has spawned countless arguments between the groups involved, evokes one of the crucial issues in Zionist ideology, especially in its "labor" version: the ostensibly commonplace, neutral distinction that is drawn between private capital and national capital. As will be seen, this conceptual dichotomy is not unrelated to the struggle among the political parties and between the owners of capital and the labor movements.

Metzer (1977) explains the difference between "national capital" as defined by positivist economics and its definition as a political value. In positivist economics, "national capital" is "the net value of the stock of the produced assets of production which are owned by all the economic units of the national economy: households, private and public firms, and the public-governmental sector" (p.2). This is countered by the "normative" definition posited by the Zionist institutions, which treat national capital as "the range of economic sources which will be available to the *institutions* in order to build the National Home in the Land of Israel in its full scope and scale" (Ulitzur, 1939, p.11, quoted by Metzer, 1976, authors' emphasis). In other words, that part of capital which is categorized as national capital is at the disposal of the official Zionist institutions. Moreover, Metzer and Gozansky (1986, pp.87–110) point out that different bodies purport to understand the term national capital differently as they vie for control. Baron Hirsch's investments through the Palestine Jewish Colonization Association [PJCA], for example, are sometimes referred to as private capital but in other instances as national capital, and in other cases it is subsumed under a separate category, "public capital." Naturally, the WZO's prerogative to define any enterprise as one that is founded on "national capital" gives it the right to intervene in its operations, while at the same time the owners, by designating an enterprise "national" can benefit from cheap financing which originates in that national capital and from legitimation by the national institutions and organized labor. The struggle by different groups to impose their definition of reality as the dominant one was central to the labor parties' ideological drive to achieve control in the Yishuv. In this context the owners of capital and the industrialists were caught in the middle. If their capital was considered "national capital," their operations would become subject to the demands of the Zionist leadership, which sometimes made little economic sense; but by the same token if their firm was perceived to be part of the Zionist project, they would become eligible for benefits not easily passed over. The elements that the industrialists introduced into the dominant Zionist discourse are here considered part of their continuous effort to define their place within its complex mosaic. Would they become part of the dominant discourse from which they were excluded, or should they continue to manage their affairs separately, driven by what the discourse held to be the profit motive? The dilemma is reflected in the struggle for the Dead Sea charter and the efforts to finance it.

The Competition for the Charter

Novomeysky waged his struggle for the charter at a critical juncture in shaping the character of the Yishuv and determining its relations with the Mandate authorities. Formally, the Weizmann-Brandeis contest had already been decided, but the two groups remained rivals and each considered it a feather in its respective cap to help found a company to exploit the country's major natural resource.[7] In the 1920s the labor parties had not yet consolidated their political hegemony; it would reach its peak in the following decade, and was also bound up with the debate over the Yishuv's character. These were also the years in which the British entrenched their rule in Palestine, though this brought about a shift in their perception of the situation. Their previous absolute support for the Zionist cause gradually gave way to the recognition that both sides, Jews and Arabs, had legitimate claims to Palestine.

These, then, were the constraints under which Novomeysky sought the charter. He pressed his case in three main spheres—political, financial, and technical—and in a range of political and organizational environments, involving the British, the Zionists, and businessmen who were potential investors in the new company.

The technical aspect was the simplest. Novomeysky had proof of his ability to extract potash from the Dead Sea. Getting the charter from Britain was the major problem. The Dead Sea was the only source of potash in the British Empire, and London was concerned that it would fall into hostile hands. Consequently, the possibility that the charter might be awarded to a non-British company generated both government and public opposition to Novomeysky. Novomeysky was a Russian national, and the fact that another Russian, Pinhas Rutenberg, had already received the electric-power charter, only compounded the situation. (Novomeysky, 1958, p.253) To muster political support, Novomeysky turned to James de Rothschild (for example, in 1924) but principally to Chaim Weizmann. The latter had met with officials of the Colonial Office and threw his support behind Novomeysky within the framework of the cooperation between the Mandate government and the WZO. Other Zionist leaders, such as Nachum Sokolov, Cohen, and Lipsky (the latter two were American Zionists) were also active in the effort to obtain the charter. (CZA Z4/3473)

The company also faced financial difficulties because of the time needed to obtain the charter. Given the extraordinary importance of potash and the Mandate government's economic and colonial interests, the British wanted to be sure that the charter awardee would be able to implement it and maximize profits, to be shared by the government in the form of taxes and royalties. In addition, even before the tender for the charter was issued, other competitors entered the picture, including the giant American business conglomerates General Motors and Du Pont,[8] and Nobles Industries of Britain. Their vast capital made them formidable rivals: Novomeysky was forced to raise a larger sum than he had originally anticipated. His funds nearly depleted, he had to find additional investors, a task made doubly difficult by Britain's reluctance, as we saw, to place its only source of potash in completely foreign hands. To avoid giving the impression that he represented Zionism exclusively, Novomeysky turned to various types of investors: private individuals and foreign companies with no Jewish or Zionist attachments, whose interests were purely economic; Jewish personalities and institutions motivated primarily by the Zionist vision, though in some cases expecting to reap a profit as well. Ultimately, ownership of the company's basic capital was divided among investors motivated by economic interests and those with Zionist affiliations, namely Keren Hayesod and the Palestine Economic Council, headed by Alfred Mond (later Lord Melchett). The bulk of the funding came from the Palestine Economic Corporation (PEC, founded, as explained above, by Brandeis's followers in the Zionist Organization of America [ZOA]), both as a corporation and from individual members; their motivations were primarily Zionist, but they hoped that the potash company would be an economic success and enjoy progressive management. (Israel Brody to Novomeysky, September 5, 1929, CZA A3 16/4) An important point is that even though much of the capital was defined, in the WZO's terms, as national capital, all the investors (with the exception of the WZO itself) considered the company a private, profit-seeking venture which should be managed as a capitalist project. Neither Novomeysky nor the Brandeis group found an internal contradiction in this approach, since they saw no reason that a profit oriented operation could not contribute significantly to Zionism. The contradiction surfaced in the labor movements' socialist, centralist doctrine, and Novomeysky had to address his arguments to the vocabulary of that discourse. In his contacts with the Zionist institutions in Palestine, Novomeysky took care to present PPL as part of the Zionist enterprise, and he based his requests for financial assistance on that argument. An example is his letter to the secretariat of the Zionist Executive in London asking its support to obtain the Dead Sea boats service charter (he won the charter—his first in the area—and it gave him an important foothold in terms of his ability to begin the trial production of potash). Economic justifications for the charter were presented as secondary. Above all, Novomeysky insisted on the importance of developing an infrastructure in transportation, tourism, and economic viability for a future Jewish community at the site, to be based on extraction of the minerals. The document, which makes no mention of Novomeysky's personal interest in the project, asks the Jewish Agency to underwrite 70 percent of the purchase. To justify this request Novomeysky asked the Zionist leaders to take into account the fact that not one dunam (four dunams equal one acre) of the soil of Trans-Jordan, which had just come under to the complete political control of the English government, was owned by a Jew, and the fact that no Jewish settlement existed in the area. For these reasons, he writes, he finds the proposal of Mr. Hasbon [the Arab seller of the land] as appearing to bear enormous national importance for the Jews (CZA Z4/3473b).

The records show that the WZO accepted this line of reasoning and agreed to invest the funds. Conquest of the land, after all, was part of its *raison d'être*.

Clearly, then, within the framework of the Jewish discourse the portrayal of the company as an element in the Zionist enterprise helped Novomeysky muster political and financial support which facilitated his efforts to obtain the charter from the British government.[9] He even undertook to will his shares in the company to the WZO in return for its assistance and as part of his contribution to the country's development. This complex picture confirms the view that the question of whether PPL was a private or a national company had nothing to do with accountancy and everything to do with political perspectives. The answer, indeed, would determine how much control the WZO would be able to exercise vis-à-vis the company. This issue was the crux of many disagreements that developed among the company and its organized workers, the Histadrut, and Yishuv institutions. In many of his confrontations with the company, the leader of the organized Jewish laborers, Yehouda Kopolovich (Almog), queried the essence of the capital which had founded PPL. He demanded that the Histadrut invest more heavily in the company to ensure that it would be controlled by national capital. He addressed his protests to Ben Gurion in a letter dated August 3, 1943: "Jews founded the potash company, Keren Hayesod extended faithful assistance to the nascent firm, but today the international aspect of the company is being emphasized from various sides." (CZA J99/3) And elsewhere: "Jewish brainpower and Jewish energy and capital founded it, Zionists and proponents of building the homeland bore the burden, and even if the circumstances of the time cast the plant in an international light, it remains a link in the chain of building the land." (Kopolovich and Vansky, 1945, p. 227)

The workers urged that the company be regarded as the product of national capital so that they could dictate policy on Jewish labor and settlement, but Novomeysky, in the face of the workers' representatives, rejected this totalistic viewpoint and challenged its validity, adducing instead a stand that seemed to contradict his original arguments to the Zionist institutions. This is implicit in a letter to Novomeysky from Berl Katznelson, the editor of the Histadrut daily paper *Davar*, in reaction to the former's objection to an article in the paper claiming that PPL had been established with national capital: "He [the writer of the article] has every right to credit Mr. Novomeysky's activity as well, not to the account of international capital but to that of the Zionist movement. Will you really be offended if we say that were it not for the Zionist movement the engineer Mr. Novomeysky would not have set his sights on the Dead Sea, of all places." Novomeysky's disavowal of the "national" character of the company's basic capital led various groups to question PPL's loyalty to the Zionist interest (as they saw it). Whenever a particular group raised specific objections about the company, the question of the investors' loyalty would be raised. Another example is Kopolovich's letter to the Histadrut's Actions Committee (June 1, 1944) warning of the danger that the company might be wrested from the Jews. The English influence is too strong, Kopolovich wrote, and he urged that Jewish capital be raised for the company to ensure continued Jewish control.

(CZA 1335 C/S53) The loss of the northern factory to the Jordanians in 1948 prompted him to write, "The management never believed in the Jewish state and does not believe in it even today. The management collaborated with the British authorities here and in London, as well as with the Trans-Jordan government."

Such challenges to the company's Zionist commitment left it in a permanent quandary. On the one hand, its categorization as part of the Zionist project was a prior condition for obtaining allocations it sorely needed: land, national funds, and especially trained manpower willing to work at Sedom (identified with the biblical Sodom) in heat averaging 42 degrees Celsius (108 degrees Fahrenheit), remote from any human habitation, at a time when the Yishuv was enjoying a boom economy. On the other hand, the company's total identification with the Zionist enterprise would also jeopardize its economic progress, in the perception of its managers and board members.

PPL's multiple aspects—its self-presentation as a full-fledged Zionist project in certain contexts, but in others as a private, profit oriented firm that shunned all things political—characterized the company throughout its existence. The need to placate different groups representing contradictory interests deeply influenced PPL's behavior and rhetoric from the beginning, when it fought to obtain the charter; at the same time, it also had an impact on the concept of the "conquest of Jewish labor."

"Jewish Labor" or "Cheap Labor"

Having secured the charter and established the operation, PPL, as noted above, found it problematic to recruit trained manpower. The brutal physical conditions around the Dead Sea and its isolation (given the transportation infrastructure of the 1930s) were not calculated to lure manpower to the site, least of all personnel with industrial experience or other relevant qualifications. PPL was adequately staffed when it opened, as its general manager reported, (General manager's report to first annual general meeting, April 21, 1931, CZA Z4/3473) but beginning in 1932, as demand for workers throughout Palestine rose, it became increasingly difficult to recruit professionals, especially to work at the Sedom site, for reasons already explained: "There are very few skilled laborers in Palestine in the sense of Western European or American standards. In the short period since industry was inaugurated in this country, skilled labor was not created in any considerable numbers and those who have learned a trade or come from abroad are already settled in the few larger undertakings, like Palestine Electric Corp., Nesher, Shemen and Grand Mills."[10] Elsewhere Novomeysky complains that the major difficulty is to find senior personnel to replace key staff who had left. (Letter to Lord Lytton, the company's chairman, July 23, 1944, CZA F43/49) Even though the terms of the charter stipulated explicitly that the company would employ an equal number of Jewish and Arab workers, PPL considered the latter unskilled, and therefore the technical staff was mostly Jewish with the assistance of a few British experts.[11]

Thus, unlike the classic case of agriculture in Palestine, Jewish laborers were a "necessary resource" for the potash company. Industry required trained, literate, educated manpower, while Arab workers were perceived as uneducated and illiterate, hence PPL's dependence on Jewish workers. [12] Another and equally important reason for such dependence was that only by employing Jewish labor could the company obtain legitimation from Yishuv institutions, whose support was critical. At this stage of the Yishuv's history, the employment of "Jewish labor" became a paramount criterion—which had the constant support of the Histadrut—for an enterprise to be categorized as "Zionist." The need to find Jewish workers willing to face the harsh conditions of the Dead Sea, while at the same time reducing labor costs, generated fascinating ideological activity focusing on one of the key symbols in the discourse: what at the time was known as "Hebrew [i.e., Jewish] labor."

PPL's involvement in the discourse relating to the "conquest of Hebrew labor" became a praxis that interwove vital interests of the workers with company interests. From the beginning, PPL raised the banner of Jewish labor, as is apparent from Novomeysky's description of negotiations he conducted with one of the British-Zionist investors, Alfred Mond (Lord Melchett): "There were three points that were important to me: first, I reminded him that Mond was to sign a letter guaranteeing the rights of Hebrew labor in the plant." Novomeysky says that negotiations actually broke down over this issue: "Mond acted above all as an entrepreneur and only in the second instance as a Zionist, whereas for me Zionism took priority." (Novomeysky, 1958, p. 308) Here and elsewhere, Novomeysky claimed that he viewed the employment of Jewish labor as an important goal.

The workers, too, explain their decision to work at PPL in terms of the "conquest of labor" and assert that they were aware of the bargaining chip they held: "We view the Dead Sea as a charter [granted by] the Mandate [authorities] for the Jewish people. Who, then, should implement the charter if not us Jews . . . ? Only Jews should work at the charter. . . . If we had done everything in our power, there would have been 400 Jewish workers." (Undated report from the General Meeting, Lavon Archives, IV 104–1–225 A) And, in retrospect: "Labor is a decisive factor in the fate of an enterprise. And here is where our role begins, the role of a kibbutz in the south. We settled in the south in order to involve ourselves in the plant's establishment. At the time, PPL faced two major, objective facts, which the company itself noted frankly a few years later: (a) 'The prosperity which prevailed in the country at the time and the resulting shortage of workers'; (b) 'The south was a wasteland at that time, and the site lacked all the comforts of life.' Of course, we, too, knew these facts, but nevertheless we saw compelling prospects: 1. To become part of a complex industrial process of cardinal importance, and 2. To carve a path both for the agricultural development of the near and distant surroundings, and for exploiting the natural resources." (Kopolovich and Vansky, 1945, p.278) And elsewhere: "One vision guided us from the time we trod on the soil of Sedom: to cling to all the operations of the plant in all its scope and without discrimination." (p. 300) This aspiration to monopolize work at the plant, including the simple, manual, unskilled tasks, would later generate bitter conflicts between the firm and its organized workers.

Paradoxically, this "vision" ultimately became a double-edged sword. The organized workers' ideological identification with the principle of the "conquest of labor" weakened their bargaining position, enabling the company to demand that they work for less and increase their productivity, even in positions where they were irreplaceable. PPL's managers were always quick to use the charter document obligating them to employ an equal number of Jews and Arabs as a whip against organized Jewish labor. Whenever the Jewish workers demanded wage increases, the company reminded them that cheaper and more productive Arab labor could have replaced the Jews in "conquered jobs." The company thus scored points against the workers without subverting completely its status as a Zionist enterprise. In the words of a member of the works committee, "Mr. Novomeysky explained that according to management's calculations, the great wage disparity does not permit its acceptance of this demand [to employ only Jews to extract the raw material, one of the simplest tasks at PPL, which in the past had been promised to Jews], and he also issued orders to the foremen at the site to put a stop to having Jews load the potash onto the boats and have Arabs do it. In response, comrade Kopolovich stated that the Histadrut will by no means forgo the rights of Jewish laborers to do the above-mentioned work. . . . He [Kopolovich] thinks that introducing technical improvements will reduce the [cost of] labor." (Flawed phrasing in the original. Archives: 982–63/H, letter from June 28, 1937) Indeed, to realize their vision of "conquering labor" the organized workers accepted lower wages, as arises from the description by Kopolovich and Vansky: "This is only seasonal work, with low pay, but we accepted it with great satisfaction because by doing so [we created jobs] for 40 more workers" (p.295).

The Dead Sea and District Committee, which was set up to examine the future of the project after its destruction the 1948 war, was also conscious of the paradox: "We cannot say that we found the salary for work at the Dead Sea to be notably lower than elsewhere, but it is not difficult to understand that most of the workers did not consider their wages to be suitable compensation for the singular working conditions resulting from the conditions at the site. . . . Moreover, the company employed a large number of Arab workers. [They] received significantly lower wages than the Jewish workers. Arguably, perhaps, the quality of their work and their productivity were inferior by the same degree that their wages were lower than those of the Jewish workers, but the very fact that the total daily wage of the Arab worker was several times lower than that of the Jewish worker may have influenced management when it assessed the demands of the Jewish workers." [Dead Sea and District Committee, 1950, Lavon Archives, IV 104–251)

Discussing more broadly the implications of the struggle for "Hebrew labor" on the Yishuv economy, Sussman (1974, p.10) puts forward a similar argument. "Despite the pressure not to employ Arab laborers," he writes, "or, if they were hired, to pay them less than Jewish workers, the very possibility of hiring Arabs created a ceiling on the wages that Jewish employers were ready to pay unskilled Jewish labor."

It is also important to point out that it is not self-evident to describe the company's operations as occurring within the framework of the discourse on "Hebrew labor." Labor leaders often accused the moneyed elements of opposing or ignoring the effort to "conquer labor": such employers were castigated for preferring "private" over "national" interests. PPL followed the pattern by vacillating in its attitude toward "Hebrew labor." For external consumption, the company consistently pointed to the parity in its employment of Jews and Arabs, though it was fuzzy about the differences in type of employment, working conditions, and wage levels between the two groups.

PPL's participation in the discourse relating to "Hebrew labor," and its success in controlling its workers by identifying with that symbol, dovetailed with the discourse on another key symbol in the dominant Zionist discourse: the "conquest of the wilderness."

Conquest of the Wilderness

All the Zionist movements had the declared intention of setting territorial boundaries for the future Jewish entity in Palestine; however, in contrast to the discourse on the "conquest of the land," with its predominantly militaristic associations, the labor movements' discourse emphasized the conquest of what they considered an "uninhabited wilderness." "Conquest of the wilderness" and "redemption of the soil" through agriculture and settlement had been core symbols in the dominant Zionist discourse since the Bilu movement in the 1880s. Industry seemed to be excluded from this discourse, but in reality PPL and other industrial concerns could join it easily enough. As noted, already in the vision of Herzl and Levinsky the Dead Sea chemicals industry was to generate Jewish settlement that would form the cornerstone for control of the road to Jericho and of the Gulf of Aqaba.

Novomeysky himself used this argument in soliciting the WZO's aid for his project. In his memoirs he associates PPL's establishment with the pioneering endeavor to conquer the land. He contemplates "establishing an industrial settlement in the heart of the remote wilderness," adding that "the very act of creating a settlement in surroundings universally known for their barrenness" attracted him because of its pioneering aspect. (1958, p.234) Novomeysky used similar rhetoric to boost his workers' morale. Speaking at the departure for Sedom of the group which was to establish the southern plant, in May 1934, he stated: "We are gathered here today to launch a new era in the history of our enterprise: conquering a new part of the wilderness. We have come to salute you as you set out for the other side of the Dead Sea to lay the cornerstone for the new settlement. In sending you to that place, which is described in such dark colors in human history, I wish you a good and successful trip and the joy of creation, knowing that you have been chosen to be the first to lay the cornerstone for a new settlement at the furthermost point in the Judean Desert." (Kushnir, 1973, p.280) In fact, the mooted settlement at Sedom was never built, but the aspiration to build it was sufficient to induce a large group of workers to choose arduous physical labor in onerous conditions and for relatively low pay at a time when, thanks to the Yishuv's economic boom, they could have easily found work close to their families and their kibbutzim and for far higher pay. Novomeysky concedes as much. In a letter to the chairman of PPL's Board of Directors, Lord Lytton, he writes that the Kibbutz Ha'artzi's workers, the firm's most loyal organized personnel, are all trained in agriculture and wish to settle down with their families near their place of work place. The only inducement for the kibbutz members, he admits, is a piece of land they can cultivate and where they can reside with their families for the rest of their lives. (Oren, 1985, p.79) Kopolovich, the workers' leader, frequently cites the doctrine of conquering the land as a paramount motive for sending the workers to Sedom: "When we went, in 1934, to the desolation of the southern Dead Sea to establish another plant of PPL, we saw the future looming before us. This settlement site that has been struck at the southern tip of the Dead Sea should become the point of departure for the Yishuv's expansion eastward . . . . Many [natural] resources await development and exploitation." (Letter to David Ben Gurion, August 3, 1943, CZA J99/3)

Indeed, the workers had warned that unless their demand to build the southern settlement was met, they would resign: "The pinnacle of the achievement of the [Labor] Battalion at Sedom will be its settlement foothold. Without a settlement foothold Hakibbutz [Hameuhad movement] has [already] fulfilled its role here to the best of its ability." (Protocol of the Battalion's Assembly, December 25, 1945, Lavon Archives, IV 104 1149/250) Here the company did not make do with rhetoric; it allocated charter land for the establishment of Kibbutz Beit Ha'aravah and for a clerks' neighborhood, Rabat Ashlag. PPL managers, by depicting these settlements as part of the Zionist vision in presentations to Yishuv institutions and to the workers, was able to win the loyalty of the latter even during periods of high demand for labor in the Yishuv. To the British government and the foreign members of the Board, the new operation was described in terms of praxis to increase PPL's productivity and streamline the channels for agricultural supplies and services to reach the company. The foreign audiences accepted this presentation as legitimate, identifying it with "welfare capitalism" practices with which they were familiar. This type of managerial practice had been widespread in nineteenth-century England and afterward in America, where it was known as "industrial betterment." It was the theoretical foundation for industrial towns such as those of Robert Owen in England and of Ford and Pullman in America. The professional literature describes welfare capitalism as a humanistic ideology spawned by the awareness of industrialists, such as Owen, that they had a paternalistic social duty to show concern for the poor on moral grounds. In time it was understood that, beyond the humanistic rhetoric, concern for the workers' welfare also served the employers' interests by increasing workers' loyalty to and dependence on the companies which employed them. Critical studies (see especially Shenhav, 1995b; and Barley and Kunda, 1992) maintain that these mechanisms of "concern for the worker" were a particularly effective method of controlling workers and increasing their productivity without the need for close external supervision of the work process. In addition to settlements, this ideology is embodied in the form of education, health care, and even factory police to look after the workers' security. By depicting the new settlements to the foreign members of the Board and to the British authorities as a praxis of welfare capitalism, PPL assured itself of financial allocations for the project and of British agreement to use charter land for settlement purposes, contrary to the original terms of the charter.

By portraying industry as a national, collectivist praxis bound up with the effort to "conquer labor" and "conquer the wilderness" through settlement, the industrialists were able to extend the boundaries of what was perhaps the most crucial concept in the dominant discourse: the "pioneer."

Pioneering as a Key Discursive Symbol

On the face of it, the image of the Jewish *halutz*, or "pioneer," in Palestine would seem to have little in common with that of the industrialist. To the ascetic pioneer—who functions within the framework of a collective, seeks the common good, shuns material gratification, and works the earth[13]—the private industrialist appears as a mirror-image: wearing a natty suit and bow-tie, he is a world traveler who moves around the country in a rare automobile, his first concern is for his and his family's well-being, and he seeks economic gain by operating as an individualist who shuns agricultural work or other physical labor. This profile, of which Novomeysky was a prime specimen, excluded industrialists from the ranks of the "pioneers" as most contemporaries perceived them, but also as they have been treated by later scholars. Fierer (1984) emphasizes the contrast between the image of the pioneer and the image of the industrialists and the owners of private capital, who stood for values at the opposite end of the pole from the pioneers. Near (1987), underlining the differences between the Yishuv *chalutz* and the American pioneer, notes the former's collectivist and socialist principles and the latter's individualistic and capitalist orientation. Still, PPL succeeded in defining itself—and in inducing its Zionist audiences to accept the definition—as a "pioneering" entity; paradoxically, that identification became a central symbol that enabled the company to obtain legitimation for its operations and gain access to resources.[14] There is no doubt that PPL's acceptance on these terms was made possible by its involvement in the practices of the "conquest of Hebrew labor" and the "conquest of the wilderness."

Kimmerling (1983: 20) analyzes the struggle to subdue the forces of nature, such as draining swamps, digging water wells, afforestation, and building towns in the dunes. Novomeysky strove to cast his personal activity and his private company's operations in a pioneering light. Here he could point to PPL's groundbreaking activity in a region previously uninhabited by Jews and the company's struggle against the natural adversities that prevailed at Sedom and in the Judean Desert. Two other aspects of the mythic pioneer—"collectivism and volunteering" and "agriculture"—also appear, in one form or another, in the company's discourse. One important way

in which the company associated itself with "agriculture" was through the establishment of Kibbutz Beit Ha'aravah in 1939. The kibbutz, which, as noted, was built
on charter land, signified PPL's involvement in "conquering the land" by working
the earth and thus endowed it with the needed agricultural "embellishment." The
company's engineers, for example, utilized technological know-how they had acquired in the manufacturing process to teach the kibbutzniks how to eliminate salt
from the desert soil in order to grow vegetables.

Novomeysky inserted himself into the Zionist project by defining PPL as part of
the effort to revive the desert and make it bloom. He fulfilled the "volunteering" aspect by declaring, as already noted, that he would will his shares in the company to
the WZO, an act which the company's spokesmen cited as proof of its Zionism.
(Brody, 1949) The overall result was that the various Yishuv publics indeed saw the
enterprise through a pioneering prism. Kopolovich, the workers' leader and at times
Novomeysky's bitter foe, calls him an "entrepreneur-pioneer," adding: "The pioneers of this enterprise certainly did not have in mind only chemical production,
they saw [the project] as the great lever which would re-imbue vast areas with the
spirit of life." And elsewhere: "The private capital that was raised to assist the plant
upon its founding had a national purpose and fulfilled a pioneering role, paving the
way for the new enterprise." (From the draft of a preface for a book on Bik'at Tso-
har, Archives, 982/66)

Novomeysky, then, consistently adopted practices which conferred on him and
his company a *chalutz* image. By framing his activity in pioneer-Zionist terms,
Novomeysky acquired legitimation in the dominant discourse. Evidence of this may
be seen, for example, in the editorial preface to an article written by Novomeysky
himself for the daily *Ha'aretz* in 1945: "A veteran Zionist, he holds very progressive
social views. These qualities imbue anything he says with immeasurably greater importance than should be attributed to warnings we have heard occasionally from
functionaries with rightist views, who want to prove the damage that is being caused
by the labor movement. . . . Here a Zionist is speaking Zionism, an engineer with
unrivaled experience who has devoted his life to building industry in the Land of Israel and whose only goal is to see it flourish." ("From Day to Day," editorial preface
to Novomeysky's article, *Ha'aretz*, July 8, 1945) The company's practices and
rhetoric not only enabled it to take part in the dominant discourse, they accorded it
a legitimate place in that discourse, enabling PPL to benefit from state resources
which were earmarked for national enterprises.

Thus far we have described how the Zionist discourse was expanded to encompass industry as an instrument to mobilize resources: capital and labor. But recruitment of workers is not enough. From the industrialists' point of view, it is essential
that the workers be productive. Here, too, Novomeysky strove to expand socialist-
Zionist ideology rather than attempting to posit an alternative ideology, such as capitalism, for example. To its external public PPL declared that it would endeavor to
increase productivity—in the accepted terms of the West—but when addressing its
internal public, the workers and their leaders in the Histadrut, PPL invoked the

terms of reference of the pioneer Zionist ideologue A.D. Gordon to describe the thrust for productivity.

Productivity

PPL's management was preoccupied with finding ways to step up production. Data released by the company (CZA A316/5, n.d.) show that worker productivity was far inferior to that of potash firms in Spain, German, and the United States. From PPL's second decade of existence, and more particularly toward the end of World War II, as the probability loomed of competition from other potash manufacturers, productivity became the nexus of discussions about the company. The definition of labor productivity as a national goal—a definition which was conditional for the existence of a "national industry" and for Palestine's economic viability—conferred on the term a meaning different from Western industry; improved productivity became a goal espoused by company and workers alike.

Zionism's linkage with productivity was not new. In the struggle to infuse the term with meaning and transform it into Zionist-type praxis, the industrialists of PPL could draw on seminal works relating to the question, particularly the writings of A.D. Gordon, though other socialists, notably Ber Borochov, also discussed the need for the Jews to become a productive people. Only work, they maintained, would bring the nation deliverance, and they urged unceasingly the overturning of the socioeconomic pyramid. The Jewish people, these thinkers argued, suffered from a surfeit of merchants, bankers, and scholars, and must become a productive nation capable of extracting surplus value from its labor. However, the Gordonian and Borochovian concept of labor, with its nationalist overtones, does not adequately account for the discourse on productivity in PPL and for industrialization in general.

Labor productivity is a multifaceted concept that assumed various forms parallel to the rise of industry and the articulation of the managerial theories it spawned. Shenhav (1992) distinguishes between a consideration of labor as a sacred task and an instrument for moral betterment, and an analysis of productivity as it finds expression in industrial engineering, that is, the ratio of output to input, which is measured statistically and is wholly bound up with the question of efficiency. The productivity generated by industrial engineering is individualistic and is based on competition between workers and on divide-and-rule strategies which proceed from the psychological assumption that workers want only to enlarge their income and savings and that in contrast to management they do not have the complete picture. The ideological change undergone by the concept of productivity is related to a more general process—the evolution of the concept of work into that of labor—which, in turn, is related to a shift from work perceived as autonomous doing to its perception as an element in the process of controlling the work force. The underpinnings of the new conception—the need for maximization embodied in the terms "more," "faster," and "cheaper"—stands in absolute contradistinction to the religious conception of work, which considers productivity from the starting point of avocation and mission, and where the profit motive is not the be-all and end-all.

A.D. Gordon and Borochov belong to the earlier, quasi-religious attitude toward work, which was influenced by both the Marxist discourse and the Narodnik discourse, with its emphasis on a return to the land. In contrast to that conception, the discourse relating to productivity in PPL forges a link between productivity in its rational and scientific sense, and nationalism which, suffused with emotion and the pioneering ethos, would appear to be its polar opposite.

It is at this nexus that the struggle over the meaning of central symbols in the discourse, as part of the ideological praxis, becomes clear: the industrialists' effort to introduce the concept of industrial efficiency and the cost-utility connection into the framework of the national goals that will enable the country's development. Shenhav (1992) notes that with America's entry into World War I the craze for efficiency also became a test of patriotism. A similar connection is created by the praxis that stretches the meaning of Zionism to encompass efficiency and greater productivity, which constitutes a method of controlling workers through national ideology. The workers, who perceived their labors to be part of the national enterprise, strove to upgrade production, accepting the term's capitalist definition. Moreover, this modified definition reflects the emergence of a deeper form of controlling the workers: normative control, which shifts the focus of control to the workers themselves without the need for more expensive—and less effective—technical or external supervision.

An example of the method by which the idea of productivity in its capitalist sense was injected into the Zionist discourse vis-à-vis PPL is found in Novomeysky's article in *Ha'aretz*, "Where Are We Bound? What Is Our Task?" There he links productivity in its Taylorist sense with the national interest, which is shared by industrialists and laborers. Novomeysky begins by explaining that he is writing in order to serve the country's future, which he claims is now in danger. "Very well," he continues, "what do we demand today from labor leaders. . . ? We want them to take an interest in the worker's productivity. This is a subject to which we attach great importance. Abroad, and especially in the United States, the cost of labor is closely linked to productivity. In fact, these elements are inseparable. The high wages that are in effect in the United States are justified by the high work productivity. Our difficulty in Palestine is the very low productive efficiency of labor. . . . I mentioned above the immense importance of work productivity and the necessity of increasing it. In the United States a new science has emerged called 'industrial engineering.' [It] has been introduced as a special subject in the higher schools of engineering, and special departments of large companies, such as Standard Oil, Du Pont, Monsanto, etc., operate according to its principles." Summing up, Novomeysky writes: "All interested parties and everyone who foresees and anticipates the imminent changes that will occur in the country's future, have the duty to act together and take the necessary measures that will soften the consequences of the crisis." (Novomeysky, *Ha'aretz*, July 8, 1945) Novomeysky is here fusing the good of the country with the need to increase productivity in its capitalist sense, a connection which afterward would become self-evident. The Histadrut itself established the Work Productivity Institute and urged the formation of joint production councils in which the workers' representatives were to cooperate with industrial engineers in introducing methods of scientific management; and the Histadrut was active in putting the new methods into practice in order to further the "socialist-Zionist project."

Conclusions

Industrialists and managers, then, took part in shaping the dominant socialist-Zionist ideology long before the state was established. PPL's ideological effort to conceptualize its operations in dominant Zionist terms is not the exception but the rule. Other private firms, such as Rutenberg's Electric Company, were (and still are) also involved in expanding the scope of central symbols within the dominant ideology. By doing so, such firms were/are able to gain access to resources, control their workers, and increase production without raising wages. The ideological framework also had the effect of creating an emotional bond between the laborers and their place of work, based on a perception of common interests and a shared destiny. "Nationalism" in its socialist-Zionist form constituted an ideology of industrialization where the nation is the supreme body under which the rival sides must serve together. Subordinating the conflicting interests of the industrialists and their workers to one common denominator blurs the basic clash of interests between the two sides and brings about the workers' identification with their managers.

Barley and Kunda (1992) distinguish between two types of control in organizations: rational and normative. Rational control is imposed on the worker from the outside, demarcates the boundaries of his function, and proposes methods for supervision; whereas normative control shifts the focus of control to the worker's psyche and feelings by binding him emotionally to the company. When those emotions are made to intersect with the organization's cultural aspect, the company effectively controls the workers' total behavior (Van Maanen and Kunda 1989). The company's ideological work became a mainstay of its organizational culture. The perception of PPL as an element in the Yishuv's pioneering enterprise endowed it with a special status in labor negotiations and in its contacts with Yishuv institutions. The company's *chalutz* image ensured it broad cooperation and the almost boundless loyalty of the workers, who believed in the Zionist idea and identified their work at PPL with the pioneering ideology. They remained steadfastly loyal even when they could easily have found more convenient work as an economic boom in the Yishuv resulted in a demand for working hands. PPL thus forged a connection between the workers' feelings for Zionism and the behavior expected of them as company employees. In effect, the company exercised a sophisticated form of control over the workers—through emotions—which ensured the workers' positive response to the company's needs. Thus, by charting the road followed by Novomeysky and PPL, we can show how the industrial discourse was embedded in the dominant socialist discourse while simultaneously taking part in its construction during the prestate, nation-building era.

A telling sign of ideological success is the ability of the carrier group to identify itself with symbols or signs that generate a sweeping emotional response in a social context. Such identification ensures that its interpretation will emerge as the dominant one, by defining the manner in which other groups are to perceive reality; in other words, the conception underlying the ideology becomes "self-evident." A case in point is the industrialists. By their success in identifying their private economic interests with the national interest they reap many legitimate benefits. They can urge Israeli consumers to demonstrate their commitment to the nation and its well-being by buying "blue-and-white" (that is, Israeli-made products), mounting a "Blue-and-White Campaign" which, again, represents private interests.

We have seen, then, how a dominant national ideology—socialist- Zionism—which was originally developed as a labor ideology, evolved into, and by and large remains, an ideology of industrialization in the Israeli context. It became an ideological infrastructure allowing for the rise of capitalism under the state's sponsorship without any sharp transformation of the dominant discourse. Today, too, industrialists who claim they are contributing to the public good by establishing enterprises in "development towns" and frontier areas, gain better access to state resources and support. This support is accepted as legitimate because of the now-taken-for-granted link between industry and national goals.

References

Aharoni, Yair. 1991. *The Political Economy of Israel*. Tel-Aviv: Am-Oved, in Hebrew.

Almog, Yehouda and Ben-Zion Eshel. 1947. *The Dead Sea Region*. Tel-Aviv: Am-Oved, in Hebrew.

Barly, Stephen R. and Gideon Kunda. 1992. "Design and Devotion: Surges of Rational and Normative Ideologies of Control in Managerial Discourse." *Administrative Science Quarterly* 37, pp. 363–99.

Beilin, Yoseph. 1987. *Roots of Israeli Industry*. Tel Aviv: Keter, in Hebrew.

Ben-Eliezer, Uri. 1996. "The Elusive Distinction Between State and Society: The Geneology of the Israeli Pioneer." *Megamot* 37 (March), pp. 207–28, in Hebrew.

Ben-Porat, Amir. 1993. *The State of Capitalism in Israel*. London: Greenwood Press.

Bendix, Reinhard. 1974. *Work and Authority in Industry: Ideologies of Management in the Course of Industrialization*. Berkeley: University of California Press.

Brodi, Israel. 1949. *The Dead Sea—What Are the Achievements of PPL*. Jerusalem: Hamadpis, in Hebrew.

Eisenstadt, Shmuel Noah. 1967. *Israeli Society*. London: Weidefeld and Nicolson.

Foucault, Michael. 1981. "The Order of Discourse." In R.Young, ed. *Untying the Text*. London: Routledge and Kegan Paul.

Fierer Ruth. 1984. "The Rise and Fall of the *Halutz* Myth." *Kivunim* 23, pp. 5–23, in Hebrew.

Gal, Alon. 1981. "Brandeis' View on the Up-building of Palestine." *Zionism* 6, pp. 97–146, in Hebrew.

Giladi, Dan. 1969. "Private Enterprise, National Capital and the Political Integration of the Right Wing." In S.N. Eisenstadt et. al., eds. *Israel's Social Structure*. Jerusalem: Academon, in Hebrew.

Grinberg, Lev Luis. 1993. *The Histadrut Above All*. Jerusalem: Nevo, in Hebrew.

Gozansky, Tamar. 1986. *Formation of Capitalism in Palestine*. Haifa: University Publishing Project, in Hebrew.

Hall, Stuart. 1982. "The Rediscovery of Ideology: Return of the Repressed in Media Studies." In Gurevitch et. al., eds. *Culture, Society and the Media*. London: Methuen, pp. 56–90.

Herzl, Theodor. 1943. *Altneuland*. Tel-Aviv: Mitzpe, in Hebrew.

Horowitz, Dan and Moshe Lissak. 1989. *Trouble in Utopia: The Overburdened Polity of Israel*. Albany, N.Y.: State University of New York Press.

Horowitz, David. 1948. *The Development of Palestine's Economy*. Tel-Aviv: Dvir, in Hebrew.

Kahane, Reuven. 1968. "Attitudes of the Dominant Ideology in the Yishuv Period Toward Science, Scientists and Professionals." In S.N. Noah Eisenstadt et. al., eds. *Stratification in Israel*. Jerusalem: Academon, in Hebrew.

Kimmerling, Baruch. 1992. "Sociology, Ideology and Nation Building: The Palestinians and Their Meaning in Israeli Society." *American Sociological Review* 57, pp. 446–460.

_____ 1983. *Zionism and Territory*. Berkeley: University of California Press.

Kopolovich (Almog), Yehouda and Ben-Zion Vensky (Eshel). 1945. *The Sodom Region*. Tel-Aviv: Hakibbutz Hameuhad, in Hebrew.

Kushnir, Shimon. 1973. *Man in the Wilderness: the Life of Yehouda Almog*. Tel-Aviv: Am-Oved, in Hebrew.

Levi-Faur, David. 1993. "State and Industry Interactions in the Industrial Development Policy 1948–1965." Doctoral dissertation, Haifa University, in Hebrew.

Metzer, Jacob. 1977. "The Concept of National Capital in Zionist Thought, 1918–1921." *Asian and African Studies* 11, pp. 305–331.

Near, Henry. 1987. "Frontiersmen and Halutzim." Discussion paper, Haifa University, in Hebrew.

Novomeysky, Moshe A. 1945. "Quo Vadis?" *Ha'aretz*, in Hebrew.

_____.1950. *The Truth About the Dead Sea Charter*. Tel Aviv: Schocken, in Hebrew.

_____. 1956. *My Siberian Life*. London: Max Parrish.

_____. 1958. *Given to Salt: The Struggle for the Dead Sea Concession*. London: Max Parrish.

Oren, Dvira. 1985. "PPL's Involvement in the Jewish Settlement on the Dead Sea Shores." Hebrew University, in Hebrew.

Ram, Uri. 1989. "Civic Discourse in Israeli Sociological Thought." *International Journal of Politics, Culture and Society* 3, pp. 255–272.

Roinger, Luis and Michael Feige. 1992. "From Pioneer to Freier: The Changing Models of Generalized Exchange in Israel." *European Journal of Sociology* 33, pp. 280–307.

Rosenfeld, Henry and Shulamit Carmi. 1976. "The Privatization of Public Means, the State-Made Middle Class, and the Realization of Values in Israel." In J. G. Perisitany, ed. *Kinship and Modernization in Mediterranean Society*. Rome: American University Field Staff.

Shafir, Gershon. 1989. *Land, Labor and the Origin of the Israeli-Palestinian Conflict, 1882–1914*. Cambridge: Cambridge University Press.

Shalev, Michael. 1988. "The Political Economy of Labor Party Dominance in Israel." In T. J. Pampel, ed. *Democratic Oddities: One Party Dominance in Comparative Perspective*. Ithaca: Cornell University Press.

Shalev, Michael. 1992. *Labor and the Political Economy in Israel*. Oxford: Oxford University Press.

———. "Have Globalization and Liberalization 'Normalized' Israel's Political Economy?" *Israel Affairs*, Forthcoming.

Shaltiel, Eli. 1990. *Pinhas Rutenberg*. Tel Aviv: Am Oved, in Hebrew.

Shapiro, Yonathan. 1971. *Leadership of American Zionist Organization, 1897–1930*. Urbana: University of Illinois Press. 1977. *Democracy in Israel*. Ramat Gan: Masada, in Hebrew.

——— 1991. *Managerial Ideology in the Age of Rationality*. Tel Aviv: Broadcasted University Series, in Hebrew.

———1992. "The Social Construction of Labor Productivity." *Annual of Labor Law* 3, pp. 195–212.

. ———1995a. "From Chaos to Systems: The Engineering Foundation of Organization Theory, 1879–1932." *Administrative Science Quarterly* 40, pp. 557–585.

. ———1995b. *The Organization Machine* . Tel-Aviv: Schocken, in Hebrew.

Sternhell, Ze'ev. 1995. *Nation Building or a New Society: The Zionist Labor Movement (1904–1940) and the Origins of Israel*. Tel-Aviv: Am-Oved, in Hebrew.

Sussman, Zvi 1974. *Wage Differentials and Equality Within the Histadrut*. Ramat Gan: Masada, in Hebrew.

Taylor, Frederick W. 1947. *The Principles of Scientific Management*. New York: Harper.

Van Maanen, John and Kunda Gideon. 1989. "Real Feeling." *Research in Organizational Behavior* 11, pp. 43–104

Notes

1. For a similar analysis, which underlines the role of the state as personified in Pinhas Sapir as Minister of Industry and afterward as Minister of Finance in generating the growth of Israeli industry, see David Levi-Faur (1993).

2. Gal, though, claims that Brandeis agreed that the natural resources and essential industrial enterprises should be reserved for the Jewish people as a whole (Gal, 1981, p. 99).

3. See Bendix (1974) for a review of the difficulties that faced industrialists as industrialization began to take off in Europe.

4. As it was perceived by the period's contemporaries: founded on primordial ethnic ties and its identity perceived to be affiliated with the Jewish religion.

5. The report appeared in 1912 in Germany, in M. Blanckenhorn: *Naturwissenschaften Studien an Toten-Mer und Jordantal.*

6. The efforts were undertaken by the Palestine Settlement Association; the manager of the EPC Bank Z.D. Levontin; and Yehoshua Hankin. On the reason for the failures, see D. Oren 1985, pp. 16–18.

7. Letter from Brandeis to De Haas, May 5, 1929, describing the creation of the potash company with the aid of the American Zionists as a victory for the Americans, particularly as Weizmann had warned Novomeysky about the involvement of Israel Brody, from the Brandeis group, in the company. Weizmann alleged that Brody was using his connections with Novomeysky to excoriate the Yishuv Zionists (CZA A316/13).

8. Behind these groups was Standard Oil (Novomeysky, 1958, p. 261). The rival companies wanted to produce bromide and not potash, but because bromide production entails the production of potash the other firms unintentionally became Novomeysky's competitors.

9. Paradoxically, Novomeysky, in putting his case before the British, tried to portray the company as a private enterprise with no attachments to the Zionist interests which had paved his way.

10. From the company's letter in reaction to the article in *Davar*, received from the private archive of Dr. Vardi, no notation or date.

11. Company Board of Directors' document to U.N. Secretary-General in 1948, Archives 980/H. No consistent hard quantitative data on the segregation between Jews and Arabs in regard to manual work were found. However, numerous documents point to the fact that the firm itself viewed the Arab workers as unqualified to conduct the necessary in-house procedures.

12. This is another phenomenon which is concealed by the historiographic emphasis on agriculture. The literature of political economics (especially Shafir, 1989), which focuses on the struggle for the "conquest of labor" in agriculture, considers Jewish workers inferior to their Arab counterparts in terms of what they contributed to the economy, hence the need for political organizing. But in industry this was not necessarily the case.

13. For a description of the mythic *chalutz*, see Eisenstadt, 1973; Fierer, 1984, Roniger and Feige, 1992; Near, 1987; and others. A genealogical analysis of the *chalutz* myth is found in Ben-Eliezer, 1996.

14. According to Foucault (1981) the dominant discourse determines who might be considered a legitimate spokesman. The *chalutz* fulfills this role in the socialist-Zionist discourse.

4

From *"Eretz Yisrael Haovedet"* to *"Yisrael Hashniah"*: The Social Discourse and Social Policy of Mapai in the 1950s

DOV KHENIN

One should stress the importance and significance which, in the modern world, political parties have in the elaboration and diffusion of a conception of the world.

Antonio Gramsci

What are the roots of the social limitations of the Israeli Labor Party? From where did the deep rift between the disadvantaged strata of the Jewish public and the Labor Party emerge? Was Labor, and its predecessor Mapai, always the political expression of the established classes? Or did the party undergo, at some point in its history, a fundamental change in its social identity and class location? And if so, when?

In this chapter I claim that Mapai did undergo a fundamental change in its class location, and that this change occurred in the 1950s. Up to the beginning of that decade, Mapai's activity and political discourse still partook in the building of a particular kind of working class. This was done primarily through the one-directional demarcation of a social "Us"—the workers—against "Them"—the employers and the rich. In this sense, regardless of the sincerity and depth of its socialist commitment, Mapai was indeed a workers' party. One-directional upward social demarcation still characterized Mapai's discourse in the election campaign of 1951, and was instrumental in forging the coalition of veteran workers and new immigrants that was responsible for Mapai's victory in those elections.

But already in the early fifties a rapid qualitative change was beginning to unfold. The socio-political decisions taken by Mapai as a governing party led to the re-establishment of a split labor market, which changed the make-up of Israeli society. In this restructured social arena, Mapai's policies defended the social status quo, the privileges of the established classes, and "law and order." Subsequently, Mapai's discourse also underwent a process of change, shifting from a one-directional upward demarcation of the social "Us," to its demarcation in two directions, both upwards and downwards. Thus Mapai—and Labor after it—was transformed from a workers' party to a party of the middle class. When *Eretz Yisrael Haovedet* (Laboring Israel, another designation of the Labor Settlement Movement) became *Yisrael Hayafa* (beautiful Israel),[1] Labor remained the political expression of the same social groups, but its policy located differently on the social map. The continuity in the human identity of the political subject matched a deep change in its social character. Still, that change was so smooth that it easily evaded social analysis.

Mapai brought many of its old symbols to *Yisrael Hayafa* of the established strata, but without the social content that they used to signify. Thus, in Israel "left" came to signify educated, well-to-do ashkenazim. The final stage of this process—the transformation of the symbols and the fragmentation of the Histadrut's organizational structure—was the "Ramon Revolution" of 1994. (See Grinberg and Shafir in this volume) But this was merely the symbolic and organizational culmination of a process which, from the social perspective, had been completed years earlier.

Why did this change occur? I will contend that the reasons are not to be found in national needs or even in Zionist ideology per se, but rather in the characteristics of Mapai's social politics: the narrowness of the way it defined the workers and the paths it chose for furthering their interests; the discouraging of all significant social change; and the interests of the strong bureaucracy. This claim certainly does not relieve Mapai and Labor of their heavy responsibility. On the contrary: the labor movement's responsibility for its contemporary social limitations is actually heightened. The reasons for these limitations are not located outside the labor movement or in fundamental factors which preceded it, but rather in the movement's internal characteristics and in historic decisions it made in its politics.

Explicating the social decisions made by Mapai in the nineteen fifties, which transformed it from a workers' party to a party of the middle class, constitutes the core of this chapter. I will explicate these decisions by examining the relationship between Mapai's political action and political discourse throughout the 1950s and making a distinction between elements of the discourse which resulted in action and those which were used to camouflage that action.

In a sense, this chapter constitutes the closing of a circle. Sociological debate in Israel set out by focusing on the center of society and took scant notice of what was happening in the periphery. In its second phase, the important analyses did focus on the periphery. The return to the center which is carried out here is an attempt to understand the interaction between the center and the periphery and its consequences. This is a type of social analysis which does not reduce politics to a dependent variable, but which aims, rather, to locate and signify politics' social influence and the social meanings of political decisions. Through Mapai's politics in the fifties, I will try to demonstrate the ways in which a political party is involved in the construction of class deployment, a deployment which, in turn, deeply influences politics.

The 1951 Elections:
A Coalition of Veteran Workers
and New Immigrants

I propose to distinguish the question of Mapai's class location up to the beginning of the 1950s from other questions, such as how sincere its socialism was. It is my contention that, until the beginning of the fifties, Mapai was indeed a working class party. In the Yishuv, Mapai's politics constructed a social environment—*Eretz Yisrael Haovedet*—that included most Jewish wage workers. More importantly, the explicit social demarcation (within a social sphere signified as encompassing the Jewish community only) was one way, in an upward direction: at first mainly against the landowners of the First Aliya, and later against the entire bourgeois stratum. This is, significantly, a type of social demarcation which characterizes a working class. To a significant degree, *Eretz Yisrael Haovedet* was, during this period, a young working class coming into being.

In what follows we shall see that in the election campaign of 1951 Mapai's discourse was still characterized by this one-directional social demarcation. Social and economic issues were the focal point of those elections. In their election campaign, the General Zionists (GZ), the main bourgeois party at the time and Mapai's main rival, deployed a stinging attack on the regime of austerity (*tsena*) established in 1950. Their election slogan was: "Let us live in this land." Mapai, for its part, defended the regime of austerity as an appropriate, feasible and proper solution to the problem of food shortages, and promised to adhere to it for as long as necessary. The party presented itself as the voice of the workers and the common people, and attacked its rivals on the right not only as political competitors, but mainly as representing the class interests of a narrow social stratum. Mapai's discourse in the 1951 campaign outlined a social coalition which, as I explain below, brought about Mapai's victory in the elections. It appealed to two characteristic social experiences and two different types of social identity: *Eretz Yisrael Haovedet* and the new immigrants.

Mapai's election discourse was connected to the milieu of *Eretz Yisrael Haovedet* on two levels. It used the common code words of *Eretz Yisrael Haovedet*—"socialism" and "*chalutziyut*"—and integrated them, as well as other conventional symbols, into its discourse. Ben Gurion spoke of Israel's "socialist character," expressed by the "conquests of the working class and the masses," and of the need for its further advancement. (*Ma'ariv*, July 7, 1951) Use of the rhetoric of "socialism in our time," such as Golda Meir's promise of May 1, 1949, to complete, within a year, the establishment of socialism as defined by Mapai, (*Davar*, May 3, 1949) continued to characterize Mapai's pronouncements in the elections of 1951. However, that "socialism" had no practical element, only a festive dimension, just like the other code words and symbols Mapai continued to use, such as the red flag and the Internationale.

The connection to *Eretz Yisrael Haovedet* was also made by appealing to its social experience. Mapai's publications were full of direct appeals to the "veteran workers," who remembered the stresses of unemployment and could appreciate the achievement of overcoming it. Through various texts, the "veterans" were lauded as being the repositories of experience and knowledge, elder brothers who could explain to the new immigrants the world in which they found themselves.

The attempt to connect with the experiences and social identities of the new immigrants could also be found on two planes. Here, too, an appeal to the immigrants' social experience was combined with the informed use of common code words and symbols. The tale, "Meiri Zachariah—What Does He Have to Say?," which was included in a Mapai election publication that appeared in *Ma'ariv*, (July 20, 1951) described the immigrant Meiri Zachariah's encounter with a series of Mapai's political opponents.

Zachariah, a religious Yemenite immigrant, head of a large family, and a laborer, settles down after work on the doorstep of his hut to rest, reading the *Zohar*. Mapai's rivals, depicted as entirely detached from the reality of Zachariah's life and mentality, show up and disturb the quiet of his repose. The GZ representative is "an elegantly dressed man" whose "car horn, like a sharp scalpel, cuts through the twilight hour," a quiet time in the *ma'abara*. Repeated emphasis of the gaps between rich and poor serve to amplify the distance between the GZ and Zachariah. Their propagandist further deepens the rift when he openly expresses nostalgia toward the good old days, before mass immigration.

The religious parties' representative is a "cleanly shaven gentleman, dressed like a nobleman . . . upon whose head sits a minuscule silken skull-cap," and he too arrives in a new car. On the face of it, his utterings—on the importance of prayer, the Sabbath and Jewish education—could well have been embraced by Zachariah. However, from the outset he adopts a condescending and paternalist attitude toward the Yemenite Zachariah, and, when he chooses to ally with the religious citrus grower who employs only Arab workers, and who drove away the Jewish workers with the help of British policemen, the social gap between the two is further sharpened. His detachment from the problems of the *ma'abara* stands out even more when he denounces the enlistment of women in the army, the same young women who, according to Zachariah, are a great help both at work and with the care of babies in the camp.

Members of Mapam, Mapai's rival to the left, are also characterized as socially distinct from the immigrants. Mapam's representative is a "red-haired fellow, with pretty eyes"—a mythological Sabra—who jumps from his jeep, "his shirt untucked from his trousers, battle-alert." However, in contrast to the conflict with the GZ, the argument with Mapam does not explicitly contain a social aspect. The emphasis is on the detached and schematic nature of Mapam's worldview, whose only sub-stantial element is international. In the 1951 elections, Mapai took care not to di-rectly engage itself with the social and economic criticism of Mapam, to the extent that such criticism existed. Any serious involvement with discussions of that nature would have necessarily challenged Mapai's pretensions not only to be the faithful representative, but also the sole expression of organized labor in Israel.

Mapai itself needed no propagandist in the Meiri Zachariah tale. It was left as the natural choice, taken for granted, the choice that every child could easily make—as seen in a "kind of song" sung by Zachariah's young children: "The most loyal man/to immigrants from Yemen/the one and only in Zion/David Ben Gurion."

Mapai's ability to present itself as the natural choice, that needs no justification or explanation, expressed a high level of self-confidence. It was the manifestation of the hegemonic standing of Mapai and its politics. However, at the root of this approach was a real weakness: Mapai did not really speak with Zachariah. It did not relate to him as a true interlocutor. It did not provide him with real reasons why he should support Mapai and no one else. As we shall see later on, this was an expression of a fundamental weakness in Mapai's discourse, a weakness that will be further mani-fested when we come to discuss that discourse's other dimensions.

Mapai's election discourse of 1951 refrained from adopting blunt patronizing at-titudes toward the new immigrants, attitudes which could already be found in Is-raeli society. Under no circumstances did the discourse contain the strong expres-sions which Mapai's leaders used in smaller and closed forums, especially with regard to the mizrachim (to whom in a forum of senior Israel Defense Forces [IDF] officers in 1950 Ben Gurion referred as "human dust"). Mapai's election discourse preferred to attribute these attitudes, as we saw, to the GZ, and mark for itself a dif-ferent narrative, at the center of which were the immigrants and veteran workers uniting against the rich. In this association, senior status was reserved for the veter-ans, the "absorbers," but the new immigrants were offered a certain level of part-nership. At the same time, in the appeal to the veteran workers, solidarity with the new immigrants was also emphasized.

Mapai's real argumentation, lacking from the conversation that did not take place with Zachariah, could be found, to a certain extent, in other texts of the election discourse. In an assembly of new immigrants, Moshe Sharett posed the following question against the slogans of the free market:

> Let us assume that an immigrant arrives in Israel and is in need of housing. Someone must build him a house. And if not a house—a hut. He will come to the free market and wait until this is offered to him. Who are the business owners for whom building houses for immigrants is worthwhile? And where is the large working public which will immediately have the money to pay for these houses? What would have been the fate of the whole wave of immigrants had not the state intervened in the matter of housing? And what would have happened had the second principle of the General Zionists—freedom from state supervision—come into being? Only because there is state supervi-

sion, and because we can concentrate the state's income in our hands, and because we can then budget dollars for imports, can we prioritize building materials and direct them to housing for immigrants. (*Ma'ariv*, July 20, 1951)

In a letter to the voters, Ben Gurion constructed an argument which relied upon many of his readers' experiences in Europe between the wars:

The "free initiative" regime of the General [Zionists] is well known in Europe as a Balkan regime, whose consequences are: alarming poverty amongst the masses on the one hand, and on the other, exorbitant abundance and wealth amongst a minority. (*Ma'ariv*, July 27, 1951)

In its publications, Mapai connected the slogans of the GZ to many Israelis' firsthand experiences of austerity: "*Free trade—in other words, speculation.*" (*Ma'ariv*, July 27, 1951) The "freedom" to which the GZ refer, said Sharett, is none other than the shattering of the national economy, unrestraint and lawlessness. (*Ma'ariv*, July 20, 1951) "Free initiative," said Ben Gurion, actually means "the violent is victorious . . . freedom for the holders of capital to get even richer at the expense of the state, the consumer and the worker . . . freedom for the few to lust after profit, to speculate and to get rich quick at the expense of the many . . . avaricious entrepreneurship of the minority, and unlimited and uncurbed speculation." (*Ma'ariv*, July 13, 1951)

Ben Gurion presented the debate with the GZ not as a conventional political debate but as a comprehensive social and moral confrontation. Mapai's election manifesto divided the world into two opposing camps: against the "organized working public" — characterized by "rising up above the petty considerations of the moment . . . faithful to the state and its missions . . . [accepting of] the yoke of the commandment to be satisfied with little"—are placed "the criminals . . . the speculators and organizers of the black market, who take advantage of the miracle of the ingathering of the exiles for their own gain." The GZ support speculation. The black market, according to the manifesto, "has spread with the moral support and the public help of the right." (Mapai's electoral manifesto, *Ma'ariv*, July 20, 1951)

Political argument becomes moral denunciation. The immorality of the GZ is not accidental. It stems from their "narrow class" interest as "holders of capital, rich wholesalers, owners of heavy industry and citrus plantations, who boycott the Hebrew worker." (Mapai's manifesto, *Ma'ariv*, July 27, 1951) Obviously, this class interest situates the GZ first and foremost against the hired worker: "The supporters of 'free initiative' . . . aspire to lower the worker's wages by creating reserves of unemployed labor." (Mapai's manifesto, *Ma'ariv*, July 13, 1951, emphasis in original) It is not accidental, therefore, that the "working public" places itself opposite the "holders of wealth." The working public rejects free initiative, which means prosperity for the few, and establishes a contrary principled standpoint—to ensure that everyone receives the essential. This is Mapai's path: "In the future, [Mapai] will continue to endeavor to realize the principle of providing essential needs, in contrast to abundance for the few, which others believe in." (Mapai's manifesto, *Ma'ariv*, July 20, 1951)

The claim that the right's policy was directed against the national interest was also repeatedly brought up in Mapai's election propaganda. As Ben Gurion wrote in his letter, (*Ma'ariv*, July 27, 1951) the choice facing the voter was sharp and clear: on the one hand, "national issues, security matters, ingathering of the exiles, and settling the desert"; on the other, only "the narrow class entreaties" of the GZ. Ben Gurion also took pains to point out that the anti-national standpoint of the GZ was not new. The GZ, he wrote, are those "who, for a period of many years, boycotted Hebrew labor and the Zionist movement."

This, he claimed, was the issue around which the "working public" could "unite most of the people [and found] an alliance of the masses" against the GZ and the right. (*Ma'ariv*, July 13, 1951)

In contrast to its affinity to *Eretz Yisrael Haovedet* and the new immigrants, Mapai did not tie itself to the experiences and identity of the middle classes. It turned to them only "to the extent that they are interested in contributing their share towards the existence of a regime of organized concern for all, instead of lawlessness from which only a few benefit." (Mapai's manifesto, *Ma'ariv*, July 13, 1951) Mapai's concern for the middle classes is described in the manifesto merely as "a state necessity and a respectful duty," a side-effect of the protection of salaried workers. Thus full employment would also protect "all of the middle classes." (Mapai's manifesto, *Ma'ariv*, July 13, 1951) In practice, the middle classes, or part of them, were no more than an additional and supplementary ingredient of the "alliance of the masses" which, according to Ben Gurion, the "working public" must set up in opposition to the wealthy in order to advance its national and class goals.

Unquestionably, Mapai's efforts in the 1951 elections bore fruit. In those elections Mapai succeeded in creating a social coalition encompassing most of *Eretz Yisrael Haovedet* and most of the new immigrants as well. Despite losing the support of many old-timers, Mapai succeeded in the elections as a result of massive support from the new immigrants—in the *ma'abarot*, the poor neighborhoods, and the immigrant moshavim. In November 1950, a few months before the national elections of 1951, municipal elections had taken place in which Mapai was heavily routed: the Histadrut list, shared by Mapai and Mapam, received only 27 percent of the vote (as against nearly 50 percent in the general elections of 1949). The GZ won almost a quarter of the votes. A large part of the immigrant population was still in immigration camps, and only a few participated in these elections. (Shapiro, 1984, pp.129–130)

The 1951 elections for the second Knesset had different results, despite the loss of support for Mapai amongst the old-timers. Old-timer settlers were less than half of the eligible voters in 1951. New immigrants made up about half of the voting public: between May 15, 1948, and December 31, 1951, 687,624 immigrants arrived in Israel—doubling the number of Jews. In the second half of 1948 most immigrants were of European origin, including the Cyprus detainees and "displaced persons" from Germany (76,554 out of 101,828). However, in the three years that followed, the number of immigrants from Asia and Africa grew greatly (232,613 and 85,759, respectively, out of 585,796). The three leading countries of origin throughout the whole period were Iraq (123,371), Poland (106,414) and Yemen (48,315). Many tens of thousands of immigrants were living in tents and shacks in immigrant camps and in *ma'abarot*. Mapai's election victory resulted from the support of those people. (Shapiro, 1984, pp.129–130)

The claim, that Mapai's *modus operandi* in securing the vote of the immigrants consisted largely of the crude use of carrot and stick, has a large measure of truth to it. However, Mapai's political discourse in 1951 represented another dimension, one which supplemented the party apparatus's activity by demonstrating a certain openness toward the new immigrants, while integrating them within the coalition of forces supporting Mapai.

Mapai's Discourse in 1951:
The Operational Limitation

As we have seen, Mapai's 1951 election discourse took part in forming a social coalition wherein "Us" were the workers and the immigrants, and "Them" were the bourgeoisie. However, the discourse most certainly did not seek to sharpen the social *struggle*, but rather the opposite: it was aimed at neutralizing the very class tension to which the party appealed in its election campaign. This was done in two ways: through a world outlook provided by the national setting, and by detaching social development from the struggle and activity of the workers themselves and attributing it to the party leadership—in the Histadrut and the government—alone.

The national setting played a double role in this context. On the one hand, it was used to strengthen the hegemony of Mapai's politics. In a nation-building society, faced with the task of immigrant absorption, it was argued, the standpoint of the right was irrelevant and unrealistic. In the reality of a young Israel—said Sharett in a radio speech—the state would simply be "betting on its life and putting an end to immigration if it relies only" on free initiative. (*Ma'ariv*, July 27, 1951) In this situation, only Mapai's strategy could really advance the national interest. On the other hand, the national framework of Mapai's world outlook influenced the character of the social confrontation marked out within it: Mapai, and the working public led by it, represented the national interest at a time described as complicated and singular, a period of building the state in a hostile environment, while absorbing an immigration of huge proportions. This was a very substantive limitation as to what it was right to demand and what could be expected to be achieved in the social sphere.

The emphasis on the nation characterized Mapai's appeal both to *Eretz Yisrael Haovedet* and to the new immigrants. It did not cancel out social/class emphases but was incorporated within them, while blunting them somewhat. This was a complicated discourse, as the social emphases were not squeezed out, and continued to occupy a significant, if moderated, place in it. The symbols and socialist slogans were preserved, as well as the direct appeal to the workers' experiences and trials. A world outlook with the unionized worker at its center remained. According to this outlook, the working public was also the leader of the nation's struggles and missions. However, such leadership was accompanied by responsibility, and this responsibility limited the possibilities for progress.

Until the beginning of the fifties, *chalutziyut* was seen as the central value of the Zionist cause, as expressed in the labor movement's discourse. Much has been written, from many different angles, on the place of *chalutziyut* in the labor movement's discourse, and I do not intend to retread this ground. For our purposes, the most important fact was that, through *chalutziyut*, the disintegrating effect of the national dimension on the social construction of the class environment was, to a certain extent, neutralized: *chalutziyut* presented *Eretz Yisrael Haovedet* as the social subject of the national cause. Using the discourse of *chalutziyut*, the national dimension did not replace the party's connection to the social environment of organized labor, but rather participated in its particular make-up.

In the election campaign of 1951 Ben Gurion expressed a clear preference for *chalutziyut*: "*This country will not be able to stand with only the state apparatus* . . . with those things alone we will not be able to do the job in hand. We must set into motion all the energy of *chalutziyut* hidden within us." (*Ma'ariv*, July 27, 1951, emphasis added) The discourse of *chalutziyut* maintained the environment of *Eretz Yisrael Haovedet*, but blunted the sharpness of its social outlook and played down the politics derived from it. It was active in strengthening national solidarity and in creating a feeling of responsibility towards the national economy on the part of the workers. It did not heighten class tension, but rather diffused it to a large extent: there was certainly room for cross-class cooperation for the sake of the nation. The Histadrut's economic enterprises (of which the rank and file members were officially the owners) were, before everything else, instruments for the furthering of national tasks. The labor unions were also directed to the needs of the national economy, no less than to those of the workers organized in them.

The second way in which Mapai's discourse sought to diffuse class tension was through the total detachment of social progress from the class struggle. The struggles of the workers themselves were given no place whatsoever in the discourse. Social progress was always attributed to the leadership: of the Histadrut, the government, and Mapai. "All the achievements," said Aharon Becker, a Histadrut official, "are the fruits of the cooperation between the government and the Histadrut, the results of Mapai's policies." (*Ma'ariv*, July 13, 1951) It was Mapai's leadership that generated improvements in the workers' conditions. All that was left to the workers themselves was to continue to support Mapai's leadership.

The discourse emphasized especially the centrality of the Histadrut, which was awarded its own chapter in Mapai's election manifesto. It was presented as the source of power and success on both the class and the national planes: the Histadrut had laid the foundations of success even before independence; it was at the forefront of building projects and social security in recent years; and it outlined future demands. In Mapai's manifesto, the workers' successes were described as Histadrut achievements. Since 1948, they were seen as the fruits of cooperation with the government, and at all times were presented as a product of Mapai. And the achievements of the past marked out the path for the future. In the future, Mapai, the Histadrut and the government would all be found in the center of social progress. The workers themselves were merely passive recipients. The working class was an object of social improvement, not its subject.

This bureaucratic take on politics was connected to the heavy weight of bureaucracy within Mapai. Relatively speaking, Mapai was a more bureaucratic party than the European labor parties. Party personnel could assure themselves of many benefits, and their standard of living was much higher than that of the rank and file. (For a detailed discussion see Sternhell, 1998) These were the sources of the bitterness, and even hostility, toward Mapai and the Histadrut that broke out into the open in the "Ramon Revolution" of 1994.

The contradiction between the bureaucracy and the workers had been endemic to the movement and characterized it from the start. But even the hard struggles that resulted from this tension were managed *within* the movement. (Avizohar, 1990) For although the bureaucracy was very conspicuous amongst the leadership, even the latter could not be entirely immune from the permeation of feelings and perceptions coming from the workers. At the beginning of the fifties, Mapai's politics was still able to contain the two patterns, despite the tension between them.

The operative dimension of Mapai's discourse in the 1951 elections was limited, therefore, in two ways. It was demarcated by the perception of the national interest, and was located in a political framework which was both bureaucratic and prescribed from above. "The realm of the possible" created by this discourse was, therefore, particularly restricted and narrow: the practical steps perceived as possible were indeed tied to the interests of workers and new immigrants, but these were isolated steps lacking any momentum and imagination.

For example, rationing, described in the 1951 discourse as a crucial economic tool, was no more than a bureaucratic response to the social problems that arose with mass immigration. It was an expression of the strong connection between the operative aspect of the discourse and the social core of the movement: it manifested, first and foremost, the world of bureaucracy, its interests, its conceptual horizons.

The quotation from Sharett cited above already hinted at the social compromise outlined by the discourse's operative dimension, that of peaceful coexistence between the bureaucracy ("rationing") and the social stratum from which other dimensions of the discourse still tried to be distinguished ("free initiative"). A coalition between the two was still far from being explicitly proposed, but the practical politics which will set it up could already be found at the center of the realm of possible politics.

Nevertheless, the new politics of social compromise was still faced with limitations. The main limitation was the policy of consumption restriction which mostly affected the established classes. In order to soften the limitations, various qualifications were introduced in the policy of rationing. On a practical level, rationing was presented as a measure of limited importance. Mapai's manifesto did promise that rationing would continue for as long as there were shortages, but the connection between rationing and the general principle of "providing for everyone's essential needs" was largely neutralized when rationing was presented as *a practical, national need, limited in time*: "as long as the ingathering of the exiles and ensuring our security demand." (Mapai's manifesto, *Ma'ariv*, July 20, 1951) Rationing, then, was not an end in itself, and not even a means of achieving equality. Its minimalistic and cautious presentation hinted at the dropping of the policy of austerity, which was to come right after the elections.

As with every Western labor party at that time, the issue of ensuring "full-employment" was central to Mapai in the 1950s. The manifesto, however, did not explicitly detail how, in practice, full-employment was to be guaranteed. It did not mention, for instance, guarantees of employment being set in law or fixed through state arrangements, nor even the continual expansion of the national economy which would, in practice, assure employment. While unemployment was depicted as the explicit goal of Mapai's social opponents, who were repeatedly and clearly demarcated, the discourse contained no references to the influences of the ways employment was organized, or of the quality and conditions of the promised employment. This angle, which Mapai's discourse completely failed to deal with, would later become central in determining the characteristics of the Israeli labor market.

The practical references in the discourse to welfare arrangements consisted of one sole concrete commitment to the most minimal of social security handouts, to mothers, pensioners, widows and the disabled. (Mapai's manifesto, *Ma'ariv*, July 13, 1951) Mapai's discourse did propose a serious housing program, however. This was the only area in which a plan for substantive social action was presented—popular housing projects based on public construction. Public construction was not directed against the well-to-do, however. It was commensurate with the outlooks and interests of the bureaucracy. Even the list of candidates for public housing did not emphasize new immigrants or the homeless, but rather certain sections of the veteran population: "workers, officials, teachers, lawyers, and the other liberal professions." Problems arising from the rent control system, highlighted as that which public housing was meant to eliminate, were also a concern of old-time residents and not of new immigrants, at least at this stage. (Mapai advertisement, *Ma'ariv*, July 20, 1951) In fact, the manifesto mainly talked about public construction as aimed at improving the living conditions of the old-timers, most of whom were established, if not well-off.

In general, the operative facets of Mapai's discourse in 1951 did not outline any program for overall social responsibility for the absorption of mass immigration. Apart from general sloganeering, the remarkable process of the doubling of Israel's population passed it by without any practical engagement. In this sphere, the weakening and softening of the discourse's operative dimension were striking, even in comparison to Mapai's 1949 election manifesto. In those days, one could still hear reasonably explicit references to an "immigration regime," implying broad social responsibility for providing housing, employment and education to the new immigrants. In the discourse of 1951, social responsibility for absorption disappeared almost entirely from the dimension of activity. Also absent were proposals to collect wealth from the rich for the sake of absorption, proposals which did appear in the discourse of 1949. In 1951, restricting the rich's consumption was not a strategic aim but at best a tactical maneuver. There were no revolutionary proposals or socialist measures in the 1951 discourse; it did not even contain an outline for any substantive social progress. Its practical outlook was static, not dynamic, and defensive as opposed to offensive. Beyond the issue of housing, and the qualified adherence to the policy of rationing, the discourse did not actually outline any practical way for advancing the interests of the workers and the immigrants.

The paucity of practical measures sketched out in the 1951 discourse is therefore striking even in comparison with the operative dimension of the discourse in 1949. In 1951 horizons of social change were not opened at all. All such visions remained utterly stunted. Capitalist free initiative was still to be restrained in 1951, but there was no explicit challenge to its existence, indispensability and contribution. As Sharett put it: "of course— freedom of initiative, but freedom of initiative within the framework of the law, freedom of initiative in fulfilling the state's mission, and not in opposition to it." (*Ma'ariv*, July 20, 1951) The discourse revealed the particular interests which stood behind right-wing criticism of the social status quo, but was far from critically identifying the interests behind the existing status quo itself.

Furthermore, the operative elements of Mapai's discourse restrained and limited its ability to commit people to it. National responsibility moderated all social demands. The discourse turned to the workers and the immigrants, but did not commit them to struggle and to social activism. In fact, the workers and immigrants did not constitute an active subject in the discourse at all. The leadership was entirely responsible for all activity, and all that was left for the workers and immigrants was simply to trust and rely upon it.

Mapai and Mass Immigration:
Why Did the Change Continue?

The tensions inherent in Mapai's 1951 discourse were brought to the fore by the mass immigration. A clear decision was then called for. It was possible to "absorb" the mass immigration in one of two ways: integrate the immigrants into one labor market on an equal basis, or split the labor market between veterans and newcomers. The first option would have actually maintained Mapai's traditional attitude against the creation of a separate sector of cheap workers within the labor market of the Jewish economy. However, this would have demanded the true socialization of immigrant absorption. In practice, such socialization would have meant a policy of social responsibility for absorption, broad protection for the new immigrants through equality of employment, substantial compensation for the unemployed, and the equal provision of housing and education. This policy would have demanded cutting more deeply into the income of the established classes through taxation.

Mapai chose the opposite way of dealing with the mass immigration. It flinched away from socializing absorption and decided on a style of absorption that would preserve Israel's capitalist model of development. This pattern of development meant treating the new immigrants as goods, as a resource. The exploitation of most of the new immigrants turned them into a cheap and mobile work force within the framework of a segregated labor market. As will be described in detail below, at the beginning of the fifties, Mapai became the standard-bearer of a policy designed to create a separate and inferior sector of cheap workers in the labor market, deviating from the path which had previously characterized it. Reducing the actual commitment to social responsibility for absorption allowed for the relaxation of restrictions on the established strata, and the removal of limitations on the ability of the holders of capital to exploit it.

The mass immigration could have been absorbed differently. The model of absorption chosen by Mapai was not forced upon it by external and objective constraints, but was rather the expression of its social characteristics. Although both models of absorption were related to some part of Mapai's politics and discourse, the part which was associated with the chosen model turned out to be more important. This distinction, between dimensions of greater and lesser importance in Mapai's politics and discourse, is critical for understanding them. Before I begin a detailed analysis of the social policy Mapai chose at the beginning of the fifties, therefore, I shall briefly discuss its motivations and the party's relationship with the politics which preceded it.

Mapai's policy at the beginning of the fifties refrained from establishing the social coalition intimated by the electoral discourse of 1951, and abstained from turning it into a stable historical bloc. Not only did the policy not sustain those elements of the discourse, it was entirely opposed to them. The policy did not even provide new immigrants with the same moderate defenses that Mapai had previously afforded the workers.

Mapai's social activity had always been more qualified than its social discourse. Firstly, the party had never been a revolutionary socialist party, but rather a party of very limited and modest reformism, at the most. Secondly, Mapai's ability to act was limited by the fact that, up until the creation of the state, it did not hold political power and therefore had restricted social power and could not determine an overall economic policy. (Shalev, 1992) But subject to these restrictions, Mapai provided a certain type of answer to the needs of the Jewish worker in the Mandatory period. Thus, for instance, in the thirties, the issue of the freedom to strike was the focal point of the conflict between Mapai and the Revisionists: Ze'ev Jabotinsky, the Revisionists' leader, saw strikes as sabotaging the building of the national economy in Israel, and therefore as fundamentally wrong. He held that labor conflicts should be settled by national "mandatory arbitration." The Histadrut, led by Mapai, opposed this, and insisted on the workers' right to strike. (Sternhell, 1998) The defense of the right to strike was not a chance element of the labor movement's credo. Indeed, it was so fundamental that even a joint effort by Ben Gurion and Berl Katznelson, the most prominent of Mapai leaders, did not succeed in limiting it: in 1934 the two failed in getting Mapai and the Histadrut to ratify an agreement with Jabotinsky, at the center of which was a degree of restriction on the right to strike.

However, even before the fifties, Mapai did not stand for social equality. The Yishuv was far from being egalitarian, and large gaps in salary between skilled and unskilled workers prevailed. (Zussman, 1974, pp.13–25) The labor movement did not strive to eliminate this inequality (neither in the economy in general nor in its own enterprises (see also Sternhell, 1998), but it could claim that, in practice, its social politics protected Jewish workers from its deepening. At the center of these social politics was a point of view with regard to the make up of the labor market. The large supply of cheap, unorganized labor was the main economic factor which enabled low salaries to be paid to unskilled workers in Mandatory Palestine. (Zussman, pp.13–25)

The answer offered to this problem by the labor Zionist movement as a whole was neither radical nor extensive: the Histadrut and Mapai did not try to unionize the Arab workers, and did not fight for pay raises and improvements in their working conditions that could have reduced the supply of cheap and unprotected labor (and thus reduce the pressure on the Jewish worker). The solution offered by Mapai and the Histadrut stood in stark contrast to this. It was an exclusionary solution: with limited success, Mapai acted to exclude Arab workers from the Jewish economy. The practical efficacy of this policy was limited, but Mapai presented it as a defense of the Jewish worker in the face of competition from cheap Arab labor. This was a fundamental element of Mapai's policy and a central pillar of its status amongst Jewish workers.

At the beginning of the fifties Mapai's policy was quite different: While continuing to exclude cheap Arab labor through the Military Administration it imposed on the Arab citizens, it also created a separate and inferior sector, made up of immigrants, within the Jewish labor market. In terms of Edna Bonachich's split labor market theory, Mapai added to its strategy of exclusion a strategy of caste, constructing a separate caste of cheap Jewish workers. (Bonacich, 1979) In both cases Mapai showed absolutely no willingness to represent the cheap workers and be truly connected to them.

This change in Mapai's social strategy can be explained by what I earlier called the operational limitation of its discourse. At one level, this change was connected to the national framework of Mapai's outlook. While this allowed the exclusion of cheap Arab workers, it also demanded the inclusion of their Jewish counterparts. Although the national dimension can contribute to explaining the absence of exclusion of the new immigrants, it cannot explain why they were made into a low caste in a split labor market. This was connected to the other limitation manifested in Mapai's political discourse: The option of social responsibility for the immigrants and their equal integration into the labor market was not explored in it at all. From this perspective, what the discourse did not mention as a possibility was no less important than what it did.

The effect of creating a social security net for the immigrants while perpetuating restrictions on the established strata—the option not chosen by Mapai—would have been substantial sharpening of class tensions. This would have forced Mapai to go beyond the bounds of the model of social-democracy that had characterized it throughout—cautiously advancing the workers' interests within an unchallenged capitalist framework. It was possible to further the veteran workers' interests, which were connected to Mapai, even when accelerated development was carried out on a capitalist basis. The vast majority of those workers, therefore, were prepared to settle for only limited restrictions on Israeli capitalism, and this is what Mapai continued to propose. Dissident groups, which had a more radical potential, were aggressively suppressed (the best known example is the sailors' strike of the early 1950s.) (Khenin and Filc, forthcoming)

The bureaucratic stratum, Mapai's other traditional social base, had an even more unequivocal interest: The continuation of restrictions on consumption threatened its standard of living. It would have been hit by any policy of seriously taxing the established strata, and it was therefore determined to prevent such policy from coming into being. Instead of being threatened by a policy of general social responsibility for immigrant absorption, it preferred to conservatively fortify the existing social order.

Isolation from the new immigrants was made easier by the way the labor Zionist movement had shaped the Jewish working class in Palestine, molding it in a narrow and restricted way, subject to "national responsibility" and striving towards class partnership. *Eretz Yisrael Haovedet* was formed as a closed cultural group. As such, it was easier to differentiate it from the new immigrants (and especially the mizrachim amongst them) than from the rich strata of old-timers.

Obviously, nationalist justifications were and still are given for Mapai's social decision. But in practice it was not dictated by the national dimension of Mapai's politics in itself. The national dimension could have been integrated into a different social politics. National aims are always achievable through a variety of social policies. Therefore, the matter resides not in nationalism itself, but rather in its specific deployment. In Mapai's discourse of 1951, nationalism and Zionism could be easily connected to the unchosen option: From the materials of the discourse, one could have built an argument why Zionism actually required that the labor market not be split among Jewish workers. Just as immigration was put forward as a national effort of the highest priority, so too could real social absorption have been presented. In practice, however, Mapai's social choice adversely affected the "central national aim"—immigration. 1951 marked a turning point in this regard: in 1951 more than 173,000 immigrants arrived in Israel, in 1952 a little more than 23,000, and in 1953 only a few more than 10,000. (For a discussion of this subject and its relationship to economic policy, see Segev, 1984, p.302, and Hacohen, 1994)

Mapai's social policy at the beginning of the fifties continued to represent the interests of the bureaucracy and, in a more limited way, those of the veteran workers.

It also continued the operative element of the party's discourse and continued to reduce the substantive contents of its symbolic element. It also contained a significant
change, however, a move to a new policy with regard to the split labor market, and,
as a result, a move to a social coalition utterly unlike the one suggested by the electoral discourse of 1951.

Changes in the Fifties: The Level of Action

The early years of the fifties represent an important junction in Israel's development.
Up until now, most research has concentrated on the international dimension, on
the move to open identification with the West. But what occurred on the internal
social level was no less important: the establishment of a new split labor market at
the hands of Mapai that shifted its policy from the exclusion of cheap workers from
the labor market to the construction of a separate and inferior sector within it. (For
a discussion of split labor market theory, see Peled, 1989, pp.9–15)

The formation of a government coalition with the GZ after the elections of 1951
expressed a fundamental *social* choice made by Mapai. That decision was not only
political, it was social as well: an opening toward the veteran middle classes, coupled
with the creation of a new split labor market, forcing a large number of workers,
mostly new immigrants, to its lower reaches. In this way Mapai gave up on forming
a social partnership with most of the immigrants and chose not to consolidate the
coalition that had brought it victory in the elections.

The first step in this social decision—the construction of *ma'abarot*—actually
preceded the 1951 elections. For many years, research into Israeli society considered
the *ma'abarot* an unavoidable necessity. (Eisenstadt, 1967; Horowitz and Lissak,
1989) S.N. Eisenstadt, for example, still related to them in this way in 1989: "The
combination of scarce economic resources together with large waves of immigration
created extremely difficult conditions for absorption." However, relating to the
ma'abarot as indispensable prevents an analysis of the social *choice* made with their
establishment. Despite the great interest shown in the *ma'abarot*, research into Israeli society has never given the essence of the *policy of the ma'abarot* the attention it
deserves.

The idea of *ma'abarot* was not invented until 1950. In March of that year, Levy
Eshkol, Treasurer of the Jewish Agency, dramatically presented a "revolutionary proposal," as he called it, to the Jewish Agency Directorate. (Hacohen, 1994, pp.
204–205) Until then, immigrants had been housed in immigrant camps, where the
state and the Jewish Agency took responsibility for their subsistence. The plan to
build *ma'abarot* was aimed at relieving the national institutions of this responsibility. In the *ma'abarot*, just as in the immigrant camps, the immigrants continued to
live in high density and in difficult conditions in temporary housing (tents, tin huts,
shacks). (Hacohen, 1994, p. 218) In many cases, the immigrants remained in the
same camps they had been living in up until then. But with the redesignation of the
camps as *ma'abarot*, the immigrants found themselves without the right to receive

food and other services. (Hacohen, 1994, p. 203) From that time onwards, the immigrants had to work in order to support their families and pay for the various services provided them, when they were provided.

During 1950, the pace at which immigrants were sent to *ma'abarot* increased steadily, but 1951 was the year in which the *ma'abarot* really grew. At the beginning of April 1951 there were sixty-five *ma'abarot*, holding 70,000 people; in July there were eighty-five, containing 138,000 people; and in September there were eighty-seven, holding 170,000 immigrants. (Hacohen, 1994, p.257) By the end of 1951 the population in the *ma'abarot* reached 257,000. (Hacohen, 1994, p.298) The first *ma'abarot* were established in central Israel, but from 1951 they were scattered around the country, in places intended to become permanent settlements. (Hacohen, 1994, p.216)

The public sector's release from responsibility for the subsistence of the immigrants—as a result of the creation of *ma'abarot*—was a central ingredient in the *specific model of immigrant absorption chosen* by Mapai. The immigrants were sent to the labor market with no preparation or training, and there was not nearly enough work for all of them. As a result, the immigrants' dependence on the bureaucracy— the *ma'abarot* managers, employment bureaus, and so on—for employment, social services, and permanent housing, only deepened. The immigrants were not afforded the protection which the unionized old-timer workers received. The social responsibility for immigrant absorption was reduced to the bare minimum. The shedding of social responsibility for absorption was accompanied by a fundamental change in immigration policy. In November 1951 the Directorate of the Jewish Agency and the coordination team responsible for immigration policy adopted a system of serious restrictions on immigration. (Hacohen, 1994, p.305) The policy of selection led to a steep fall in immigration, beginning in November 1951. In December 1951 fewer than 4,000 people arrived. In February 1952, less than 1,500. In the whole of 1952 only a few more than 23,000 immigrants came to Israel, and in 1953 just over 10,000 (compared to more than 171,000 in 1951).

In 1951 Mapai reined in—and very quickly dissolved—the principle of "preferring the minimum for all over abundance for a few." By 1951 the importation of capital in the form of commodities for sale in the free market, without the obligation to convert currency at the official exchange rate, had been permitted. A decision was taken to close the Ministry of Supplies and Rations, which had been responsible for the policy of austerity, dividing its responsibilities between the ministries of Agriculture and of Trade and Industry. This meant the eradication of the supervisory framework which, despite its many bureaucratic defects, played a central role in the former economic policy. The new economic policy was introduced in February 1952 and brought with it, among other things, the lifting of most of the rationing and supervision regulations. (Segev, 1994, p.300)

As opposed to what might have been understood from its 1951 electoral discourse, Mapai refrained from creating a substantive system of protection for the new workers. In particular, the failure to legislate unemployment benefits stands out.

Unemployment rates were relatively high throughout the fifties, especially among mizrachi immigrants. (Bernstein and Swirski; Halevy and Klinov-Malul) In the absence of unemployment benefits, masses of immigrants were reduced to dependence on welfare payments which, through the fifties, remained especially meager. Despite the large number of needy people, the subject of welfare remained at the margins of Mapai's social policy, as evidenced by its willingness to place it in the hands of religious parties.

From time to time, racist justifications were given for both the failure to institute unemployment benefits, and the minimization of the allocations to the needy. Practically, however, their combination was a key element in a social policy which helped turn the immigrants, and particularly the mizrachim amongst them, into a cheap, mobile and powerless labor force. This trend was strengthened by a reduction in the scope of relief work, brought about by a cut in government expenditures in the 1950s. (Carmi and Rosenfeld, 1993, p.292)

The establishment of a new split labor market brought about what Lev Grinberg has called "split corporatism" in the Israeli economy. During the fifties, Mapai remained committed, through a system of social defenses, to restraining capitalism in the upper sectors of the labor market. Workers' conditions in these sectors (skilled workers, technicians, and most public service employees) improved: A system of labor relations was founded on the basis of collective agreements; these workers greatly benefited from public housing construction (around two thirds of the total spent on construction in the fifties), from health care provided by the Histadrut's sick fund, and from cheap elementary education.

Workers in the lower sectors of the labor market, however, were far from having equal access to the social policies that Mapai continued to implement for *Eretz Yisrael Haovedet*. Throughout the fifties, differences in wages and working conditions between the old-timer and the immigrant workers kept increasing. (Swirski, 1981) Many of the immigrants were not included in the framework of collective agreements, and the health and educational services they received were of inferior quality. Even though new immigrants could benefit from the extensive public construction, the location, quality and general conditions of their housing were far lower than those of the old-timers. (Bernstein and Swirski, 1982)

During the fifties, the split labor market became the central characteristic of Israeli society; at the bottom end of the ladder new rungs were quickly created for immigrants in general, and for the mizrachi immigrants in particular. To a growing extent, they constituted the lion's share of the cheap and mobile work force that was a central element in the accelerated development of Israeli society. The new workers' strata became pivotal to the process of speedy economic development, firstly in agriculture and construction, and later on in industry as well. (Bernstein and Swirski, 1982) And once the central part of the country had had its fill of cheap labor, development towns in the periphery began to replace *ma'abarot* as the new immigrants' destinations.

The new working classes had a completely different social experience in the split labor market from that of *Eretz Yisrael Haovedet*. Their struggles were different too.

In many cases, state institutions and the Histadrut were their opponents in these struggles: not only as those responsible for social services (or the lack thereof), but also as direct employers (in an economy which, at that time, was mainly "public"), exploiters and repressors. The clash with state institutions also stemmed from the latter's central role in driving the new immigrants to the geographical periphery— as development towns began to replace the centrally located *ma'abarot*—and to the more deprived areas of the split labor market.

These experiences and struggles did not characterize *Eretz Yisrael Haovedet* of the fifties, which was concentrated in the relatively protected and preferred spheres of the split labor market. It was the main source of employees for the growing public service sector (which grew from 18.9 percent of the work force in 1948 to 26.6 percent in 1961) and especially for the growth in government employment, whose numbers augmented from 12,683 at the end of March 1948 (a rate of 12.1 for every 1000 inhabitants) to 38,310 at the end of March 1955 (21.9 per 1000 inhabitants). In industry and construction as well the old-timers held the more senior positions— skilled workers, technicians, clerks and managers. (Bernstein and Swirski, 1982)

The split labor market made possible a substantive change in social alignments. It brought about a conflict of interests between old-timer and the newcomer workers, and ruled out the option of forming a unifying historical bloc combining the two groups, an option which, in 1951, was still indicated in Mapai's discourse. Parallel to the development of the split labor market, the opposite alternative—that of deepening the rift between the two groups—became characteristic of the discourse.

Changes in the Fifties:
The Level of Discourse

The most significant change in Mapai's discourse during the fifties was the shift from one-directional upward demarcation of the social "Us" to its demarcation in two directions. However, the definition of the "Us" in relation to both directions was not static: The downwards demarcation with regard to the new workers, and mainly the mizrachim, sharpened, while the upwards demarcation gradually blurred.

As we have seen, Mapai's discourse in the 1951 elections still presented a world outlook in which "the unionized working public" is set against the "corpulent". But even then that world outlook—fundamentally class-based—was placed within a national framework, which also took part in demarcating the existing, the possible and the desirable. The discourse took part in fashioning a class identity, but its national dimension framed, limited, and dimmed it. Even at this point in time the national dimension weakened the discourse's social/class outlook. Even then a strong emphasis was placed on the fact that Mapai's standpoints were not only moral and suited to reality (a reality with which Mapai's enemies were simply out of touch), but also the only ones that advanced the broad national interest. However, at the beginning of the fifties the discourse of *chalutziyut* still fulfilled the role of combining the preservation of the special social identity of *Eretz Yisrael Haovedet* with the world outlook's national framework.

The social change of the beginning of the fifties was accompanied by an increase in the use of the national dimension in restraining social demands. At the beginning of 1952, due to "national needs," the Histadrut agreed to make pay raises conditional on rises in productivity and efficiency, and to abstain from cutting work hours "in the face of the manpower shortage." (This decision was adopted on January 6, 1952. See Ben Gurion, 1969, p. 434) This manpower shortage was, obviously, relative. The unemployed masses of immigrants were not seen as an answer to existing needs. The only solution was more efficient use of the existing labor pool— capitalist rationalization of labor par excellence. For Ben Gurion, as for the other Mapai leaders, this Histadrut decision was the pretext for once more pointing out ("willingly and in tribute," as he put it) the "responsibility for the fate of labor and the workers and for the fate of the national economy" expressed by its policy. (Ben Gurion, 1969, p. 434) The Histadrut's role in restraining the workers strengthened throughout the fifties.

The rise in the centrality of the state and the changing role of *chalutziyut* were the outstanding expressions of the new demarcation in Mapai's discourse. The fifties were characterized by the evolution of an outlook that placed the state as the key value and espoused its strengthening at the expense of organizations of the Yishuv period. But on a practical level, the shift to *mamlachtiyut* (politics of state centrality or *etatism*) had begun already behind the rhetoric of *chalutziyut*. In the election campaign of 1951, while Ben Gurion was singing the praises of *chalutziyut*, he had already completed the first stage of its conversion—the dismantling of the *Palmach*. The second major stage—dismantling the Histadrut's primary school system and the closing of the state educational system to the left-wing youth movements—was actually part of the new social choice which came into effect immediately after the 1951 elections. The implementation of these moves—and others parallel to them— preceded the completion of the change in the discourse. The process of change in the discourse carried on throughout the fifties: *Mamlachtiyut* gradually took the place of *chalutziyut* as the central element in Mapai's discourse. Characteristically, Ben Gurion continually refrained from presenting *mamlachtiyut* as a substitute for *chalutziyut*, insisting on describing it as complementary to it. Thus: "The criticism of the approach of *mamlachtiyut* in Mapai at the end of the fifties was . . . a late ideological response to reforms, most of which had already been implemented." (Yanai, 1982, p. 65)

The shift to the discourse of *mamlachtiyut* expressed the conversion from limiting class identity to its fast and active undermining. In contrast to *chalutziyut*, *mamlachtiyut* placed the social subject of the national project in the state itself, not in *Eretz Yisrael Haovedet*. The shift to *mamlachtiyut* was another step in transferring the emphasis from the particularity of social class to the generality of the state. It directly contributed to the process by which *Eretz Yisrael Haovedet* was worn away as a social environment. The exclusion of the discourse of *chalutziyut* was part of the formation of a new social coalition and a new demarcation of the social "Us": *Eretz Yisrael Haovedet* ceased to be demarcated as a working class and began to dissolve into the new Israeli middle class. The discourse of *chalutziyut* was not entirely squeezed out, however. Certain of its elements remained in use, mostly symbolic expressions. But from this point on they were mainly employed in order to reinforce the social distinction from the new working strata (and to strengthen the ethnic superciliousness that accompanied it).

Mamlachtiyut had already captured a respectful position in Mapai's discourse in the elections of 1955. In its electoral propaganda, Mapai presented itself as expressing the centrality of the state, unlike others who merely represented narrow sectoral interests. The list of Mapai election meetings published in Davar on July 1, 1955 was headlined: "State Responsibility Versus Sectarian Reckoning." The electoral discourse of 1955 differed from that of 1951 primarily in what it portrayed as possible and proposed politics. Differences could also be found in the social demarcation suggested by the discourse. At the level of code words and symbols the change was much more moderate, however.

The change was particularly pronounced at the level of possible politics. For instance, Mapai's election propaganda revealed that it was not Mapai that was responsible for the rationing policy, but rather the GZ. The disclosure was made by none other than Dov Yosef, former Minister of Supplies and Rations, known as "Mr. Austerity." An assembly he attended was reported in *Davar* under the headline *"Bernstein,* [a prominent GZ leader] *the father of rationing."*

> The [GZ], now loudly declaring that they removed the restrictions while they were in government, are throwing sand in the public's eyes and denying the truth. The Trade and Industry Minister of the [1948] Provisional Government was Peretz Bernstein, and it was he who led the supervision and rationing in the face of the large commercialization which then prevailed over our commodities. (*Davar,* July 10, 1955)

As opposed to the GZ, the party of rationing, Mapai was the party that encouraged private wealth. As Prime Minister Moshe Sharett said: "Through the Treasury, at the head of which have always stood comrades of ours, the state . . . has done the maximum to attract private capital, and expended great efforts to facilitate the establishment of new private capital enterprises." (*Davar,* July 11, 1955)

Mapai, then, led the efforts to encourage private capital. And what exactly was the difference between Mapai and the GZ? It was no longer a class difference, nor was it a difference of politics. The GZ, said Sharett, simply have no skill or ability to *do.* (*Davar,* July 11, 1955) Attracting private capital and smoothing its course— this is the politics required by reality. That is the way to show concern for "the economy of the whole people." (*Davar,* July 11, 1955) Encouragement for private wealth need not harm the economy of the Histadrut, but rather should combine with it for the sake of development. For this there is no alternative. Supporting private capital is, in fact, the economic expression of *mamlachtiyut.* (*Davar,* July 11, 1955) For encouraging private wealth does not harm the workers. Au contraire, it provides for continued development, full employment and stability, while guarding against a fall in wages, all aims to which Mapai continued to be committed in its electoral discourse.

Since the beginning of the fifties Mapai's policy already enabled the formation of a social coalition between private capital and the old-timer workers, but Mapai's discourse in the 1955 election campaign still did not explicitly indicate this coalition. Rather it implied it, mostly through the way it related to the middle classes. No longer were the middle classes located in the middle ground, but rather they were an inseparable part of the "popular classes," to which Mapai was committed. (Levy Eshkol, "An Assembly of the Middle Classes," *Davar*, July 5, 1955). "The productive and working public" included the educated and the self-employed. (Levy Eshkol, "An Assembly of Craftsmen," *Davar*, July 8, 1955) The new demarcation united the workers and the middle classes, distinguishing them not from the wealthy, but from all those who neither produce nor work.

Simultaneously, Mapai's leaders took pains to give the traditional code words and symbols prominence in the election campaign. They carried on, calling their party "the party of the working class," (see, for example, Sharett, *Davar*, July 11, 1955) appealing to Mapai's base of support amongst veteran workers. In 1955 much weight was still given to an appeal to that public. Thus *Davar* carried full-page advertisements calling for hundreds of workers' committees to support Mapai: "We must strengthen the class party, fighting daily to further the vital interests of the worker, and for the nation's historical needs." (Workers' Committees call, *Davar*, July 9, 10, 24, 1955)

To summarize, Mapai's discourse in the 1955 elections was changed significantly in its operative dimension: from the restriction of private wealth to its vigorous encouragement; from a willingness—tactical and qualified—to restrict the established classes' consumption to a vehement negation of any such restriction, combined with emphasizing stability. Change was also indicated through the demarcation of the social "Us." A social coalition between the old-timer workers and the middle classes was outlined, but in it a special status was still reserved for the former. At the symbolic and organizational dimension the change was much more limited. Mapai continued to talk about itself as a class party, and carried on speaking about the "conquests of the Histadrut" and the "vital interests of the worker."

*   *   *

The 1959 election campaign demonstrated the completion of the change in Mapai's discourse. The line of argument according to which Mapai was the true expression of private wealth and individual initiative was sharpened even more: "In the absence [of the GZ] from the coalition, the government has done much more in organizing, encouraging and helping private capital and initiative than in those years when representatives of that party did participate." (Levy Eshkol, *Davar*, November 1, 1959) Mapai did incomparably more in this respect than the GZ, who merely purported to represent the interests of private wealth: "When he was Trade and Industry Minister, P. Bernstein did not attract even one capital investor to Israel, while 'Eshkol the Socialist' is bringing in many investors, who are opening large industrial enterprises." (Sharett, *Davar*, November 1, 1959) Eshkol is obviously acting for the good of everyone, for encouraging private capital advances the national interest. It is the way to create jobs and develop Israel. It is the path of Mapai, "the only bearer of free initiative for all." (Pinchas Lavon, *Davar*, October 18, 1959)

Mapai continued to talk about full employment, without referring to wages and working conditions in different sectors, and without relating to the split labor market. It made do with general allusions to full employment and tied it to the policy of encouraging private capital. Those two elements were presented as two sides of the same coin. The transition from rationing to abundance was presented as an achievement of Mapai's. Mapai promised to pull the country out of the curse of austerity, and fulfilled that promise. (Mordechai Namir, *Davar*, September 13, 1959) That is the mark of Mapai's politics. It stands with two feet firmly on the ground. What is said is what is possible to achieve. What is offered is what will be done: "We carried out what we promised—we promise what we can carry out." (*Davar*, September 9, 1959)

As Foreign Minister Golda Meir put it:

[Mapai is not] trying to promise things it will not be able to stand by. It is not telling fairy tales to the nation, that anyone who votes "X" will receive everything, more work, housing and schools. It does not claim that the need for efficiency and greater labor productivity will cease. (*Davar*, November 1, 1959)

More work, housing and schools—over and above what Mapai offers—are just fairy tales. What reality demands is efficiency and greater labor productivity. Mapai's path is the only realistic one, as opposed to the castles in the air built by its rivals. In the face of demands for housing, higher wages and improved working conditions, the party stated: "We are educating the citizen self-restraint, to make sacrifices in the present for the sake of the future . . . and we reject the demagogic propaganda which calls for loosening the reins, which makes demands but does not provide answers [to the needs] of the times." (Yonah Keseh, *Davar*, October 11, 1959)

According to Ben Gurion, the positions of Mapai's left-wing rivals, Mapam and Achdut Ha'avoda, are riddled with contradictions:

On the one hand they want many houses for the new immigrants, but on the other hand they demand that the worker who will build those houses only work seven hours a day instead of eight. On the one hand they want foreign capital investments, but on the other, to impose such high taxes on capitalist investors that will drive them away from Israel. (Ben Gurion, *Davar*, November 1, 1959)

The conclusion is clear. The parties to the left of Mapai are irresponsible, lack a comprehensive perspective, and are detached from reality.

The sharpest attack is reserved for Mapam's proposal to legislate for unemployment insurance. Unemployment benefits, which Mapai supported in principle in 1951, are now seen not only as deceitful and as social demagoguery; they are presented as seriously damaging to the worker:

Mapam . . . offers a cure: unemployment insurance . . . Why is Mapam coming out
with this deceitful slogan? After all, Mapam knows full well that the government cannot carry out public works projects on such a scale while giving handouts to the unemployed . . . Mapam knows that the main burden will fall on the workers' shoulders.
(Pinchas Lavon, *Davar*, October 18, 1959)

The extent to which Mapai is removed particularly from the conditions of the
workers at the bottom of the split labor market stands out when its discourse talks
about "preserving full employment," without relating to the quality and conditions
of employment or to the existing pockets of unemployment; (for example, Aharon
Becker, *Davar*, September 6, 1959) when it mentions "preserving a realistic wage,"
while at the bottom of the market, workers earn no more than their subsistence; and
when it refers to "broad social welfare," limited in practice to workers insured by
pension plans, while it rules out the need for unemployment insurance.

Although Mapai's discourse deals less and less with the problems of *Yisrael Hashniah* it continues to defend the achievements of the split labor market's higher
reaches. This defense is particularly striking in the debate with Herut, identified in
1959 not only as Mapai's main rival but also as a threat to the achievements of the
established workers—the workers' provident and pension funds, Kupat Holim and
the Histadrut. (Akiva Govrin, *Davar*, September 6, 1959)

In contrast to the GZ in the elections of 1951, in 1959 Herut posed a threat from
below, not from above. Mapai tried to challenge *Yisrael Hashniah*'s growing support
for Herut by describing that party as serving the interests of the rich. (Reuven Barkat,
Davar, October 11, 1959) But Mapai remained unable to see things as they really
were and understand why the disadvantaged strata were using their vote as a protest.

The core of the argument against Herut and the right-wing in general turned on
a defense of the Histadrut's organizational and economic power. According to the
Histadrut Secretary-General, Pinchas Lavon:

The "Liberals" amongst us say: everything in the hands of individuals is holy and must
not be nationalized, whereas we should nationalize all that is held by the workers'
movement . . . [this is merely] a cover-up for a clear purpose—to narrow and dismantle the labor movement's power sources. Everything done to fragment that power is
called "liberalism" . . . Why should the Histadrut be forbidden to have its own sick
fund? (*Davar*, October 18, 1959)

His quarrel, Lavon emphasized, was not with old-style liberalism. In the era of restrained capitalism's hegemony one could not talk seriously about lifting all the restrictions from private wealth. Old liberalism was dead, and there was no need to
relate to it. It was the militant struggle to weaken the Histadrut which must be
dealt with, and for this purpose Lavon was prepared to adopt an anti-nationaliza-
tion stance.

By 1959, however, Mapai was no longer confined to one way of talking about the
Histadrut. The strong and direct defense of that institution was left by and large to

its own functionaries. The emerging group of Mapai "Youngsters" took a much more reserved stance, and Moshe Dayan even agreed that "there is room to discuss future revisions in the division of labor between the state and the Histadrut." (*Davar*, October 18, 1959)

In his final appeal to the voter, Ben Gurion summed up Mapai's economic policy: "we support every productive initiative of private, workers' or state capital—and oppose a monopoly on enterprise for those who only seek personal profit." (*Davar*, November 1, 1959)

In 1959 Mapai's propaganda did not propose awarding new rights to the workers. Its only proposal was aimed at generalizing arrangements for severance pay, which, in any case, was already provided in most instances. In the domain of labor law, Mapai proposed to establish Labor Courts, a move which in the past it had opposed as narrowing the Histadrut's sphere of responsibility. A headline over a list of Mapai election meetings in *Davar* summed up the first ingredient of the new discourse: Mapai was no longer for social change, however limited, but rather for preserving the social status quo: "*Security, stability and welfare* for the state and the family." (*Davar*, October 20, 1959)

An article in *Ma'ariv* analyzing Mapai's election victory was headlined: "What has changed in Mapai." Its subtitle was: "The victory of the large workers' party does not mean that the public moved to the left—but rather that Mapai moved to the right." The author summarized Mapai's new socio-economic policy and its connection with the new voters as follows:

> Many shopkeepers and small manufacturers, tradesmen and artisans gave their vote to Mapai this time, not because they began to feel disgust towards free private enterprise, but because this workers' party . . . is seen by them as largely an agent of protection and encouragement for free private enterprise . . . broad middle classes have not only ceased to fear Mapai's socialism, but see it as a serious insurance against socialism. (Y. Gilboa, "What Has Changed in Mapai? *Ma'ariv*, November 9, 1959)

Mapai's election campaign discourse of 1959 was full of direct appeals to the middle classes, connecting them to the established veteran worker strata: "Every housewife well knows the difference between the time of rationing and the present period of plentiful food, when the shops are full of products and all is well," claimed Pinchas Sapir, Minister of Trade and Industry. (*Davar*, October 11, 1959) Who was this housewife Sapir talked about? She was certainly not a resident of a *ma'abara* or slum neighborhood. She was a housewife from an urban bourgeois family, or from an established family of workers.

Aharon Becker, head of the Histadrut's Trade Union Department, addressed the workers in the following way:

> The condition of the worker in 1959 is radically different. His standard of living is immeasurably high, he is protected by an intricate system of social benefits, labor legislation is so developed that it may even provide an example to developed countries all over

the world . . . Social benefits are guaranteed both by collective agreements and by law; by the institutions of Kupat Holim; and in addition—by the new system of state [social security] insurance. Today, nearly 70 percent of all workers are covered by pension funds, which guarantee them a pension at a maximal rate of 70 percent. (Becker to Mapai union activists, *Davar*, September 6, 1959)

Who is the worker about whom and to whom Becker is talking? This worker is actually employed; his standard of living is indeed "immeasurably higher" in comparison with what it was just a few years ago; he is "protected by an intricate system of social benefits"; he is covered by a collective agreement; he is a member of the Histadrut and insured by its sick fund; he is a member of a pension fund which guarantees him a pension at a maximal rate of 70 percent. Becker is not talking to or about the unemployed, the workers employed in relief work, those who are not included in collective agreements, or those not covered by a pension fund. The experiences of all the latter categories of workers are excluded from the discourse of Mapai.

When Mapai chooses "The people will not endanger its achievements" as a slogan, it is demarcating the people about whom and to whom it is speaking. (*Davar*, October 23, 1959) These are the people who *have* achievements and who are, therefore, interested in stability, not in social change. The poor are not part of these people. Mapai talks to them from a position of superiority: "encouraging the *backward* (*nechshal*) concern for the individual and the public." (*Davar*, September 18, 1959) The backward are not really part of the nation. They are not talked to, but rather talked about. At most, they raise pity among the listeners, who themselves are situated not only outside the cycle of poverty, but above it.

Providing solutions to the hardships of the backward is a favor Mapai is benevolently doing to them. But it can only be done within the limits of possibility. On the other hand, as we have seen, encouraging private wealth is not subject to any restriction. Mapai's discourse justifies this through a clear distinction: Private wealth is encouraged for the good of all and in the name of the national interest, while at the end of the day, the hardship of the poor is a private matter. Moreover, the poor share responsibility for their fate, and should be held to account accordingly. In this spirit, Finance Minister Eshkol criticizes the young generation in the peripheral towns for their unwillingness to take advantage of professional training and integrate into the places designated for them in the split labor market. (Levy Eshkol in Sderot, *Davar*, October 25, 1959)

When relating to the experiences of *Yisrael Hashniah*, created by the policy of the fifties, a superior position is adopted. Mapai's encounters with *Yisrael Hashniah* are characterized by paternalism and condescension, by looking down on those whose "cultural standards need to be raised." (Joseph Almogi in Wadi Salib, *Davar*, October 11, 1959) In front of residents of Wadi Salib, the Haifa slum where mizrachi residents had clashed with police, Mapai boss Joseph Almogi mentioned the harbor workers, who, thanks to the Histadrut, led by Mapai, had been awarded the status of "stable" workers, and promised that they would soon become "permanent." (*Davar*, October 11, 1959) Mapai's clientelist approach is completely open by now: From our position of superiority, we can provide solutions to whoever knows how to behave. One must just know which side the bread is buttered on, and act accordingly.

Mapai activists visiting development towns were forced to deal with the tension between the reality experienced by the residents and the reality described by Mapai's discourse. Their common rhetorical technique was to localize the problem rather than generalize the achievements. The residents of Tirat Hacarmel, another Haifa slum, where "there are also things that need to be done," may not feel it yet, but the large picture does exist, and it is important. It is also real: "Heaven forbid that we should underestimate the great deeds carried out in this country so far". (Bechor Sheetrit, *Davar*, September 9, 1959)

Mapai is prepared to give problems local recognition, but is not at all prepared to legitimize protest. The tone of the manifesto published by Mapai at the beginning of the 1959 campaign is extremely blunt:

> As with every community in Israel, this community [of North African Jews] has its hills and its valleys. Those striving for the hills, clutching at working life in Israel and striking root in it, are rising in number and importance compared to those rolling to the valley—down the slippery slope of riots and violence. Tens of thousands of our brothers, North African immigrants, therefore, will not carry the burden of the violence of a few of their community. (Mapai advertisement, *Davar*, August 7, 1959)

The demonstrations that had taken place in Wadi Salib were the riots of a minority. The protest represented rolling into the valley. The only option is to grit one's teeth and, despite the difficulties, carry on striving for the hills. The relationship with the Jews of North African descent is, in this case, external. They are not "Us," but just "our brothers" (almost like "our cousins"). They are looked at from above: from our lofty heights we can see that most of them are quite all right. The cultural tension, whose most striking expression was the demonstrations in Wadi Salib at the start of the election campaign, is continually reflected on the pages of *Davar* through headlines such as: "Ethnic list leaders interrupted Sapir in Kiriyat Gat"; "Attempt to break up meeting at which Sheetrit spoke failed." (*Davar*, October 18, 1959)

Social protest is not only false messianism and adventurism; it divides the nation. "Ethnic" political parties also divide the nation, and Mapai uses primarily mizrachi activists against them. In contrast to the divisive parties, Mapai represents national unity: "We want Jewish unity and are opposed to ethnic splits and schisms." (Ben Gurion's appeal to the citizens, *Davar*, November 1, 1959) Mapai is unity. Mapai is the state: "A victory for Mapai is a victory for the state!" (*Davar*, October 30, 1959) Opposition parties and ethnic lists are all shown in an absurd and ridiculous light, for after all: "There are not 24 ways to manage the state!" (*Davar*, October 27, 1959)

*   *   *

However, the messages of national unity and *mamlachtiyut* do not yet exclude the old rhetoric, the rhetoric of the party of the working man, from Mapai's discourse in the elections of 1959: "At the center of the current regime stands the working man, building the state and the nation with the help of the Histadrut." (Reuven Barkat, in Tirat Hacarmel, *Davar*, October 11, 1959) That rhetoric particularly characterizes Histadrut functionaries:

> The Israeli laborer showed concern for the fate of the economy, and so put his faith in Mapai, the party working for additional achievements which will guarantee utter stability. This is the reason why Mapai is certain that on the day of judgment the laborer will not let it down . . . the working public will know how to lead the battle to repel fascism, which had set itself the purpose of destroying the Histadrut's enterprises. (Yerucham Meshel to workers committees in Ramle, *Davar*, October 25, 1959)

In this appeal to the worker, the "guarantee of utter stability" is the purpose, and "concern for the fate of the economy" is the starting point. Once more, emphasis is placed on repelling "fascism's" attack on "the Histadrut's enterprises."

Beyond seeing off the attack on the Histadrut, this rhetoric is only used to repeat general slogans, from which no real commitment could be derived: "The state should not be made up of a sect of rich people and profiteers, and opposite them the poor of the land and penniless workers". (Joseph Almogi, *Davar*, September 13, 1959) This statement is not meant as a description of Israel in 1959, only as a warning that Israel should not become like that in the future. As Ben Gurion put it: "We wish for a society built on freedom, equality, tolerance, mutual help and love for mankind—and we oppose a regime of class discrimination, deprivation and exploitation." (Ben Gurion's appeal to the citizens, *Davar*, November 1, 1959) We can conclude, therefore, that Mapai's 1959 discourse represented the completion of change in its first two dimensions. On the operative level, emphases were placed on free initiative, encouragement of private wealth and capital investment, opposition to unrealistic schemes for social change and to a network of social security which would ameliorate the effects of the split labor market. The operative direction indicated in the discourse of 1955 was very much strengthened and sharpened. The social "Us" demarcated in the 1959 discourse was first and foremost differentiated from those down below, from the backward, from the social parasites, from those rolling down into the valley, and from the rioters. On the symbolic level, however, the general declarations about egalitarian society, about opposing class discrimination, deprivation and exploitation, and about the working man, remained.

Epilogue: Into the Nineties

Mapai's social choice at the beginning of the fifties was meaningful not only for society as a whole, but also for the development of the party itself. A key element in the party discourse played an active role in undermining the identity of *Eretz Yisrael*

Haovedet and the symbolic dimension of the discourse itself. The social environment to which the party was connected, that of salaried workers, was detached from the new working strata and quickly lost its working class characteristics to a middle class identity. As *Eretz Yisrael Haovedet* dissolved itself into the Israeli middle class, it was worn away and lost its independent status. The cultural characteristics and organizational patterns of *Eretz Yisrael Haovedet* survived for few years, but they were gradually emptied of all significant social content.

Thus Israeli society's class deployment was fundamentally changed. The Jewish working class of the Mandatory period disintegrated, and was mostly recreated as a large and broad middle class. In the absence of explicit class tension, the dimensions of ethnic alienation, otherness and difference became central in the social construction of the new working strata. In the absence of a consolidated working class, it would become easier in the eighties and nineties to wheedle away at the achievements of organized labor in the established sector as well.

The consequences of the creation of the new split labor market for Mapai's own development were substantial. In the social choice Mapai made at the beginning of the fifties, can be found the deep roots of the schism between the deprived social strata of the Jewish public, mainly mizrachim, and the labor movement, a rift that would lead to political revolution and the overthrow of the Labor party in 1977.

With the expansion of the low social strata, populated mainly by mizrachi immigrants—strata which Mapai was no longer connected with—the symbols and code words of Mapai's discourse were emptied of real social content and mainly served to disguise the social policy that was actually implemented. Clearly, in those circumstances, the new working strata were characterized more and more by distance and alienation from those symbols and code words. *If, in the thirties and forties, Mapai had succeeded in containing the tension between the bureaucracy and the large working public, from the fifties on, that tension—along with the new working strata—was gradually shifted outside the party.*

In the fifties and sixties, Mapai continued, to a degree, to speak for the interests of the established workers, the higher tier of the split labor market. But it did this in the framework of middle class politics, positioning the established workers, alongside other strata, in the broad middle class. *Eretz Yisrael Haovedet* turned into *Yisrael Hayafa*, Israel of the established and the well-to-do.

The broad Israeli middle class, which since 1977 has provided the Labor Party with the vast majority of its votes, has no connection—apart from nostalgia—with *Eretz Yisrael Haovedet*. As the party of the middle and upper classes, Labor gradually became the main expression of the aspiration to capitalist normalization. It thus came to lead the way to diplomatic settlements and a vision of Israel's integration into a new Middle Eastern order. The social strata represented by Labor no longer need the party-Histadrut bureaucratic system, and the party's political path has, therefore, become more and more detached from it. Back in the fifties, Mapai's "Youngsters" gave the first expression to this distancing. In the seventies and eighties—years in which issues of foreign policy dominated the electoral struggle—the detachment between the vast majority of Labor supporters and the Histadrut, whose organizational base had remained intact, deepened. On the political plane, this detachment erupted only in 1994. However, the Ramon affair and the Histadrut elections of 1994 merely completed a process which had ripened long before.

References

Avizohar, Meir. 1990. *In The Cracked Mirror: Social and National Ideals and Their Reflection in Mapai's World*. Tel Aviv: Am Oved, in Hebrew.

Ben Gurion, David. 1969. *The Restored State of Israel*. Volume One. Tel Aviv: Am Oved, in Hebrew.

Bernstein, Deborah and Shlomo Swirski. 1982. "The Rapid Economic Development of Israel and the Emergence of the Ethnic Division of Labor," *British Journal of Sociology* 33, pp. 64–85.

Bonacich, Edna. 1979. "The Past, Present, and Future of Split Labor Market Theory" in *Research in Race and Ethnic Relations* 1, pp. 17–64.

Carmi, Shulamit and Henry Rosenfeld. 1993. "The Political Economy of Militaristic Nationalism in Israel," in Uri Ram, ed. *Israeli Society: Critical Aspects*. Tel Aviv: Breirot, in Hebrew.

Eisenstadt, S.N. 1967. *Israeli Society*. London: Weidenfeld and Nicolson.

_____. 1985. *The Transformation of Israeli Society*. Boulder: Westview.

Hacohen, Deborah. 1994. *Olim in a Storm: The Great Immigration and Its Absorption in Israel, 1948–1953*. Jerusalem: Yad Ben-Zvi, in Hebrew.

Halevi, Nadav and Ruth Klinov-Malul. 1968. *The Economic Development of Israel*. New York: Praeger.

Horowitz, Dan and Moshe Lissak. 1989. *Trouble in Utopia: The Overburdened Polity of Israel*. Albany, N.Y.: State University of New York Press.

Khenin, Dov and Danny Filc. Forthcoming. "The Sailor's Strike" in *Teoriya Uvikoret* 15, in Hebrew.

Peled, Yoav. 1989. *Class and Ethnicity in the Pale: The Political Economy of Jewish Workers' Nationalism in Late Imperial Russia*. London: Macmillan.

Segev, Tom. 1984. *1949 – The First Israelis*. Jerusalem: Domino, in Hebrew.

Shalev, Michael. 1992. *Labor and the Political Economy in Israel*. Oxford: Oxford University Press.

Shapiro, Yonathan. 1984. *An Elite Without Successors: Generations of Political Leaders in Israel*. Tel Aviv: Sifriat Hapoalim, in Hebrew.

Sternhell, Zeev. 1998. *The Founding Myths of Israel: Nationalism, Socialism, and the Making of the Jewish State*. Princeton, N.J.: Princeton University Press.

Swirski, Shlomo. 1981. *Israel: The Oriental Majority*. London: Zed.

Yanai, Nathan. 1982. *Political Crises in Israel*. Jerusalem: Keter, in Hebrew.

Zussman, Zvi. 1974. *Gaps and Equality in the Histadrut*. Ramat Gan: Massada, in Hebrew.

Notes

1. "*Eretz Yisrael Haovedet*" refers to the Labor Movement; "*Yisrael Hashniah*"—the second, or second class citizens of Israel.

PART TWO

Liberalization

5

Economic Liberalization and the Breakup of the Histadrut's Domain

LEV LUIS GRINBERG AND GERSHON SHAFIR

At the end of the 1970s, despite the fact that the Labor Party lost the Knesset elections in 1977, the Histadrut was at its peak. It owned or controlled 25 percent of Israel's economy, its membership was above 100 percent of the labor force, it was involved in almost all wage negotiations and collective agreements, from the local to the national level, and the state subsidized its economic activities and services. Powerful trade unions supported the Histadrut's leadership and propelled it to radicalize the struggle against the Likud government's half-hearted policies of economic liberalization. The weak unions continued to depend on the representation by the Histadrut in collective bargaining as well as on its welfare services, mainly its health care and pension funds.

The most striking display of the Histadrut's authority occurred on May 1, 1980, when masses followed its call against the Likud government's economic liberalization and participated in one of the largest demonstration in Israel's history. The willingness of thousands to protest was particularly impressive considering that the Likud's electoral support came mainly from working class mizrachi voters and that Menachem Begin, the Prime Minister, enjoyed broad popularity in the wake of the peace agreement he signed with Egypt.

By May 1994, fourteen years after this historic demonstration, the Histadrut leadership had sold almost all its economic assets (those that remained under its control were in a severe financial crisis), and found itself in the eye of biting public criticism. It failed to initiate new collective bargaining agreements with the employers' Coordinating Bureau and was preempted as negotiator by the powerful trade unions which used the 1985, 1989, and 1994 Histadrut elections to gain long postponed wage increases. Finally, despite the sympathetic attitude of the ruling Labor government which signed a generous collective wage agreement in the public sector on the eve of the elections, the Labor Party lost control over the Histadrut for the first time in its 75 years of existence. A broad based coalition—"New Life"—led by Labor Party reformers, who split from the party just one month before the elections, won almost 46 percent of the vote, while the old leadership received the confidence of just over 30 percent of the voters.

Upon assuming power, the new leaders of the Histadrut discovered that they inherited an empty shell: The Histadrut was with almost no real assets, its budget was in the red, and its financial balance was well-nigh bankrupt. Of its members, only about 400,000 were covered by a collective wage agreement.

The aim of this article is to describe and analyze the economic, political, organizational, and trade union-related transformations which led to the crisis of the Histadrut. Our thesis is that the Histadrut, a semi-autonomous quasi-state institution, was the direct victim of the Israeli state's reassertion of autonomy, which began with the 1985 stabilization policy, as part of its economic liberalization policy. Given the Histadrut's quasi-state characteristics, priority was accorded to its privatization at the early stage of economic liberalization. Until the 1960s and maybe the 1970s, it was possible to present the Histadrut as the promoter and protector of the national good, itself identified as the overriding public good, and consequently the Histadrut, we believe, is best treated as part and parcel of the public sector in Israel. By the 1980s for certain, the Histadrut became an easy target for the neo-liberal state not only under Likud governments but especially when the Labor Party, whose image was damaged by its association with the Histadrut's apparatus, was in power. It was no longer possible to sustain the subsidization of its activities, since these were viewed as aimed towards particular and political goals and not national priorities. The Histadrut suffered simultaneously from financial and legitimational deficits.

The Histadrut's Quasi-State Structure

The Histadrut was constructed from its inception as a proto-state institution of member "citizens" entitled to various services, such as health, education, housing, pension, employment, etc. This structure was created to facilitate Zionist colonization, namely to build with the funds provided by the World Zionist Organization [WZO] an institutional framework for the absorption of Jewish immigrants, and ultimately to form a Jewish economy and state. The Histadrut was the conduit for financing and the focus of economic initiatives, in part organized in cooperative form and in part publicly managed. In the absence of a Jewish state, the Histadrut's services were vital and its members joined up mostly to receive its services. (Grinberg, 1991; Shalev, 1992)

The recruitment of members and the financing of the Histadrut's activities were freed from the need to organize the workers at their places of employment and represent them in collective bargaining. The size of the Histadrut's membership, consequently, was not tied to its activities as a trade union. The ensuing "miracle" was that at times the Histadrut's membership rolls exceeded the number of wage earners in the economy. After all, the Histadrut provided services not only to its Jewish members but also to other groups of the Jewish population: worker's families, the unemployed, self-employed, retired, and to co-operative members.

The Histadrut, on its part, was dominated by Mapai *(Mifleget Poalei Eretz Yisrael*—The Eretz Israeli Workers Party), the largest party in the Jewish community, which ruled in coalition with other Zionist workers' parties that also engaged in colonization, but retained control of the Histadrut's bureaucratic apparatus and economic enterprises. (Horowitz and Lissak, 1978; Shapiro, 1976) Mapai was also the dominant party of the WZO since 1933, and after Israel's establishment governed it for thirty years. The division of labor between the Histadrut and the government served Mapai in preserving and strengthening its power. (Medding, 1972) During periods of full employment the Histadrut became the main agency for moderating the workers' demands, and frequently was removed from and conflicted with them. (Grinberg, 1993)

In order to ensure the proper functioning of the labor market in spite of the fact that the Histadrut was not an ordinary trade union, the state came to its help by institutionalizing two types of legal arrangements: labor courts and extension orders *(tzav harchava)*. Labor Courts allowed, on the one hand, the workers to sue their employers and, on the other hand, the employers and the Histadrut (which had equal representation on the Courts) to regain control over unions which defied the Histadrut (which alone possessed legal standing as the workers' representative). Expansion orders issued by the Minister of Labor made the working conditions and wages negotiated between the Histadrut and the employers binding on all employers, and thus both benefited all workers and narrowed gaps which could have led to internal divisions in their ranks. For example, the government made mandatory for the whole economy the provisions of national collective bargaining agreements on standard-of-living increases, working hours and holidays, minimum wage, etc. in spite of the fact that in most enterprises no collective bargaining was conducted and neither the Histadrut nor the employers' organizations had any enforcement capacity of their own.

The elaborate legal and institutional framework which buttressed the Histadrut's authority by linking it with the state, was required, and intended to compensate for, the proto-state-like character of the Histadrut itself which hampered it from becoming an effective representative of its rank and file vis-à-vis the employers and the state. The Histadrut's leverage over the workers derived in equal, if not in greater share, from the unique structure and dynamic of the labor market of an immigration society. Long periods of migration contributed to the old timers' social mobility, but competition with the new immigrants, who were in the process of absorption into the host society, also depressed unskilled wages. Both of these processes lowered the level of labor market conflict.

Absorption of new immigrants into the Jewish community was multi-faceted. The Histadrut itself provided multiple services, but immigrants needed to join the

Histadrut to become eligible mostly for two benefits: the services of Kupat Holim, its health insurance provider, and the employment bureau. Only the employment bureau referred job seekers to potential employers, but informal assistance, that is, "political absorption," for finding employment, was provided by the political parties in the Histadrut coalition. Those not satisfied with the Histadrut turned to the opposition parties, mainly Herut, which condemned the Histadrut for its socialism and stayed out of it. In view of the Histadrut's success in reaching practically the whole working population including their family members, the retired and the unemployed, Herut realized that it had no choice and in 1965 participated in the Histadrut elections for the first time. (Shapiro, 1989)

The Histadrut's contribution to the stability of the Yishuv's political life was repaid in high direct and indirect state subsidies. Labor governments collaborated with the Histadrut and subsidized its economic enterprises and social services. First and foremost they subsidized the Histadrut's health insurance, but also those of its economic activities, construction and agriculture and later industry and military industry, that were central to the project of nation-building. (Klinov and Halevi, 1968; Bichler, 1992; Peri, 1983; Shalev, 1992) The form these subsidies took varied: Some were direct outlays from ministry budgets; the most important one followed a more indirect route.

The major source of domestic investment capital in Israel was personal savings deposited in pension or provident funds (*kupat gemel*), most of which belonged to the Histadrut. Upon embarking upon a policy of industrialization in 1957, the Israeli government and the Histadrut agreed that 65 percent of the amount accumulated in the latter's provident funds were to be invested in government "approved investments," a portion that increased steadily until it reached 92 percent by 1977. (Aharoni, 1991, p.118; Grinberg, 1991, p.91) The Histadrut was required to use 50 percent of that sum to purchase non-tradable government bonds, which the government invested in its own or private firms or otherwise used at its discretion and, in return, consented to the Histadrut's continued investment of the remaining 50 percent in fixed-yield bonds and thus in further developing the enterprises of Hevrat Haovdim, the holding company of all Histadrut-linked economic entities. This agreement served as the basis for Hevrat Haovdim's yearly "financial plan." The exposure of the Histadrut-generated funds to risk was limited by the consent of the Ministry of Finance in 1962 to tie the value of the bonds' yield to the standard of living index thus, in effect, equalizing them with government issued non-tradable bonds (*igrot chov meyuadot*) and guaranteeing them an about 5 percent real yield. (Grinberg, 1993, pp.43–55; Aharoni, 1991, pp.20, 117–119; *Ha'aretz*, July 16, 1996) by legally permitting the Histadrut's pension funds to finance the activities of Hevrat Haovdim.

The private sector did not question but, in fact, supported the subsidization of the Histadrut and its mechanisms of control over the workers because it benefited from both. Under pressure, the government also authorized the Industrial Development Bank and the Manufacturers Association to issue bonds under similarly favorable conditions. Simultaneously, the government required all other long-term institutional savers, such as pension funds and life insurance companies, to participate in its bond program. In sum, capital formation in Israel was a circular affair which made available to the government the Histadrut's pension and provident funds for loans to public and private investors for investments approved by the government itself.

Cracks began to show in this system only with the industrialization and full employment in the 1960s. The unions became stronger and began asserting their independence whereas the industrialists sought to establish a pro-business party. (Grinberg, 1993; Shapiro, 1989) The political response to these threats on the part of the Labor movement was the formation of a united front of the workers' parties, whose power was based on their control of the Histadrut, in the form of a "small Ma'arach" (Alignment) between Mapai and Achdut Ha'avoda on the eve of the 1965 elections, and a "broad Ma'arach" (including Mapam and Rafi) for the 1969 elections. Economically, the government sought to punish the workers' autonomous activities (through wages) and the industrialists (through prices) by implementing a policy based on state autonomous capacities in the 1966/67 years. (Shalev, 1984, 1992)

The year 1967 signaled a turning point in both the form taken by the subsidization of capital and services for the Histadrut and private sectors, and the form of control over the workers. The new structure emerged in response to the integration of the Palestinian labor force of the newly occupied territories into the Israeli labor force, in effect creating a lower caste of unorganized and cheap labor. (Semyonov and Lewin-Epstein, 1987) The integration of the Palestinian laborers also enhanced the collaboration between the Histadrut and branches of the government, especially the security apparatus and the Ministry of Labor, whereas the legitimation for the continued denial of civil, political, and social rights from the Palestinians employed in Israel was based on national and security arguments. (Grinberg, 1993)

Economic expansion after 1967 contributed to the creation of an elaborate institutional network of capital subsidization by the state in the form of unindexed loans (namely loans whose repayment was uninfluenced by the rate of inflation). After the inflationary expansion of the 1970s they became the lion's share of the internal debt. Part of these loans were directly granted to the private sector and the Histadrut, but their largest share were unindexed state-subsidized loans paid out of the Histadrut's pension funds. The expansion of the state's boundaries after 1967 stabilized the political system, increased profits for the Histadrut's economic sector and, through it, for the private sector as well, but eventually led to a fiscal crisis for the state. (Grinberg, 1991)

The Economic Stabilization Plan of 1985

The degree of the Histadrut's autonomy and capacity to preserve its influence was the mirror image of limited state autonomy and the inability to attend to interests it deemed vital for its institutional functioning. The institutional split between the state and the Histadrut's quasi-state, which played such a crucial role in the Israeli state's establishment and contributed much to the economic and political absorption of the mass immigration of the 1950s and early 1960s, became an impediment to state autonomy and an obstacle after 1967, and especially after 1973, with the onset of global inflationary pressures.

In the 1980s, with the growing emphasis on monetary policies and the recovery of markets from inflation, another set of global incentives came into play. The volume of international trade, direct foreign investment, and finance grew manifold, but to benefit from integration with the global market and the new wave of growth it offered, much of the idiosyncrasy of Israeli economy, the result of the state-building drive associated with the Histadrut, had to be abandoned. The first, and most crucial, phase in Israel's response to the growing global pressures in the 1980s was the securing of state autonomy. Such autonomy is a precondition for the adoption of economic decisions, especially decisions to promote and protect the state qua institution. Among these were the reduction of the public debt, the augmentation of foreign currency reserves, and the balancing of the budget.

Institutional autonomy is not a permanent feature but rather a state potential, one which is not always realized. (Skocpol, 1985) The attainment of such autonomy serves state interests but at the same time might de-legitimate the state which is now more likely to be involved in conflict with various population and interests groups. Consequently, states usually wait for times of severe crisis to assert their autonomy. To assert themselves with a measure of confidence, states also need to possess technical skills, namely a professional stratum of high-ranking civil servants, and financial resources, that is, financial resources not dependent on the groups the state is about to confront. (Skocpol et al., 1985) Finally, states that persist in their autonomous actions are usually those that possess a sufficiently broad legitimation which will deter the joining of forces between opposition parties and the interest groups which are most likely to suffer from the state autonomous economic policies (Grinberg and Shalev, 1989).

All these conditions were met in the summer of 1985. The economic and fiscal crises were at their height as inflation was spiraling out of control and the U.S. government demanded that an anti-inflationary policy be adopted. In return it promised a safety net of a $1.5 billion and the transformation of its annual loans of about $3 billion to outright gifts. In the national political arena, the 1984 elections led to the formation of a national unity government which neutralized most of the opposition; and the May 1985 Histadrut elections returned the Labor Party to power thus ensuring that for the next four years its control would not be threatened. The professional resources were mobilized when a directing team (*tzevet higuy*) was formed, headed by Professor Michael Bruno, and including prominent economists from the Ministry of Finance, the universities, and the Bank of Israel.

After the adoption of the Economic Stabilization Program in July 1985, heavy pressures were exerted on the government from various quarters, but it successfully withstood them. The first was over the exchange rate. The industrialists, who became used during the heavy inflationary years to see the wage raises they conceded evaporate rapidly through price hikes and the devaluation of the shekel, demanded already at the end of 1985 that the government undertake a further devaluation. This time, however, the government was able to dig in its heels and head off the devaluation until January 1987. The refusal to cave in to the exporters' pressure was due to the American safety net and was one of the key factors that promised the success of the stabilization program. When the devaluation came, it was part of a comprehensive agreement with the Histadrut and the employers in which wage and price restraint were also pledged. (Grinberg and Shalev, 1989; Grinberg, 1991; Shalev, 1992)

. One of the central institutional consequences of securing the state's autonomy was the crystallization of the autonomy of the Bank of Israel. The new bank Governor, Professor Bruno, relied on two sources of authority: legal and wrested or usurped. First, the Bank of Israel Law was revised to forbid the bank to finance deficit, that is, "to print money," and thus laid the basis for the first time for a monetary policy. A second tightening took place with the adoption in 1991 of a law, anticipating part of the Maastricht plan, which restricted the budget deficit to a certain percentage of the government's budget. Finally, a purported technical change, altering the mechanism for setting the exchange rate in December 1991, was transformed into a main policy tool. A horizontal exchange rate band (with upper and lower limits of 3 percent around a central parity, which ensured a 3 percent yearly devaluation) was replaced with a diagonal, or upward-crawling, band whose slope was determined by the difference between the local and international inflation rates. But since accepting the prevailing local rate would have been counterproductive, a yearly "inflationary target" (*yaad inflatziyoni*) was used instead. This technical target now assumed a life of its own: It became a political necessity to offer a lower or at least equivalent yearly goal. When Rabin's Finance Minister, Avraham Shohat, sought to undermine the use of such official "targets" he found this to be politically too late. Price stability required the bank to be independent and was justified as seeking the common good of making the economy more efficient. (Interview: David Klein, Bank of Israel, March 26, 1998)

The Bank of Israel and the Finance Ministry were able to use their autonomous influence by exerting decisive influence on the formation of monetary and fiscal policies with almost no public debate or attention to the political and social dimension of economic policy. The clearest expression of the neo-liberal economic consensus of the Finance Ministry, the Bank of Israel, the universities and the media may be found in the similar policies of the Likud and Labor Finance Ministers, Nissim and Shohat, respectively. The predominance of the higher bureaucratic economic echelon is the clearest and most real expression of state autonomy, and left its imprint not only on the stabilization of the economy after its inflationary bout, but also in the form of far-reaching structural reforms, not only in the reduction of the subsidization of the Histadrut and the private sector but also on the defense budget. (Shalev, 1998)

The Histadrut's Economic Crisis

One of the most far-reaching and yet expected consequences of the economic stabilization policy of 1985 was the crisis of almost all the Histadrut's economic institutions. It is possible to state without exaggeration that the only two institutions that avoided this fate—Bank Hapoalim and the pension funds– were either nationalized or bailed out already. The construction companies, Solel Boneh, the industrial enterprises and the largest of them—Koor, the insurance company Hasneh, the kibbutz and moshav movements, Kupat Holim all found themselves in the throes of a gripping crisis and in one form or another were forced to undergo reform or privatization, and sometimes both.

The reasons for the financial crisis of the Histadrut's institutions were the termination of subsidized credit at the end of 1980 by the Likud's Minister of Finance combined with their tendency to ignore the pressures to reform themselves so as to fit the requirements of the new situation. A combination of factors: lack of professionalism, old-fashioned managerial approaches and structures, self-confidence in the knowledge of their historical importance and large size, and the undying hope that the return of the Labor Party to power would rescue them all led to the denial of the crisis' severity. Consequently, these institutions chose to finance the repayment of their low interest loans by borrowing high interest ones. (Grinberg, 1991) The problem was compounded by the decision of the Bank of Israel to maintain high interest rates in the economy to ensure the success of the Economic Stabilization Program. This high interest policy also precipitated the bankruptcy of many privately-owned companies and was held responsible for preventing renewed economic growth.

The Histadrut itself could no longer transfer resources between its own companies and thus help its failing institutions. The Histadrut lost its control over its main financial institution, Bank Hapoalim (the body which in the past allocated the funds from its pension funds by means of Hevrat Haovdim's annual financial plan) when the government intervened in the capital market in October 1983 to save the major Israeli banks from the consequences of their failed attempt to regulate their own stocks. The government's plan to gain control over the bank's stocks amounted to their de facto nationalization.

The necessity for such drastic governmental action is a proof of its lack of autonomy before 1983 and especially in the 1980–83 years. As a consequence of such governmental deficit in its ability to prevent reckless economic activity, not only had the original intentions of its own liberalization policy not been carried out (Ben Porath, 1982) but the very obverse happened. First, the capital market was de facto nationalized when the flow of investment from the Histadrut's pension funds was halted in 1980. Second, the transfer of control over the major bank's stocks to the government as part of their bailout program in effect nationalized them as well. The post-1985 liberalization did reverse much, though not all, of this. It reduced the role of the government in the capital market through the partial privatization of the banks, and by ending government issued and secured bonds for the provident funds (though not for pension funds) propelled companies to invest in the market. This, as we argued, was made possible through the most significant institutional consequence of the Economic Stabilization Plan: the construction of the autonomous control of the Bank of Israel over interest and exchange rates which perforce led to budgetary restraint.

Practically all the Histadrut's enterprises were privatized or closed (government-owned companies started to face the same fate only in the second half of the 1990s) in the 1980s. An overview of the transformation of the Koor corporation from the Histadrut's, and indeed Israel's, largest industrial conglomerate to Israel's first multi-national company will illustrate the shift of power from the Histadrut to the government and the market. Koor was established a few years before Israel's independence with the intention of building labor-intensive factories to provide employment to Jewish immigrants, in the time-honored fashion of the Histadrut. With privileged access to labor, land, and capital, it emerged already in the mid-1950s as a major conglomerate. As a provider of jobs, not of growth or profits, for example, Koor purchased Alliance, a tire producer, that was threatened with liquidation by its creditors, in 1983. Koor's subsidiaries, furthermore, mutually guaranteed each other's debts and through an internal clearing-house in effect subsidized the loss-making ones (Gross, 1994, p.1) and ensured that wages remained roughly even among their workers. Without any strategic plan or vision, Koor entered into many unrelated fields but assigned an especially important role to its military industries.

In the 1970s, under the management of Meir Amit, Koor began to emphasize profits, seeking in his words, to balance profit and the company's social mission by, for example, experimenting with profit-sharing. On one occasion, the Histadrut consented to the closing of an unprofitable plant and the firing of its 100 workers and thus of transferring more power to the management. But, in fact, these were piecemeal changes and "most important matters [were] cleared with the union," which was the company's legal owner. (*International Management*, 1974, p.18)

For twenty years Koor reported profits. Its 1987 sales of $2.7 billion represented more than 10 percent of Israel's gross national product and its employees accounted for nearly 11 percent of the country's labor force. But already in 1986 it had a loss of $100 million, in 1987 these climbed to $188, and in 1988 to $369 and in October Koor defaulted on its loans. At the time the ratio of debt to equity was 72:1. Koor's future became doubtful when the financial reports of 1987 revealed a debt of $1.4 billion and one of its American debtors asked for its liquidation. (*Multinational Business*, No.1, 1989, pp.28–29) In 1988, 126 out of Koor's 130 subsidiaries were money-losing and were bailed out by the remaining profit-making subsidiaries, most of which were in military production.

Benny Gaon, who set up in 1976 Koor's foreign trade division, the largest Israeli company in Europe, with 15 branch offices and $100 million in yearly sales, and later helped restructure the Histadrut's Co-op—the largest supermarket chain in Israel, was appointed the new CEO. Negotiations between May 1988 and September 1991 with 32 Israeli and foreign banks, in what seemed like the last possible minute, led to a comprehensive agreement; debtors wrote off $330 millions of its bad debt and the Israeli government reluctantly agreed to provide a new loan of NIS [New Israel Shekel] 175 million for the duration of the reorganization. (Asa-El, 1997) Though the government offered some support, it was relatively small and was offered in the context of changing Koor's ownership structure.

Under Gaon's management Koor was radically and brutally transformed. The mutual guarantee and the internal clearing arrangement among Koor's subsidiaries, which ensured the employment and relative wage equality of its workers, was abolished. The Histadrut conceded that profitability must be viewed as the top priority and consequently consented to the sale of assets, to the shutting down of loss makers, and to firing 40 percent of Koor's workers, that is 4 percent of the Israeli labor force. Even the *Wall Street Journal* compared the effect of the new found "capitalist creed" on Koor, which saved the company by shedding so much of its labor force, to that of a "neutron bomb." (July 3, 1991) And the *New York Times* quipped that Koor turned into a "lean-and-mean conglomerate that sheds money-losing businesses faster than you can say 'Charles Darwin.'" (January 1, 1992) Though the layoffs were accompanied by worker demonstrations and protests, the repudiation of the workers control, nay, the firing of the workers who under Hevrat Haovdim's constitution were the putative owners, and its transfer, in the *Jerusalem Post's* writer's words, to "the unabashedly greedy ownership of Wall Street financiers—hardly [caused] anyone to raise an eyebrow." (Asa-El, 1997) Hevrat Haovdim's 97 percent stake in Koor, already reduced to 71 percent in the reorganization's wake, was dramatically reduced by selling close to 60 percent to the public and to the Shamrock Group of the Shamrock Holdings investment company, wholly owned by the Disney family. In March 1995, Shamrock purchased Hevrat Haovdim's remaining shares, thus ending Koor's close to 50 year-long association with the Histadrut.

But an even more severe and, on the long term, the most significant crisis for the Histadrut and the state was that of Kupat Holim, due to the fact it provided health care to 70 percent of the population and to the special place it occupied as the linch-pin of the Histadrut's institutional network. The Histadrut's tax bureau collected Kupat Holim's dues and handed over to the health care provider about 70 to 75 percent of the total. The transfer of these funds was not always done in a timely manner or in full, due to the financial shortages of the Histadrut itself. Among other causes of the crisis was the unequal competition between Kupat Holim and rival health insurance funds which bit into its membership. Other health care insurers had two advantages over the Histadrut's Kupat Holim. First, they used all the fees they collected to provide health care since they did not have to share it with a political apparatus. Second, the Histadrut's Kupat Holim was obligated by its nationalist and socialist nature to provide insurance to the whole population, whereas other insurers were able to exclude population groups, such as the elderly, that cost more.

The Israeli government could not accede to Kupat Holim's collapse, and yet its financial outlay for the health care provider's continued subsidization was enormous. The state, consequently, had a vested interest in bringing about the kind of structural change in Kupat Holim's operation which would lead to the reduction of its ever-growing subsidies. It was not possible, however, to separate the reform of health insurance from the restructuring of the Histadrut and the place of the Histadrut in Israeli society. After all, the identity of the membership in the Histadrut and Kupat Holim meant that subsidies for the health insurer amounted to indirect subsidies to the Histadrut's apparatus and through it to the political parties, especially the Labor Party, represented in Histadrut.

The Labor Party's Organizational Revolution

The Labor Party was so closely tied with the Histadrut that the latter's crisis could not have passed without severely affecting the former. Whereas the 1984 Knesset elections took place under conditions that were practically ideal for the Labor Party (the Likud mired Israel in the Lebanon War and inflation reached triple digits), the opposite was true for the elections of 1988. Four years of cohabitation between Labor and Likud in a national unity government blurred the differences between them. The peak of high inflation had already passed, and the institutions engulfed in crisis were associated with the Histadrut, that is, with the Labor Party.

In 1988, the Likud's electoral campaign zeroed in on the failings of the kibbutz movement, Hevrat Haovdim and Kupat Holim, and claimed that the Labor Party's wish to return to power was motivated by a desire to bail out its network of institutions from the public coffer. In fact, Shimon Peres was enticed to join the new national unity government in 1988 by the promise of being awarded the Ministry of Finance, and he sought to use the position to salvage the Histadrut and its institutions from their economic crisis. When the Likud governed alone, during 1990–1992, one of the major accusations leveled against it by the Histadrut was that it had refused to transfer sufficient funds to allow the routine operation of Kupat Holim. Whether this was true or not is difficult to determine, but it is obvious that Likud propaganda was able to use to its advantage the continued crisis of Kupat Holim and its dependence on the Labor Party.

This dependence and its detrimental consequences were also a source of concern to some of the leaders of Labor, especially the younger ones, but also to Yitzhak Rabin. The status of Peres, Rabin's arch rival, as Finance Minister turned him into an ally of the Histadrut's apparatus which supported the continued presence of the Labor Party in the national unity government. The Histadrut apparatus also continued to dominate the representative bodies of the Labor Party which appointed the candidates for Knesset membership, the cabinet Ministers and the party leader. The younger Knesset members, known as the *tzeirim*, who congregated in the dual political circles of *Chug Mashov* and *Hakfar Hayarok* quickly defined as their objective the weakening of the Party's dependence on the Histadrut's apparatus and the

repudiation of the virtual identity between the two. *Chug Mashov*, the more intellectual of the two coteries, was led by Yossi Beilin, Avrum Burg and Yael Dayan,
whereas the *Hakfar Hayarok* group, led by Haim Ramon, sought to represent important social sectors and exert its influence through such involvement: Amir Peretz
in development towns, Chagai Meron in kibbutzim, Shmuel Avital in the
moshavim, and Nawaf Massalha in the Arab community.

The main common denominator of the younger Labor Party Knesset members
was their distinctly moderate, or "dovish" position in the Israeli-Palestinian conflict.
And in this they were closer to Shimon Peres then to Yitzhak Rabin. Yet in regard
to their attitude towards the Histadrut, Rabin was their partner, though instead of
leading their struggle he only sympathized with it. Rabin, for example, expressed his
approval for the symbolic change in the Labor Party's constitution, sponsored by the
tzeirim in the Labor Party's 1991 Congress, to abolish the requirement that only
Histadrut members could become party members.

An opportunity for further cooperation with the aim of weakening the influence
of the Histadrut's apparatus presented itself upon the disintegration of the national
unity government in the summer of 1990. Since Rabin and the *tzeirim* enjoyed a
great deal of support within the rank and file party members, they proposed the democratization of the party through the adoption of primaries for the election of
Knesset candidates and party leader. Initially, however, Rabin and the *tzeirim* were
divided in regard to the breaking up of the government, since its rationale was
rooted in a foreign policy initiative: to establish a government with a narrow base
which would advance negotiations with the Arab states and the Palestinians. After
Peres's failure to accomplish this aim and the return of the Labor Party to opposition, Rabin and the *tzeirim* turned into allies in the attempt to renew the party's
image by unburdening its dependence on the Histadrut's apparatus. The circumstances surrounding the break up of the national unity government and the failure
of the attempt to establish a dovish coalition highlighted severe shortcomings in the
functioning and public status of the Labor Party and thus legitimated the need to
undertake internal reforms in the party.

In the course of the negotiation for the establishment of a dovish coalition by
Peres, an ugly picture was revealed of individual Knesset Members holding the
party's fate hostage to their personal interests. The pronouncement of various rabbis
and the dependence of the party on small religious parties also became a central
public issue. The debate following these events called into question the party system
and its ability to represent the public and its wishes. Various civic action groups put
forth demands to adopt a constitution or change the electoral system. These debates
within and pressures from civil society set in motion processes which generated a
number of important results, among them the direct election of the Prime Minister
and the adoption of "fundamental" or constitutional, civil rights laws. Another
change, generated by the demand for increased democratization of the political system, took place within political parties. In the Labor Party the primaries system was
adopted soon after and in the Likud in the wake of the defeat in the 1992 elections,

which was attributed, among other causes, to the fact that the more openly elected Labor candidates were more popular than many of their Likud counterparts.

As a result of the adoption of primaries, Rabin and the *tzeirim* accomplished their personal and organizational goals and improved their public image. Many of the *tzeirim* were elected to high places in the party list, and they succeeded to weaken the influence of the Histadrut and party's apparatus on the election process and the party in general, and helped transform the image of the party from a machine dominated by the Histadrut's particularistic interests to a young and renewed organization which represented a plurality of groups. As a consequence of the Histadrut's preoccupation with its financial crisis, and public animus against the traditional machine-dominated party system, the internal party reorganization took place with relative ease.

Since the adoption of the primaries system amounts to the 'privatization' of the political system, the countervailing reaction in the Histadrut apparatus was practically identical—turning its resources to advance the individual career of some of its own leaders. The full scope of this phenomenon was revealed after the 1994 elections, when the police undertook a series of investigations into the misuse of funds for the benefit of people associated with the Histadrut. Various Histadrut-affiliated candidates were sponsored for the Knesset, and Israel Keisar, the Histadrut's Secretary General was put forth as a Prime Ministerial candidate against Peres and Rabin. Though it was expected that Keisar will not defeat the two historical leaders of the Labor Party, it was thought that if he could force runoff elections he would be able to wrest concessions favorable to the preservation of the Histadrut apparatus. But the depth of the crisis in which the Histadrut found itself was brought home by a split among its own apparatchiks: one wing supported Keisar, who received only 18 percent of the vote, the rest voted for Peres who commanded 35 percent of the vote in the Labor Party. Pooling their support, they could have defeated Rabin, but the latter, receiving 40 percent of the votes for the Labor Party's candidate for Prime Minister, won in the first round. The Histadrut's crisis gave the Labor Party the opportunity to renew itself, adopt a sharper socio-economic and foreign policy profile, and win the elections.

The Labor Government and the National Health Insurance Bill

The Labor Party's victory in 1992, in spite of its narrowness, was of a far-reaching nature, similar in many ways to the 1977 elections which brought Likud to power for the first time. In both of these elections the ruling parties collapsed and lost about a third of their power (and about 25 percent of the electorate) and the main opposition, which posed comprehensive internal and foreign policy alternatives, grew and garnered almost 40 percent of the vote. In both cases the ruling party had to move into opposition whereas the winning party faced little difficulty in forming a new parliamentary majority coalition since its victory was so clear cut.

By promising to reach an accord with the Palestinians within nine months, which would lead to Israeli-Palestinian territorial separation, the Rabin-led Labor Party coalition government presented in 1992 a clear alternative to Shamir's intransigent and inflexible foreign policy. Not less importantly, it offered to change the order of Israeli priorities by focusing on domestic needs such as economic growth, health care, education, road construction, and immigrant absorption. These were presented as alternatives to the wasteful expenditure of funds on the West Bank settlements and their infrastructure. The Likud was no longer able to sling mud at the Labor Party for the Histadrut's failures and tainted image and perforce focused on the two parties' different visions of Israeli-Arab and Israeli-Palestinian relations of which, however, the public chose Labor's more appealing version. After its electoral victory, the new government began seeking ways to implement both its peace and economic growth policies.

One of the leaders of the *tzeirim* who backed Rabin and assisted him to his victory was Haim Ramon. Ramon received the central role in undertaking the policies expected to complete the organizational restructuring of the Labor Party, the portfolio of Health Minister. He promised, with Rabin's explicit support, to pass a bill of National Health Insurance, in spite of the opposition of the Party's bodies. Ramon tied his political future to the fate of this bill, and thus to the goal of dismantling the Histadrut apparatus which still dominated the Labor Party, by promising that if the bill did not pass he would resign his ministerial post.

The new bill was novel both in its content and the process of its genesis. The Knesset's Labor Committee, headed by Amir Peretz, Ramon's ally, invited the input of concerned citizens groups, thus involving civil society in its deliberations and generating broad-based public support for the proposed bill. The bill was to make health insurance more accessible and egalitarian by promising to provide health care to all the population free of charge and by financing it out of a progressive tax. The bill also combined principles of competition between the health care providers over customers with a "capitation cost," calculated differentially for age and socio-economic groups and location. By equalizing conditions for competition the bill would have favored the Histadrut's Kupat Holim at two levels: 1. the Law compensated Kupat Holim for its elder and weaker members through the capitation system, 2. the Law liberated Kupat Holim from financing the Histadrut apparatus. The Health Law was laying the foundations of a stable financing system which could free the government from the continuous threat of public health care's collapse.

Significantly, not the innovative aspects of the bill, such as the broadening of health insurance and the lowering of costs for lower socio-economic groups (or the higher tax to upper middle classes), became the center of the public debate. The focus of the debate was the political implication of the proposed legislation, namely the severing of Kupat Holim from the Histadrut. The strongest and well-nigh lone opposition to the bill originated in the Histadrut which rightly felt threatened by a law which would wrest away its source of funding.

The two concrete issues around which the debate was centered were the "abolition of the [Histadrut-Kupat Holim] bond" (*bitul hazika*) and the "separation of
collection" (*hafradat hagviya*). The former signaled the end of the practice which required Kupat Holim members to be also Histadrut members. At one fell swoop the
Histadrut's major recruiting tool was to be gone, and it would have to prove that its
existence was necessary for its members or cease to be. The latter referred to the bill's
intention of collecting the health tax by the government and no longer by the health
insurance providers. The government would also be responsible for allocating the
tax to the various health insurance companies according to the size of their membership and the "capitation" level of various population groups.

The Histadrut apparatus threw all its weight behind efforts to prevent the bill's
passage, in spite of its support by the majority of the government and the Knesset
and its immense popularity which was due precisely to the revulsion from coerced
membership in the Histadrut. To block the bill, the Histadrut demanded that the
Labor Party's Convention, in which the apparatus still controlled the majority, debate the subject. Knowing only too well that this partisan body would stop the legislative process, Finance Minister Shochat (nicknamed Beige) offered a compromise
according which collection would be transferred from the Histadrut to the government, but the ties between Kupat Holim and the Histadrut would be retained. This
compromise would be implemented by instructing the National Insurance Institute
(Israel's equivalent of the Social Security Administration) to collect in addition to
the health tax also 0.8 percent of the payroll for trade union dues which would be
remitted to the unions connected with the health insurers.

Although "Beige's Compromise" would have laid solid foundations for financing
both Kupat Holim and the Histadrut, it would have had the perverse effect of giving incentives to all health insurers to establish their own trade unions in competition with the Histadrut. The Histadrut's leadership, encouraged by the government's partial retreat, rejected the compromise and sought to scuttle the bill
altogether. The first chapter in the saga of the national health insurance bill ended
with the Histadrut's victory. Rabin, caving in to the pressure exerted by the Histadrut in the party convention in March 1994, withdrew his public support, and
the great majority of convention members instructed the party ministers and members of Knesset to oppose the bill. Ramon, the Minister of Health, delivered a fiery
speech at the Convention in which he announced his resignation. But the second
chapter, which was concluded with the defeat of the Histadrut's apparatus, was to
begin soon.

The 1994 Histadrut Elections

The upcoming Histadrut elections, scheduled for May 1994, linked the battle over
the National Health Insurance bill and the battle of the young Labor reformers
against the Histadrut apparatus. Since 1961, with one exception (Ben Aharon,
1969–1973), the candidate for post of the Histadrut's Secretary General was se-

lected through "bureaucratic advancement," thus depriving the Labor Party of exerting its influence on the Secretary's selection or policies. According to the new method adopted by the Labor Party in 1991, the candidate for the Secretary General was to be picked, for the first time, through primaries among party members.

This reform and the growing unpopularity of the leaders of the Histadrut apparatus propelled Amir Peretz to declare his candidacy against the apparatus' candidate, Haim Haberfeld. The group of the *tzeirim* from *Chug Mashov* and *Hakfar Hayarok* and the Knesset Members affiliated with them—now known as "the group of eight" (*shminiya*)—joined the struggle on Peretz's side. Their support was based less on an agreement as to what to do in the Histadrut if Peretz were to win than on the desire to use the elections as a lever to weaken the influence of the Histadrut apparatus in the Labor Party. Within the "group of eight," some wished only to free the Labor Party from the negative image and bureaucratic influence attached to the Histadrut, whereas Peretz hoped to use the Histadrut to advance the long neglected interests of the workers. Peretz, in short, wished to be the workers' leader not only to weaken the influence of the Histadrut apparatus on the party.

The contest was one-sided because within the Labor Party the apparatus was still powerful and cohesive and knew clearly that this was a do or die struggle. The primaries between Haberfeld and Peretz were held at the beginning of 1994 and Peretz won considerable support—he received the votes of 35 percent of the voters, only 5 percent less than Rabin who became Prime Ministerial candidate with about 40 percent of the party members' votes. But against Peretz and within the Histadrut's own stronghold the apparatus was fully mobilized in support of its leader. The fateful decision to withdraw the National Health Insurance bill in the Knesset was adopted by the Labor Party's Convention following Haberfeld's impressive victory with 65 percent of the vote.

Haim Ramon's resignation from the post of Minister of Health, which happened a short while before the Histadrut elections, roused a great deal of public support for his struggle. Ramon and Peretz's political future was clouded after their failed public challenge to the Histadrut's old leadership in both the Histadrut and the Party, and the morale of their opponents was raised. Under these circumstances, the two decided that they had little to lose and sought another venue for continuing their campaign, this time with the more radical goal of wresting the Histadrut itself away from its apparatus. They hastily improvised a new party under Ramon's leadership (called "New Life") and joined it with the Labor Party's two coalition partners in the government—Meretz and Shas. Both had their own party apparatus but had vastly different constituencies: Meretz attracted educated middle class ashkenazi voters mostly in the large cities whereas Shas appealed to the lower class mizrachim, mostly in peripheral development towns.

The ability of such diverse bodies to cooperate was fueled by their shared desire to bring about the demise of the hated Histadrut's apparatus which foiled the nationalization of health insurance. At the center of the electoral campaign stood the double goals of punishing the Histadrut apparatus for its domineering stance and of opposing the practice of making membership in the Histadrut a precondition for membership in Kupat Holim, that is, opposition to the imperious and coercive aspects of the Histadrut. The character of the Histadrut after the legislation of a National Health Insurance bill was rarely addressed by New Life. Even Ramon and his allies were not unified in their views in this respect.

Ramon's party received the tacit support of both his remaining allies from the "group of eight" who remained in the Labor Party and of Rabin who also wished for the reduction of the Histadrut's apparatus influence but were weary of struggling against it as openly as Ramon and Peretz chose to do. The results of the elections demonstrate that support for New Life's was broad based: The new party bit significantly into the pool of Labor voters, attracted Meretz and Shas voters, but also received a significant portion of Likud supporters. The balance of power after the elections—46 percent for New Life and 32 percent for the Labor Party—enabled Ramon's rebels and their supporters to incorporate a significant part of their program into the coalition agreement and, subsequently, to start implementing it.

It seems impossible to explain the defeat of the Histadrut's apparatus without recalling the erosion of its organizational muscle and public image in the 14 years that passed subsequent to Finance Minister Hurwitz's decision in October 1980 to terminate the agreement permitting the Histadrut's pension funds to finance the activities of Hevrat Haovdim. Just as the 1985 stabilization program exposed the depth of the financial imbroglio or difficulties in which the Histadrut's institutions were stuck, so the 1994 elections and the legislative battle over the National Health Insurance bill revealed the hollowness of the Histadrut's organizational framework.

The Histadrut's new leadership, upon assuming power, declared its intention to extricate the Histadrut from its multiple crises and redirect its resources to the realization of aims which better serve its membership. The new leadership rapidly discovered, however, that the Histadrut's resources had been significantly depleted and, further, that it was very difficult to sell its assets or significantly reduce its activities. The Histadrut's crisis was aggravated by the consent of the new leadership to adopt the National Health Insurance bill in its original version and the conclusion of an agreement with the government concerning the repayment of the Histadrut's accumulated debts to Kupat Holim.

The Implications of
National Health Insurance for the Histadrut

Following the adoption of the National Health Insurance bill, a comprehensive debate broke out concerning the Histadrut's role, legitimation, structure and influence, its relationship with political parties, the quality of the workers' representation and, above all, the basis of membership (and the collection method of membership dues). The new leadership was quick to answer one of the main questions: Upon the separation of the Histadrut and Kupat Holim and, consequently, upon ending the Histadrut's dependence on the government's largesse, the new Histadrut's central role would be that of a regular trade union. The Histadrut, Ramon announced, should become a federation of trade unions, and half of the Histadrut's budget was planned to be spent on its union-related functions.

A telling move was the appointment of Amir Peretz as the head of the trade union department, the traditional jumping board for the Histadrut's future secretary generals. Whereas Ramon chanced upon his role as the Histadrut's Secretary General, Peretz sought this job for many years. The division of labor between the two was clear: Ramon saw his mission as undoing the old Histadrut, Peretz as building the new Histadrut. The two tasks were connected, but not identical. Ramon directed his sight to the government which he wished to rejoin as a cabinet Minister instead of staying on as a workers' leader. Consequently, the manner in which he broke the Histadrut up was drastic, rapid and decisive. Peretz, on his part, began to lay the foundations for the new body as soon as he assumed his role at the head of the trade union division.

The new Histadrut's reform committee adopted a series of substantive and symbolic changes concerning the composition of the Histadrut's organs. The Convention was deprived of its powers, which were transferred to the standing House of Representatives. The proportional electoral system, favoring political parties, was replaced with a system of direct personal elections of 1/2 to 1/3 of the House of Representatives which was planned to be implement in the 1998 elections, but never was. Delegates of trade unions and workers' committees were given greater influence on the coordination and implementation of policies while the trade union division received direct and broad authority to oversee labor conflict negotiations. At the same time, the proposals to eliminate or to limit party representation in the Histadrut's House of Representatives and the trade unions and replace it with the directly elected workers' representatives were postponed and are still the main bone of contention between the New Histadrut leadership and the political parties which wish to maintain their influence even in the new body.

The most important task in building the new Histadrut was the creation of a new approach to membership and to the collection of dues. The trade union department conducted talks with the government and the employers' Coordinating Bureau of Economic Organizations, in order to find an acceptable method of dues collection. It seems that the employers' organizations no less than the Histadrut were concerned lest the Histadrut as a centralized body, which alone can impose corporatist discipline, would disappear and the trade unions and the most powerful workers' committees would step into the vacuum. Out of this shared concern a new accord was worked out. Starting on January 1, 1995 (the implementation date of National Health Insurance), the employers began collecting dues of 0.9 percent from the wages of Histadrut members (that is, those who were members of Kupat Holim until December 31, 1994), and 0.7 percent as a "handling fee" (*dmei tipul*) from non-members for a basket of services to be provided by each and every trade union and guaranteed by the Histadrut. The legal basis for this arrangement was the "organizational tax" (*mas irgun*) of 1 percent, collected until then as payment for the

Histadrut's trade union services from non-members, though in the past the main group on which this payment (as well as others) was imposed were Palestinian Arab workers from the occupied territories employed in Israel. This accord has served as the basis for the financing of the Histadrut's activities since the National Health Insurance went into effect.

As we argued in this paper, the membership dues collection system was the aperture through which it was easiest to observe the peculiar and unchanged quasi-state character of the Histadrut into the 1990s. By examining the weaknesses of the new dues collections method we again will be able to observe the problems the New Histadrut faces and by examining the way it tackles them will be equipped to foresee its future course. The Histadrut employers' accord, indeed, left two unanswered questions: Who is covered by the new collection system? Is it possible to avoid payment? The way these questions were tackled and resolved showed that in spite of the radical restructuring of the Histadrut there was reluctance on the part of other institutions to do away with some of its traditional characteristics.

First, who is obligated to participate in the new taxation system which provides the new Histadrut finances? In the past, all wage-earners who belonged to the Histadrut through their membership in Kupat Holim were obligated to pay dues. In the past, in order to ensure that payment was required of all wage earners, including non-Histadrut members, the government imposed an extension order. This order extended to the whole economy the collective wage agreement signed between the Histadrut and the employers' Coordinating Bureau thus obligating employers to collect this tax even from those of their employees who were not Histadrut members. In the past, it didn't matter if the Histadrut signed plant-level wage agreements with every private employer, many of whom were small or medium sized, because it did not depend on the employers but on Kupat Holim for its dues. Furthermore, the governmental extension order granted anyway all employees the conditions attained through negotiations with the large employees.

In 1995, the government, however, decided that it could no longer resort to extension orders in order to have membership dues or their equivalent collected from all wage earners. Its reasoning was legal and part and parcel of other changes which transformed Israeli society at the same time the Histadrut itself underwent its own reform. The public dissatisfaction in the wake of the dissolution of the national unity government in 1990 served as the catalyst, as we argued, for the adoption by the Knesset of fundamental, or constitutional, laws. The Supreme Court began invoking them in justifying, for the first time in Israeli legal practice, the judicial review of the legality of various public, including governmental, actions. Government ministers expressed fear that an appeal to the Supreme Court by employers who were not part of the employers' Coordinating Bureau would lead the Court to use the fundamental laws: "Man's Dignity and Liberty" and "Freedom of Occupation" to strike down the extension order. The anxiety expressed was genuine enough, though it is not possible to tell what other factors influenced the government's decision not to issue an extension order and thus test its powers in the new legal context.

The implications of the end of the use of extension orders for taxation were far reaching. Together with the implementation of National Health Insurance, this decision was the one that finally severed the Histadrut from its dependence on the state. Had the government issued a new extension order, the Histadrut would have received all its dues via its agreement with the employers and the government's extension of that agreement, and it would have remained dependent on them and would not have had to try and recruit new members through the improvement of its services. But just how little the Histadrut could depend on its old membership base became clear when it was revealed in January 1995 that the agreement for the collection of membership and handling dues covered only 400,000 individuals, their overwhelming majority in the public sector.

This dire state of affairs pushed the Histadrut's apparatus, for the first time in many years, to sign plan-level collective bargaining agreements in order to broaden the basis of dues collection. This initiative was undertaken under the real threat of layoffs; for many months the Histadrut's income was only one third of its expenditure. The result of this massive effort was a 50 percent growth of collection and the increase of dues and handling fees payers to 600,000 within two years. Even so, not all parts of the apparatus lent a hand to this recruitment effort; it was the work of one of its divisions.

But the most significant component of the Histadrut which abstained itself from the recruitment drive was the trade unions. The fact was that membership in trade unions had no real meaning; members in the past were affiliated with the Histadrut at large, and some Histadrut members were registered in a number of unions. The unions themselves received their budget from the Histadrut not on the basis of their membership roaster, which they systematically inflated, but on the basis of their relative strength and ability to pressure the Histadrut's leadership. The unions, especially the strong ones among them, jointly with the big workers' committees, also conducted their own negotiations with their employers, since they held the key to industrial peace (Grinberg, 1991).

The Histadrut's new leadership, consequently, faced a serious dilemma. It wished to change the basis of Histadrut membership and its relationship with the trade unions in order to attain their support for the drive to recruit new members. At the same time, the Histadrut did not wish to clash with the stronger unions all at once, especially since these now served as the only justification for the Histadrut's continued existence. In spite of the importance given to the unions in the new Histadrut, the latter also didn't want to empower the unions too much since direct membership in the unions would have loosened the members' ties with the Histadrut itself and would have encouraged or allowed the trade unions to insist on the collection of and, consequently, on keeping the members' dues. The unions on their part were leery of deserting the Histadrut since they could not be sure whether the members would follow them or elect to stay in the Histadrut. And yet they had no incentive to join the recruitment drive and enlarge the Histadrut membership. In the new, as in the old Histadrut, the leadership's main "weapon" in its tug of war with the unions were the workers' committees which, though connected with the unions, could have served as the nuclei of new unions, friendly to the Histadrut, if the trade unions left the Histadrut.

Under these conditions an uneasy balance of power was achieved between the Histadrut and the trade unions, as they all chose to retain the old definition of membership at large in the Histadrut, disconnected from direct union membership. Even as the Histadrut was renewing itself, some of its key aspects—its umbrella character—could not be undone.

Second, was it possible for wage-earners to avoid payment to the Histadrut? Would non-members continue to be obligated to pay? The question who was a member of the new Histadrut was resolved relatively easily: All those who belonged to Kupat Holim were defined as continuing members. Though it was possible to withdraw from the Histadrut, this phenomenon remained marginal because most members were unaware of this option and remained members through inertia. The main loss of dues was the result of non-payment by workers employed in enterprises which had no plant-level collective bargaining agreement with the Histadrut, or their agreement was negotiated by trade unions which were not part and parcel of the Histadrut, namely the teachers, physicians, academics, and journalists unions. In the past, many members of these unions were simultaneously Histadrut members by virtue of their membership in Kupat Holim; the implementation of National Health Insurance in fact canceled their membership in the Histadrut even if they didn't desire that.

The question of the avoidance of payment, therefore, concerned mainly those required to pay the "handling fee." The Histadrut and employers agreed that every enterprise that signed a collective bargaining agreement was required to collect either Histadrut membership dues of 0.9 percent of the monthly wage or a handling fee of 0.7 percent from its employees. In such an enterprise the decision of a worker to quit the Histadrut, consequently, would reduce his or her payment only from 0.9 percent to 0.7 percent, that is, so minimally that most would hardly bother to make the choice. The real question became, therefore, whether it was possible to pay nothing but still enjoy the employment conditions, overtime and other benefits, cost of living allowances, etc. negotiated between the Histadrut and the employers which continued to be implemented through a governmental extension order.

The law contained such a lacuna. If the worker belonged to a trade union not affiliated with the Histadrut, he or she was not required to pay the handling fee. Indeed, a number of trade unions established prior to 1948 by the rivals of Histadrut and the Labor movement, namely the religious Mizrachi and Hapoel Hamizrachi, and Herut's National Workers Organization, were based on the same partisan principle as the Histadrut. The Histadrut recognized their special standing under the agreement with employers. It didn't, however, extend this recognition to a new quasi-union established now by Kupat Holim Maccabi, an independent health insurance provider for the middle class.

Kupat Holim Maccabi sought to reverse the pattern characteristics of the old Histadrut. As part of its preparations for the implementation of National Health Insurance, under the "Beige compromise," it established a quasi-union named "Amit" which, though it did not seek to unionize enterprises or sign collective bargaining agreements, offered legal counseling to individuals who were employed through personal contracts and also covered by Maccabi's complementary insurance. 150,000 members of Kupat Holim Maccabi signed Amit's application form to join it as a workers' organization. When the government began collecting the handling fee from non-members of Histadrut, Maccabi requested the Labor Court to ensure that it received the portion it was entitled to in its view.

The court case on the issue of the handling fee was highly significant for the Histadrut as it determined the criteria of membership and the basis of its financing, in short, whether it was possible to avoid payment to it by non-members. If Amit was recognized as a *bona fide* union without the requirement that it was to conduct collective bargaining, willing workers could have used it as a "tax shelter." Such turn of events would have also given an incentive to the setting up of other organizations which would have provided very limited trade union services but would have collected only very small sums for membership since their members would have been "free riders" on the Histadrut's collective bargaining agreements. This situation would have meant not only the disintegration of a unified trade union body but also open competition for members by new bodies. Hence not only the Histadrut but also the trade unions, including those not part of the Histadrut, the government and the employers organizations rallied against Amit.

The trial lasted more than a year, and after the decision of the Labor Court was handed down included an appeal to the Supreme Court. On both levels the trial was accompanied by many exceptional if not irregular features. The Labor Court, composed of three professional judges, two judges appointed by the Histadrut and two additional ones by the employers' Coordinating Bureau, decided by a majority of four to three to recognize Amit as a trade union. The irregularity of this decision consisted of the fact, as pointed out in the minority opinion, that it emptied the definition of trade union from its content. The Histadrut appealed this decision to the Supreme Court which unanimously overturned the lower court's decision. The exceptional character of the higher court's decision may be seen both in the fact that not only part of the court but also all of its nine members sat in judgment and all concurred in the decision. It was further surprising that in this case a regular court overturned a legal opinion given by a Labor Court against the Histadrut. The Supreme Court's own decision provided the Histadrut with the necessary tool to prevent members from leaving the Histadrut and Amit disintegrated shortly afterwards. Again, the final legal decision confirmed the collective character of labor relations and saved the Histadrut.

The new Histadrut shed those of its institutions that made it into a quasi-state structure and succeeded in its attempt to create a legal basis for membership due to the collective agreements with the private employers and the state, thanks to the Supreme Court's decision. The new Histadrut thus is a much weaker body and is less able to oppose the liberalization of the Israeli economy and the privatization of many of the previously publicly-held companies. However, the Histadrut's dependence on the state could not be completely undone due at once to the problematic relations between the political parties and Histadrut apparatuses and to the interests of workers, worker committees and trade unions. Since the new leadership was unable to reduce the power of the former, it also failed to solve the financial deficit, because it could not fire apparatchiks who served at the behest of the parties or close divisions controlled by these political parties. The new leadership also failed to change the electoral system in its House of Representatives (that was assumed to give direct representation to workers' representatives) and was unable to remove partisan control within the trade unions. Since December 1996, in fact, the new leadership was pressured by powerful worker committees and some non-party ruled unions to adopt a confrontational policy of strikes in the public sector. Recently some Histadrut leaders also organized a Workers Party which will run in the Knesset 1999 elections. The Histadrut's transformation, and in some areas privatization, is still an open problem.

Conclusion

The crisis and decline of the Histadrut's institutional network and power between 1980 to 1994 was the last chapter of the peculiar relation between the Labor Settlement Movement and the Zionist process of state building (Shapiro, 1976; Kimmerling, 1983; Shafir, 1989; Shalev, 1992; Grinberg, 1993). Before 1948, as the Zionist state-in-the-making, the Histadrut's institutions played a crucial role in establishing a separate Jewish economy and supplied welfare and employment services to Jewish immigrants. After the establishment of the State of Israel this quasi-state structure became problematic, but was retained by the ruling Labor Party to serve its manifold interests, for example, to help absorb new immigrants and rein in wage demands. At the same time, the blurred institutional boundaries between the state and the Histadrut and the continued pressure on the state to subsidize the Histadrut's national functions were among the most salient obstacles to the autonomous capacities of the state.

Despite the fact that the Histadrut continued to carry out its state-building role after 1948, the Labor Movement became alienated and disassociated from the workers during the fifties and sixties. Two of the causes of this process of disassociation were the radical change in the social composition of the working class due to migration, and the growing power of the rank and file workers to organize their own representative committees under conditions of full employment. In spite of the Histadrut's reduced legitimacy and the growing support of lower classes for the right wing opposition (Herut and later Likud), the Histadrut's strong ties to the state, and claims on its purse, were not weakened because of the role it played in shoring up the Labor Party. As long as the Labor Party governed both the Histadrut and the state, the Histadrut remained shielded from pressures of reform. The Histadrut's own decline began only after the Labor Party lost its role as Israel's dominant party.

Seven years of Likud governments and Labor opposition (1977–1984) led party apparatchiks to the conclusion that in order to save the Histadrut, the Labor Party had to join a national unity government with the Likud, even at the price of postponing political accommodation with the Palestinians and accepting the unprecedented rotation of Prime Ministers. Yet the formation of the national unity government in 1984, and the implementation of the economic stabilization plan in 1985 in order to solve the inflationary crisis, facilitated for the first time the construction of a political basis for state autonomy. This autonomy provided the capacity to reduce the state budget and subsidies, to neutralize the power of groups that in the past penetrated state apparatuses, and to open up the Israeli economy to global financial markets and forces. The most prominent victim of this policy—due to its quasi-state character and dependence on state subsidies— was the Histadrut.

The 1985 economic stabilization program was widely supported by the public fearful of the uncertainty created by the hyperinflation. One of its most important by-products was the depoliticization of economic policies. From 1985 on, the two large parties by and large abandoned any semblance of a public debate on economic and distributional issues, and the authority on economic issues was transferred to the "specialists"—to Treasury and Bank of Israel officials and to professional economists at the universities. This process was obviously part of an international trend which saw the depoliticization of the economy (or, by the same token, the politicization of the economists), but one of its local consequences was the inability of the Histadrut leadership to present a sustained struggle or coherent ideological opposition to the reduction of their subsidies. In addition, the weakening of the Histadrut was caused by the lesser relevance of the project of state-building, and the expansion of the power of the state, the private sector, and the military. After 1967 the quasi-state institutional structure of the Histadrut became irrelevant for state-building purposes, and since 1977 it became politically vulnerable.

Not only did the Histadrut lose its historical role to the state, the military and the private capital, the Labor Party did too. The return of the Labor Party to national leadership, consequently, was directly related to the severance of its bond with the Histadrut. Despite the struggle of the veteran apparatchiks against this process, it was on-going and ultimately coherent; its leadership was taken by the reformist young leaders of Labor and by Yitzhak Rabin, all supporters of neo-liberal economic order. Peretz, the only non-liberal leader, remained the leader of the Histadrut at the time when the Labor Party happily abandoned it. The fate of the Histadrut and Israel's organized workers remains uncertain at the end of this century.

References

Aharoni, Yair. 1991. *The Israeli Economy: Dreams and Realities.* New York: Routledge.

Asa-El, Amotz. 1997. "Koor Grabs the Future." *Jerusalem Post* (February 19).

Ben Porat, Yoram. 1982. "The Conservative Turnabout that Never Was. Ideology and Economic Policy in Israel Since 1977." *Jerusalem Quarterly*, no.115.

Bichler, Shimshon. 1992. "The Political Economy of National Security in Israel." Ph.D. dissertation., Hebrew University. (Hebrew)

Grinberg, Lev Luis. 1991. *Split Corporatism in Israel.* Albany, N.Y.: State University of New York Press.

_____. 1993. *The Histadrut Above All.* Jerusalem, Nevo Publications, (Hebrew).

Grinberg, Lev Luis and Michael Shalev. 1989. "Histadrut-Government Relations and the Transition from a Likud to a National Unity Government, Continuity and Change in Israel's Economic Crisis." *Sapir Center For Development.* Discussion Paper No. 14.89.

Gross, Joseph. 1994. *Koor Industries Inc.: The Reorganization Process and the Capital Market.* Tel Aviv University, School of Management. (Hebrew).

Horowitz, Dan and Moshe Lissak. 1978. *Origins of the Israeli Polity: Palestine Under the Mandate.* Chicago: University of Chicago Press.

International Management. 1974. "Union-Owned Firm Stresses Profits." (February)

Klinov, Ruth and Nadav Halevi. 1968. *The Economic Development of Israel.* New York: Praeger.

Medding, Peter. 1972. *Mapai in Israel: Political Organization and Government in a New Society.* Cambridge: Cambridge University Press.

Peri, Yoram. 1983. *Between Battles and Ballots.* Cambridge: Cambridge University Press.

Semyonov, Moshe and Noah Lewin-Epstein. 1987. *Hewers of Wood and Drawers of Water: Non-Citizen Arabs in the Israeli Labor Market.* New York: ILR Press.

Shafir, Gershon. 1989. *Land, Labor and the Origins of the Israeli-Palestinian Conflict, 1882–1914.* Cambridge: Cambridge University Press.

Shalev, Michael. 1984. "Labor State and Crisis: An Israeli Case Study." *Industrial Relations*, no. 23, pp. 362–386.

_____. 1992. *Labour and the Political Economy in Israel.* Oxford: Oxford University Press.

_____. 1998. "Have Globalization and Liberalization 'Normalized' Israel's Political Economy ?" *Israel Affairs.*

Shapiro, Yonathan. 1976. *The Formative Years of the Israeli Labor Party.* London: Sage.

_____. 1989. *The Road to Power.* Albany, N.Y.: State University of New York Press.

Skocpol, Theda. 1985. "Bringing the State Back In: Strategies of Analysis in Current Research," in Skocpol, et. al. eds., *Bringing the State Back In.* Cambridge: Cambridge University Press.

Skocpol, Theda, Dietrich Rueschemeyer and Peter Evans. 1985. *Bringing the State Back In.* Cambridge: Cambridge University Press.

6

Liberalization and the Transformation of the Political Economy

MICHAEL SHALEV

Surely, nothing in Israel has changed more dramatically than the economy and the assumptions underlying the state's economical policies. Fifty years ago Israel was a poor new state hopelessly indebted to the outside world. Thirty-five years ago it could be described as a rapidly growing developing country undergoing successful industrialization. Fifteen years ago it was an extreme case of an economically over-burdened state incapable of stemming stagnation and spiraling inflation. But as the century comes to a close, the guardians of the "Washington consensus" hold Israel up as a model of economic liberalization and successful adaptation to globalization and technological change.[1]

In the course of the 1990s the economy experienced a wave of growth that was comparable in pace to the Asian tigers and brought average living standards within reach of the rich OECD democracies. Starting in 1992 when mass immigration from the former Soviet Union peaked, and ending after the 1996 elections, Israel's real per capita GDP grew by a remarkable 4 percent per annum. But since then the economy has moved into a deepening recession. As usual, the economic pundits at-tribute the recession to policy errors—some point to erroneous economic policies while others blame the deadlock in the peace process.[2] But from a longer historical perspective the rhythm of the ongoing business cycle is not surprising. Ever since the onset of modern Jewish settlement in Palestine, geopolitics, immigration and capital inflow (the assets brought by immigrants, or foreign gifts) have driven the economy's major episodes of boom and bust.

Although this pattern continued after the establishment of the State of Israel half a century ago, the fundamental parameters of the relations between state and econ-omy remained remarkably stable. Neither wars nor political upheavals appeared ca-pable of altering the extensive scope of public employment and expenditure, the state's generous subsidization (for Jews) of both businesses and households, or its dominant role in mobilizing and allocating capital. Periodic attempts to contract the economic dimensions of the state and create conditions for self-powering capitalist growth proved unsuccessful.

The endurance of the basic political-economic patterns during the first four decades of Israel's existence as a sovereign state rested on a broad and durable policy consensus among policymakers regarding the indispensability of open, organized and subsidized Jewish immigration; the need for the state to underwrite the economic security of all Jewish citizens and to "close gaps" between different Jewish ethnic groups; the necessity to meet Israel's defense "imperatives" irrespective of economic considerations; and the desirability of the state playing an active developmental role in the economy.

Over the past ten or fifteen years these four consensual pillars, especially the last, have for the first time been confronted by a comprehensive and vigorously articulated alternative: the (neo) liberal view which glorifies individual acquisitiveness and views the state as an impediment to the workings of the market economy, a conviction hitherto voiced only by economists or by disaffected businessmen lacking the right political connections. Both Labor and Likud are now committed to reducing the economic role of government, making the economy more attractive to foreign investors and other shibboleths of contemporary economic liberalism. In order to understand why Israel has taken the path of liberalization, and what this might mean, this chapter will attend to both the stable and the dynamic elements of the country's political-economic history: the inner logic characterizing its past and present political-economic regimes, and the tensions and conditionality built into them.

Historical Origins

The conditions of Jewish immigration and settlement required that the political institutions of the Zionist movement and the Yishuv dominate the mobilization of capital and the purchase of land. Because of their common interest in neutralizing an unfavorable labor market, the Labor and Zionist movements cooperated intensely. Organized Zionism supported the workers' movement, which shielded Jewish workers from Arab competition by providing subsidized employment and social services. A wide consensus developed around the view that economic collectivism was indispensable to the success of Jewish colonization but that it could and should coexist with a capitalist market economy. (Kimmerling, 1983; Shafir, 1989; Shalev, 1992)

The Labor movement dominated Zionist politics for so long that it was tempting to identify Zionist collectivism with socialist ideology. In fact, the world-view of Labor Zionism was only secondarily socialist; its central theme was Jewish nationalism. (Sternhell, 1995; Shalev 1996) The arrival of sovereignty reinforced the collectivist consensus, rather than weakening it. The ruling Labor Party adopted a highly interventionist economic stance but embraced neither of the innovations associated with Western parliamentary socialism after the war—nationalization and the welfare state. The government was committed to assisting the private sector, along with state- and Histadrut-owned enterprises; in any case, the Israeli bourgeoisie was neither able nor willing to bear principal responsibility for economic development, and private industrialists were the first to demand a controlled (protected and subsidized) economy. In the domain of social policy, attempts to introduce a modern system of social insurance along the lines of postwar British reforms were stillborn. (On economic policy see Barkai, 1964, pp.15–77; Plessner, 1994. The failure of early welfare state initiatives is discussed by Doron and Kramer, 1991)

State intervention was rationalized by specifically Israeli constructions: the challenges of arming and defending the country, settling huge waves of new immigrants, penetrating frontier regions of the country where Arabs lived or which bordered Arab countries, and developing an economic infrastructure that would permit immigrant absorption and eventually eliminate Israel's dependence on charity and loans. This constituted what may be thought of as the "demand side" of the interventionist state in Israel. The "supply side" was no less compelling. It rested on Israel's singular capacity to attract *gift capital* from foreign donors stemming partly from its active alignment with the West in the East-West struggle, but even more importantly from the Jewish character of the state which enabled it to make claims on Jewish communities abroad and obtain substantial financial compensation from Germany on behalf of world Jewry. (Bialer, 1989; Yago, 1977) These "unilateral transfers," as well as a relatively favorable borrowing capacity for a struggling new economy, provided the Israeli state with the means to steer economic development and play a very active role in distributional processes. Economic growth was powered by the state's ability to mobilize money and people from abroad. Under these conditions, it is not surprising that liberal arguments in favor of "free" markets and self-interested private investment enjoyed limited appeal among policymakers.

Perhaps the clearest indication of the structural underpinnings of the role of the state in the Israeli economy was the continuity evidenced after the 1977 elections, when Labor's long period of uninterrupted rule was abruptly brought to a close. Despite the new Likud government's claims to be embarking on a radical program of liberalization, widespread expectations of a fundamental shift in economic policy priorities proved to be premature. (Sharkansky and Radian, 1982; Ben-Porath, 1983) The enduring parameters of economic policy included the following: (Halevi and Klinov-Malul, 1968; Ben-Porath, 1986, pp.1–23; Aharoni, 1991)

1. High levels of government expenditure and employment (biased by commitments to defense and immigrant absorption), relative to the economy's level of development.
2. Extensive state control of savings, investment and foreign currency.
3. Modest public ownership alongside a high degree of public subsidy of private and Histadrut-owned business.
4. Corporatist delegation of state functions to the Histadrut, with the state trading subsidies for policy cooperation and legitimation.

This is not to suggest that Israel's political economy has been immutable to change. Rather, changes have not necessarily been coupled with policy proclamations, and they must be understood more broadly than exclusive concentration on policy allows. It is more useful to think in terms of political-economic *regimes*, an analytical construct which abstracts the underlying "model" of political economy in a given epoch from the broad ensemble of economic, political and institutional variables which supports it.

For an understanding of the background to contemporary economic liberalization in Israel, two such regimes are noteworthy. The first, characterizing the period of rapid growth from the mid-fifties to the mid-sixties, rested on the synergy created by the meeting of two imported influences: German reparations and other foreign gifts, and the arrival of masses of propertyless immigrants who (among other things) expanded the markets for housing and consumer essentials and simultaneously provided a cheap labor force for their production. (Bernstein and Swirski, 1982) The state was positioned strategically, as the factor that directed immigration and settlement, the disposal of foreign gifts, and housing and industrial policy. It created a highly politicized and closely regulated economy with partially competing blocs of public, private and Histadrut capital, and a high degree of labor market segmentation parallel to ethnic and national divisions in the working class. These arrangements awarded both the state and the party that dominated it considerable autonomy—that is, the capacity to steer business interests and civil society rather than be steered by them. (Shalev, 1992; Evans, Rueschemeyer and Skocpol, eds., 1985)

After a decade of rapid growth, this regime was exhausted. The shift to full employment upset power relations by reducing the dependence of ordinary workers on the state and the ruling parties. The winding down of immigration and German aid persuaded the state to cut back both the scope of its presence in the economy, and the extent of its subsidizing role. It was thought necessary to discipline both labor and capital. The instrument for exercising this discipline was a recessionary economic policy—the *Mitun* or slowdown of 1966–1967. (Shalev, 1984)

Post-1967 Modifications

This cooling-off period proved to be short-lived, however. The aftermath of the 1967 war fundamentally altered key elements of Israel's political-economic regime. Although senior politicians and bureaucrats developed a sudden fondness for laissez-faire rhetoric, and some elements of economic regulation did become less direct, there was no undermining of the state's role as the central pivot of the economy. Instead, this pivot found a new axis in the "military-industrial complex." (Mintz, 1983; Barkai, 1987) The basis for this development was a potent combination of government-subsidized local military procurement, the burgeoning world market for arms, and (from 1970) U.S. government financing of Israel's foreign arms purchases. The occupation of the West Bank and Gaza also played an important part in reviving growth along new lines, both by extending the scope of Israel's "domestic" product market, and by providing a source of cheap labor to replace increasingly scarce Israeli manual workers, especially in construction.

During the 1970s the structure of the Israeli economy, and its labor market, became increasingly dualistic. "Big business" developed in the *bureaucratic sector*, nominally controlled by the state or the Histadrut, frequently linked to military requirements, and employing exclusively Jewish labor under the favorable conditions of a sheltered or "primary" labor market. The more competitive economic periphery, smaller-scale and privately-owned, operated a "secondary" labor market employing a mixed. (Jewish and Arab) work force. (Farjoun, 1983; Aharoni, 1976; Semyonov and Lewin-Epstein, 1987)

As in the past, economic growth under the post-1967 regime relied heavily on state subsidization of both capital and labor. The most compelling claims to subsidy were made by the bureaucratic sector. The key actors in this respect were the big banks and the big conglomerates under their control: the "strong" Workers' Committees in the employ of the state; and the Histadrut (simultaneously representing big business and "big labor"). The state found itself increasingly indebted to these powerful interests and unable to assert its will and extract benefits in return for the rising tide of subsidies. Under the conditions prevailing in the world economy of the post-1973 period, and given the earmarked nature of U.S. aid, economic policy became strikingly "undisciplined." Symptomatic of this was the public sector's excessive deficit spending, frequent recourse to corrective devaluations, and government lending policies that favored borrowers at the state's expense. The result of these policies was to exacerbate Israel's immanent condition of stagflation after 1973, while paradoxically enriching its big banks and conglomerates. (Grinberg, 1991; Shalev, 1989; Bichler, 1991)

This is the background to the Emergency Economic Stabilization Plan of June 1985. (Bruno, 1993) In hindsight, the astonishing success of the plan in bringing the Israeli economy back from the brink of hyperinflation is of lesser importance than the structural change that it inaugurated—the contemporary liberalizing shift in Israel's political-economic regime. Just like the *Mitun*, the stabilization plan was a radical attempt by the state—led by senior economic policy mandarins and sages—to regain autonomy by strengthening market discipline. (Shalev and Grinberg, 1989; Barkey, 1994) The plan and the structural reforms temporarily hidden in its shadow constituted a frontal attack on mechanisms that had previously protected societal interests, directly or indirectly, at the expense of the state: devaluations, protectionism, wage indexation, unlinked public lending, and diffuse investment incentives.

Why had it taken the state so long to develop a coherent policy response to the problems of economic stagnation and hyperinflation? Only by 1985 had the economic crisis come to pose tangible threats to the state itself—its fundamental legitimacy and, no less importantly, its economic viability. While critics cast doubt on the plan's macro-economic effectiveness, (Razin and Sadka, 1993) its consequences for the viability and autonomy of the state were very substantial indeed. Talk of the need for a "strong leader" (an ominous threat to the political regime) disappeared; state extraction of economic resources through taxation was restored to effectiveness; it was possible to set in motion a long-overdue flattening of military expenditure; and a worrying hole in Israel's foreign reserves was filled, in large part by virtue of enlarged U.S. aid.

This is not to argue that the acute crisis which economic instability posed to core state interests was the only relevant factor. As is often the case when history turns at a major crossroads, multiple causal forces converged in mid-1985. First, many of Israel's largest corporations and investors began to believe that there were limits to the profitability of military-based demand and inflationary subsidies, and that the time was ripe for a new and more outward-looking economic strategy. (Bichler and Nitzan, 1996)[3] Second, the political conjuncture in mid-1985 was especially favorable to radical policy initiatives. (Grinberg, 1991). There was little scope for profiting from party rivalry under the National Unity government which was then in its early stages. And the leadership of the Histadrut, the most vocal potential opposition to the stabilization plan given that it was expected to slash real wages, was politically indebted to the government for its aid in a recent election. All of these circumstances together offered exceptional leeway to the professional economists in state agencies and university economics departments who prepared and lobbied for the stabilization plan. The architects of the plan cannily grasped the opportunity to go beyond crisis management and engineer a strategic reorientation of economic policy. (Keren, 1993)

State Contraction

The principal goal of liberalizing economic reforms in Israel, as elsewhere, has been *state contraction*, a fundamental alteration of the division of labor between markets and the state by means that include privatization, expenditure and tax cuts, sectoral "deregulation," etc. To the extent that this aim is achieved, the state's ownership, regulatory and distributional roles are diminished in favor of the market and the private sector. The conventional wisdom assumes that combining state contraction with increased exposure to international competition causes markets to become both more important and more competitive.

The decline since the mid-1980s in the share of national resources distributed by the Israeli state is quite remarkable. Total public expenditure had been equivalent to at least three-quarters of the national product since the 1973 war. But two years after stabilization the figure fell to 62 percent, and by 1994 it had troughed at only 54 percent. Almost all of the decline in government spending since the early eighties can be traced to defense (a drop of over 10 points of GNP), capital subsidies (down 8 points) and debt service (down nearly 5 points).[4]

The decline in capital subsidies is especially significant, given that much of the increase in transfer payments during the seventies—which was the major factor behind the fiscal crisis of the early eighties—consisted of payments and benefits to business. (Shalev, 1992) One element in the cutback, already noted, has been the termination of subsidies specifically targeted to exporters. Subsidies on production for the domestic market have also been sharply reduced. During Israel's initial inflationary spurt in the mid-1970s the burden of these subsidies jumped fourfold to 8 percent of GNP, remaining at this level through the early 1980s. Phased reductions over the next decade brought their share back down to 2 percent.[5]

Because of their indirect effects on the business sector, the implications of the other principal budget cuts—in debt service and defense—have been no less portentous. Servicing the government's debt became a major source of profitability for Israel's biggest banks, especially during the 1983–1988 period when it preempted an average of nearly a fifth of GDP.[6] Reductions since stabilization in the domestic defense budget, which had showered lucrative cost-plus contracts on large-scale local suppliers, (Hadar, 1990) may also be assumed to have indirectly eroded the profitability of big business. From 1985 the domestic military procurement budget failed to increase in real terms, so that its share of Israel's growing GNP fell substantially. (BOI–96, Appendix Table *Hay*-1a)

All of the data reviewed thus far appear to signify massive retrenchment of the "welfare state for business." But a fuller assessment of this issue also requires us to consider whether the apparent harshness of post-1985 policy toward business has not been mitigated by two developments that would not necessarily show up in these data: compensatory "tax expenditures," or the replacement of old subsidies by new ones.

Regarding taxation, as D. Swank has recently noted in a comparative study of OECD economies, despite the pressures exerted by mobile global capital on state managers, they continue to "defend the treasury.". Accordingly, although governments have found it necessary to cut taxes on business, the primacy of markets has also been invoked to justify the withdrawal of investment incentives. (Swank, 1996) The same is true in Israel, where the other side of the equation is also evident: in aggregate, massive cuts in subsidies have been offset by tax cuts of similar magnitude.[7] One of the immediate effects of stabilization was to revive the state's capacity to extract revenues from the business sector—a capacity which had been badly undermined by rapid inflation. Revenues from corporate income and payroll taxes rose sharply relative to national product immediately following stabilization, but since then taxes and subsidies have been declining more or less in tandem. A major reform in the mid–1980s and gradual additional cuts since then have brought the tax rate on undistributed profits down from an internationally high level of 61% in 1984 to the rich-country norm (only 36%) in 1996. (See the annual report of the State Revenues Administration for 1996, Table *Kaf*-12) In addition, employer contributions to the social security system and other payroll taxes have been either reduced or taken over by the Treasury in order to help employers lower their labor costs.[8]

Finally, while automatic and indirect capital subsidies have been dramatically cut, targeted incentives are more generous than ever. For example, direct investment grants issued by the Ministry of Industry and Commerce, especially assistance to startup companies in high technology fields, was three times higher in real terms in 1992–1994 than in 1985–1987. (Yosha and Yafeh, 1996)

At the same time, there is no evidence that aggregate *social* spending in Israel has fallen during the contemporary era of liberalization—an irony that holds for other countries as well.[9] Following a period of budget cutting in the eighties, in the first half of the nineties spending on the major categories of social services—health and education—rose, returning to approximately the same share of GNP as a decade earlier. (See also Schuldiner, 1996) Expenditure on housing and immigrant absorption (important components of Israel's generosity toward Jewish newcomers) increased by well over 3 points of GNP, in response to the wave of immigration from the former USSR. Transfer payments to households also grew, by about one and a half points of GNP.

The record of annual fluctuations in real social expenditure over the last fifteen years shows that in addition to immigrant absorption, increased commitments have come about for a variety of reasons. The cost of the key income maintenance branches has grown mainly because of automatic benefit adjustments and demographic shifts (a larger and older population). In other instances, specific programs have experienced innovations that caused sudden steps in expenditure. The most notable example is the national health insurance law adopted in 1994 (see below). There have also been a few cases where spending rose when liberal demands for equality coincided with increased political clout, leading to a broadening of the universal basis of social security.[10] Finally, one of the social services—a very expensive one, education—actually expanded during the nineties. The Labor government elected in 1992 restored per capita spending to the level that prevailed before cuts were instituted in the eighties. (Schuldiner, 1996) This momentum has however stalled in several recent years.

None of this necessarily means that there has been no rollback of the welfare state, broadly-conceived. At least one significant form of social protection has been all but eliminated since the stabilization plan—consumer subsidies on food and public transportation, which at their peak in 1984 amounted to $1.4 billion. (Karger and Monnickendam, 1991) The Treasury has also sought and sometimes succeeded to erode entitlements (child allowances have been a favorite) or stymie the implementation of costly political promises (such as extension of the school day). As in most other countries, eligibility rules for unemployment insurance have become more restrictive, although this has not prevented rising take-up.[11]

In addition, it has been widely observed in Israel that private expenditure on social services has increased in the last decade to compensate for inadequate public provision.[12] The public school system both requires and encourages parents to pay a range of fees and subsidies in public education. In the health field supplementary insurance schemes have recently proliferated, and the Treasury has tried to cut the cost of national health insurance by authorizing additional membership fees and service charges to be collected by healthcare providers (in addition to the health tax collected by the National Insurance Institute).

Critics see these signs of privatization of welfare as part of a broader project of undermining the generosity and universality of the welfare state. (Doron, 1995, 1997; Schuldiner, 1996) No less important but less noticed so far are the implications of the ascendancy of market-oriented criteria in relation to public sector employment and government policy toward outlying Jewish areas. So long as the bureaucratic sector sheltered key parts of the defense industries and other key industrial sectors that exclusively employed Jewish citizens, it was a haven for government-subsidized occupational welfare. (Farjoun, 1983; Doron, 1988) The retrenchment of both the scope and conditions of blue-collar employment that tends to follow privatization seriously threatens this system of welfare. Regional development incentives constituted a second element of the state's traditional role in supporting the living standards of Jewish citizens. The claim that these incentives are inefficient and no longer justified by security considerations has generated ongoing policy changes that threaten to substantially erode direct and indirect subsidies to housing, employment and public services in peripheral "development towns."

Opening up to the World Economy

Trade liberalization should be evidenced at the macro level by buying more from the outside world and selling more to it, and at the micro level by the elimination of import restrictions and export incentives. The scope and regulation of trade can only tell part of the story, however, especially in Israel, where politicization has been the most salient feature of external economic relations. In the Israeli context, liberalization would also imply a change in the character of capital inflow, from state to market-sponsored and from gifts to loans or investments.

Since its establishment as a sovereign state, and in fact well before that, Israel has been chronically dependent on imported goods and services yet unable to pay for them from export revenues alone. The total value of trade (imports plus exports) relative to national product has always been exceptionally high compared to other countries, three-quarters or more of GNP. Setting aside fluctuations, it is evident that this ratio experienced a *declining trend* between the late 1970s and the early 1990s. The seeming absence of a tendency towards increasing openness is again unusual from a comparative perspective.[13]

Part of the puzzle is resolved by recognizing that Israel's relatively strong growth rates in the 1990s hide a major increase in the absolute volume of trade. Since stabilization the dollar value of both imports and exports has surged upwards, even taking account of rapid population growth. In addition, two elements of Israel's trade that arguably warrant separate consideration—the diamond-processing industry and arms imports—have been contracting. The Bank of Israel estimates that setting these elements aside, during the 1990s the scope of trade increased from roughly 50 percent to 70 percent of national product. (BOI–96, Diagram *Vav–1*) No less significant than the quantitative trend, foreign sales have altered qualitatively—more high-tech yet less military-centered; less dependent on the European market and more on "emerging" markets in Eastern Europe and, especially, Asia.[14] Nevertheless, during the nineties exports have failed to keep pace with rapidly rising imports as trade barriers came down and cheap imports became a de facto mainstay of Israel's anti-inflationary policy. Consequently, the civilian "import surplus" (excess of imports over exports, again net of diamonds) has risen to a staggering 15 percent of national product—far above OECD standards.[15]

Between 1985 and 1990 there was a 30 percent increase in the penetration of domestic markets for manufactured goods.[16] Still, the impact of greater openness to imports on competition has been weakened by monopolistic tendencies among importers. Moreover, while after much foot-dragging Israel honored its free trade agreements with the European Union (1975) and the United States (1985), defenses against competing imports from other countries (mostly NICs) were actually fortified for a time. However, during the 1990s these barriers have gradually come down. (Halevi, 1994) On import duties, see the annual reports of the State Revenues Administration. On the other side of the trade ledger, export subsidies—at least those for which statistics are available—have been phased out. At their peak in the period 1970–84 these subsidies averaged 3 percent of GNP, but by 1990 they had been virtually eliminated.[17]

"Unilateral transfers" from foreign sympathizers and governments have always been crucial both for meeting Israel's external obligations and for financing the role of the state in the economy. One variety of gift capital, that which emanates from Diaspora Jewry, has gradually declined in importance.[18] Since the beginning of the 1970s the U.S. government has become the pre-eminent source. By the late 1970s the import of American arms had plateaued at around 8 percent of GNP, and American aid was effectively paying for them in full.[19] In 1984 and 1985 Israel's foreign economic relations took a dramatic new turn. A wide gap emerged in Israel's favor between what it receives from the U.S. government and its purchases of U.S. arms. In the first half of the 1990s net U.S. aid averaged over 3 billion dollars a year, up by a billion dollars from a decade before. At the same time Israel's purchases of imported arms were declining, especially in relation to the rapidly growing national product. As the combined result of these two trends, for more than a decade the ratio of aid to arms has been at least 2:1.

Not only has the pure gift element in U.S. aid increased substantially since the mid-1980s, but following the transition to a Labor government after the 1992 elections, Israel was able to obtain official U.S. guarantees for $10 billion worth of future commercial loans. Like the peace process which was also inaugurated following the 1992 elections, the loan guarantees have helped raise Israel's commercial creditworthiness abroad. (BOI–95, p.238) So far, in most years of the 1990s, this has helped give the state the resources and flexibility to maintain or increase non-defense spending while actually reducing the budget deficit and the public debt and accumulating very high levels of foreign reserves.

The political-economic implication of these changes is multi-dimensional. The increase in the gift component of U.S. aid and the addition of the loan guarantees has enhanced the scope and autonomy of the state in the economic arena. At the same time, by helping relieve the budget deficit and the shortage of hard currency that reached crisis proportions prior to stabilization, American aid created necessary (although not of course sufficient) conditions for liberalization of the capital market and the foreign exchange regime, which in turn opened up new possibilities for capital inflows and outflows through the market.

Foreign direct investment (FDI) has been the most novel and noticed element of Israel's contemporary integration into the world economy.[20] Net FDI was insignificant until the early 1990s and only at mid-decade did it reach substantial levels (1.5–2.0 billion dollars a year). (BOI–96, Appendix Table *Vav*–13) In the past the Israeli economy was too small and resource-poor to interest most foreign investors, and many big financial and corporate interests also stayed away because of the chronic state of war or their fear of the Arab boycott. The little FDI that did enter Israel typically involved Jewish businessmen with connections to Zionist philanthropy and the Israeli political establishment, who were induced to invest by a combination of generous subsidies and patriotic appeals. (Levi-Faur, 1993) Investments in Israel by Volkswagen, Nestle's, Mc/Donald's and numerous other well-known transnational enterprises indicate a substantial departure from this tradition, although not its elimination. The recent acquisitions, led by Charles Bronfman and Ted Arison respectively, of controlling interests in Koor and Bank Hapoalim—arguably the two most important corporate entities in Israel—are eloquent testimony to the continuing role of well-connected Jewish magnates. (*Yediot Acharonot-Mamon*, October 1, 1997)

There are additional reasons why the features of the new foreign investment warrant careful scrutiny. The effective scope of the capital inflow accompanying FDI is far more modest than the imagery conveyed by government and business discourse suggests. The largest deals (including those just mentioned) have been financed almost entirely by Israeli banks. (Lipson and Peretz, *Ha'aretz*, October 28, 1997) The mushrooming of franchise operations in consumer markets also takes place, by definition, with a minimal financial commitment on the part of the foreign investor. Another significant limitation of FDI is that the state continues to generously subsidize showcase foreign investments. Intel's decision to open a major production facility in Israel was conditional on a government subsidy so large ($600 million) that the Investment Incentive Law had to be amended to make it legally possible.[21]

FDI is of course not the only means by which overseas investors channel capital to Israel. Indeed, it has been complemented by an equal or larger stream of foreign purchases of shares issued by Israeli firms. Both, in turn, are overshadowed by the liquid capital (much of it "hot money" originating in Israeli companies) which has been attracted simply by high interest rates and convenient opportunities for "laundering."[22]

It is still too early to assess the scope or durability of Israel's new status as a target for foreign investment, but there is no gainsaying the growing international orientation of Israeli business (mainly big business, but also smaller high-tech firms), which in the last few years have become much more committed to raising capital via foreign banks and stock markets, undertaking joint ventures with foreign firms, and in some cases even setting up branch plants abroad. Reports of such activities fill the business-oriented media in Israel, although it is hard to gauge their scope with any precision. Aggregate data confirm, however, that like incoming FDI, outward direct investment has risen far above previous levels. For instance, in the period 1994–1996 alone, industrial firms in Israel purchased one billion dollars worth of equity in foreign concerns. (MAI, 1997; BOI–96, Appendix Table *Vav*–13)

Competition Policy:
Privatization and Deregulation

The industrialization of Israel was both directed and financed by the state, working through the managers of the private, state and Histadrut sectors. (Kleiman, 1964; Bregman, 1987; Levi-Faur, 1993) This *dirigisme* was practiced in a fashion which strongly encouraged the monopolistic tendencies that characterize capitalism in general, and small-country capitalism in particular. (Pryor, 1973) Since the late 1960s a very substantial and quite integrated sector of big business has emerged in Israel. At the apex are only a handful of "business groups" constituted by very large conglomerates and banks. These two wings—the financial and non-financial—are moreover closely connected by virtue of bank ownership or simply as a result of the banks' multiple roles as investors, creditors and stockbrokers. The two biggest banks account for a majority of the country's highly diversified banking business, while conglomerates and other large firms have typically dominated the branches in which they operate.[23]

The period between the 1973 war and the stabilization plan furnished hothouse conditions for growth in the profitability and power of the big business groups. (Bichler, 1986; Shalev, 1992) Direct incentives and capital subsidies, cost-plus procurement contracts, and windfall profits from the government's practice of lending unlinked money and borrowing linked money all contributed to an impressive increase in capital accumulation at the apex of the business sector, despite the dampening effect of economic stagnation on profitability as a whole. The changing profile of state expenditure since stabilization undoubtedly hurt the profitability of the large banks and conglomerates.[24]

No less important, the government's nominal ownership of the largest banks—the result of the bailout which followed the stock market collapse of 1983—offered the reformers an opportunity to force the big banks to divest their controlling interests in industrial and service enterprises. This demand is part of a wider recent tendency for Treasury officials to place the issues of monopoly power and ownership concentration on the public policy agenda and to advocate tighter regulatory inhibitions on big business.[25] Together with the inflow of competing imports discussed in an earlier section, the result has been a decline in the monopolistic character of the market for manufactured goods.[26]

The recent "trust-busting" activities of the state, so alien to its traditional role of fostering concentration, should not however be over-dramatized. The Treasury's attempts to limit bank ownership of non-financial firms are only the latest round in a long-running battle.[27] There are a number of indications that the status quo is highly resistant to reform. First, by offering the banks postponements, special exceptions, tax incentives, and compensatory approved rises in bank fees and rate spreads, the state has gone to considerable lengths to sweeten the bitter pill of divestiture. (See two articles by Sami Peretz in *Ha'aretz*, March 29, 1996) Second, even though new local and foreign private investors have acquired controlling interests in segments of big business, the existing groups were also strengthened in the 1990s by opportunities for expansion furnished by some major privatizations and by boom conditions in construction and infrastructure. Third, the top executives who formerly ran firms in the state and Histadrut sectors continue to be major players in big business.

Although the personal wealth of members of the former managerial oligarchy and their potential role as capitalists in their own right have grown substantially, their struggles for control have not always been crowned with success.[28] But internationalization need not threaten the interests of the local business elite, whether owners or managers. They are equally likely to utilize it as a resource in struggles for personal and institutional wealth and power.[29] Koor, which came close to bankruptcy in the eighties, illustrates the renewed vitality of big business in the era of globalization. Like other big manufacturing interests, Koor has evidently benefited from economic trends of the nineties—diversification away from arms production, penetration of new overseas markets, increased financial ties with overseas capital, and booming local and global stock markets. *(Ha'aretz, July 26, 1996)*

Liberalization is directed not only at stimulating competition but also at reducing the scope of *state ownership* of firms and organizations producing marketable goods and services. Summing up developments in Israel prior to the mid-1980s, one survey concluded that in this period "no serious effort was made to privatize public corporations." (Eckstein, Zilberfarb and Rosowitz, 1993] A recent study suggests that in the 1968–1988 period, Labor and Likud governments were equally inactive in privatization. [Harris, Katz and Doron, 1997. Additional sources on privatization are Katz, 1991; Hasson, 1995) The first major initiative occurred in 1988, when the cabinet embraced an ambitious privatization program drawn up by an international consulting firm. Yet as in other countries, privatization has been hampered by the problem of finding a method of sale that would be at once feasible, politically acceptable and make a worthwhile addition to the state treasury, as well as the need to overcome opposition from employees, executives and responsible cabinet ministers in corporations targeted for privatization.

Beginning in 1990 the government budget has included sizable projected revenues from privatization, but until recently only 15 to 20 percent of the targeted revenues were actually raised. (Hasson, 1995) The first few major sales, based on hastily-concluded deals with local and foreign investors, netted disappointingly low revenues. Several subsequent public offerings on the Tel Aviv Stock Exchange were more successful but this outlet was closed off when the market collapsed in 1994. The Likud-led government that assumed office following the May 1996 elections has carried the process much further, most notably by the sale in September 1997 of the government's controlling stake in the country's largest bank (Hapoalim) to a consortium of foreign and local investors. A number of other major privatizations in banking, arms production and transportation appear imminent, but could yet run into obstacles of various kinds.

Deregulation, a second catchword of neoliberal reform programs, has been carried out at least partially in several areas, notably by the dismantling of producer boards in agriculture. (Schwartz, 1995) As part of their recent "trust-busting" frenzy, the authorities have launched specific measures designed to eliminate monopoly "rents" created by licensing and rationing mechanisms that were operated by or with the consent of the state. Current examples include the markets for insurance, pay TV, overseas and cellular telephones, and taxis. However, insofar as barriers to entry other than licenses are high (as in most of these examples), the result is typically an expanded market capable of supporting a few more large-scale players, rather the substitution of many small players for one big one.

By far the most important locus of deregulation in Israel has been the attempt to roll back the state's domination of what in the past could only euphemistically be called the "capital market.". It will be recalled that prior to 1985 the state was the dominant source of investment capital; both reinvestment of undistributed profits and unregulated bank credit played very limited roles. The disposal of long-term savings (in bonds, pension funds and bank savings plans) was heavily regulated in ways that funneled the lion's share of these assets to the state, with the result that the stock market played virtually no role in the mobilization of investment capital for the business sector.

Two different factors account for the state's historic domination of capital flows. Its ability to acquire extensive foreign gifts, part of which took the form of donated capital goods or raw materials, naturally encouraged the state and its political masters to prefer institutional and political modes of allocation. Both the state bureaucracy and the governing party benefited greatly from their resultant ability to directly steer the course of economic and indeed societal development right down to the micro level. However, once erected this interventionist bias proved highly durable even when the state's ability to cover the costs by foreign gifts and the political profits to be reaped from intervention both diminished. The 1967 and 1973 wars were turning points after which the state's commitments grew far beyond its extractive capacities, with the result that budget deficits and the cost of servicing accumulated public debt greatly increased.

This fiscal crisis reinforced the state's long-standing preference for meeting its commitments by pre-empting private savings through regulations requiring banks, pension funds and other institutional investors to automatically convert the bulk of their accumulations into government securities. (Leiderman and Bufman, 1994)

Under these circumstances the state's relationship with the big banks became characterized by competition to attract private savings, as well as by collaboration (the banks were charged with the profitable tasks of mobilizing funds for the state and distributing credit on its behalf). The authorities' seeming inattention to the banks' extensive manipulation of their own share prices in the early eighties was one of the ways by which the state's economic managers attempted to handle this mix of competition and collaboration.[30]

In addition, to protect the state's autonomy in fixing domestic credit and interest rates, international currency flows and the holding of foreign currency inside Israel were limited or banned outright. While most foreign currency controls were removed by the first Likud government in 1977, it was still necessary to finance a growing deficit, and as a result controls were gradually reinstated. (Leiderman and Bufman, 1994; Tov, 1988)

As this example demonstrates, lowering fiscal indebtedness was a necessary condition for capital market deregulation. With the abrupt ending of hyper-inflation by the stabilization plan in 1985, public sector costs were reduced and state revenues enhanced. Along with other elements of the plan (such as large cuts in price subsidies and the partial de-indexation of wages), these developments virtually wiped out the domestic budget deficit. Since then, Treasury and Bank of Israel officials and the responsible cabinet ministers have been committed to ending the various forms of government regulation of savings and credit and to easing the local capital market into the international market. The measures already implemented or decided upon include eliminating "directed credit" and encouraging businesses to turn instead to banks and the stock market, and cutting the state's claims on (and obligations to) pension funds, provident funds and insurance companies. In addition, foreign currency flows and holdings have been partially deregulated, so that while the Israeli shekel is still not fully convertible, foreign interest rates now exert a stronger influence over local ones.

That the state today makes a diminished claim on domestic savings, and that it has devolved the setting of important financial parameters onto the market, cannot be in doubt. Yet it remains uncertain whether the still ongoing process of capital market reform will be fully completed. (See the conclusions reached by Yosha and Yafeh, 1995; Leiderman and Bufman, 1994). As I have emphasized, the competitiveness of the enlarged capital market is significantly bounded, especially given the obstacles facing attempts to limit the role and power of the big banks. On the other hand, both sides have reason to be satisfied by the partially liberalized status quo. The Treasury and the Bank of Israel have been at least partly freed of the necessity of propping up financial institutions and bidding up the cost of attracting private savings, and are themselves among the potential beneficiaries of the accessibility of foreign capital markets.

At the same time, the new avenues for raising capital (especially the stock market) which have been opened up by the state's withdrawal and deregulation measures have widened the scope for at least the very largest concerns to lessen their traditional dependency on both the government and the banks. Yet this enhanced flexibility need not promote a radical break with past patterns of ownership and control of business. Companies that "went public" during the stock market boom of 1992–1993 by and large continued to be dominated by the same individual owners or holders of controlling blocks of shares. Similarly, the increased role of stock markets—domestic and overseas—in the 1990s has not eliminated either government subsidies or bank credit as mainstays of investment finance. Reliance on the New York exchanges is realistic only for big or "hot" enterprises, while the local market is operated largely by, and to an important extent for the benefit of, the large banks. It is a testimony to this continued domination that independent brokers, nonbank financial institutions and foreign commercial banks have all made very limited inroads into the market for financial services, despite facilitating changes in the rules of the game. (These assertions are empirically supported by a recent wave of research sponsored by the Bank of Israel. See especially Yosha and Yafeh, 1997.)

Radical Restructuring of the Labor Market

As the historical introduction emphasized, the labor market was the stimulus and original site of many of the most distinctive features of Israel's political economy. The problem of creating jobs for propertyless Jewish settlers and insulating them from Arab competition led to the creation in 1920 of the Histadrut as a unitary, multifunctional, politicized national labor organization that for more than half a century played a dominant role in politics, the economy and social protection. The need to generate work for settlers also stimulated the public and Histadrut economies, where Israel's bureaucratic sector took root. The drive to provide immigrants with jobs and prevent emigration encouraged a political consensus on the desirability of full employment, as well as the readiness of successive governments to subsidize an inefficient business sector provided that jobs were created.

Given this background, the labor market sphere has generated what must be judged as perhaps the three most remarkable signs of contemporary change in Israel's political economy. First, revolutionary transformations of the structure and rationale of the Histadrut have been so radical that some observers have cast doubt on its continued viability. In the last few years the labor organization has experienced an internal political upheaval, massive membership losses, and the paring down of its mandate to trade union representation. Second, the government has violated an enduring nationalist taboo by admitting large numbers of foreign *Gastarbeiter* who have replenished and enlarged Israel's stock of cheap non-citizen labor. Third, privatization of public and Histadrut-owned business enterprises accompanied by reduction or "casualization" of employment, together with diminished activity by the public sector (including the military) in creating new jobs, have retrenched the bureaucratic sector.

It is hard to exaggerate the importance of the Histadrut, prior to the 1990s, in diverse spheres of Israel's political economy: power-brokering in the Labor Party;

shaping the formation of economic and social policy; monopolizing the national-level representation of labor and centralized collective bargaining; nominally directing the country's main health fund and several of its largest financial and industrial enterprises; and leading an irresistible "distributional coalition" by coordinating the demands of private and Histadrut business and siding with privileged public sector workers. (Grinberg, 1991, 1993; Shalev, 1992) The decomposition of the Histadrut's complex role-set had multiple sources, but the most salient (and mutually reinforcing) developments may be summarized as follows.

1. In 1979, after failing to gain the vital cooperation of the Histadrut for restrictive wage and economic policies, the Likud government's Minister of Finance revoked a long-standing arrangement whereby the Treasury authorized and subsidized the Histadrut's use of its pension fund accumulations to finance investment by its corporate affiliates. This act eliminated the principal source of Bank Hapoalim's leverage over its largest client, the Histadrut economy. Then in 1983, following the bank share collapse, Hapoalim suffered major losses and was effectively nationalized pending privatization. Along with contraction of military-related demand in Israel and worldwide, and the effects of deflation, the loss of favorable pension fund financing also precipitated an acute crisis in Koor, the Histadrut's flagship conglomerate.

2. In the labor relations sphere, determined employers—including Koor—embarked on the same road to decentralization and flexibilization of labor relations followed by their counterparts in other countries. Preoccupied with rearguard struggles to defend its affiliated pension funds, health service and business enterprises, as well as its position inside the Labor Party, and sensitive primarily to pressures from powerful groups of workers who could threaten its representational monopoly, the Histadrut leadership did little to counter layoffs and clawbacks in crisis-stricken firms, or the growth of individual employment contracts, subcontracting and temporary employment. Then, partly for conjunctural political reasons and partly with an eye to obtaining aid for Koor's ailing enterprises, the Histadrut cooperated with a key element of the 1985 stabilization plan—the dismantling (albeit incomplete) of wage indexation. This removed the most significant aspect of its role in countrywide wage negotiations. In addition, the "framework agreements" hitherto negotiated for the whole of the business sector between the Histadrut and the Manufacturers Association were scrapped.[31] The combined result of the twin crises in the Histadrut's economic and labor-representation roles was that it lost not only economic assets and trade union legitimacy, but also the ability to pivot an alliance of big labor and big business against the state.

3. Finally, a long-brewing political crisis inside the labor complex came to a head in the run-up to the 1994 Histadrut elections. Because of its un-

popularity and the pressure on Labor cabinet ministers to prioritize aid to Histadrut enterprises and services over other policy goals, the labor organization had become a political liability. A group of younger liberals who had risen within the Labor Party independently of (and in conflict with) the old Histadrut-based "machine," openly articulated this tension. They succeeded in ousting the party-appointed Histadrut oligarchy, and given the labor organization's desperate fiscal crisis and the government's unwillingness to bail it out, the result was not only a severing of the traditional political ties between the Histadrut and the party, but also the selling off of the Histadrut's business assets, the cessation of its responsibilities for healthcare, and consequently its loss of hundreds of thousands of captive members.[32]

Current attempts to reformulate a role for the Histadrut as a trade union and to add roots from below to its corporate and centralized traditions are best understood as a belated adaptation, almost half a century after the event itself, to the challenge which statehood presented to the Histadrut's prestate mode of operation. In contrast, the presence of some 200,000 foreign "guest workers"—perhaps one eighth of business sector employment—poses a stark contradiction to a core feature of Israel's state tradition, its hostility to the entry of non-Jews other than for tourist purposes. Following the occupation of the West Bank and Gaza, in an effort to prevent unrest in the territories and meet unmet demand for construction and agricultural labor, the government sanctioned the entry of Palestinian day laborers on a commuter basis. In the late 1980s and early 1990s, when this flow was disrupted by Palestinian strikes, Israeli retaliations and security closures during the *intifada*, the number of Palestinians employed in Israel remained high (around 100,000, down by only 20 percent). But in 1993 security-related prohibitions were tightened considerably. Over the next two years the escalating scarcity of Palestinian labor was compensated almost precisely by increased quotas for "temporary" imported laborers.[33]

The scope of the guest worker phenomenon has rapidly outgrown the problem of substituting for Palestinians, however, and observers agree that today there are probably as many illegal as legal immigrant laborers in Israel. Not only is this an indication of internationalization affecting yet another of Israel's markets, but in consenting to labor importation and delegating responsibility for its operation to private manpower companies, the state has yielded capacities that include but go well beyond its role in regulating the economy. Yet in contrast to other reforms, Israel's opening to the global market in cheap labor does not reflect a strategic embrace of liberalization by state elites. The decision to open the floodgates to foreign labor is the consequence of the state's contradictory interests. The political economy of Palestinian pacification—whether under conditions of reconciliation and self-rule, or continuing Israeli occupation—requires that the Palestinian proletariat be able to earn a living inside Israel, but the real and perceived threat of terrorism leads policy in the direction of shutting the Palestinians out.

Another dimension of liberalization of Israel's labor market is the diminished (although by no means exhausted) role of the state in furnishing employment. Privatization and deregulation, although incomplete, have putatively lowered both the scope and the sheltered quality of employment in public corporations, military industries, infrastructural monopolies, and the former Histadrut enterprises. Employment in the public services (health, education, government administration etc.) has declined somewhat during the 1990s, and there has been a pronounced growth of new jobs in the business sector. (BOI–96, Appendix Table *Dalet*–8) In particular, industry has responded to the low cost of employing experienced skilled labor and highly specialized scientists and engineers from the former Soviet Union.[34] The third component of the public sector is the military, which like public corporations and services has played a significant role in the past in absorbing excess (Jewish) labor. In 1983 the regular army (including conscripts) and reserve duty together accounted for over 12 percent of the total (civilian plus military) labor force. By 1995 this proportion had fallen to 8 percent.[35]

Conclusion:
Winners and Losers from Liberalization

As in other countries, liberalization measures in the context of increasing globalization have a high potential for generating distributional "shocks." The obvious winners are capitalists (new or old) and business executives, along with the foot soldiers of liberalization—the middlemen and women of the "professional," "service" or "new" class. In Israel the vast majority of the beneficiaries are Jewish and Ashkenazi; most are also men. The biggest losses (in descending order of magnitude) have been suffered by Palestinian commuter laborers,[36] the Palestinian Arab minority inside the Green Line, and those mizrachi Jews (perhaps still the majority) who remain stuck on the country's geographical and/or economic periphery. Few hard facts are available concerning the changing spatial, social and political ecology of the distribution of wealth and advantage in Israel today, but we do know that the fruits of the 1985–95 cycle of prosperity have been unevenly and regressively distributed (Achdut, 1996; Gottschalk and Joyce, 1997).

The potential for political backlash against the material consequences of liberalization in Israel is difficult to gauge because it is bound up with the complex interplay between "foreign" and "domestic" policy. Distributional politics in Israel are filtered by its peculiar stratification and citizenship regimes and the political inequalities and competing symbolic realms that are part and parcel of those regimes (Shafir and Peled, 1998). Political and media discourse separates status and identity politics from class politics, with the latter focusing on phenomena like the demise of traditional, labor-intensive industries in "development towns" or the salary and benefit increases recently lavished on prominent CEOs. These are good examples of the wider trend. There is little likelihood of steps to limit the gains of the wealthy, but because mizrachi Jews are the most salient floating voters for the two main parties, and because their interests are also represented by potentially king-making smaller parties, the plight of the development towns periodically becomes a major political issue. In some circumstances a similar dynamic also comes into play for parties representing new immigrants or Israel's Palestinian Arab citizens.

In general, major economic policy transitions are propelled by a combination of endogenous and exogenous pressures for change; unintended and undesired consequences of existing policies and institutions accumulate, while changing external conditions add new opportunities and constraints. A long-term perspective on contemporary trends in Israel reveals that in both the mid-sixties and the mid-eighties the Israeli state found itself unable to revive a failing growth model that imposed heavy burdens on the state itself. In both cases it was no longer possible to resolve the contradictions by taking advantage of windfalls of imported financial and human capital. Given a political conjuncture that made it possible to ignore or even attack entrenched interests, the state responded with radical breaks from past habits. Its new policies were aimed at shedding economic obligations to powerful interests and defending its capacities to manage both the public economy and the wider national economy.

Theoretically, this dialectic fits well with a view of public policy as grounded in the state's interest in autonomy. When the pendulum swings and the state becomes burdened by commitments that no longer empower it vis-à-vis social groups and economic sectors, it may cast off these fetters by devolving responsibilities to the market arena. The apparent paradox of willful liberalization—that *states willingly shed power in order to regain it*—makes sense analytically if we recognize the difference between *power as resources* and *power as autonomy*. Forfeiting resources may be the price which has to be paid for regaining lost autonomy.[37]

This perspective sheds light on the *origins* of radically liberalizing policy initiatives like Israel's *Mitun* and its current liberalization drive. It is less helpful in dealing with the question of how *durable* such policy realignments are likely to be. After little more than a year, even before the June 1967 war and its consequences propelled Israel toward a new political economic regime, the liberalizers of the time encountered serious difficulties in sustaining recessionary discipline and reaping the expected harvest of export-led growth.[38] However, in the dozen years that have elapsed since 1985, the structural reforms which were the subtext of the stabilization plan have been partially and sometimes haltingly implemented, but incontrovertibly so. Israel's political economy has changed, in ways that did not seem possible in the past.

To understand how a new political-economic regime becomes viable, we need to focus on the formation of mutually profitable coalitions that link (sectors of) the state with (sectors of) society. (Gourevitch, 1986; Swenson, 1991) Established patterns are unlikely to be broken for long unless the state's interest in initiating change connects with compatible interests (or at the very least, encounters a low probability of resistance) in important power centers outside of the state. This survey has identified trends during the 1980s and early 1990s that furnished precisely this condition.

1. The multifaceted political exchange between the Histadrut and the state—key to the persistence of the collectivist/interventionist bias in economic policy—was undermined by the Histadrut's decomposition, which also wore away the common political destiny which had bound the labor organization and the Labor Party.
2. Several key centers of the "big economy"—the major banks and the Koor conglomerate—were weakened by serious crises.
3. Globalization offered new opportunities to market, produce and finance business activity—opportunities that were greatly enhanced by free trade agreements on the one hand and the "peace process" on the other.[39]

The first two of these developments weakened the capacity of the most powerful beneficiaries of "excessive state intervention" to resist retrenchment; the third trend is indicative of a new global strategy for big business no less profitable than the previous regime. Indeed, the new turn in state/economy relations opened the way to transforming what had been vicious circles into virtuous circles. From the state's viewpoint, its new profile in the economy not only greatly eased fiscal strains,[40] but also contributed to the new 1990s formula for rapid economic growth led by the export-oriented hi-tech sector. For big business a slimmer state meant fewer capital subsidies but also turned out to offer significant advantages. Privatization offered opportunities for private takeover of public enterprises and weakened the pressure from the bureaucratic sector on private sector wages. A smaller state budget led to lower taxes and a far more open capital market. But the budget has remained big enough to sustain vigorous state intervention helpful to business, including absorption of masses of cheap and productive immigrants, and educational and industrial policies that enhance Israel's edge in technology and expertise.

The role of the state thus remains crucial even though it is less obvious. In particular, it remains true that the state's management of the national conflict continues to impact on the political economy. The state plays a decisive trail-blazing role for Israel's arms industry, which remains the world's fifth largest exporter.[41] Perhaps most important of all, if the state were to turn its back on the peace process, then internationally-oriented business strategies would be hampered, and the military burden on the budget would rise again. Not only the national conflict but another traditional extra-economic state function—its "demographic interest"—continues to be invested with major economic implications. The conjunction of liberalization with the immigration wave of the early 1990s did not end state intervention but instead transformed its instruments. Most of the privileges earmarked for immigrants have been dispensed as entitlements to financial aid rather than (as in the past) by bureaucratic allocation of state-provided goods, services and exemptions. Similarly, the shift in industrial policy from blanket subsidies to "picking winners" in hi-tech fields is testimony to the renewed (albeit "market-conforming") steering capacities of the state.

Still, there is ample room for tension between the state and business. The Treasury, for example, performs a dual role, both orchestrating diminution of the state and attempting to appropriate some of the benefits of liberalization for the state. In the specific cases of taxing capital gains on stock-market profits and diminishing the holdings of the big banks in industrial and service corporations, this "clawback" dynamic has resulted in sometimes acrimonious and still unsettled conflicts with big business.[42]

It is not difficult to imagine other potential threats to the institutionalization of liberalization. The decline of hitherto protected industries, shrinkage of the bureaucratic labor market, and the mass importation of non-Jewish guest workers could all give rise to politically potent reactions.[43] The 1996 elections have already demonstrated that the losers from liberalization can crystallize into a substantial political force, although so far this force has been focused on issues relating to peace/borders and identity politics.

In any event, it is by no means obvious that the new growth model is sustainable, or even that it is entirely new. The economic downturn that began in 1996 raises the possibility that in the future Israel's strong economic performance in the 1990s may come to be seen as only a conjunctural success, a latter-day version of the old-fashioned growth machine powered by inflows of human and financial capital. Even if the market-driven and globally anchored growth model envisioned by the champions of economic liberalization really has taken root, it remains vulnerable should the collapse of the "peace process" and tension between the United States and Israel cause foreign investors and financial institutions to revise their favorable view of Israel's economic potential.

The hegemony of the liberal model of political economy cannot be taken for granted anywhere. Experience in the OECD countries indicates that some specific processes of liberalization have been incomplete or only skin-deep, a testament to the continuing ability of states to retain nationally distinctive institutions and policy paradigms (albeit within limits set by global pressures). At the ideological level liberalization has become the sole economic program favored by all major political parties, yet the employees and beneficiaries of the welfare state oppose its retrenchment and the mass public remains much more positive towards state expenditure than the politicians and their economic advisors. The politics of liberalization, like the politics of economic policy generally, is rooted in the conflicting interests of winners and losers; furthermore, these interests are just as likely to be camouflaged as revealed by the contenders' ideological positions.

In Israel both the left and right wings of the political spectrum favor liberalization, but they hold opposed positions on how to resolve long-standing boundary disputes. The "expansionist" position requires considerable state activism and funneling of economic resources to consolidate and defend territory, a requirement patently at odds with state contraction.[44] The right in Israel is also political home to Jewish social groups whose precarious economic standing would be deeply threatened by a rollback of Israel's settler-society welfare state and the triumph of merito-cratic individualism.

The left, which in Israel means the liberal "peace camp," holds out the prospect of further reducing military spending and altogether eliminating the costs of oc-cupying and settling Palestine, as well as profitable exploitation of the regional and international economies formerly blocked by the Arab-Israeli conflict. Yet, except for Arab-backed parties, the left remains committed to continued military strength and Jewish territorial, demographic and cultural predominance. It is thus both unable and unwilling to contemplate an alternative to the active settler-soci-ety state.

. The logical option for the left—a "post-Zionist" vision of Israel as a politically liberal state in the service of (all of) its citizens—is fundamentally at odds with al-most the entire spectrum of Jewish opinion, both at the elite and the mass levels. It is especially at odds with the religious-nationalist ethos of the right, on which the socio-political standing of the economic losers from liberalization is so dependent. But both right and left share a commitment to the Zionist consensus. The triumph of economic liberalization may eventually overpower this hegemony, unintention-ally and perhaps even unconsciously.[45]

The liberalization of Israel's political economy is thus at one in the same time dramatically far-reaching, and yet fraught with contradictions. Radical institu-tional reforms have been carried out, there have been major moves in the direction of an economically smaller and less intrusive state, and individualism, efficiency and laissez-faire dominate economic policymaking talk. Yet the reformed state con-tinues to confront the consequences of being a settler society, and its most com-pelling discourse continues to mandate acceptance of these collective responsibili-ties. The increasingly important high-tech sector of the economy in particular thrives on an uninhibited marketplace exposed to the outside world. But the human capital windfall and construction boom associated with an immigration wave were critical to recent growth—and its current exhaustion. The economic benefits of peace in the sphere of foreign trade and investment cannot far outlast the peace process, and unless that process continues, costly renewal of confronta-tions with the Palestinians and the neighboring Arab states will become a distinct probability. Add to these uncertainties the usual ones located in the ups and downs of the world economy, and it will be evident why it is impossible to assume that economic liberalization has constructed a stable growth-inducing political-eco-nomic regime.

Bibliography

Aharoni, Y. 1976. *Structure and Performance in the Israeli Economy.* Tel Aviv: Cherikover, in Hebrew.
_____. 1991. *The Israeli Economy: Dreams and Reality.* New York: Routledge.

Amir, S. 1996. "Unemployment in Israel 1964–1989: An Analysis Based on the Beveridge-Curve Model." Discussion paper No. 96.04 Falk Institute for Economic Research, Jerusalem.

Arian, A. 1981. "Health Care in Israel: Political and Administrative Aspects." *International Political Science Review* 2, pp. 43–56.

Barkai, H. 1964. "The Public, Histadrut, and Private Sectors in the Israeli Economy." *The Falk Project for Economic Research : Sixth Report, 1961–1963*. Jerusalem: Falk Institute for Economic Research, pp. 15–77.

_____. 1987. "The Defense Industries at a Crossroads." Research Paper No. 197. Jerusalem: Falk Institute for Economic Research.

Barkey, H.J. 1994. "When Politics Matter: Economic Stabilization in Argentina and Israel." *Studies in Comparative International Development* 29 (Winter), pp. 41–67.

Bartram, D.V. 1998. "Foreign Workers in Israel: History and Theory." *International Migration Review* 32, pp. 303–25.

Bebchuk, A.L., L. Kaplow and J.M. Fried. 1995. *Concentration in the Israeli Economy and Bank Investment in Commercial Companies.*

Ben-Porath, Y. 1983. "The Conservative Turnabout that Never Was." *Jerusalem Quarterly* 29 (Fall), pp. 3–10.

_____. 1986. "Introduction." In Yoram Ben-Porath, ed. *The Economy of Israel: Maturing through Crisis*. Cambridge, Mass: Harvard University Press, pp. 1–23.

Berg, A., B. Rosen and G. Ofer. 1996. *Changes in Household Expenditure on Health*, Research Report No. RR–246–96. Jerusalem: Brookdale Institute of Gerontology.

Bernstein, D. and S. Swirski. 1982. "The Rapid Economic Development of Israel and the Emergence of the Ethnic Division of Labor." *British Journal of Sociology* 33 (March), pp. 64–85.

Bialer, U. 1989. *Between East and West: Israel's Foreign Policy Orientation, 1948–1956*, Cambridge: Cambridge University Press.

Bichler, S. 1986. "The Political Economy of National Security in Israel: Some Aspects of the Activities of the Dominant Blocs of Capital." Masters thesis, The Hebrew University of Jerusalem, in Hebrew.

_____. 1991. "The Political Economy of Military Spending in Israel." Ph.D. dissertation, Department of Political Science, Hebrew University of Jerusalem.

Bichler, S. and J. Nitzan. 1995. "The Great U-Turn: Restructuring in Israel and South Africa." *News from Within* 11 (September), pp. 29–32.

Bregman, A. 1987. "Government Intervention in Industry: The Case of Israel." *Journal of Development Economics* 25, pp. 353–67.

Brodet, D. 1995. *Report of the Committee to Examine Structural Changes in the Capital Market*. Jerusalem, in Hebrew.

Bruno, M. 1993. *Crisis, Stabilization, and Economic Reform: Therapy by Consensus*. Oxford: Clarendon.

Chinitz, D. 1995. "Israel's Health Policy Breakthrough: The Politics of Reform and the Reform of Politics." *Journal of Health Politics, Policy and Law* 20 (Winter), pp. 909–932.

Doron, Avraham. 1988. "The Histadrut, Social Policy and Equality." *Jerusalem Quarterly* 47 (Summer), pp. 131–144, in Hebrew.

_____. 1995. *In Defense of Universalism: The Challenges Facing Social Policy in Israel*. Jerusalem: Y.L. Magnes, in Hebrew.

_____. 1997. "The Contradicting Trends in the Israeli Welfare State: Poverty, Retrenchment and Marginalization." Paper presented at 19th Meeting of the ISA Research Committee on Poverty and Social Policy, Copenhagen.

Doron, A. and H. J. Karger. 1993. "The Privatization of Social Services in Israel and its Effects on Israeli Society." *Scandinavian Journal of Social Welfare* 2, pp. 88–95.

Doron, A. and R. Kramer. 1991. *The Welfare State in Israel—the Evolution of Social Security Policy and Practice*. Boulder: Westview.

Eckstein, S., B.T. Zilberfarb and S. Rosowitz. 1993. "The Process of Privatizing Public Corporations in Israel: Survey and Evaluations for the Future." *Rivon Lekalkala* (May), pp. 31–47, in Hebrew.

Evans, P., D. Rueschemeyer and T. Skocpol, eds. 1985. *Bringing the State Back In*. Cambridge: Cambridge University Press.

Farjoun, E. 1983. "Class Divisions in Israeli Society." *Khamsin* 10, pp. 29–39.

Gaon, B. 1997. *He Who Dares Wins*. Tel Aviv: Yediot Achronot, in Hebrew.

Garrett, G. D. Mitchell. 1996. "Globalization and the Welfare State: Income Transfers in the Industrialized Democracies, 1966–1990." Paper presented at Annual Meeting of the American Political Science Association, San Francisco.

Gourevitch, P. 1986. *Politics in Hard Times: Comparative Responses to International Economic Crises*. Ithaca. N.Y.: Cornell University Press.

Granovetter, M. 1994. "Business Groups." In N.J. Smelser and R. Swedberg, eds. *The Handbook of Economic Sociology*. Princeton, N.J.: Princeton University Press, pp. 453–475.

Grinberg, L.L. 1991. *Split Corporatism in Israel*, Albany, N.Y.: State University of New York Press.

_____.1993. *The Histadrut Above All Else*. Jerusalem: Nevo, in Hebrew.

Hadar, S. 1990. "Blurring of the Boundaries between Public and Private in Relations between State and Industry." Ph.D. dissertation, Department of Political Science, Hebrew University of Jerusalem.

Halevi, N., ed. 1994. *Import Policy and Exposure of Israeli Industry*. Jerusalem, in Hebrew.

Halevi, N. and R. Klinov-Malul. 1968. *The Economic Development of Israel*. New York: Praeger.

Harris, M., Y. Katz and G. Doron. 1997. "Ideology and Privatization Policy in Israel." *Environment and Planning C: Government and Policy* 15 (August), pp. 363–72.

Hasson, M. 1995. "The Privatization Policy of the Government of Israel: Declarations versus Action in Practice." Masters thesis, Hebrew University of Jerusalem, in Hebrew.

Karger, H.J. and M. Monnickendam. 1991. "The Radical Right and Social Welfare in Israel." In James Midgley and Howard Glennerster, eds. *The Radical Right and the Welfare State: An International Assessment*. Savage, Md.: Barnes and Noble, pp. 124–40.

Katz, Y. 1991. "Privatization in Israel: 1962–1987." *Medina, Memshal Veyachasim Benleumim* 35, pp. 133–45, in Hebrew.

Keren, M. 1993. "Economists and Economic Policy Making in Israel: The Politics of Expertise in the Stabilization Program." *Policy Sciences* 26, pp. 331–46.

Kimmerling, B. 1983. *Zionism and Territory: The Socio-Territorial Dimensions of Zionist Politics*. Berkeley: Institute of International Studies.

Kleiman, E. 1964. "The Structure of Israel Manufacturing Industries 1952- 1962." Unpublished paper for the Falk Project for Economic Research in Israel, Jerusalem (December).

Lederman, J. 1995. "Economics of the Arab-Israeli Peace Process." *Orbis—a Journal of World Affairs* 39, pp.549–66.

Leiderman, L. and G. Bufman. 1994. *Financial Reform in Israel: A Case of Gradualism.* Tel Aviv: Pinhas Sapir Center for Development.

Lustick, I. 1989. "The Political Road to Binationalism: Arabs in Jewish Politics." In Ilan Peleg Ofira Seliktar, eds. *The Emergence of a Binational Israel—The Second Republic in the Making.* Boulder: Westview, pp. 97–123.

Manufacturers' Association of Israel. 1997. *Globalization in Israeli Industry: Report of the Committee for Strategic Thinking.* Tel Aviv: Economic Division, MAI, in Hebrew.

Mintz, A. 1983. "The Military-Industrial Complex: The Israeli Case." *Journal of Strategic Studies* 6 (September), pp. 103–128.

Murphy, E.C. 1996. "The Arab-Israeli Peace Process: Responding to the Economics of Globalization." *Critique* (Fall), pp. 67–91.

Peled, Y. and G. Shafi. 1996. "The Roots of Peacemaking—the Dynamics of Citizenship in Israel, 1948–93." *International Journal of Middle East Studies* 28, pp. 391–413.

Plessner, Y. 1994. *The Political Economy Of Israel: From Ideology to Stagnation,* Albany, N.Y.: State University of New York Press.

Pryor, F.L. 1973. *Property and Industrial Organization in Communist and Capitalist Nations.* Bloomington: Indiana University Press.

Razin, A. and E. Sadka. 1993. *The Economy of Modern Israel: Malaise and Promise.* Chicago: University of Chicago Press.

Regev, H. and S. Bar-Eliezer. 1994. "Control over the Domestic Market and Economic Performance in Israeli Industry." Discussion Paper No. 94.05. Jerusalem: Falk Project for Economic Research.

Retzky, A. 1995. "Peace In the Middle East—What Does It Really Mean For Israeli Business?" *Columbia Journal Of World Business* 30, pp. 26–32.

Rowley, R., S. Bichler and J. Nitzan. 1988. "Some Aspects of Aggregate Concentration in the Israeli Economy 1964–1986." Working paper No. 7/88, Department of Economics, McGill University.

Schuldiner, Z. 1996. *A Look at the 1996 Budget.* Tel Aviv: Adva Center, in Hebrew.

Schwartz, M. 1995. *Unlimited Guarantees: History, Political Economy, and the Crisis of Cooperative Agriculture in Israel.* Beersheba, in Hebrew. Ben Gurion University Press.

Semyonov, M. and N. Lewin-Epstein. 1987. *Hewers of Wood and Drawers of Water: Noncitizen Arabs in the Israeli Labor Market.* New York.: ILR Press.

Shafir, G. 1989. *Land, Labor and the Origins of the Israeli-Palestinian Conflict 1882–1914.* Cambridge: Cambridge University Press.

Shalev, M. 1984. "Labor, State and Crisis: An Israeli Case Study." *Industrial Relations* 23, pp. 362–86.

———. 1984. "The Mid-Sixties Recession: A Political-Economic Analysis of Unemployment in Israel. *Machbarot Lemechkar Ulebikoret* 9 (February), pp. 3–54, in Hebrew.

———.1989. "Israel's Domestic Policy Regime: Zionism, Dualism, and the Rise of Capital." In Francis G. Castles, ed. *The Comparative History of Public Policy,* Cambridge: Cambridge University Press, pp. 100–48.

———.1992. *Labor and the Political Economy.* Oxford: Oxford University Press.

———. 1996. "Time for Theory: Critical Notes on Lissak and Sternhell," *Israel Studies* 1, pp. 170–88.

Shalev, M. and L.L. Grinberg. 1989. "Histadrut-Government Relations and the Transition from a Likud to a National Unity Government: Continuity and Change in Israel's Economic Crisis." Discussion Paper 19–89, Pinhas Sapir Center for Development, Tel Aviv University.

Sharkansky, I and A. Radian. 1982. "Changing Domestic Policy 1977–1981." In Robert O. Freedman, ed. *Israel in the Begin Era.* New York: Praeger pp. 56–75.

Sharon, D. 1994. "Wage Policy and its Implementation." *Kalkala Veavoda* 9 (October), pp.97–115, in Hebrew.

Sher, H. 1996. "After the Revolution." *The Jerusalem Report* (October 17), pp. 37–41.

Stephens, J.D., E. Huber and L. Ray. 1995. "The Welfare State in Hard Times." Paper presented at Conference on the Politics and Political Economy of Contemporary Capitalism, Humboldt University and the WZB.

Sternhell, Z. 1995. *Nation-Building or Social Reform? Nationalism and Socialism in the Israeli Labor Movement 1904–1940.* Tel Aviv: Am Oved, in Hebrew.

Sussman, Z. and D. Zakai. 1996. *The Decentralization of Collective Bargaining and Changes in the Compensation Structure in Israel's Public Sector.* Jerusalem: Bank of Israel Research Department.

Swank, D. 1996. "Funding the Welfare State, Part I: Global Capital and the Taxation of Business in the Advanced Market Economies." Paper presented at Annual Meeting of the American Political Science Association, San Francisco.

Swenson, P. 1991. "Bringing Capital Back in, or Social Democracy Reconsidered—Employer Power, Cross-Class Alliances, and Centralization of Industrial Relations in Denmark and Sweden." *World Politics* 43, pp. 513–44.

Tov, I. 1988. "The Economic Upheaval of 1977–Implementation of Operational Goals." *Rivon Lekalkala* 135/6 (April), pp. 33–47, in Hebrew.

Yago, G. 1977. "Whatever Happened to the Promised Land? Capital Flows and the Israeli State." *Berkeley Journal of Sociology* 21, pp. 117–46.

Yosha, O. 1995. "Privatising Multi-Product Banks." *Economic Journal* 105, pp. 1435–53.

Yosha, O. and Y. Yafeh. 1995. *The Capital Market Reform and Its Influence: An Analysis from the Angle of Industrial Structure.* Jerusalem: Bank of Israel Research Department.

_____. 1996. "The Capital Market Reform 1985–95 and Modes of Finance in Israeli Manufacturing." *Rivon Lekalkala* 43, in Hebrew.

_____. 1997. "Capital Market Reform." In H. Ber, Y. Yafeh and O. Yosha, eds. "Conflicts of Interest in Universal Banking: Evidence from the Post-Issue Performance of IPO Firms." Jerusalem: Bank of Israel Research Department, Discussion Paper 97.05.

Zilberfarb, B.Z. 1994. "The Effects of the Peace Process on the Israeli Economy." *Israel Affairs* 1, pp. 84–95.

Notes

1. This paper is based on work previously published in *Humboldt Journal of Social Relations* (No.1–2, 1998) and *Israel Affairs* (No. 4, 1998). It is based on information available as of early 1998. I acknowledge the financial support of the Israeli Science Foundation, founded by the Israel Academy of Sciences and Humanities. Note that throughout this article, annual reports of the Bank of Israel in Hebrew are cited in the form "BOI–96" (for the 1996 edition).

2. This debate is exemplified by the contrasting opinions of the two senior economic commentators of the quality daily *Ha'aretz,* Abraham Tal and Nehemia Strasler.

3. The shift in opinion among key figures in the business elite has been retrospectively confirmed by a series of interviews carried out by Yehezkel Lein and myself during the summer of 1997.

4. Comparison is between the five years preceding stabilization (1980–1984) and a more recent five-year period (1992–1996). BOI–96, Appendix Table *Hay-1a*.

5. BOI–96, Appendix Table *Hay-7*. In addition to subsidies granted under the Investment Incentive Law, the main formal means of capital subsidy—since abolished—was "directed credit" channeled through the commercial banks. Already by 1990 the cost to the government of directed credit was less than a quarter of its 1984 level in real terms.

6. Data are based on budgetary allocations and are derived from Tables 1 and 2 of the statistical appendix to Y. Kop. (ed.) *Allocation of Resources to Social Services 1996* (in Hebrew), Jerusalem, 1997. According to the same source, in the 1990s the ratio of debt service to GDP fell by about 6 points. The Bank of Israel's estimates of the ratio of debt service to GNP (BOI–96, Appendix Table *Hay-2b*) are much more conservative, but they also indicate a major drop in the burden of both domestic and foreign interest payments.

7. Compare the data on subsidies in BOI–96, Appendix Table *Hay-7*, with data on direct and indirect taxes on business that appear in the annual reports of the State Revenues Administration.

8. Schuldiner (1996) estimated that relief of employer contributions to social security and health insurance, along with a wage subsidy paid to employers for the first two years of new hires, accounted for 12.5 percent of the government's "social expenditure" budget for 1996.

9. For comparative discussions, see Stephens, Huber and Ray, 1995; P. Pierson, "New Politics of the Welfare State".

This section relies on data presented in the annual report of the Center for Social Policy Studies in Israel; Y. Kop, (ed.) *Allocation of Resources*. The estimates from this source, which are based on substantive definitions of expenditure categories and refer to budget allocations, are more conservative (especially regarding income maintenance) than the national accounts data published by the Bank of Israel and referred to earlier.

10. Retired women who did not work outside the home are now entitled to pensions, and an economically significant form of discrimination against Palestinian citizens has been ended with the decoupling of child allowances from military service.

11. While rules for the receipt of unemployment benefits were toughened with a view to making refusal of job offers more difficult, this failed to reduce the number of unfilled vacancies during the period of high unemployment in the early 1990s. Amir, 1996 .

12. For a general discussion, see A. Doron and H.J. Karger, 'The Privatization of Social Services in Israel and its Effects on Israeli Society", *Scandinavian Journal of Social Welfare* 2 (1993), pp.88–95. It is hard to find reliable indicators of expenditure on "gray" health and education services. One analysis of the Household Expenditure Survey has shown little change in expenditure on private health services between 1986/7 and 1992/3, but this conclusion is probably already outdated. See A. Berg, B. Rosen, and G. Ofer, *Changes in Household Expenditure on Health*, (1996), Research Report No. RR–246–96, Brookdale Institute of Gerontology, Jerusalem.

13. For the sake of comparability I cite data from The Penn World Table (Mark 5.6), as made available at http://datacentre.epas.utoronto.ca:5680/pwt/pwt.html. Bank of Israel data covering the same period (1975–92) exhibit almost identical trends but have much higher absolute values. The idiosyncratic nature of the Israeli trend is emphasized by the fact that during the 25 year period ending in 1990, in the average OECD member-state the ratio of trade to GNP rose by 10 points. Garrett and Mitchell, 1996. The Penn Tables cover 40 countries in Europe, the Americas and East Asia, excluding East Germany and Puerto Rico. Israel's rank on openness declined from 6 in 1975–1984 to 7 in 1985–1989 to 10 in 1990–92.

14. For detailed data on manufacturing exports, see the annual *HaTa'asiya Beyisrael* published by the Ministry of Industry and Commerce's Planning Administration.

15. The OECD's *Main Economic Indicators* indicates that Austria and Switzerland have the highest import surpluses—at around only 3 percent of GDP.

16. Regev and Bar-Eliezer, 1994. Significantly, the overall rise between the low of 1980/81 and the peak reached in 1990 was quite widely diffused. Increases were posted in this period for 20 of the 22 disaggregated branches investigated by Regev and Bar-Eliezer, although in three cases the change was only negligible.

17. Both the figure cited here and the presentation in Chart 2 are based on data published in BOI–95, Appendix Table 12 which include both explicit supports and implicit credit subsidies. However, many other traditional elements in government aid to exporters, such as the provision of subsidized land, infrastructure and labor, are not included in the figures.

18. A high estimate of philanthropic aid, based on the category "foreign transfers to the national institutions and non-profits" in Appendix Table 11 of BOI–95, put it at under 2 percent of GNP throughout the last decade. In an article in *Yediot Acharonot* on August 20, 1996, former Deputy Foreign Minister Yossi Beilin wrote that Israel's receipts from the United Jewish Appeal had declined to less than $300 million a year, and that the Israel Bonds had become a more expensive way of raising money than free market loans.

19. Compare the data on inter-governmental transfers with the series on defense imports in BOI–96, Appendix Tables *Hay-1a* and *Hay-1b*.

20. For an optimistic survey of foreign investment, which dates the breakthrough to the Madrid peace conference of 1991, see Sher, 1996. I have also benefited from conversations on this topic with two Israeli bankers, Yair Saroussi and Nir Oliver.

21. The dubious economic benefits to Israel of the gigantic Intel subsidy have been noted in many media commentaries (e.g., Oded Lipschitz in *Davar Hashavua*, March 29, 1994). Another noteworthy case is the 38 percent subsidy promised to Volkswagen (the government paid for $133 of its nominal $350 million investment) for a joint magnesium production venture with the Dead Sea Works (*Jerusalem Report*, June 27,1996).

22. In a communiqué dated November 6,1996, the Economics Desk of the Government Press Office reported that investment in Israeli shares by foreign citizens had reached $5.5 billion, whereas other financial assets held by foreigners amounted to $14 billion.

23. On the theory and the Israeli experience of business groups, see Granovetter, 1994. Until recently, the striking role of big business in Israel and of banking within it was rarely mentioned by mainstream economists and never studied by them. Yair Aharoni and Shimshon Bichler were the first scholars to definitively establish the dualist character of Israeli capitalism. Rowley, Bichler and Nitzan, 1988. More recently, hyper-concentration in banking and the big banks' multiple roles as owners, financiers and investors have been explored by Bebchuk, Kaplow and Fried, 1995,unpublished typescript; and by O. Yosha and Y. Yafeh, "Capital Market Reform." Indirect indications of the market domination of big business are furnished by H. Regev and S. Bar-Eliezer, *Control over the Domestic Market.*

24. The most up to date source of data on big business profits is Bichler and Nitzan, 1995, but these figures are not entirely consistent with earlier publications by Bichler cited in previous notes. According to Bichler and Nitzan, big business profits declined precipitously after 1984 and experienced only a very modest recovery through 1993 (the latest date of the series).

25. The "Brodet Committee" on bank ownership of non-financial corporations was a milestone in this respect. (Brodet, 1995) The unprecedented activism of the current directors of two units of the Treasury—the Supervisor of the Capital Market and the Antitrust Com-

mission—also constitute a sharp break with past practice. See for example *Ha'aretz* weekend supplement, November 28, 1997.

26. Between 1982/3 and 1990 the three-firm concentration ratio fell from 43 percent to 34 percent of total domestic sales. H. Regev and S. Bar-Eliezer, *Control over the Domestic Market*, Appendix Table 1.

27. As long ago as 1981 the Banking Law tried unsuccessfully to prohibit banks from holding more than 25 percent of the equity of any non-financial corporation. See O. Yosha, "Privatising Multi-Product Banks", *Economic Journal*, vol. 105, no. 433 (1995), pp. 1435–1453. The recommendations of the Brodet Committee, endorsed by the government at the end of 1995, postponed the deadline for implementation of the Banking Law to the end of 1996, although the ownership ratio is supposed to be further reduced (to 20 percent) by the end of the century.

28. Privatization of the Histadrut-linked Koor conglomerate is a case in point. The June 1995 sale of the Hevrat Ovdim's 22.5 percent stake in the Koor group to Shamrock Partnerships, an American investment company, was immediately followed by the distribution of options to Koor's management with a theoretical value of close to $30 million. Shamrock later sold out, for a considerable profit, to a consortium led by the Bronfman family. Benny Gaon, the aggressive CEO of Koor, initially kept his position under the new regime but was subsequently unseated by one of the new owners. See *Globes*, February 5 and February 27, 1996 and July 24, 1997. For a perceptive commentary on the changing position of the managerial elite, see Ephraim Reiner in *Ha'aretz*, November 20, 1997.

29. As Benny Gaon has candidly pointed out, one of the uses of internationalization has been the possibility of countering dependence on traditional bank partners (in Koor's case, Bank Hapoalim) by exploiting new opportunities to raise capital abroad. (Gaon, 1997)

30. Despite the judicial discourse of individual culpability in which it was framed, the report of the commission of inquiry into the bank shares collapse made this abundantly clear. See Commission of Inquiry into the Regulation of Bank Shares, *Final Report* (in Hebrew), Jerusalem, 1986.

31. Between 1980–1984 and 1992–1993 the role of cost of living adjustments in business sector wage increments was reduced by almost half (69 percent to 37 percent) and national-level wage increases (formerly 13.5 percent of the total increment) were eliminated altogether. Sharon, 1994: see also Sussman and Zakai, 1996.

32. The decline of the Histadrut has hardly been investigated systematically. See however the symposium in *Rivon Lekalkala*, April 1995. For earlier developments (through the late 1980s) see L.L. Grinberg, *Split Corporatism in Israel*. On the traditional political functions of the Histadrut health fund and its ultimate loss, see respectively Arian, 1981; Chinitz, 1995.

33. On the factors accounting for the entry of Palestinian labor to Israel and its implications, see L.L. Grinberg, *The Histadrut Above All Else*, Chap. 6; M. Semyonov and N. Lewin-Epstein, *Hewers of Wood*. For an overview of the foreign worker phenomenon, see Bartram, 1998. Further documentation may be found in *Ha'aretz*, March 22, 1996; *Skira Kalkalit* (Bank Hapoalim Economic Department), August 29, 1996; and the *Kav LaOved* website, a source of current information on the employment of Palestinian as well as foreign labor (http://www.aic.org/org/kav-oved).

34. Annual surveys of immigrant employment in industry conducted by the Manufacturers' Association have revealed the scope of immigrant employment in industry. Indirect evidence from the surveys, as well as media reports, point to the role of downgrading (such as the

employment of qualified engineers as technicians, and technicians as skilled manual workers), low pay, and government wage subsidies in rendering immigrants attractive to employers.

35. My calculations based on estimates of the number of conscript and career soldiers published in *The Military Balance* (International Institute for Strategic Studies, London) and the extent of absence due to reserve duty as estimated by official labor force surveys.

36. The Palestinians have been hurt by the abandonment of one form of liberalization in favor of another. Israel refused on security grounds to honor its commitments to a free flow of labor from the Palestinian territories to Israel, and subsequently, in a radical departure from previous policy, it opened its gates to foreign labor.

37. I recognize, but have not investigated, a parallel (and complementary) dialectic located *inside* the state apparatus: the economic-policy bureaucracies favor a slimmer public economy with fewer commitments, because this enhances their autonomy by trimming the sails of other departments of state.

38. These difficulties derived from the resistance of the business sector to operating without state subsidies, and challenges posed to the legitimacy of the recession by popular unrest and individual out-migration. Shalev, 1984.

39. The links between economic liberalization and globalization and the peace process have been emphasized by Peled and Shafir, 1996. For other discussions of the "peace dividend," see Lederman, 1995; Retzky, 1995; Zilberfarb, 1994; Murphy, 1996.

40. Comparison of experience in the 1990s with a decade earlier shows that the state not only reduced its claims on the national product but also changed the profile of public finance: capacities of tax extraction were enhanced and reliance on debt and gifts reduced. (BOI–96, Appendix Table *Hay-1b*)

41. Israel's rank in arms exports as reported by Israel Radio on October 14. 1997, based on International Institute of Strategic Studies data. A good example of the state's role in facilitating military exports is an agreement reached between the Israeli and Polish governments for refurbishing helicopters in Israel (*Yediot Acharonot*, October 15, 1997), a $600m. deal that pressure from another trail-blazing state—the United States—might ultimately force Israel to yield.

42. The Finance Minister of the 1992–1996 Labor government was forced by business pressure to reverse the government's decision to tax stock market gains. The saga is documented and analyzed by Yehezkel Lein in a forthcoming masters thesis in the Department of Political Science at the Hebrew University.

43. At the end of 1997 a major confrontation developed between the Histadrut and the Ministry of Finance. Although a dispute over pension reform was the central issue nominally at stake, the deeper source of tension was the attempt by the country's strongest groups of organized labor in the public sector to preempt state attacks on their privileged position by allying themselves firmly with the Histadrut.

44. Although "expansionism" requires an interventionist state, some of the means of this intervention can and have been effectively "liberalized," that is, delegated to the market. In the heyday of Jewish settlement in the occupied territories, the state used massive subsidies to attract private contractors and home buyers on the basis of financial self-interest.

45. Compare the similar argument made by Lustick on the implications of competition between the main Zionist parties for their de facto orientation toward Israel's Palestinian-Arab minority. Lustick, 1989.

7

Change and Continuity in the Israeli Political Economy: Multi-Level Analysis of the Telecommunications and Energy Sectors

DAVID LEVI-FAUR

Since the mid-1980s and increasingly during the 1990s Israel, seems to have been experiencing a neo-liberal revolution. The discourse of deregulation, liberalization, and privatization has gradually, but steadily, occupied large areas of the intellectual, media, and political agendas. Two decades after the colossal failure of Simcha Ehrlich's liberalization program, in November 1977, the Israeli economy and the interaction between the state and the economy, are "finally" being radically transformed. The "revolution that wasn't" has come into sight. Now, in contrast to the past, the process of liberalization is led by the professional elite in the state bureaucracy and is backed by a relatively wide consensus that includes the major parties in the Knesset, the business community, and the media. The process of liberalization is very gradual and is marked by a series of "little bangs" rather than one "big bang," yet the accumulation of these small changes in various parts of the Israeli politics, society, and economy adds up to nothing less than a radical change and the creation of a "new Israel".

The process of change, namely the sources, scope, and implications for the division of power in Israel's political economy, are the subject of this paper. Its focus is on the liberalization of the Israeli telecom and energy sectors by various Israeli governments from the end of 1970s, especially from the second half of the 1980s. These reforms were directed at sectors which used to be considered ill-suited for competition either because they were a "natural monopoly" (telecom) or of primary military importance and capital intensive (energy). Liberalization is the introduction of competition to arenas which before were not competitive or only partially competitive. The introduction of competition requires a new governance structure, that is, re-writing the rules, changing the economic allocation mode, and transforming the policy network.

Although the introduction of competition into both the telecom and energy sector involved similar aims and political strategies, the two cases differ in one important respect. Whereas in the telecom sector it resulted in intensive competition in major segments of the market and in widely distributed costs-savings for the users of telecom services, in the energy sector it did not produce more competition or meaningful benefits for most consumers. While the case of telecom reflects relative success, the case of energy reflects relative failure. True, in both cases the state privatized and opened the door to new business players. But when the changes are examined with respect to the ability of the state to "nurture" competitive markets, and to force competition on defiant business actors, the different outcomes are striking. The variation in outcome serves as the puzzle that guides the discussion.

It is suggested here that in order to understand the changes in these two sectors and the differences between them one has to examine process and actors in three arenas, the sectorial, the international, and the national. This paper unites the policy sector approach, the national policy patterns approach, and the international regime approach. Each of these approaches concentrates on a single level of analysis, and although it usually acknowledges the importance of the other two levels, the analysis tends to be restricted to one or two levels.

The policy sector approach suggests that sectors are expected to exhibit typical characteristics which constrain and shape their political dynamics, hence also their propensity to liberalization. Their specific technology (one or many, extent of innovations, ownership patterns), their economic dynamics (expanding, stable, declining) and the extent of concentration (monopoly, cartels, open markets) may shape and constrain the sector's policy regime. State capacities and the organization of business and labor power may differ and thus also constrain the effects of liberalization. In the literature of political economy and public policy, it is the "policy-sector" approach that emphasizes the relatively autonomous political characteristics of distinct policy sectors, and thus the multiplicity of political patterns in any single polity. (Lowi, 1964; Atkinson and Coleman, 1989; Hollingsworth, Schmitter and Streek,1994)

At the same time, however, the liberalization of the two sectors may reflect global rather than sectorial dynamics. (Keohane and Nye, 1977). Neither the liberalization of telecom nor the liberalization of energy is a unique phenomenon. Both are part of a broader change that affects many sectors and many countries and may suggest a causal relation between global forces and national and sectorial policy making. This process may be conceptualized under banners such as globalization, "paradigm change," and the retreat of the state. Although the mechanisms and scope of these changes are highly contested, there is a wider agreement that national and sectorial politics should be examined in a broader framework. Israeli telecom is not alone in experiencing changes, nor is the Israeli energy market alone in resisting them; the picture is reasserting itself on the international level. Although a number of international agreements have ensured liberalization of the world telecom market, nothing much has changed in the energy sphere. The European Union [EU] has succeeded in opening its member countries' telecom markets, but it has largely failed to do likewise in energy. Thus, an alternative approach to the study of change in the Israeli telecom and energy sectors would be to examine the international regimes that govern telecom and energy. (Aronson and Cowhey, 1988: Krasner, 1983)

Finally, the national level, rather than the sectorial or global levels, may explain the different outcomes of the liberalization processes in telecom and energy. The national level is composed of a set of institutions that are the product of a nation-specific trajectory of development, itself the product of a unique national mixture of economic, social, and cultural features. These different trajectories created different national structures of interest intermediation that were characterized as strong states (that is, France), weak states (that is, the United States), and corporatist states (that is, Germany, the Netherlands). (Shonfield, 1965; Katzenstein, 1984) They are also reflected in the conflicting notions of developmental states (that is, Japan, France, South Korea, Taiwan) on the one hand and liberal non-interventionist states (United States, United Kingdom) on the other. (Evans, 1995; Weiss, 1988)

These institutions also reflect and shape a unique national policy style that determines qualities such as consensusalism, activism, pragmatism, improvisation, and secrecy. (Richardson, 1982; Vogel, 1986) The combination of policy styles and specific patterns of interest-intermediation gave birth to the national-patterns approach. (van Waarden, 1995) According to this approach, the differences in the outcomes of liberalization in Israeli telecom and energy reflect specific power structures, national interests, and policy capacities that are neither specific to the sectors nor outcomes of global forces. At least three primary arenas of politics and economics must therefore be considered in order to understand the dynamics of change in the Israeli telecom and energy sectors. The task of the researcher is to contrast and at the same time integrate the forces and processes in the three arenas in order to present a comprehensive picture of the changes in the Israeli political economy.

The International Telecommunications and Energy Regimes

Regime change and increasing competition are evident in the international telecom and energy markets, but for different reasons. While globalization is the driving force behind increasing competition in telecom, it is hardly a factor in the case of energy. Technology, which plays a prominent role in the opening up of the telecom market, has a marginal role in energy. Ideology and knowledge-based arguments, which play an important role in telecom, play a negligible role in energy. The U.S. government, which took a relatively reactive role in the change of the energy regime, took a very active role in the creation of a new international telecom regime. Governments on the periphery of the world economy that were prominent in the transformation of the international energy regime assumed a reactive role in the transformation of the telecom.

The Dynamics of Change in the International Telecommunications Regime

The old international telecom regime was based on the principle of national autonomy in the provision of services on the one hand, and, on the other, international
coordination of international transfers of voice, video, and data between these na-
tionally-organized providers. The major actors were large, state-owned, government
controlled monopolies known as the Post, Telegraph, and Telephone administra-
tions (PTTs). The industry, however, has been radically changing, and competition
in today's telecom markets is more evident than ever before. This is most clearly expressed in (a) opening the domestic markets for foreign direct investment; (b) the
creation of global alliances between the most dynamics operators (that is, Global 1,
Concert) and (c) the collapse of the old arrangements, which prevented international traffic from moving through the least-cost routes. Changes in the market level
are reinforced and reflected by a set of new international agreements. These include
the World Trade Organization agreement on the liberalization of government procurement (1994), the Information Technology Agreement (1996), and the WTO
agreement on telecom trade (1997).

The old international telecom regime was initially developed around the functional necessity to coordinate international calls. The central institution of the
regime was the International Telecom Union [ITU], which was created in 1932 by
a merger of the International Telegraphs Union (founded in 1865) and the signatories to the International Radio Telegraph Convention of 1906. The ITU is the old-
est international organization operating today and, with 166 members in the late
1980s, it has density of participation which is even greater than that of the United
Nations. The International Consultative Committee for Telephones and Telegraph
(CCITT) operated under the auspices of the ITU, acting as a virtual telephone cartel for the national PTTs. According to Cowhey, the CCITT's rules served as an anchor for the old regime's policies "that facilitated bilateral monopolistic bargains, reinforced national monopolies, and limited the rights of private firms in the global
market". (Cowhey, 1990, p. 176)

There were American reservations about the old international telecom regime
and the politics of the ITU, but for a long time these reservations were not translated into action. The United States in practice embraced the old regime and
changed its preferences only in the early 1980s. The origin of this change was largely
the divestiture of AT&T in 1984. This was first designed and perceived as a domestic issue, but soon enough its implications were felt across the world. The domestic
developments in the United States coincided with the progress of the European
Union toward a single market for telecom. The process which began very slowly in
the 1980s reached the point of no return with the decision to open the European
telecom markets. The leading role that the European Commission took in this effort made it possible for the Europeans to play a counter-role to the United States
and to create bilateral EU-US dynamics in which the proponents of liberalization
on the two sides would support each other and share the "managerial" or "diplo-

matic" costs of bringing other parties into voluntary negotiations on the opening of the international markets.

Soon after the AT&T divestiture the domestic policy of deregulation turned into an international strategy in which the American government combined unilateral moves, bilateral pressures, and multilateral negotiations in order to bring about change in the basic rules of international trade in telecom services and information technology equipment. The Americans acted unilaterally in the case of Intelsat and enforced a regulatory change in satellite communication services when they allowed the creation of privately-owned satellite systems. In this they took a significant step toward eroding the Intelsat monopoly position. (Krasner, 1991) In the new competitive situation American companies had technological and economic advantages that put them in a position to collect bigger slices of the rewards of a highly expanding market.

The unilateral American moves were backed by multilateral bilateral strategy. In the context of bilateral trade and economic negotiations, the Americans urged their Japanese and German colleagues again and again to open their markets. Simultaneously, in multilateral bodies they raised a whole new agenda, namely the opening of service industries to competition. The most important forum in which such a demand was raised was GATT. Until 1986, trade in services, including telecommunications, was not regulated by GATT. In that year the United States government undertook to stretch the sphere of "free trade" a bit farther, to include services in general and telecom services in particular. The increase in the importance of services (finance, telecommunication, transportation, media, and software) has shifted American priorities regarding the rules of the international economic order. (Aronson and Cowhey, 1988) The extension of free-trade principles into the sphere of services led first to negotiations on the General Agreement on Trade in Services (GATS) and then, with their successful conclusion, to the establishment of the World Trade Organization (WTO) as the successor of GATT. The negotiations on new agreement on free-trade in telecom that came under the auspices of the WTO marginalized the role of the ITU, the key organization of the old regime, and with it its most basic principles. In February 1997 negotiations were concluded in an accord on free trade in telecom services signed by 69 governments (including Israel).

The international accord sponsored by the WTO has not radically opened world telecom to competition. It reflects a domestic decision taken by governments in Britain, Japan, and the United States and by the European Union commission to move toward liberalization. Yet at the same time it enforces the domestic decision by commitments in the international level, it legitimizes these policies, and it encourages countries that lag behind to move faster. The current regime for telecom services is much more competitive than ever before. It is still far from being "fully" competitive, but this is not a situation that is unique to telecom. All in all, the change on the international level is indeed impressive and points to the "global" context in which the Israeli liberalization was conducted.

Dynamics of Change in the International Energy Regime

The oil crisis of 1973 resulted in a radical change in the potential for competition in the international oil markets. At first, shortage of supply created a seller's market, and competition was more prevalent among buyers than sellers. However, the emergence of the Organization of Petroleum Exporting Countries (OPEC), and the assertion of the rights of the national governments concerned in setting the prices for their most valuable natural resource, changed the rules of the game in this market. The new situation of competition is not the result of less government intervention in the international oil markets. It is more the accidental consequence of a rise in the intervention of some governments, the proliferation of actors, and the increasing difficulties in the coordination of collective behavior.

A common characteristic of both the old and the new international energy regimes is their low degree of institutionalization. International institutions from the United Nations to GATT, the World Bank to the IMF, are negligible actors in determining the course of development in the international oil market. The ascendancy of OPEC as a major political actor, with ambitions for cartel formation, is an indication of extent of institutionalization. (Skeet, 1988) OPEC was established in 1960 and its expansion on the one hand, and the interest aggregation of non-OPEC oil exporting countries on the other, promise some degree of institutionalization in the international energy regime. Moreover, institutionalization of international cooperation is also observable among the consumer countries. This was enhanced by the creation of the International Energy Agency in 1974. (Keohane, 1984) In addition, in July 1991, a meeting of the world's major oil producers and consumers was held in Paris in an effort to restore "mutual confidence at all levels of the oil industry chain." Thus, although a slow trend toward some degree of institutionalization can be observed in the international energy regime, its long-run implications for setting prices and governing markets are still uncertain.

The collapse of the multinationals' control of oil pricing and production was to a large extent the outcome of political efforts by Third World nationalists who were hostile to the old order in which the natural resources of their countries were controlled by Western companies. To some extent, OPEC was not only an expression of collective efforts by the producing countries to enlarge their economic slice of the cake, but also an expression of nationalist feelings and interests. (Skeet, 1988) Third World nationalism in general and Arab nationalism in particular were not interested in competitive markets (much as they were not in the interest of the Seven Sisters). The current competition is the result of a failure of both sides to control the market rather than any logic of globalization of markets.

The low degree of institutionalization of the old and new regimes is also a matter of choice, basically the choice of the hegemonic power, the United States. For them the challenges of private interest government of the old regime and the OPEC cartel of the new regime were best dealt with by unilateral and bilateral options. In the postwar period, economic power was in the hands of a few major multinationals that acted as a vertically integrated oligopoly and restricted competition. Following the 1973 crisis, economic power became much more dispersed. Through political means the OPEC countries managed to created a situation in which two new types of actors—national companies and independents—consolidated their place in the fields of oil exploration and production. Together, the national oil companies (NOC) and the independents expanded the free market for the production, refining, transportation, and marketing of oil products. The dominance of the multinationals became radically altered, and the total share of the Seven Sisters in the oil market declined drastically—from over 60 percent in 1972 to less than 20 percent in 1989. (Hartshorn, 1993, p.115)

A radical change is also evident in the economic allocation mechanism of the international energy regime. The postwar energy regime was authoritative primarily in the vertical integration of the majors. The integrated structure included in-firm control of the various stages of processing of crude oil. In fact, most crude oil that circulated on the international market was never sold at all: "It was simply transferred between subsidiaries of these groups, at prices that could be adjusted to minimize the total tax exposure of the parent company across all the countries where it operated."(Hartshorn, 1993, p.115) Market transactions were concluded very late (downstream as possible), while critical stages of the process were shielded from the market and managed by the multinationals' officials. In addition, the dominance of few majors created an oligopoly, in which market-sharing agreements and informal rules for constraining competition (hence of free market conditions) created an authoritative allocation mode rather than a free-market allocation. As was revealed by the United States Senate hearings in 1952, and again in 1974, the operation of the major multinationals, at least in the Middle East, was governed by strict (extra-market) rules constructed to constrain supply and protect price by constraining competition.

The new international energy regime, in contrast to the old, is more transparent and competitive. First, the extra-market transactions in crude oil, which characterized the vertical integration of the Seven Sisters, were radically narrowed down. In the early 1990s, probably 85 percent of the crude circulating in international trade was available to all. (Hartshorn, 1993, p.115) The vertically integrated channels and the long-term contracts were replaced by a much more fragmented structure and by short-term contracts of the spots markets. There also emerged a new kind of middleman, a trader in oil who runs the spot markets. These markets have become the main price indicators for the international oil trade. The rise of an international open market, which is much freer than ever before, is the major sign of the new international energy regime.

The stability of the new competitive regime in the international oil market is still uncertain. The degree of scarcity of resources is in itself uncertain, and on the other hand, the extent of growth in demand for oil products is also uncertain. Two important trends are especially important in this respect. One is the relative decline of the oil industry. After more than a century of expansion, which was far faster than growth in both energy and the world economy, the industry is now in its third decade of relative decline, compared with most other forms of energy. (Hartshorn, 1993, p.1) Declining industries face growing pressures for price reductions and competition, but the same forces that compelled competition are also those that will supply incentives for greater coordination among the sellers in the future. At the moment there are some indications for a reintegration of the market (hence restriction of competition). Major multinationals are increasing their cooperation in the form of joint ventures, mergers, and acquisitions. In addition, there is a new trend to joint ventures between the NOC and the multinationals—which may help to create a convergence of interests and restriction of competition. Finally, it seems that while multinationals are increasingly leaving the midstream markets of refining and transportation, the exporting countries, through their national companies, are replacing them. The new international energy regime may prove less stable than its predecessor, and the future of competition in it in the long run is uncertain.

From Developmental State to a Competition State?

Changes in the role of competition in the Israeli economy are evident in the national arena as well. In what follows, the dynamics of this change is conceptualized as a transformation of the Israeli developmental state to a competition state. This dynamics captures only part of the changes in the Israeli political economy, but it still reflects the most important developments with regard to changes in the sectors to be discussed later. While liberalization is indeed a clearly observed process, it does not necessarily challenge either the autonomy of the state or its commanding position in the economy. This dominance is the most salient feature of the Israeli political economy, and represents the continuity between the old and the new regimes.

Despite its late formation (that is, its being one of the new post-colonial states), the Israeli state was born "strong." (For the distinction between strong and weak states, see Katzenstein, 1978; Migdal, 1989, as well as the critique by Atkinson and Coleman, 1989) The strong state was formed on the basis of the institutions of the labor movement (primarily the Histadrut, that is, the Federation of Labor) and the national Zionist institutions (primarily the Jewish Agency). During three decades of British rule these institutions acquired a strong developmental character: They were engaged in economic promotion of the Jewish society by subsidies for labor as well as business. When sovereignty was obtained in 1948 it was used with even greater effort for the expansion and consolidation of the developmental machine of the pre-state institutions. Thus, in its formative period (in which basic institutional rules are set and are most likely to be endured) the Israeli state was designed as a developmental state, one pushing toward rapid economic growth. The viability and importance of the economic growth is reflected in the relatively limited resources that were allocated by the state, governed by a social-democratic party, to welfare purposes. Indeed, only in the 1980s did the Israeli welfare state mature in terms of social spending. The developmental character of the state was expressed in a tightly controlled financial system, protectionism, and extremely high subsidies for industrial investments.

The consolidation of the regime rested on all three structures, and for almost a quarter of a century these were highly integrated and consistent. The primacy of ideology in setting the terms under which the Israeli policy regime was shaped was expressed in and manifested by consensus over the practice of *mamlachtiut* (etatism). Under this ideological orientation, a wide and extensive set of functions and organizations conducted by non-governmental organizations—such as the political parties and the Histadrut—were transferred to the hands and responsibility of the state. At the same time, a rapid process of expansion of the state into ever new spheres of activity was also taking place. At the end of 1973 the old regime came to its end. The development budget was cut drastically in order to finance the heavy burdens of military and energy imports. The new fiscal reality was accompanied by a new generation of politicians. With the retirement of the old-guard Finance Minister Pinhas Sapir in January 1974, a whole new economic philosophy—neoclassical rather than mercantilist—was on the rise.

The demise of the old policy regime did not automatically generate the birth of a new one. The crisis period of 1974–1977, in which adjustment efforts were successfully made, was followed by the governability crisis of 1977–1985. In May 1977, for the first time in the history of the Israeli democracy, electoral change brought about the transfer of political power to a right-wing government. This was followed by a period of political crisis, itself succeeded by stagflation and record-breaking inflation (over 400percent). It would be futile to discuss this period in terms of a new economic regime since it is hard to find any coherent set of norms that guided the new policy making, let alone a coherent policy of goals and actions. After a decade of economic and political upheavals, a new order was set in the Israeli political economy, and with it a new era began. On July 1, 1985, a stabilization program was successfully implemented and almost immediately managed to get inflation under control. State autonomy was reinforced and the governability crisis came to an end. (Barkey, 1994) The remarkably successful plan that brought inflation down with only (relatively) minor costs in terms of unemployment was designed and implemented by professional economists.[1] The epistemic community of economists became a highly influential policy community, and the rise in its status, influence, and power clearly indicates, perhaps more than anything else, the transformation of the Israeli policy regime.

The fact that the chief actors who promoted privatization and liberalization were economists of the Ministry of Finance raises the question of the extent to which the new regime is more liberal. The answer requires us to distinguish market-led competition from state-made competition. This will serve the argument that the new competition state has strong mercantilist features and that the rise in the scope of the competition in the Israeli economy does not necessarily mean that the Israeli state is becoming more liberal in its relation with the economy.

One may identify the birth of a "competition state" when and where state officials take an active role in the restructuring of the national economy by introducing and even enforcing competition. The obvious but not necessarily the most important evidence for competition policies is a rise in the role of the anti-monopoly authorities. Another indication of this change is a legislation, following the recommendations of a committee chaired by David Brodet, that required the banks to sell their non-financial holdings. This move, which significantly contributes to a more decentralized economy, was again led by economists at the Ministry of Finance. Still, the Israeli competition state is in its very initial stages of development. It is not necessarily replacing or directly attacking old features and norms but is struggling to take its place alongside them. Thus it adds another visage to the multi-face institution that we call "state."

All in all, the regime change in Israeli policy making is best analyzed through changes in the state's preferences and through the largely successful efforts of the economic and legal elites to impose certain procedural norms of policy making, nowadays competition, on the central organs of state power. This kind of change may be characterized as a "change from within"—for it is being devised, initiated, and finally even enforced, by "insiders." But it is also important to understand that change in the Israeli policy regime comes about through a reforming and evolutionary process rather than as an abrupt and revolutionary step. Despite the very turbulent environment and an intensive and crisis-ridden politics, the old styles of policy making, the institutions of allocation and of governance, and the balance among the major powers are proving remarkably stable. This stability, together with the fact that the regime change in Israeli policy making is a "change from within," reflect the limits of change and the importance of continuity in the Israeli political economy.

Sector-Level Analysis:
Telecommunications and Energy in Israel

Regime change is evident in both the Israeli telecom and energy sectors. This part of the study examines the sources, trajectories, outcomes, and implications of the changes. The reforms in telecom and energy have several common features, mainly in regard to the reform agenda, the timing and length of the reforms, the actors who have led the process, and the decline in the power of organized labor as the results of the reforms. They differ, however, in the degree of success in introducing competition into these sectors and in the role of technology and business actors. The comparison reveals the advantages and limits of sector-level analysis. Starting with telecom, the dynamics of change is conceptualized here through a distinction between the old regime (1920–1984), the intermediary regime of corporatization and partial privatization (1984–1994), and the new competitive regime (1994–).

The Dynamics of Change in the
Israeli Telecommunications Regime

The Old Israeli Telecommunications Regime

As in most other countries, the Israeli telecom sector was dominated by a state-administered monopoly. The government served as the policy maker, regulator, and provider of telecom services. The origins of the Israeli etatist regime date to the early 1920s when the first civil telephone network was established by the British government in Palestine. Several important features of the old regime were evident already under the British (that is, tendency of the system to fall short of the demand for telephones from its very inception; organization of the sector according to the classic PTT model; practice of cross-subsidization; and important role of the unions).

The British withdrawal from the country in 1948 was followed by a rapid construction of the system. The annual average growth rates of the system as measured by the number of subscribers was around 15 percent between 1951 and 1960 and 19 percent between 1961 and 1970. (Bezeq, *Annual Statistics: 1994*, Jerusalem, 1995) Developmentalism and economic nationalism are reflected in the governance and provision of telephony. Telephony was used by the government to nurture the creation of a national telecom industry as a means of import substitution. Instead of importing terminals, switching, and cables, a national industry was established. Two manufacturers of telephone and switching equipment and two manufacturers of cables had dominated the Israeli scene already in the 1950s.

Despite the fast growth of the system in the 1950s and 1960s and the rapid catch-up of the Israeli system with major European systems, there was widespread public dissatisfaction with the performance of the system, especially the quality of service. In 1963 the Dinstein Committee recommended corporatization of the telecom services. But it took at least three more committees (all recommending corporatization) for the government to finally decide (August 19, 1979) to corporatize the telephone company. Four more years were needed before the new corporation, Bezeq, was ready to take legal and practical responsibility for the telecom sector.

The corporatization took place against the background of a severe performance crisis in the system and the changing ideological mood in Israeli politics and society. Growing budgetary constraints in the early 1970s and a severe physical crisis following the 1973 war and the oil crisis severely affected the country's economy. Instead of catching up, Israel's telecom at the time was in stagnation. From 1970 to the corporatization of the telecom services in 1979, the average growth rate of supply lagged behind the growth of demand. (Bezeq, *Annual Statistics: 1994*, Jerusalem, 1995) The gap between supply and demand became immense. Between 1971 and 1980 the growth of demand (measured as standing applications) was double the growth of supply. The major reason for the delays and the crisis of supply was a strain on the government budget, hence on investment in the sector. The outcome was decline in public support for the state monopoly in the sector and a crisis of confidence among employees and managers. In addition, a combination of political change in Israel and a "paradigm shift" in the economic elite of the world led to a re-examination of the role of government in the telecom sector. Both the ideology of privatization and the rise to power in 1977 of a new right-wing government legitimized the corporatization of the telecom services.

Corporatization had to be hard fought for by government officials (among whom officials of the Ministry of Finance played an important role) against the unions. With the backing of the Histadrut, the sector's unions proved to be a powerful actor. Only when their demands for significant benefits were met (in the form of wage raises, stability of work, and more influence on day-to-day management), did corporatization become possible. Corporatization was thus the product of a compromise between the two most powerful actors of the sector: the bureaucrats and the unions. Both sides had reason to be satisfied at the time. Working conditions were improved for the workers and corporatization ensured a business-oriented strategy and efficiency in telecom. However, as will be shown below, the new regime again became a target for conflicts.

The Intermediary Telecommunications Regime

The legislation of the Telecom Law in 1982 and the operation of the new corporation from February 1984 radically transformed the structure of the old regime. In the new regime there was separation between the policy making, supervision, and regulatory functions, which were kept in the hands of the Communications Ministry, and the service provision, which was handed over to Bezeq. Noteworthy, too, is the partial privatization of Bezeq in 1990 and 1991. There were also radical changes in its performance, but paradoxically these did not contribute to the legitimization of the regime. Pressures for a more radical reform, which would promote competition and not merely privatization and efficiency, began to be felt from the late 1980s. They were expressed most clearly in a major report by the Boaz Committee published in April 1991, which called for immediate liberalization of the telecom market (except for the local loop). These recommendations were subject to intense and sometimes violent conflict, which in March 1994 resulted in the victory of the proponents of competition.

The radical improvements in the performance of the Israeli telecom sector following the corporatization of Bezeq are primarily evident in the rapid reduction in the number of standing applications for telephone lines, from a record 257,000 in March 1984 to 41,000 in 1989 and 18,000 in 1991. While performance greatly improved, the first years of Bezeq's corporatization were followed by a crisis of governance in the policy and regulatory capacities of the communications ministry. As the ministry had changed its role from an operating department to policy maker and regulator, it had to develop new skills to reorganize its functions. This proved to be a slow and energy-consuming process, which is not yet over.

Side by side with the corporatization, the intermediary regime was characterized by partial privatization of Bezeq. As in other cases, this was a slow process. Only in

1990 and 1991 were 25 percent of the corporation's shares transferred to private hands on the Tel Aviv Stock Exchange. This partial privatization did not proceed further for the next six years for four reasons. First, was the vehement opposition of labor to further privatization. Second, was the indecisiveness of Bezeq's management about selling control to foreign telecom companies. Third, were the security considerations that the state faced over transferring control to foreign investors. Fourth, was growing recognition that privatization as such was not a panacea for the Israeli economy in general or the telecom sector in particular. (Arnon and Preschtman, 1992)

The intermediary regime promoted privatization, and the promotion of competition was a marginal goal. This is evident in the introduction of cable television, which allowed exclusive franchises for the provision of multichannel broadcasting through cables. The operators were all private companies, and there was wide agreement among the legislators and policy makers that the public purse should not defray the heavy investment in building the cable infrastructure. The goals of competition were secondary. The intermediary regime was not about change in the distribution of power as compared with the old regime but about reassertion of its power in changing circumstances and pressures for improvement in its performances. This was evident in respect of Bezeq's senior management, the interests of the equipment industry, and the power of Bezeq managers. Outside the constraints of civil service regulations, Bezeq's senior management won wage raises and managerial autonomy it had not known before. The rapid expansion of investment in the sector under conditions of protectionism and generous government subsidies for research and development and investment had a positive impact on the equipment industry's revenues and profits. At the same time, the reality of technical change at a time of economic expansion allowed newcomers to enter the closed circle of the Israeli telecom industry.

The unions, which at first had opposed corporatization, later negotiated an attractive deal (which included better working conditions and higher wages, and did not reduce employment stability). From 1984 to 1994, employees' wages consistently rose higher than the average rise in the economy as a whole. (Bank of Israel, 1995. *Annual Report*. Jerusalem: The Government Printing House, p.90) Cuts in the labor force were hardly painful, as they were based on voluntary retirement under conditions of highly attractive financial emoluments. Considering the desirability of the intermediary regime for labor and business, as well as the successful accommodation of new technologies and the great improvement in services, it is quite puzzling to see that already at the end of the 1980s, soon after it was established, it faced serious challenges. It took a while for the opponents of the intermediary regime to change the rules of the game, but at last they had their way after bitter and at one point even violent conflict. The new regime of competition was designed and enforced by the state, particularly through cooperation between the bureaucrats of the communications ministry and the eco-bureaucrats of the ministry of finance. These policy entrepreneurs worked in a changing environment which helped them carry out the reforms and bring about a regime change.

A critical turning point in the life of the intermediary regime came with the appointment of the Committee for the Examination and Reorganization in the Structure of the Telecom Sector. This body was established in February 1990 by the Minister of Finance, Shimon Peres and the Communications Minister Gad Ya'acobi. It was chaired by David Boaz, head of the powerful Budget Department in the Ministry of Finance. The committee's recommendations, which were published in April 1991, placed the issue of competition at the top of the regime's agenda. They called for the liberalization of supply and installation of telephone equipment, and for opening international telephone services, cellular phones, data transmission, and value-added services to competition. The committee also recommended that Bezeq's monopoly over the operation of the local system not be changed, but that to guarantee fair competition and avoid cross-service subsidies, substantial parts of its operations be organized as autonomous subsidiaries.

These recommendations were again a subject of bitter conflict between the Communications Ministry on the one hand and Bezeq's management and union on the other. A new committee was appointed to examine the issue, this time chaired by the economist Ilan Maoz. This committee's recommendations, which were published in September 1992, in general reasserted the recommendations of the Boaz Committee on competition and again opened the door to a regime change in Israeli telecom . The political machine of the labor government thereafter moved more rapidly, with the intensive involvement of the late Prime Minister Yitzhak Rabin. In December 1992 an amendment in the Bezeq law to end Bezeq's monopoly control over international calls and cellular phone services was placed before the Knesset. After a struggle that Bezeq's union and its supporters in the Labor Party Knesset faction lost, the amendment to the law was approved. This allowed the Communications and Finance ministries to move on to draft a new general license for Bezeq. In March 1994, after a long delay, the new general license was signed by the Communications Minister, Shulamit Aloni. Bezeq fought the new general license in the Israeli high court of justice, but in June 1994 the court handed down its decision to uphold the new general license and so opened the door to a new regime of "regulated competition" in Israeli telecom.

The New Telecommunications Regime

Bezeq has come under intense pressure of competition. After years in which labor was well protected, the company is now passing through the very difficult process of dismissing 20 percent of its 8,400 workers. In the next two years the Israeli government will most probably reduce its shares in Bezeq to less than 50percent. The first 25 percent of Bezeq's shares were offered to the Israeli public in 1990 and 1991. In 1997, another 12.3 percent of the shares were sold to the American investment bank Merrill Lynch, which intended to resell them in 1999. In March 1998 the government sold another part of the company, and it now holds about 60 percent of the shares. The remaining shares are held by the public (20 percent), Cable and

Wireless (10 percent), and Merrill Lynch (10 percent). Although Cable and Wireless is certainly a candidate to acquire control over Bezeq, the issue is not yet settled.

A recommendation to create an independent regulatory authority in the style of the FCC has been raised since the mid-1980s in various reports. On August 31,1993, the government decided to establish a committee of experts to present recommendations for the establishment of a regulatory agency in the telecom. The committee recommended that the communications ministry be dissolved and most of its responsibilities transferred to a new National Telecommunication Authority (NTA) to be headed by up to seven commissioners and to be responsible, like the FCC, for telecom and for the media field. A government decision of May 29,1996, gave a green light to the preparation of draft legislation by December 1996. However, the political upheaval that brought the right-wing government to power in mid-1996 was a pretext for delay in the establishment of such an authority. Yet, judging by the consensus on the issue as expressed in various reports, it seems fairly certain that in the next couple of years such an authority will be created.

As mentioned, 1994 was a critical year not only in regard to the symbolic act of the new general license but also in regard to the enforcement of competition in important markets. The first to be liberalized was the terminal-equipment market. Indeed, initial steps toward the opening of the equipment market were taken during the first years of the intermediary regime. But the most meaningful step was in July 1994, when for the first time the Communications Ministry forced Bezeq to allow new customers to freely choose who would supply their first telephone set. At the same time, the type-approval regime was becoming more and more flexible. Now manufacturers and importers of terminals can test their equipment in private laboratories, they are not required to test for quality (only for compatibility and safety), and testing results from Europe and the United States are recognized by the Ministry.

Although the equipment market was the first to be liberalized, the benefits of liberalization were first widely felt by the Israeli public in the cellular market. The policy makers of the old regime gave the first cellular operator a monopoly over the provision of the service until 1994. Following the recommendation of the Shiloh Committee, a tender for a second cellular operator was published in November 1993. The winner, Cellcom, a joint venture of BellSouth, Safra Brothers, and Discount Investments, started to offer its services to the public in December 1994. The entry of the second operator radically transformed the sector. While prices fell to a quarter of what they had been before, the penetration rate increased by an even greater factor. The current penetration rate is 30percent (that is, 30 out of 100 people have mobile phones), a rate second only to the Nordic countries. In February 1998 a third operator, Partner, won the first GSM license in Israel, and is expected to start its operation by the beginning of 1999.

The outstanding growth in the cellular market following the entry of Cellcom made the benefits of competition in the international market clearly visible to the policy makers and the public. This in turn encouraged the Communications and Finance Ministries to continue with their liberalization plans. The next target on the government agenda was the market for overseas calls, which represented about 30 percent of Bezeq's revenue and about 40 percent of its net profits. To make liberalization possible, Bezeq's labor union opposition had to ironed out. From the entry of the new Labor government into office in July 1992 until June 1995. Bezeq's workers and the Finance and Communications ministries were engaged in bitter and to some extent violent conflict. This conflict became "manageable" only with the promise of the late prime minister Yitzhak Rabin and the ministers of finance and communications that the "financial solidity" of Bezeq would be preserved. Even then Bezeq's workers engaged in strikes aimed to obstruct the process of opening the market for international calls. However, the state officials eventually had their way, and in October 1995 a tender for two licenses to operate international services was finally launched.

Six groups entered the competition. The two winning groups represent joint ventures between first-class international actors and local business. The new companies started to offer their services on July 1, 1997, and immediately revolutionized this segment of the telecom market. Prices of international calls went down by an average of 60 to70 percent. Overnight, the Israeli public found itself enjoying one of the lowest rates, if not the lowest, anywhere for international telephony. The market grew by 50 percent in the terms of number of minutes. In two months Bezeq International lost about 45 percent of the market. At present Bezeq International holds 55 percent of the market, and the newcomers, which are less than a year old, hold 30 percent (Barak) and 15 percent (Golden Lines).

The next stage in the liberalization and introduction of competition to the Israeli telecom market aims at opening the local loop to competition. The policy process in this regard moved ahead during 1996 when Communications Minister Shulamit Aloni and Minister of Finance Avraham Shohat charged their respective directors-general, Shlomo Waxe and David Brodet, to examine whether the national infrastructure should be exposed to competition, and if so when and under what terms. The committee's report was published in December 1996 and included recommendations (a) to open the Israeli domestic market to competition from January 1999, and (b) to open multi-channel satellite broadcasting to competition. The 1998 agenda of the ministry has been devoted to setting the rules for regulation of competition in the local loop. Although a major decision has been made—new operators will not be able to use the current network but will have to build their own—much still has to be decided before the design of new regime will be complete.

The liberalization program of the telecom sector was liberalization from "above"; in other words, a "state-led" liberalization. While labor opposed it, business—including those that most benefited from it—were relatively passive actors. The new regime is therefore the product of government policy and government regulation. It is thus hardly surprising that the liberalization of the telecom sector did not result in deregulation. Instead of eliminating rules and minimizing control, the government found that in order to liberalize the sector without totally destroying the old players or creating a private monopoly instead of a public one, exit and entry should be regulated. Thus, the bureaucrats found themselves in a long and laborious process of re-regulating the sector. The government's re-regulations under the new telecom regime cover a wide range of issues: from detailed quotas over the number of public telephones to be installed, through the authorization of new services, to determining the rates for various services. The process of the telecom reform, therefore, demonstrates that despite its liberal rhetoric, the government is heavily involved in market-enforcing policies.

The Dynamics of Change in the Israeli Energy Regime

Liberalization, namely the introduction of competition, has been the aim of state-led reform in the Israeli energy sector since the second half of the 1980s. The driving force behind the reforms was the Ministry of Energy, especially the economists in its Planning and Policy Department. Almost 15 years after the start of the reform effort, success in terms of introduction of competition to the market remains very limited. Currently, the government is still heavily engaged in the implementation and enforcement of the new rules it set for the game, and the regime lacks a stable governance structure. The reforms were targeted mainly at the major market of petroleum.[2]

Israel's petroleum production is marginal, and import supplies almost all the consumption of petroleum. The absence of (proven) natural resources of petroleum excludes Israel from the upstream stages of the industry. From 1948 the Arab boycott excluded Israel from the midstream component of the industry as well. A major pipeline that once connected the Iraqi oil field of Kirkuk with the Haifa port stopped working in 1948, following the establishment of the state of Israel. An entrepreneurial initiative by the state led to the construction of a pipeline from the Eilat port on the Red Sea to the Mediterranean in the1960s. This pipeline made it possible to transfer Iranian oil, first to the center of Israel, and, after the closure of the Suez Canal in 1967 (following a capacity enlargement), even to western Europe. To increase the returns from this pipeline, a tanker service was established under effective Israeli control. However, the Islamic revolution in Iran in 1979 abruptly halted the supply of Iranian oil. This, together with the reopening of the Suez Canal (following the Egyptian-Israeli peace agreement), made the pipeline useless and again minimized the Israeli presence in the midstream petroleum market. In the downstream component of the petroleum market Israel is constrained on the one hand by its small size—equal that of a major city in the United States—and on the other hand, by its trajectory of industrial development toward low-energy and high-tech industry rather than toward of high-energy and heavy industry.

The Old Israeli Energy Regime

The old Israeli energy regime was closed and restrictive, with high barriers to both entry and exit. The limited degree of openness and competition in this market was to some extent, the legacy of British colonialism (1918–1948). The practices of monopoly concession by colonial government for oil exploration and the common agreements among Western multinationals to limit inter-firm competition in the Middle East are part of this legacy. Israel's integration into the world oil market was characterized by limited efforts to explore for oil on the one hand, and the establishment of midstream and downstream facilities on the other. A concession in 1933 granted the Iraqi Petroleum Company the right to lay a pipeline connecting the Iraqi oil fields to the port of Haifa on the Mediterranean. The Haifa Refineries were also established as a joint project of the Anglo-Persian Company (from 1954, British Petroleum) and Royal Dutch/Shell. A major reason for their establishment was the needs of the British navy and army in the eastern parts of the Middle East.

Unbridled competition was considered a "danger" by the multinationals that operated in the Middle East in the interwar period. To avoid its ruinous implications, cartel and market share settlements (frequently sponsored by the British government) were agreed upon. To some extent it was not a unique Middle Eastern practice, and as the "As-Is" agreement of 1928 can teach us, sharing the market among the major oil companies was also a general practice. (Yargin, 1991, pp. 260–265) However, in the Middle East the practice of cooperation to avoid competition was highly developed. The "Red Line Agreement" that split the future resources of the defunct Turkish empire (including the territory of Palestine) among the major players, including British, American, and French oil interests, served as a framework for future restrictive practices and in effect almost to the elimination of competition.

Because upstream operations (exploration and production) were negligible in Palestine at that time (as well as later) most of the impact of the major multinationals fell on the midstream and downstream portions of the market. In the midstream part, activity was divided between the two British majors, British Petroleum and Royal Dutch/Shell. The two shared in both the investment and profits from the Kirkuk-Haifa pipeline as well as in the Haifa Refinery. The downstream market of wholesale distribution was controlled by the Royal Dutch/Shell jointly with two smaller American companies, Socony Vacuum and Esso. Because they had to purchase their products from the Haifa Refineries, monopoly was another constraint on competition.

The Israeli government inherited an uncompetitive energy sector, and basically did little to change the situation. The problems of shortage of supply gave considerations of security and continuity of supply higher priority than the goal of a competitive market. The Israeli experience of rationing, limited supply, and scarcity of oil (at least until July 1949) added their weight to the creation of an uncompetitive market. Arab pressures on the major oil suppliers to curtail connections with Israel were high on the agenda of the policy makers during the 1950s. The limited scope of the international oil market not controlled by the majors largely made the oil import to Israel a matter for intergovernmental agreements.[3] In 1951, three years after the establishment of the state of Israel, the government embarked on the establishment of an Israeli national oil marketing company. The shares of the new company, named Delek, were allocated to the Histadrut (45 percent), the private sector (45 percent), and the government (10 percent). Delek entered an agreement with the existing companies on sharing the market: Shell (later renamed Paz) was to receive 45 percent of the market, Sonol 25 percent, and Delek 30 percent. Today, 45 years later, this market allocation remains very much the same. The ownership of Shell and Sonol, the subsidiaries of the two major multinationals that operated in the country, changed during the 1950s, but the structure and the practice of market sharing remained the same. Sonol was owned by Socony Vacuum (later Mobil) of the United States.[4] In late 1956, under threats by Saudi Arabia to terminate the company's concession, Socony Vacuum sold its assets in Israel to a minor American player, Sonneborn Petroleum Associates. The two other major oil companies, British Petroleum and Shell, followed the Americans, again under the pressures by the Saudis, and left the country in 1958. By the time the multinationals left the country the restrictive norms and practices they had established were firmly institutionalized. The norms of the old regime left a little place for market competition either as a disciplinary method or as an organizing principle—let alone as a normative order.

The "old regime" was represented and to some extent protected by the Fuel Administration, the old regulatory department that was created in the early 1950s in the Ministry of Finance and transferred to the Ministry of Energy when it was established in the mid-1970s. A central element of the old regime was the government's entrepreneurial role. Planning and central management were a critical norm, at least in regard to the supply of petroleum. Entrepreneurial activity of the government was a major characteristic of the upstream part of the market (petroleum exploration), as local energy sources promised to save the country's foreign currency. The Eilat-Ashkelon pipeline, to carry Iranian oil, was another instance in which the government acted as an entrepreneur. In the downstream part of the market the government was involved as a shareholder in Delek, and after 1958 also in Paz (this company was under effective government control until its privatization in 1988). An Israeli stake in the oil shipping industry was perceived as critical for national security and the government developed a state-owned oil transport company. In the late 1950s the government's ownership of the Haifa Refineries enabled it to develop a petrochemical industry, which was based on the remainders of the refined oil.

In the absence of competition, prices were regulated by the government. "Cost-plus" arrangements were introduced in order to ensure the oil marketing companies an adequate return for their operations. Like all cost-plus arrangements, this one, too, was considered to contain a negative incentive for efficiency—why should the companies work hard when their profit was assured?. Nonetheless, pressure for change hardly arose. From time to time consumers' complaints could be heard, but hardly any calls for change came from powerful interests. Above all, the government's ability to set prices just about at will gave it strong leverage over any business contender on the one hand and, on the other, the capacity to respond to complaints by business by manipulating the price of products. Although marketing companies had an obvious interest in the restriction of competition, large consumers had negative incentives to change this situation. It so happened, then, that for reasons that are beyond the scope of this paper, the large consumers were the government itself or government-owned corporations that worked under similar cost-plus arrangements. The Israel Defense Forces, for example, had no economic incentive to obtain the fuel it consumed at competitive prices. This was also the case with other big consumers such as the Israel Electric Corporation, which was state-owned and also operated under cost-plus arrangements. The state-owned Israel Chemicals Ltd., yet another large oil consumer that had positive incentives to press for price reduction (as it did not operate under cost-plus arrangements) could hardly challenge the policy of the government—which was also its owner.

The Intermediary Energy Regime

The current regime in the energy sector was born and shaped in the Ministry of Energy between 1985 and 1988. There are clear signs (discussions, deliberations, committees) that the process was initiated by the ministry's officials, and there is no public evidence for behind-the-scenes intervention of societal interests. Although one can clearly identify certain beneficiaries from the reform (the new oil marketing companies), and probable beneficiaries (the oil refineries and the owners of the gas stations), it is still not possible to point to direct, or even indirect, relations between them and the initiative for reform. The intensity of conflict over the reform, the plurality of conflicting interests, and the high public visibility of the reform, all ensure a degree of transparency, and so allow reliable policy analysis.

Internal discussions on regulatory reform that would enhance competition and reduce market restrictions were evident in the Ministry of Energy's bureaucracy since the late 1970s. Back then, it was believed, at least by a few of the ministry's officials, that the sector's structure and its operative rules were both democratically inadequate (that is, secretive and closed) and inefficient (that is, lack of competition is believed to produce less than optimal allocation of resources). To the economists in the Planning and Policy Department, the practice of cost-plus arrangements was a challenge to basic professional tenets. Together with the economists from the Budget Department in the Ministry of Finance they formed a strong bureaucratic coalition in favor of competitive pro-market rules. Officials of the Fuel Administration opposed the reform. But with the nomination of the new Minister of Energy, Moshe Shahal, the supporters of reform got the upper hand. Shahal's ambition was to run for the chairmanship of the Labor party and for the post of Prime-Minister, and the reform in the energy sector was considered beneficial for the new party image, and personally for his own public image. It is doubtful that he understood the complexities of the energy sector or had a realistic political estimate of the extent of opposition from entrenched interests in the sector.

The coalition of a reform-oriented minister on the one hand, and professional economists in the Ministry of Energy and the Ministry of Finance on the other, thus set out to enforce a set of new regulations to induce competition among the three majors and between them and the oil refineries. A fierce opposition of the three majors caused long delays in the policy-formation stages of the reform. The adversarial style of negotiations practiced by the participants at this stage did not prevent them from reaching a compromise in the end. According to it, reform would be enforced in two stages. The first would go into effect in 1988, the second in 1990. The compromise over the timing did not allow the establishment of a new consensus in the energy market. Stormy relations still characterize the policy field, as well as the stubborn opposition of the Big Three.

Now, a decade after the start of the reform, its aims have evidently been realized only to a very limited extent. An examination of the normative change and the structure, depth, and scope of competition, as well as of policy outcomes, reveals that modest changes have occurred. On the normative side, there is still disagreement between market actors and public officials over the very necessity of competition and its benefits. The Big Three, the owners of the gas stations and the oil refineries, are willing to accept competition, but not in their own segments of the market. Structural changes are marginal. There is still a high concentration of and a monopoly situation in midstream facilities. Competition exists with respect to the big consumers but has not reached the small consumers who fill their car tanks at local gas stations. Although service may be improving, there is no competition over prices. Despite the entry of new competitors to the gasoline market, they seem to have been swallowed by the old cartel. All this has resulted in a situation where petroleum products sold through gas stations represent only 25 percent of the sales but account for almost 49 percent of the industry's profits. (State Comptroller's Report 1993, cited in the *Jerusalem Post*, May 1, 1993, p.10) All in all, a marketing cartel still exists, the refineries are still a monopoly, and the Organization of Gas Station Owners still stymies competition.

Under the new circumstances of the intermediary regime, it is the workers of the Big Three who have lost the most. The proposed rules of the game served to legitimize unilateral actions by the companies to revoke collective wage agreements, cut wages, reduce the work force, and erode the union's power by the enforcement of "personal contracts" as the basis of workers' rights. According to the largest oil company's spokesman, the new measures were aimed to "bring the workers closer to the changing reality"! (*Jerusalem Post*, November 8, 1994, p. 8) Despite protests by the hundreds workers of the Big Three, and despite the Histadrut's backing, the power of labor is, by any criterion, on the decline in this sector. Business power, by contrast, seems to be hardly changed. The past cozy relationship with the government may perhaps not be quite as it was, but profits do not seem to have been declined. True, there is still uncertainty regarding the future of the industry should competition be enforced. But even in such a case diversification to other businesses and markets is possible.

Despite the very limited success of the liberalization of the energy sector, the state seemingly had the upper hand in it. The government is still the owner of critical actors in the sector as well as of strategic facilities. It clearly has not retreated from managerial and ownership roles. Moreover, for the last decade the government has been on the offensive rather than the defensive. The veto power of the Big Three has gradually worn away, and it seems very likely that they will be defeated eventually. The pattern of state-led liberalization that was found also in the case of the telecom regime shows that the government holds the power of discretion—or at least the power derives from being in a position of discretion. Even with a full enforcement of the reform, the government will most probably end up setting new rules rather than simply abolishing the old ones. Instead of deregulation, the result will be reregulation. It is most likely that the introduction of competition into the market will eventually result from the maintenance and strict enforcement of new regulations. According to this scenario, then, the Israeli energy market will eventually develop into a free market—albeit with more, rather than less, regulation.

Multi-Level Analysis:
Telecommunications and Energy Compared

Four sector-oriented explanations may be raised to account for the relative success of the introduction of competition into the telecom sector and its relative failure in energy. First, the autonomy of the state varies across sectors, and different state capacities in different sectors may explain the different outcomes. I examined the structures of the ministries involved, their patterns of recruitment, the legal power of state officials in the two sectors, the coherence of policy making, and the frequency of changes of directors-general and ministers in the two ministries, but no conclusive evidence arose of differences in state capacities in the two sectors to support such a hypothesis.

Differences in the organization of business and the organization of labor in the two sectors may offer a better explanation. Business power was most salient in the energy sector but much less so in telecom. In both cases workers and managers only rarely cooperated to prevent the reform. Nonetheless, while in case of Bezeq the labor union took the initiative and was the major contender for the government policy, in the energy case the unions were relatively silent. In both cases, labor power was not strong enough to prevent the change in the regime. It is not likely that the less powerful and less active unions in the energy sectors succeeded where the more organized, the more powerful unions, failed. If the differences in the political structures in the two sectors is to explain the differences in the success of the reforms, business power, not labor power, should be considered.

Business power in the telecom sector includes the power of Bezeq as well as that of the major suppliers (the two oligopolies of cables and telecom equipment companies). In practice, however, it was only Bezeq that conducted the struggle against the regulatory change, and it did so in a very understated manner. Bezeq's power was limited because its managers had to take into account the policies of its shareholder—the government. Being a public corporation, Bezeq's managers were not free to act as they would have liked. By contrast, in the energy sector, the Big Three had extensive room for maneuver that enabled them to fight the government policies. They were connected to the most powerful conglomerates in the Israeli economy, and they did not hesitate to put heavy pressure on Members of Knesset to achieve their goals. In one case, their contribution to an association which was headed by the former chairman of the Knesset Economics Committee, Tzachi Hanegbi (later the Justice Minister!) is under investigation by the police. It might be argued on the basis of the Big Three's strong opposition to the reforms that business power is the critical element in the change of the regime. Although this argument seems highly reasonable, it is difficult to accommodate it with the statist tradition of policy making in Israel. Hence, without denying the importance of business power, a complementary explanation is suggested.

Differences in the propensity of telecom and energy for competition may well explain the differences in the success of the state's liberalization efforts. Energy and telecom include a various number of veto points along the chain linking producers to consumers. In the case of energy, prior to the reform, the veto over competition was in the hands of the government, but it was also in the hands of the cartel of the Big Three, the gas station owners, the refineries, the international oil companies, and the oil producing countries. During the process of regime change, some of the actors lost their veto power whereas others changed their preferences and started to support competition. By contrast, the number of veto points over competition is much smaller in telecom. The differences in the number of veto points are specific to a product and to a sector. Their number considerably determines the outcomes of the process. Yet, while the length of the energy sector chain has some impact on its propensity for competition, there is no reason to believe that it acts as an insurmountable barrier to a more competitive market. More rationed preparations and planning of the liberalization of the energy market, and primarily the establishment of a regulatory body with appropriate policy powers, may result in the success of liberalization in energy as well.

Sector-centered explanations are indispensable when one considers differences in the success of reforms, as reflected in the extent of competition and allocation of benefits between large and small consumers. Yet they leave a few basic questions that cannot be answered looking at the sectors. First, and this is hardly contestable, liberalization is not unique either to energy or to telecom. It is grounded in forces and actors that are well beyond sectors and nations. Second, none of the sectors' prominent actors pushed for liberalization. Indeed, the political process was one of state-led liberalization. To explain these aspects of the changes in the two sectors one has to move to the "global" and "national" levels of inquiry.

Competition was found to play a greater role in the international markets for both telecom and energy. However, the factors that shaped this new reality were different. In energy, competition was the unintended outcome of a failure to create a governance structure to replace the old mechanisms of hierarchical allocation by the multinationals. In telecom, competition was an outcome of three factors. First, technological innovations, especially the convergence of the computer, media, and telecom industries, are the most commercially spectacular advances of the last two decades. The new technologies did not create any imperative for competition, but they opened the window and provided challengers of the monopolies with incentives. Second, the interest of American corporations and the U.S. government in more competitive markets was a critical factor in determining the outcomes. Even without the use of political power, the unilateral deregulation of the British and American markets made it impossible for other governments to ignore the benefits of competition. Finally, the "paradigm change" from Keynesianism to Monetarism also had an impact on the normative aspects of the regimes. The ascendancy of the economists as the strongest epistemological group dealing with that market gave the final push, as well as legitimacy, to the more competitive order.

However, increasing competition in the international regimes for telecom and energy did not create any imperative for change on the national and sectorial levels of policy making. It both cases it made change possible rather than enforcing it. Nothing in the competitive international market in the two sectors obliged the Israeli government to enforce competition in either the domestic energy market or the domestic telecom market. But the role and influence of events and actors in the international telecom regime were more important than in the international energy regime. Epistemological and ideational change in the international arena has legitimized the creation of competitive markets in telecom around the world. Their marginal place in the international energy regime made it more difficult for the Israeli policy makers to promote the liberalization in that market. Note that the proliferation of international bodies and the creation of a legal framework of competition in telecom do not constrain national choice but reflect consensus over desired regimes. This level appears to have some merit in explaining the flow of ideas and the creation of global epistemic communities, but is less successful in accounting for some of the most important political and economic mechanisms that transform global ideas into political action.

The national level of analysis best explains the similarities in the sources, processes, and outcomes of the liberalization of the two sectors. First, the state-enforced changes clearly reflect a deep-rooted pattern of policy making in Israel. The developmental state of the past, which undertook to guide Israeli society and economy to rapid development, is now changing its strategy: competition is perceived as an important tool for optimal allocation of resources, hence growth. The dynamics of a fall in the power of labor and a rise in the power of state-nurtured business is a long-term trend. This trend was devised, coordinated, and facilitated by the state, which extended its power and autonomy almost continuously. Second, the common goals of the reforms in the two regimes are attested by the existence of criteria of policy management that are external to the sectors themselves. The tendency to enforce competition as a guiding rule for the management of such diverse sectors as telecom and energy seems to support the national patterns approach, which predicts a national dynamics of change rather than a fragmented pattern of sectorial changes.

The study of the differences and similarities between the dynamics of change in telecom and energy enables us to integrate the three levels of analysis to one coherent explanation of change and continuity in the Israeli political economy. The multi-level analysis adopted here was found to be essential in order to understand the politics of liberalization in Israel. The two liberalization programs involve multi-level processes, with multi-level sources and multi-level outcomes, so each of the three levels has some explanatory merits. Although it is clear that sectorial dynamics determine the different outcomes of the reforms, the important similarities in the sources, processes, and styles were determined on the national (state) level. Finally, the more competitive regimes in the national and sectorial levels were encouraged and supported by more competitive international regimes. Although changes in the international regimes were necessary conditions for the changes on the national level, they were not sufficient. To make change possible, a hard and a bitter struggle between state officials and labor and business groups was required.

Conclusions:
The Contradictions and
Limitations of Liberalization

Competition was found to play a greater role in the new regimes than in the old in both telecom and energy, and on all three levels of the analysis. State manufactured competition is the result of state-led efforts to restructure the market and encourage newcomers. Competition has increased not only in telecom but also (to some modest degree) in the defiant energy sector. More competition is evident all over the economy in sectors such as health services, education, finance, and the labor market. Security considerations, which were used to legitimize monopoly and state ownership, now seem to be interpreted in a narrower and more critical manner. The dominance of the discourse of privatization and liberalization, as well as the change in public preferences towards capitalism and away from socialism, support the change in the policy regime. The dominance of the Israeli economists in the making of public policy is perhaps a still more significant thing as it reflects an epistemological change: from the economic nationalism of the past to the economic liberalism of the 1990s. All these changes reflect a decisive move toward a relatively more competitive allocation of economic power in Israeli policy making. But more competitive allocation of economic power does not necessarily imply any radical shift in performance of the Israel economy—not growth and not social justice. The

victims of the competitive regimes are the workers, and the agonies of the unfortunate victims, which have not been addressed in this paper, have to be taken into account as well.

The creation of the new telecom and energy regimes resulted in a governance
structure that represents a mixture of deregulation, reregulation, and new regulations. The Israeli experience is hardly unique in this respect; Steven Vogel pointed
out similar dimensions of liberalization in his book *Freer Market, More Rules.* (1996)
Vogel made the assertion that states and markets may be mutually supportive rather
than antagonistic entities. Indeed, this was already suggested long ago in Karl
Polanyi's seminal study, *The Great Transformation.* (1944)

Yet Vogel's suggestions, which are restated in this study, are important as they tell
us that these mutually supportive relations between state and markets are important
in the current processes of globalization and internationalization.

If this is indeed the case, and states and markets are mutually supportive, then
the old Developmental State in Israel is not likely to disappear but is more likely to
assume some features of a Competition State, which reflect mercantilist principles
as much as liberal ones. Not only does liberalization involve some measures that
contradict the assertions of the retreat of the state, but states and regimes are complex constructions which are subject to change only by adding new layers to old.
Like coral reefs that take shape by deposits over long periods of time, states and
regimes are shaped by the accommodation of complex sets of institutions and
rules. Rather than being centrally and rationally pre-devised, these institutions and
rules reflect a patchwork of different styles, different fashions, and different normative orders. Policy, legal, and economic changes interact with preexisting structures, which are more likely to adapt to the new circumstances than yield to the
forces of transformation.

Thus, the new Israel is still statist in its structure of interest intermediation. At
the same time, the value orientation of the dominant epistemic communities is
becoming more neoliberal than ever before. Changes are more evident in the
value orientations and policy goals of the regime than they are in policy instruments, policy styles, and policy actors. This reflects some of the limits of neo-
liberal and conservative approaches to the economic role of the state. Although
these approaches perceive the interaction between state and markets as zero-sum
relations, the realities of liberalization do not support their views. Liberalization
and competition do not entail a retreat of the state. The passionate love affair of
Israeli society with the ideas of market competition and liberalization is doomed
to end in tears insofar as it expects the retreat of the state. Not only is liberalization a product of entrepreneurial state bureaucracy, the current competitive telecom regime involves more (state) rules rather than less. Markets and states may
thus be mutually supportive rather than antagonistic. In the new Israel the role of
the state in the economy is expected to be as important and as critical for the
country's economic development and the welfare of the citizens as it used to be in
the past.

Bibliography

Arnon, Arye and Haim Preschtman.1992. *The Privatisation of Natural Monopolies*. (Discussion Paper 14/92). Jerusalem: Research Department, Bank of Israel.

Aronson, D. Jonathan and F. Peter Cowhey. 1988. *When Countries Talk: International Trade in Telecommunications Services*. Cambridge, Mass.: American Enterprise Institute.

Atkinson, Michael and William Coleman. 1989. "Strong States and Weak States: Sectorial Policy Networks in Advanced Capitalist Economies." *British Journal of Political Science* 19, pp. 47–67.

Barkey, J. Henry, 1994. "When Politics Matter: Economic Stabilization in Argentina and Israel." *Studies in Comparative International Development* 29, pp. 41–67.

Cowhey, F. Peter . 1990. "The International Telecommunication Regime: The Political Roots of Regimes for High Technology." *International Organization* 44.

Evans, Peter. 1995. *Embedded Autonomy: States and Industrial Transformation*. Princeton: Princeton University Press.

Hartshorn, J.E., 1993. *Oil Trade: Politics and Prospects*. Cambridge: Cambridge University Press.

Hollingsworth, J. Rogers, C. Philippe Schmitter. and Wolfgang Streeck. 1994. "Capitalism, Sectors, Institutions and Performance." In Holligsworth et al., eds., *Governing Capitalist Economies*. Oxford: Oxford University Press, pp. 3–16.

Katzenstein, J. Peter, ed. 1978. *Between Power and Plenty*. Wisconsin: University of Wisconsin.

Katzenstein, J. Peter. 1984. *Corporatism and Change: Austria, Switzerland and the Politics of Industry*. Ithaca: Cornell University Press.

Keohane, O. Robert. 1984. *After Hegemony: Cooperation and Discord in the World Political Economy*. Princeton: Princeton University Press.

Keohane, O. Robert and Joseph Nye. 1977. *Power and Interdependence*. Boston: Little Brown.

Krasner, D. Stephen.1983. *International Regimes*. Ithaca: Cornell University Press.

_____. 1991. "Global Communications and National Power: Life on the Pareto Frontiers." *World Politics* 43, pp. 336–366.

Lowi, Theodore. 1964. "American Business, Public Policy, Case Studies, and Political Theory." *World Politics* 16, pp. 677–715.

Migdal, Joel. 1989. *Strong Societies and Weak States: State-Society Relations and State Capabilities in the Third World*. Princeton: Princeton University Press.

Polanyi, Karl. 1944. *The Great Transformation*. Boston: Beacon Press.

Richardson, Jeremy, ed. 1982. *Policy Styles in Western Europe*. London: George Allen and Unwin.

Shonfield, Andrew. 1965. *Modern Capitalism: The Changing Balance of Public and Private Power*. Oxford: Oxford University Press.

Skeet, Ian. 1988. *OPEC: Twenty-Five Years of Prices and Politics*. Cambridge: Cambridge University Press.

Vogel, David. 1986. *National Styles of Regulation: Environmental Policy in Great Britain and the United States*. Ithaca: Cornell University Press.

Vogel, Steven. 1996. *Freer Markets, More Rules: Regulatory Reform in Advanced Industrial Countries*. Ithaca: Cornell University Press.

Waarden, van Frans. 1995. "Persistence of National Policy Styles: A Study of Their Institutional Foundations." In Brigitte Unger and Frans van Waarden eds., *Convergence or Diversity?* Aldershot: Avebury, pp. 333–372.

Weiss, Linda. 1988. *The Myth of the Powerless State.* Cambridge: Polity.
Yargin, Daniel. 1991. *The Prize: The Epic Quest for Oil, Money, and Power.* New York: Simon and Schuster.

Notes

1. This success gave the economists a dominant position among the Israeli policy actors. Not that they were insignificant policy actors before, but from then on they were to have a clear advantage over anyone else in the policy community.

2. The markets for electricity generation and coal were excluded from the program and are not considered in this paper.

3. For example, oil supply contracts with Russia were signed in exchange for Israeli oranges and bananas. Over 30percent of the German reparations were devoted to the purchase of crude petroleum.

4. Esso, a major American oil company, withdrew from the country in the early 1950s.

8

The Great Economic-Juridical Shift: The Legal Arena and the Transformation of Israel's Economic Order

RAN HIRSCHL

Introduction

Deregulation of domestic markets, recommodification of public services, and the gradual transition toward a more "flexible" market structure have become worldwide phenomena during the last twenty years. These processes have been described by legislators and bureaucrats as inevitable steps in the constant battle of capitalist markets, especially those in small trade-dependent countries, to remain competitive and viable in the global economy. In many countries, the gradual adoption of more flexible production conditions has been accompanied by the rise of a neo-liberal ideology emphasizing extreme social atomism, by the emergence of an international stock-exchange culture, and by placing the values of efficiency, flexibility, and economic rationality in the highest possible esteem. In the legal arena, many countries have enacted provisions to facilitate the adaptation of domestic markets to the demands of the global market, and have revived a laissez-faire interpretation of labor law as well as economic and social rights. In short, a new economic and legal order has been establishing itself in the arenas of production, labor, and social entitlement.

This wide-ranging process has not left the Israeli polity untouched. There are five main particularities of its impact that make the Israeli case interesting: the long tradition of "Hebrew labor" and collectivism as central values of Zionism; the historical role of the Labor Movement and especially the Federation of Jewish Labor in Israel (hereinafter, the Histadrut) in the formation of the state; the deeply collectivist

The research for this article was supported in part by the Yale Center for International and Area Studies. I am grateful to Caroline Chapman, Dan Friedman, Gershon Shafir, Rogers Smith, and especially to Ayelet Schachar for their helpful comments on earlier drafts of this paper.

roots of Jewish ethno-republicanism underlying the country's political culture; Israel's involvement in a fragile reconciliation process with its neighbors; and the accompaniment of the nation's transition to a market economy by fundamental legal changes in the constitutional, labor, and corporate law arenas. These changes are marked by the "constitutional revolution" of 1992: the enactment of Basic Law: Human Dignity and Liberty and Basic Law: Freedom of Occupation that, in lieu of a formal bill of rights in Israel, were aimed at securing entrenched legal status for civil liberties and human rights. (For preliminary critical assessments of the expected impact of the new Basic Laws on the status of human and social rights in Israel, see Marmor, 1997; Raday, 1994a; Ben-Israel, 1994c)

The constitutional revolution in Israel is usually seen as an act within the political arena and as a response to previous legislation and legal practice. The new Basic Laws recognize some basic human rights, establish a path for potential disqualification of "unconstitutional laws" by the Supreme Court, and clearly manifest the dual character of Israel as a Jewish and a democratic state. However, an important dimension of the revolution is often ignored by scholars of the Israeli polity: the constitutional revolution's relationship to the emerging economic order in Israel. In this article, I suggest that the fundamental changes in Israel's legal arena during the last decade—most notably the constitutional revolution of 1992 and its interpretation by the Israeli judiciary—reflect and promote a neo-liberal, individualist, "free enterprise" worldview which co-exists uneasily with the country's foundational values and experiences. The major legal changes in Israel since the mid-1980s are part and parcel of a fundamental change which is gradually transforming Israel from a collectivist state with a mobilized (Jewish) society and centralized economy into a more individualistic society with a free market orientation and culture. The trend toward the deregulation of Israel's economy both shapes and is shaped by the constitutional revolution and the neo-liberal values that underlie it.

In order to develop this argument, the article advances in four stages. I begin by describing Israel's new economic and legal order and the rise of an American-style economic and legal culture in contemporary Israel. Next, I analyze the gradual devaluation in the status of collective labor rights in Israel and discuss the emergence of legal mechanisms that have reinforced a neo-liberal conception of labor relations in the workplace since the mid-1980s. In the third part, I examine the selective interpretation given by courts to the two new Basic Laws. Under this interpretation, the economic sphere is perceived as a distinct sphere which is protected from state intervention. As a result, the right to private property is awarded a supreme constitutional status and the constitutionally protected rights to "human dignity and freedom" and "freedom of occupation" are exclusively understood by the courts as a bundle of "negative" rights. This neo-liberal line of interpretation of the two new Basic Laws is not exclusive to labor-related rights. As I illustrate, it is clearly evident in other realms such as education, health, housing, and welfare. I conclude, in the fourth part, with an examination of the *prima facie* tensions between the prevailing neo-liberal ideological and economic momentum in Israel, recent legislation and adjudication which regulate, at least to some extent, competition in the market-place and the "egalitarian" adjudication of the Supreme Court in several recent civil-liberty cases.

Israel's New Legal and Economic Order

Israel, like several other countries that inherited the Common Law tradition, has no written constitution or entrenched Bill of Rights. (For detailed accounts of the historical roots of this situation see Gavison, 1985, 1997; Strum, 1995; Goldberg, 1993; Gutmann, 1988; Ackerman, "1981) Instead, a web of 11 Basic Laws, which are for the most part immune to parliamentary majority rules, serve as the formal core of Israeli constitutional law. (For further discussion see Rubinstein, 1996; Jacobson, 1993; Elazar, 1990). Until recently, the legal nexus of Basic Laws did not include a basic law for civil liberties and human rights.[1]

Several attempts, beginning in the 1950s, to pass a bill of rights in Israel, failed due to vigorous opposition from religious parties, to a wide consensus among Israel's Jewish (secular and religious) population regarding Israel's definition as a Jewish state, [2] but mainly due to the institutional disincentive of the legislature until the 1980s to delegate power to the judiciary. In 1992, however, a group of Knesset members,[3] representing an explicitly secular, neo-liberal agenda, coordinated the 1992 enactment of two basic civil rights laws—Basic Law: Human Dignity and Liberty, and Basic Law: Freedom of Occupation,[4] and the amendment of Basic Law: The Government. (Basic Law: the Government (S.H. 1396, p. 214, 1992) The latter was the first law to be fully entrenched, followed by the full entrenchment of Basic Law: Freedom of Occupation. Both the Basic Law: Freedom of Occupation, and Basic Law: Human Dignity and Liberty contain a limitation clause forbidding infringement of the declared rights "except by a statute that befits the values of the State of Israel, for a worthy goal, and not exceeding what is necessary." These enactments paved the institutional way for active judicial review in Israel, and awarded the Supreme Court the authority both to monitor Israel's political arena closely and to disapprove of "unconstitutional" primary legislation enacted by the Knesset.

Although the two new Basic Laws on human rights do not constitute an official bill of rights, they are widely understood to fulfill the functions of a bill of rights: they protect the right of every citizen or resident of the state to engage in any occupation, profession, or business; and they protect the right of the same people to property, due process of law, freedom of movement, life, personal freedom, privacy, and human dignity. The rights protected by the two new Basic Laws are described as legal norms of preferred status, much like their constitutional status in the United States, Canada, and many other countries.

Aharon Barak, Chief Justice of the Supreme Court of Israel, asserted that the two laws would enable the Court to be more vigilant in its efforts to protect political and civil liberties in Israel: "Similar to the United States, Canada, France, Germany, Italy, Japan, and other western countries, we now have a constitutional defense for Human Rights. We too have the central chapter in any written constitution, the subject-matter of which is Human Rights . . . [w]e too have judicial review of statutes which unlawfully infringe upon constitutionally protected human rights." (Barak, 1997, p.3) Other judges and legal scholars have also emphasized on many occasions that the two new laws firmly guarantee the Israeli public its civil liberties and serve as Israel's bill of rights. (On the function of the two new Basic Laws as Israel's bill of rights, see also Barak, 1996; Maoz, 1996; All the articles in *Bar-Ilan Law Studies* 13, 1996, in Hebrew; All the articles in *Mishpatim* 28, 1997, in Hebrew; Barak, 1993, 1994a, 1994b; Goldberg, 1994; Lahav, 1993; Kretzmer, 1992a) These developments have led scholars to identify a "constitutional revolution" in Israel. The institutional and academic legal discourse in Israel characterizes this revolution as a new era in Israel's quest for a comprehensive bill of rights, and as a key element in the establishment of human rights and civil liberties as law.

The two new Basic Laws also establish the constitutional definition of Israel as both a Jewish and democratic state, thus re-emphasizing and formalizing the duality that has already been expressed in Israel's Declaration of Independence, in the Supreme Court landmark decisions regarding the *El-Ard*, *Ben-Shalom* and *Rabbi Kahane* parliamentary list cases, and article 7a of Basic Law: The Knesset. (Basic Law: Freedom of Occupation, Article 2; and Basic Law: Human Dignity and Liberty, Article 1a.) The political and legal consequences of the constant tension between Israel's status as a Jewish state and its democratic character have been thoroughly discussed by scholars of Israeli society. (Kimmerling, 1985, 1989; Klein, 1987; Kretzmer, 1990; Hofnung, 1996b; Peled, 1992; All articles in the 1995 *Tel-Aviv University Law Review*. Analyses of Israel's Basic Laws and the Supreme Court's judicial interpretations and decisions reveal that both the state and the courts take great pains to obscure the inherent and ingrained contradiction between these two poles.) The place of the recent fundamental legal changes in the emerging neo-liberal economic order in Israel, however, has been much less discussed.

Israel has traditionally been thought of as a country with a strong state apparatus. The state exhibits its strength through the kinds of controls it can exercise over various aspects of its citizens' lives. Until the late 1980s scholars of Israel's political economy claimed that "Israel's government dominates the national economy like none other outside the socialist bloc. (Sharkansky, 1987, p.3; For a general discussion of the state's central role in the Israeli economy until the mid-1980s, see Aharoni,1998; Plessner, 1994; Arian, 1989; Shimshoni, 1982, ch. 5.) In many cases, extensive state intervention served the partisan interests of the Labor Party, and political and economic interests of the Histadrut. (For critical historical analyses of the central role of the Labor Movement and the Histadrut in maintaining Jewish hegemony in the labor market, in shaping patterns of labor market segmentation on an ethnic basis, and in shaping patterns of state intervention in the market, see Shafir, 1989, 1996; Shalev, 1989, 1992; Grinberg, 1991, 1993).

Nonetheless, by the late 1960s, the pro-market voice was "imported" to Israel by a whole generation of Israeli economists, trained abroad and educated in neo-classical economics. Since 1968 economists have encouraged the state to withdraw from its extensive intervention in the market, dismantle welfare policies, develop a competitive private sector, and curtail the size and power of the public sector and the Histadrut. (Barnett, 1996; on the important role of the academic economists in Israel in promoting the neo-liberal economic ideology in Israel, see also Aharoni, 1991) In recent years this neo-liberal worldview, has become dominant in influential fields beyond academic economics and the business sector. Over the past two decades, the developing Israeli economy, funded to a large extent by foreign aid and other external financial resources, has gradually weakened the Histadrut's economic authority in favor of private business interests. As in other Western countries, there has been a sustained attempt in Israel in recent years to dismantle the country's local version of Keynesian economics and to install a more market-oriented economic pattern. This process accelerated in the aftermath of the 1996 elections.[5]

The state's roll-back from the formerly state-controlled public services arena, as well as an increasing recommodification of formerly decommodified services, indicate Israel's movement toward a variant of neo-liberal market economy.[6] Examples of these two processes are the new Medicare Law (1994); the recent privatization of health (for an informative discussion of the new public health arrangements in Israel, see Zalmanovitch, 1997; Chernihovsky, 1993; Peleg, 1994. On neo-liberalism and the privatization of the health services in Israel, see Doron, 1995, pp. 179–202; Filk, 1995, pp. 3–15); media and telecommunication services, and state owned banks (the largest Israeli bank, Bank Ha'Poalim, was privatized in August 1997); the gradual deregulation of the land market; the complete deregulation of the foreign currency market; and the emergence of private medical services and private higher education institutions. In addition, the local market has been opened to multinationals and imported goods; consumption patterns have become "Americanized"; and a "stock exchange culture" has arisen. In short, individualism, consumerism, and the market values of competition and efficiency have gained the status of cultural totems. These transitions have been accompanied by changes in the traditional power bases of the Labor Movement and by a reorganization of the Histadrut. (On the changes in the traditional power bases of the Labor Movement and the decline of the Histadrut, see Grinberg, 1996; Peled and Shafir, 1996) Patterns of political competition and political marketing have changed as well, mainly due to the amendment of Basic Law: The Government in 1992 allowing for the establishment of a new electoral system in Israel. (Basic Law: the Government (S.H. 1396, p. 214, 1992; Brichta, 1998; Hazan, 1996)

Israel's legal culture has also witnessed an "Americanization" characterized, *inter alia*, by a rise of a "culture of rights[7] and voluminous civil litigation,[8] by a dramatic increase in the number of lawyers and in the caseload of the Supreme Court,[9] and by a revival of the debate over the legitimacy of judicial review. For recent accounts of the implications of the constitutional revolution on the unique form of judicial review in Israel, see Hofnung, 1996a, 1997; Segal, 1997; Clein, 1997. [10]As Alexis de Tocqueville observed with regard to the United States, there is hardly a public-policy question in present-day Israel that does not sooner or later turn into a judicial one.

In the labor and welfare spheres, the shift toward a neo-liberal position is also evident. A new poorly-paid, largely unprotected labor force (which consists of an estimated army of more than 220,000 foreign workers, of whom only 85,000 have legal status) has been created;[11] human-power entrepreneurship and private employment services have increased; individual and special labor contracts have proliferated; collective bargaining agreements have become less common; and minimum-wage and other mandatory social security laws are no longer rigorously enforced.[12] Simultaneously, a so-called "structural unemployment" and a growing economic recession have been establishing themselves over recent years.[13] Israel's socio-economic inequality, as measured by the Gini Index (0.0 = perfect equality), worsened from 0.222 in 1982 to 0.328 in 1991, to 0.344 in 1994, and to 0.357 in 1996 making Israel one of the two most unequal societies among western democracies. The pattern of these phenomena exemplifies Israel's gradual transition toward a new social and economic order.

In sum, despite the long tradition of collectivism within Israeli political culture that provided a unique context for and consequently a unique form of neo-liberalism in Israel, the characteristics of the new order are moving toward what is called in the literature of political economy "the post-Fordist project" or "the Schumpeterian Workfare State." Schumpeterian Workfare State objectives can be summarized, in abstract terms, as the promotion of production, organization, and market innovation; the enhancement of the structural competitiveness of open economies mainly through supply-side intervention; and the subordination of social policy to the demands of labor market flexibility, structural competitiveness, and the removal of market rigidities. (Jessop, 1993; Kosonen, 1995) In the following section, I examine the legal status of collective labor rights under this new economic order.

The Devaluation of the Status of Collective Labor Rights

Historically, the values of (Jewish) collectivism and the redemption of land through labor ("Hebrew labor") were embedded in a unique form of Zionist socialism that was highly influential in Israeli politics from the foundation of the state.[14] Within this ideological context, the historical status of the Labor Movement, and the centrality of the Histadrut in the Israeli political arena, among other factors, led to extensive labor legislation in Israel during the 1960s and 1970s. During those decades, a semi-independent system of labor courts was established (1969); a system of collective labor relations came under legal regulation; some basic labor-related rights were awarded cogent legal status; and the enactment of other legal protections for organized labor was relatively widespread.[15] Nonetheless, during the last fifteen years, and as a result of domestic as well as international political and economic factors, this trend has gradually changed (often with the tacit assent of the Histadrut) toward what has been called a "more flexible" market economy, which emphasizes neo-liberal economic values and the removal of market rigidities. This transition has, in many cases, eroded the collective bargaining power of labor in Israel.[16]

Since the early 1980s, at least four basic legal mechanisms have contributed to the weakening of collective bargaining power of labor in Israel. The first mechanism is the erosion in the unique legal status of the Histadrut as the primary representative of workers in the collective bargaining arena. The second is the increasing application of contractual assumptions with regard to legal relations in the marketplace and in the workplace. The third mechanism is the relative rights doctrine and the balancing of contradictory rights that derive from this doctrine. The fourth is the devaluation of the legal protections to which strikers are entitled.

First, the erosion in the legal status of the Histadrut has contributed significantly to the weakening of collective bargaining power of labor in Israel. Until the late-1980s, the *de facto* legal status of the Histadrut as the primary representative of workers in the collective bargaining arena was unique. This can be seen, for example, in the fact that most labor statutes confer special authority on the employee organization that represents the greatest number of employees in the country, that is, the Histadrut. Moreover, the Collective Agreements Law (1957), enacted during the heyday of Mapai and the Histadrut, confers upon the representative employee organization the power to determine conditions of employment on all workers in a given workplace or profession. In most collective agreements this power has been exercised by the Histadrut. In addition, the Collective Agreements Law permits the Minister of Labor and Social Affairs to issue an extension order which will impose the provisions of a collective agreement upon workers and employers who would not be subject to the collective agreement without that order.[17] Even though the order is issued by the Minister of Labor, the initiative may come from the parties to the general collective agreement whose provisions are to be extended. Utilizing the combined legal mechanism of implied authority and extension orders, the Histadrut was able to generalize benefits reached by collective bargaining and to maintain its pervasive influence in the labor market.

In recent years, however, the sharp drop in the number of Histadrut members has weakened the Histadrut's hegemony in the collective bargaining arena by eroding its implied authority to determine conditions of employment on all workers in a given workplace or profession.[18] The simultaneous erosion of the legal status of collective bargaining in general, and the Histadrut in particular, have been intensified in recent years as a result of Israeli government policy. Its adoption of a new agenda of social and economic values, which is based upon a neo-liberal, anti-collectivist ideology, has resulted in, among other things, a significant drop in the frequency and scope of governmental use of extension orders. This dual process has led to the demise of the Histadrut's historical hegemony in the labor market, and to a severe erosion in the status of collective bargaining, thus encouraging the increasingly prevalent laissez-faire conception of labor relations in Israel.

Second, the new conception of labor relations in Israel presumes freedom of contract between employers and employees. A contract is usually characterized as the result of free and voluntary negotiation in which a binding legal relationship is created. In the labor relations sphere, it is increasingly assumed that working conditions are determined by way of such voluntary negotiations in the free market. Based on specific underlying assumptions (that is, the autonomy, rationality, and free will of unencumbered agents) agreements between employers and laborers are assumed to represent the common will of the negotiating parties. In Israel, as in other common law countries, courts are seen merely as arbitrators, and the ideal of freedom of contract generally takes precedence over court interventions. In the labor sphere, as in other social spheres, this contractual presumption often proves at best unrealistic, and at worst a tool of domination. When labor agreements are seen to represent a "common will" between parties, the a priori power relations between the two parties are often ignored.[19]

Third, the balancing of contradictory rights is an important mechanism in devaluing workers' bargaining power in Israel.[20] For example, the relative-rights doctrine gives equal weight to the workers' right to strike and the public's right to receive essential services. In this case, the key question is which services are to be defined as "essential services." Although courts tend to narrow the scope of rights to which workers are entitled, they tend to give a wide interpretation to the definition of essential services. Moreover, battles caused by the adversarial positioning of "contradictory" rights weaken workers' claims that their right to strike should be regarded as a fundamental right. Striking workers are pitted against an abstract notion of the supposedly universal "public." The definition of essential services that the "public" should receive is given a wide interpretation by courts. When the "public's" need for essential services is weighed against workers' fundamental rights, the former prevails over the latter. In more abstract terms, the legal recognition of rights as "contradictory," but nonetheless potentially "balanceable," implies that no right has a superior value which necessarily gives it priority over another right. When an equation between different rights is drawn, the decision about which right should prevail depends, at least to some extent, on the "holders" of that right. Thus, in the example discussed above, the equation gives a preliminary advantage to the public's· supposedly "universal" interest over workers' "particularistic" concerns. Rather than engendering discussions based strictly on rights, balancing blurs the focus of the decision-making process by including another variable—the identity of the holder of a particular right.

In a recent case, for example, the Jerusalem Regional Labor Court ruled that workers of the Ministry of Interior, who were participating in a legal strike during the period of bargaining for a new collective agreement, had to return to work because their right to strike must be balanced against the fundamental right of every person to freedom of movement, which had been guaranteed by the 1992 Basic Law: Human Dignity and Liberty. In other words, the public's right of free movement (that is, the right to have passports issued by the Ministry of Interior, and so forth) has constitutional priority over workers' right to participate in a legal strike. (State of Israel, Ministry of Interior—Histadrut Hakelalit, Jerusalem Regional Labor Court, given on May 25, 1992 (unpublished). The decision in this case followed the logic applied in H.C. 372/84 *Klopfer-Na've v. Israel Broadcasting Authority*, 38(3) *Piskey Din* (Supreme Court Decisions 1985) 233, in Hebrew.) By this logic any strike is a strike against the public good.

Fourth, the actual and practical right to strike—the primary right to which workers in democratic countries are entitled—has been weakened in Israel. (On the general erosion of the legal protection of the right to strike see Ben-Israel, 1994d) This erosion can be illustrated by focusing on a new mechanism regarding the liability of trade unions in torts. In the case of a lawful collective action, trade unions are generally exempted from liability for damages caused by the action. However, if the collective action is unlawful according to definitions of collective labor law, then trade unions or individual workers who have supported the strike can be held responsible for damages caused by the strike. In extreme cases they can be forced to pay for such damages. In recent years the boundaries of employee liability in torts have been significantly extended in many of the Western industrial countries that have undergone a "removal of market rigidities" process. In Israel, a similar process of narrowing strikers' immunities also has begun. (For a discussion of the erosion in the legal status of strikers in this regard, see Ben-Israel, 1994a; Raday, 1995)

Until recently, the Israeli legislature granted labor unions and individual workers full immunity for lawful strikes and lockouts, based on the pre-1980s assumption that a breach of contract is the only tort for which trade unions are liable.[21] Since the 1980s, however, claims for damages have been submitted to courts against strikers based on civil wrongs, such as misappropriation of personal property, negligence, or trespassing. A new and narrow interpretation of the freedom to strike has emerged, holding strikers liable in torts for damages that were caused to third parties by even lawful strikes. It was held in one case that striking is only a *relative* freedom that could be narrowed not only when public interests are threatened, but also when the right of third parties to reasonable economic expectations is threatened. (See Supreme Court Appeal 593/81 *Ashdod Vehicle Enterprises v. Tsizik*, 41(3) *Piskey Din* (Supreme Court Decisions 1984), 169, in Hebrew.) In more recent cases, strikers have been held responsible in tort cases, despite their legal immunity, for causing a breach of contract and breach of statutory duty between the employer and third parties.[22] In a landmark ruling in 1995, the Israeli Supreme Court further weakened the right to strike by declaring that the right to strike is not a constitutionally protected right, and by defining the right to freedom of association in a labor union as an individual, not a collective right, thus decreasing the collective bargaining power of labor in Israel. (H.C. 1074/93 *Attorney-General v. National Labor Court*, 49(2) *Piskey Din* (Supreme Court Decisions, 1995), 485, in Hebrew)

Interpretation of the New Basic Laws

The above-mentioned adjudications mark the turn of Israeli courts toward neo-liberal conceptions of the market and the workplace. The new Basic Laws further reinforce the neo-liberal position which informs the new Israeli economic order. Basic Law: Freedom of Occupation was enacted on March 3, 1992, and amended two years later, on March 9, 1994. It protects the right of every citizen or resident of the state to engage in any occupation, profession, or business. Given the ambiguity inherent in the law's wording, the range of rights it protects is potentially quite wide. Nonetheless, the new Basic Law has been selectively interpreted by the Israeli Supreme Court in a way that protects the autonomy of the economic sphere and the rights of employers but almost none of the rights of employees. This selective interpretation clearly reflects and promotes the emergence of individualism and free-enterprise as central to the new social and economic order in Israel.

One right, for example, that has gained a constitutional status under the judicial interpretation of the new law is the employers' right to hire and dismiss workers. While the interpretation establishes the constitutionality of this right, it does not allow that employees possess a constitutional right to be employed. Stated differently, freedom of occupation upholds employers' right to dismiss workers, but not employees' right to keep a job or to be employed. (Barak, 1994a; Eliasoff, 1994; Goldberg, 1994) In Chief Justice Barak's words: "Freedom of occupation is not the right to be employed, nor the right to work. Freedom of occupation is also not the right not to be dismissed from a job; tenure in a job does not derive from freedom of occupation but from freedom of contract. Freedom of occupation is the freedom to employ or not to employ." (Barak, 1994b, Part III, 597, author's translation) Following this logic, the National Labor Court recently ruled that the dismissal of four mechanics after a labor dispute did not violate their right to be employed. In addition, the Court decreed that the Basic Law: Freedom of Occupation cannot be interpreted to include the workers' right to be employed, though it includes employers' right to employ or dismiss workers.[23]

Other rights that could protect employees and job seekers are also ignored. For example, the Court's interpretation of the new Basic Law: Freedom of Occupation does not include a complementary constitutional obligation for employers (or the state) to create economic, geographic, or social conditions for full employment, or to provide access to employment opportunities. This lack of commitment to full employment, demonstrates that while freedom of occupation is guaranteed to employers, "market forces" are left to determine the fates of employees and job seekers.[24]

Furthermore, the law has not been interpreted by the Court to include mandates for state authorities or employers to provide professional training to job seekers, or to provide unemployment benefits if they fail to find an appropriate job. Such mechanisms do exist in Israel, but they have not been granted a constitutional status. Furthermore, judges have not interpreted freedom of occupation to include the right of employees to fair working conditions. The right to a guaranteed minimum wage, the right to work under minimally safe conditions, or the right to be informed about factors in the workplace that are potentially hazardous to workers' health, have all been interpreted to fall outside the boundaries of the new law.

Another right that the Israeli Supreme Court could have recognized as a complement to employers' freedom of occupation is the employees' right to be informed, if not consulted, by the employer before the employer makes decisions (that is, with regard to investments, expansion plans, or plant closing) that significantly affect workers. On the other hand, collective labor agreements often contain a no-strike or "peace" clause which stipulates that no strikes or lock-outs will take place for the duration of a collective agreement, thus protecting employers against workers' decisions that may significantly affect the employer. Furthermore, it is now the general opinion that even if a collective agreement does not explicitly contain such a clause, workers have a moral obligation to maintain "peace" in the workplace. Thus, strikes in contravention of collective agreements are in principle unlawful. The assumption that workers should uphold "peace" is in turn based upon the assumption of "good faith" (*bona fides*), a general principle of contract law. Nonetheless, other, much narrower assumptions are applied in the legal interpretation of the *bona fides* obligations of employers. Thus, a surrounding community, even one dominated by and dependent upon, a major enterprise cannot claim a legal interest to participate in or be protected from crucial capital investment decisions the company makes affecting that community. Recent cases in Israel indicate that this is not merely a theoretical problem but a real one that has allowed large companies to ignore major stake-holders.[25]

On the other hand, the Israeli Supreme Court has interpreted freedom of occupation as marking the boundaries between the autonomous economic sphere and the interventionist state. In one of the first cases that dealt with the new law, the Supreme Court ruled that the state's mandatory licensing and payment requirements for companies providing erotic telephone conversation services were unconstitutional, based both on the notion of freedom of occupation and on the proportionality requirement in Article 4 of the new law. (H.C. 987/94 *Euronet Gold Lines (1992) Ltd. et al. v. Ministry of Communication*, 48(5) *Piskey Din* (Supreme Court Decisions 1994), 412, in Hebrew) Based on the same anti-statist sentiment, the Supreme Court has recently nullified a section of a new Knesset law which regulated the licensing of investment consultants, based on their freedom of occupation.[26]

The "Meatrael affair" provides another illustration to the rise of an anti-statist sentiment in the judicial review discourse in Israel. (H.C. 3872/93 *Meatrael Ltd. v. Prime Minister and Minister of Religious Affairs*, 47(5) *Piskey Din* (Supreme Court Decisions 1993), 485, in Hebrew; H.C. 4676/94 *Meatrael Ltd. v. The Knesset*, 50(5) *Piskey Din* (Supreme Court Decisions 1996), 15, in Hebrew) In its first decision in the Meatrael affair in 1993, the Supreme Court declared the government's refusal to license the import of non-Kosher meat to Israel as unconstitutional since it stood in contradiction to the principles of the Basic Law: Freedom of Occupation, and thus infringed upon the right to engage in any legal economic initiative. Following this

decision, the Basic Law was amended by the Knesset in 1994 in the spirit of the famous Canadian "notwithstanding" override clause, (Section 33 of the Canadian
Charter of Rights and Freedoms, 1982) to allow for future modifications by ordinary laws in the instance of an absolute majority of Knesset members supporting
the amendment. Such an amendment, forbidding the import of non-Kosher meat,
was subsequently enacted. Based on the new "Meat Law," the government renewed
its refusal to license the import of non-Kosher meat. In reaction, the Meatrael company appealed again to the Court in 1996, arguing for its right to engage in any
legal economic initiative, and for the unconstitutionality of the new Meat Law. Following an immense political pressure on the Court not to allow further erosion of
Jewish values as Israel's most fundamental norms, the Court ruled this time against
the company, based on the reasonableness of the new Meat Law, given the conditions for modification mentioned in the amended Basic Law. The interesting point
in this chain of judicial events, however, is that the state had to initiate an amendment of Basic Law: Freedom of Occupation and to rely on Israel's core values as a
Jewish state in order to justify a partial regulation of the meat market.

The Israeli National Labor Court, once the bastion of unionized workers' rights
and a symbol of the strength of "Hebrew labor" and collectivism in Israel's Jewish
population, has adjusted rapidly to the decline in the political power of the Labor
Party and the Histadrut—which have together pulled the strings of the collective
bargaining system in Israel for four decades—and to the recent changes in the basic
structure of the Israeli economy with its demand for greater flexibility.[27] In several
recent cases, the National Labor Court has adopted an individualist perspective to
analyze traditional collective labor law situations, and in some of its decisions the
Court has presented a more neo-liberal position than the Supreme Court. For example, following the logic of the British verdict in the "Associated Newspapers"
case,[28] the National Labor Court recently held that individual workers have a constitutional right to establish new labor unions in enterprises in order to compete
with an already established representative labor union. Further, it ruled that a labor
union does not necessarily have to engage in collective bargaining in order to be recognized as a union.[29] As the discussion in the following pages illustrate, this pattern
of selective, neo-liberal judicial interpretation of Israel's new Basic Laws is not limited to the labor law arena.

Another new law, the Basic Law: Human Dignity and Liberty, enacted by the
Knesset on March 17, 1992, two weeks after the enacted Basic Law: Freedom of
Occupation, follows the same line of reasoning. The Basic Law: Human Dignity
and Liberty provides for personal freedom, human dignity, the right to freely enter
and leave the country, privacy and freedom of property. Other human rights are still
not explicitly anchored in legislation, but may conceivably be deduced as included
under the umbrella of "human dignity" defined by the new law. As the Supreme
Court's interpretation of Basic Law: Human Dignity and Liberty indicates, however, the neo-liberal line of interpretation is not exclusive to the realm of labor-related rights.

Chief Justice Barak of the Israeli Supreme Court has recently specified guidelines pursuant to which the new Basic Law: Human Dignity and Liberty should be interpreted. (Barak, 1994c) According to Barak, fundamental human dignity in Basic Law: Human Dignity and Liberty should be interpreted as including formal equality of opportunity, due process of law, freedom to pursue one's own life plan, the right to own property, freedom from state intrusion into one's physical and mental privacy, and the perception that each individual is a moral being. Under this definition, however, the protection of basic human dignity translates primarily into a legal right to noninterference—a negative right.[30] Barak explicitly noted that "[s]ocial human rights such as the right to education, to health care, and to social welfare are, of course, very important rights, but they are not, so it seems, part of 'human dignity.'" (Barak, 1994b, Part III, 419, in Hebrew, author's translation)

A distinction has been drawn by political theorists between "negative rights" and "positive rights." Rights are spoken of as "negative"—entailing noninterference with an activity—or "positive"—entailing the provision by some individual or institution of a valued trait. Whereas the former consist of fundamental freedoms like freedom of speech or freedom of association, the latter traditionally consist, *inter alia*, of social rights such as the universal right to services which meet basic human needs, that is, health care, basic housing, and education. The term "positive rights" is often used to describe these basic social rights, since they require the state not merely to refrain from acting, but to act positively to promote the well-being of its citizens. (On "third order rights," see T. H. Marshall's classic discussion, 1965) The right to be employed, to fair payment and working conditions, and to social security and welfare, also fall under this category of rights. Some conservatives and libertarians argue that positive or social rights are not really human rights at all, because they are not universal, paramount, or categorical; but social rights do now enjoy wide acceptance, as evidenced by the UN Covenant on Economic and Social Rights, the Conventions and Recommendations of the ILO, the European Social Charter of the Council of Europe, and the European Community's Charter of Fundamental Social Rights.

Although positive rights were widely recognized by international covenants and treaties, all attempts by various political activists in Israel to challenge the dominant anti-statist conception of human rights in court or parliament have failed. A proposal of a group of Knesset members to enact a third new Basic Law which would grant constitutional status to various social rights and guarantee minimal humane living conditions to every citizen or resident was defeated in 1992 by a rare coalition of religious and neo-liberal Knesset members. A narrow legal interpretation of the meaning of human dignity as defined by the already existing Basic Law has also contributed to the institutional disregard for positive rights in Israel. (On the different alternatives in interpreting Basic Law: Human Dignity and Liberty, see Karp, 1995, and the discussion in H.C. 454/94 *The Women's Lobby in Israel v. Government of Israel*, 48/5 *Piskey Din* (Supreme Court Decisions 1994) 501, in Hebrew.) For example, the Court has seldom dealt with a key positive right—right to education, and in the rare cases that it did, the Court consistently refused to grant it constitutional status. Recently, the Supreme Court explicitly declared that the rights to basic education and care (in this case, basic care for underdeveloped toddlers) have no constitutional status in Basic Law: Human Dignity and Liberty or in any other constitutional source in Israel. Thus, the Court held that the state is not constitutionally obliged to provide any sort of basic education, or even equality of opportunity in education, to its citizens. (H.C. 1554/95 *Gilat v. Minister of Education*, 50(3) *Piskey Din* (Supreme Court Decisions 1996), 2, in Hebrew) In the Court's words: "A constitutional right requires a constitutional source to that right. Basic Law: Human Dignity and Freedom does not anchor the right to education. The claim that human dignity includes the right to education presumes a wide model of the right to dignity which implies great difficulties. This wide model entitles the individual to a right vis-à-vis the government for better life. Therefore, the right to education cannot be deduced from the general right to human dignity." (H.C. 1554/95 *Gilat v. Minister of Education*, 50(3) *Piskey Din* (Supreme Court Decisions 1996), pp.25–26, in Hebrew. Author's translation) Moreover, despite the huge inequality and clear discrimination in education between Jews and ethnic minorities in Israel, the Court rejected claims of discrimination in governmental funding of educational programs raised by Arab-Israeli municipalities. (H.C. 3954/91 *Agbaria v. Minister of Education*, 45(5) *Piskey Din* (Supreme Court Decisions 1991), 472, in Hebrew)

In this context, it is important to note that Arab-Israeli citizens and Arab residents of the Occupied Territories have seldom been perceived by the Court as entitled to human dignity guarantees specified in Basic Law: Human Dignity and Liberty.[31] In a series of cases the Court has rejected claims raised by human rights organizations who argued that the use of systematic torture and inhumane treatment by the Israeli security services toward Arab-Israeli and Palestinian detainees, is unconstitutional and contradicts the provisions of Basic Law: Human Dignity and Liberty.[32] In December 1997, for example, the Court upheld the constitutionality of administrative detention and interrogation of twenty Lebanese detainees held in Israel since the mid-1980s without trial. The Court rejected the claim that such an administrative detention violates the provisions of Basic Law: Human Dignity and Freedom. (The Court's decision was released only on March 1, 1998 *(Ha'aretz,* March 2, 1998, p. A6). See also "Without Status or Protection: Lebanese Detainees in Israel," *Human Rights Watch/Middle East,* vol. 9, no. 11 (October 1997). The claims of Muslim political activists arguing their basic right not be deported from the Occupied Territories, (H.C. 5973/92 *Association of Civil Rights v. Minister of Defense*, 47(1) *Piskey Din* (Supreme Court Decisions 1993), 267, in Hebrew) or the claims of nomadic Bedouins arguing their right to basic housing have also failed.[33]

Although judges have excluded positive social rights and other fundamental human rights from the boundaries of Basic Law: Human Dignity and Liberty, the Court held that the law strengthens some individual property rights. In the spirit of Robert Nozick's anti-taxation argument in *Anarchy, State and Utopia,* judges and members of the Israeli legal academy have recently suggested that taxation in general, and the income tax in particular, contradict a person's or a corporation's basic freedom to own property. (Nozick, 1974) In other words, redistribution of wealth through taxation violates one's basic freedom and dignity. Following this interpretation it has been argued that the new Basic Law empowers courts to examine, and, if necessary, to abolish existing and new tax laws enacted by the Knesset. (Yoran, 1994) In a landmark decision in 1993 in the Mizrahi Bank affair which was described by scholars as the Israeli *Marbury v. Madison,* the Supreme Court ruled that based on Articles 3 and 8 of the Basic Law: Human Dignity and Liberty,[34] the right to private property has, in principle, constitutional priority over laws enacted by the Knesset.[35]

. This selective constitutionalization by way of legal interpretation has much in common with a neo-liberal, Nozickian conception of fundamental human rights. Although this conception is one logically legitimate position, it is hard to see why it should best represent "the enduring values of society," or "the historical spirit of the nation,"[36] or "a participation-oriented, representation-reinforcing approach to judicial review" (Ely, 1980)—as the institutional discourse of judicial review and proponents of constitutionalization of rights in Israel usually claim.

New Regulatory Legislation and "Egalitarian" Adjudication

The fact that neo-liberal values underlie both the new economic and legal order in Israel raises at least two important questions. First, if the prevailing ideological and economic momentum in Israel can indeed be characterized as neo-liberal, then how can we explain both the recent Supreme Court adjudication and the recent enactment of legislation which regulate, at least to some extent, the competition in the marketplace? The recent amendment of the Corporate Law and the Securities Law, a series of landmark Supreme Court rulings during the last decade that regulate the corporate and stock-exchange sphere (for detailed accounts of the recent regulatory developments in corporate law legislation and adjudication in Israel see Haviv-Segal, 1994, 1996; Gross, 1994), and the elevation of the *bona fides* requirement in contract law, the tort of negligence in tort law, and the reasonableness requirement in administrative law into quasi-constitutional standards ostensibly seem to contradict the neo-liberal stance. (For further discussion of these developments, see Mautner, 1993, 1994.

I would suggest, however, that the above mentioned legal developments that regulate, at least to some extent, the economic sphere, should be understood as establishing the basic legal nexus necessary for transition into a free-enterprise economy. As Max Weber has noted, the fundamental building-block of every successful capitalist market is a secure predictability interest. (Weber, 1978) Without this, investors lack the incentive to invest. Scholars have shown how entrenched legal rights that enhance investors' trust have led to economic growth in various historical contexts. Douglas North and Barry Weingast, for example, illustrate that the legal security of expectations allowed rulers in early-capitalist Europe to borrow capital from lenders who were protected by law from the seizure of their capital. (North and Weingast, 1989. For further discussion of the relations between secure legal rights and economic growth, see Weingast, 1993; Olson, 1993; Barzel, 1992; Milgrom, North & Weingast, 1990; Kreps, 1990) A parallel conclusion regarding the enactment of laws and the accumulation of recent Supreme Court adjudication regulating the Israeli market is that a "wild" or completely unregulated market defeats its own long-term interests.[37]

The second, and perhaps more complex question is how to explain the "egalitarian" adjudication of the Supreme Court in several recent civil-liberty cases.[38] Some scholars and political activists view recent decisions which safeguard the individual from state intrusion into his or her physical and mental privacy (that is, a decision to strictly limit the use of secret listening by the police; or a decision that an individual's sexual preferences belong to the private sphere, and therefore should not be "invaded" by the public, the state, or by one's employer) as a major step forward in protecting civil liberties in Israel. Here too, however, such adjudications should be understood as an effort made by the judiciary to protect the private sphere from a malevolent interventionist state. The principle of nonintervention is now being applied both to the free market and to the family unit, since both the market and the family are thought of as part of "private" civil society, as opposed to the "public" state. (See Olsen, 1983; Gavison, 1992. See also Horowitz, 1982.) As Frances Olsen has observed, "the classic laissez-faire arguments against state regulation of the free market find a striking parallel in the arguments against state interference with the private family." (Olsen, 1983) Thus, progressive adjudications with regard to sexual preferences are decided using the same logic that protects the autonomy of the economic sphere.

In the case of the interpretation of Basic Law: Freedom of Occupation, labor relations nest within a private sphere, ruled by contractual relations and property rights. The attempt to protect this private sphere has strengthened employers' autonomy. On the other hand, in the case of the interpretation of Basic Law: Human Dignity and Liberty, the same neo-liberal impulse to protect the private sphere has kept positive social and economic rights from earning constitutional status. The recent progressive Supreme Court adjudications protecting the human body, sexual preferences, and so forth, are thus part and parcel of the same neo-liberal impulse that relegates labor relations to the private sphere. Hence, the constitutional revolution, its current judicial interpretations, recent human rights adjudications, and the above-mentioned shift toward recommodification, are all symptomatic of the emerging neo-liberal ideology in present-day Israel.

Conclusion

Although the Israeli state's retreat from the economic sphere is not yet complete, Israel is rapidly moving away from the local version of Keynesianism toward a neo-liberal ideology. The emerging neo-liberal economic and legal order in Israel emphasizes the autonomy of the economic sphere from state intervention and calls for the state's withdrawal from the labor relations, collective social and welfare spheres, and other formerly decommodified spheres.

The fundamental legal changes in Israel since the mid-1980s reflect and promote this emerging individualist "free enterprise" worldview. The constitutional revolution of 1992 and its interpretation by the Israeli judiciary, and other recent legal changes which have significantly modified Israel's legal arena and culture, are all part and parcel of a fundamental change which is transforming Israel from a collectivist state with a mobilized (Jewish) society and centralized economy into a more individualistic society with a free market orientation and culture.

The great economic-juridical transformation in Israel is still in its generative stages. However, it provides an illustration of the reciprocal relations between law and society whereby legal changes reflect social structures and opinions prevalent in a society, and simultaneously induce social change. Israel's transition into possessing a less regulated economic sphere both shapes and is promoted by the comprehensive legal reform in Israel and the neo-liberal values that underlie it.

References

Ackerman, Bruce. 1981. "The Lost Opportunity?" *Tel-Aviv University Studies in Law* 10, pp. 53–69.

Aharoni, Yair. 1998. "The Changing Political Economy of Israel." *The Annals* 555, pp. 127–146.

Aleinikoff, Alexander. 1987. "Constitutional Law in the Age of Balancing." *Yale Law Journal* 96, pp. 943–1005.

Arian, Asher. 1989. *Politics in Israel.* Chatham, N.J.: Chatham House.

Barak, Aharon. 1993. "A Constitutional Revolution: Israel's Basic Laws." *Constitutional Forum* 4, pp. 83–84.

_____. 1994a. "Basic Law: Freedom of Occupation," *Mishpat U'mimshal* 2, pp. 195–217, in Hebrew.

_____. 1994b. *Legal Interpretation.* Jerusalem: Nevo, in Hebrew.

_____. 1994c. "Human Dignity as a Constitutional Right." *Ha'Praklit* 41, pp.271–290, in Hebrew.

_____. 1996. "The Israeli Constitution—Past, Present and Future," *Ha'Praklit* 43, pp. 5–24, in Hebrew.

_____. 1997. "The Constitutionalization of the Israeli Legal System as a Result of the Basic Laws and its Effect on Procedural and Substantive Criminal Law." *Israel Law Review* 31, pp. 3–21.

Barnett, Michael, ed. 1996. *Israel in Comparative Perspective: Challenging the Conventional Wisdom.* Albany: State University of New York Press.

Barzel, Yoram. 1992. "Confiscation by the Ruler: The Rise and Fall of Jewish Lending in the Middle Ages." *Journal of Law and Economics* 35, pp. 1–13.

Barzilai, Gad. 1997. "The Supreme Court in Israeli Legal Culture." *International Social Science Journal* 152, pp. 193–208.

Barzilai, Gad, Ephraim Yuchtman-Yaar, and Zeev Segal. 1994a. *The Israeli Supreme Court and the Israeli Public.* Tel-Aviv: Papyrus, in Hebrew.

_____. 1994b. "Supreme Court and Public Opinion: General Paradigms and the Israeli Case." *Law and Courts* 3, pp. 3–6.

Ben-Israel, Ruth. 1994a. "The Place and Function of Labor Courts in the Israeli Legal System." *Ha'Praklit* 40, pp. 431–442, in Hebrew.

_____. 1994b. "Israel." *International Encyclopedia for Labor Law and Industrial Relations.* Dventer-Boston: Kluwer Law and and Taxation Publishers, Vol. 7: pp. 1–184, 35–41.

_____. 1994c. "The impact of Basic Laws on Labor Law and Industrial Relations." In Ruth Ben-Israel, ed. *Labor Law Yearbook 1994.* Tel-Aviv: The Israel Association for Labor Law and Social Security, pp. 27–49.

_____. 1994d. "Introduction to Strikes and Lock-outs: a Comparative Perspective." *Bulletin of Comparative Labor Relations* 29, pp. 1–29.

_____. 1996. "Development of Labor Law 1994–1996." In Ariel Rozen-Zvi, ed. *Yearbook of Israeli Law 1996–97.* Tel-Aviv: Papyrus, pp. 543–576, in Hebrew.

Bickel, Alexander. 1962. *The Least Dangerous Branch: The Supreme Court at the Bar of Politics.* Indianapolis: Bobbs-Merril.

Brichta, Avraham. 1998. "The New Premier-Parliamentary System in Israel." *The Annals* 555, pp. 180–192.

Chermesh, Ran. 1995. "The Role of Labour Courts in Strengthening Labor as a Social Status." *Labor Law Yearbook 1995.* Tel-Aviv: Israel Association of Labor Law and Social Security, Vol.5, pp. 89–109, in Hebrew.

Chernihovsky, Dov. 1993. "Health System Reforms in Industrialized Democracies: An Emerging Paradigm." *Social Security* 39, pp. 5–38, in Hebrew.

Clein, Clode. 1997. "After the Bank Ha'Mizrahi Case—the Constituent Power as Seen by the Supreme Court." *Mishpatim* 28, pp. 341–358, in Hebrew.

Dagan, H. 1996. "Interpretation of Property Law, Condominiums, and Collective Action Problems." *Tel-Aviv Univesity Law Review* 20, pp. 45–92, in Hebrew.

Doron, Abraham. 1995. "Health Services in Israel: A View to the 1990s." In Abraham Doron, *In Defense of Universality.* Jerusalem: The Magnes Press, pp. 179–202, in Hebrew.

Doron, Abraham and Henry Karger. 1993. "The Privatization of Social Services in Israel and its Effects on Israeli Society." *Scandinavian Journal of Social Welfare* 2, pp. 88–95.

Dotan, Yoav. 1997. "The Constitutional Status of the Right to Private Property." *Mishpatim* 28, pp. 535–579, in Hebrew.

Edelman, Martin. 1994. "The Judicalization of Politics in Israel." *International Political Science Review* 15, pp. 177–186.

Elazar, Daniel. 1990. *Constitutionalism: The Israeli and American Experiences.* New York: University Press of America.

Eliasoff, Itzhak. 1994. "Basic Law: Freedom of Occupation." *Mishpat U'Mimshal* 2, pp. 173–193, in Hebrew.

Ely, J. H. 1980. *Democracy and Distrust: A Theory of Judicial Review.* Cambridge, MA: Harvard University Press.

Filk, Danny. 1995. "Health Goes to the Market: Public Health Between the State, Civil Society, and the Market." *Theory and Criticism* 6, pp. 3–15, in Hebrew.

Gal, Johnny. 1994. "Privatization of Services in the Welfare State: The Israeli Case." *Society and Welfare* 15, pp. 7–24, in Hebrew.

Gavison, Ruth. 1985. "The Controversy Over Israel's Bill of Rights." *Israel Yearbook of Human Rights* 15, pp. 113–150.

_____. 1992. "Feminism and the Public-Private Distinction." *Stanford Law Review* 45, pp. 1–45.

_____. 1997. "The Constitutional Revolution: a Reality or a Self-Fulfilling Prophecy?" *Mishpatim* 28, pp. 21–148, in Hebrew.

Glendon, Mary Ann. 1991. *Rights Talk: The Impoverishment of Political Discourse.* New York: Free Press.

Goldberg, Giyora. 1993. "You Don't Need a Constitution to Plant Trees: On State-Building and Constitution-Framing." *State Government and International Relations* 38, pp. 991–1056, in Hebrew.

Goldberg, Menachem. 1994. "Freedom of Occupation: From Fundamental Right to Basic Law." *Ha'Praklit* 41. pp. 291–345, in Hebrew.

Grinberg, Lev Louis. 1991. *Split Corporatism in Israel.* Albany, N.Y.: State University of New York Press.

_____. 1993. *The Histadrut Above All.* Jerusalem: Nevo, in Hebrew.

_____. 1996. "Weak Workers, Strong Workers: Development in the Israeli Political Economy 1967–1994." *Theory and Criticism* 9, pp. 61–80, in Hebrew.

Gross, Emanuel. 1996. "The New Constitutional Rights of the Defendant in Israel." *Bar-Ilan Law Studies* 13, pp. 155–182, in Hebrew.

Gross, Joseph. 1994. "Toward a Revolution in Corporate Law." *Ha'aretz.* October 21, in Hebrew.

Gutmann, Emanuel. 1988. "Israel: Democracy Without Constitution." In V. Bogdanor, ed. *Constitutions in Democratic Politics.* Brookfield, Vt.: Gower, pp. 290–308.

Haviv-Segal, Irit. 1994. "Corporate Law." In Ariel Rosen-Zvi, ed. *Yearbook of Israeli Law 1994.* Tel-Aviv: The Israel Bar Press, pp. 77–110, in Hebrew.

Haviv-Segal, Irit. 1996. "Corporate Law and the Constitutional Umbrella of the New Basic Laws." In Ariel Rosen-Zvi, ed. *Yearbook of Israeli Law 1996–97.* Tel-Aviv: Papyrus, pp. 105–165, in Hebrew.

Hazan, Reuven. 1996. "Presidential Parliamentarism: Direct Popular Election of the Prime Minister, Israel's New Electoral and Political System." *Electoral Studies* 15. pp. 21–37.

Hofnung, Menachem. 1996a. "The Unintended Consequences of Unplanned Constitutional Reform: Constitutional Politics in Israel." *American Journal of Comparative Law* 44, pp. 585–604.

_____. 1996b. *Democracy, Law and National Security in Israel.* Brookfield, Vt.: Dartmouth.

_____. 1997. "Authority, Influence and Separation of Powers—Judicial Review in Israel in Comparative Perspective." *Mishpatim* 28, pp. 211–238, in Hebrew.

Horowitz, Morton. 1982. "The History of the Public/Private Distinction." *University of Pennsylvania Law Review* 130, pp. 1423–1428.

Jacobson, Gary. 1993. *Apple of Gold: Constitutionalism in Israel and the United States.* Princeton: Princeton University Press.

Jessop, Bob. 1993. "Towards a Schumpeterian Workfare State? Preliminary Remarks on Post-Fordist Political Economy." *Studies in Political Economy* 40, pp. 7–39.

Karp, Judith. 1995. "Questions on Human Dignity according to the Basic Law: Human Dignity and Freedom." *Mishpatim* 25, pp. 129–159, in Hebrew.

Kimmerling, Baruch. 1985. "Between the Primordial and the Civil Definitions of the Collective Identities." In Eric Cohen, ed. *Comparative Social Dynamics.* Boulder: Westview.

_____. 1989. "Boundaries and Frontiers of the Israeli Control System." In Baruch Kimmerling, ed. *The Israeli State and Society.* Albany: State University of New York Press.

Klein, Clode. 1987. *Israel as a Nation-State and the Problem of Arab Minority: In Search of a Status.* Tel-Aviv: International Center for Peace in the Middle East.

Kosonen, Pekka. 1995. "European Welfare State Models: Converging Trends." *International Journal of Sociology* 25, pp. 81–110.

Kreps, D. 1990. "Corporate Culture and Economic Theory." In J. Alt and K. Shepsle, eds. *Perspectives on Positive Political Theory.* New York: Cambridge University Press.

Kretzmer, David. 1990. *The Legal Status of the Arabs in Israel.* Boulder: Westview.

_____. 1992a. "The New Basic Laws on Human Rights: A Revolution in Israeli Constitutional Law?" *Israel Law Review* 26, pp. 238–246.

_____. 1992b. "Political Agreements—A Critical Introduction." *Israel Law Review* 26, pp. 407–437.

Lahav, Pnina. 1993. "Rights and Democracy: The Court's Performance." In Ehud Sprinzak and Larry Diamond, eds. *Israeli Democracy Under Stress.* Boulder: Lynne Rienner Publishers.

Maoz, Asher. 1996. "Constitutional Law: The Constitutional Revolution." In Ariel Rozen-Zvi, ed. *Yearbook of Israeli Law 1996–97.* Tel Aviv: Papyrus, in Hebrew.

Marmor, Andre. 1997. "Judicial Review in Israel." *Mishpat U'Mimshal* 4, pp. 133–160, in Hebrew.

Marshall, T.H. 1965. *Class, Citizenship, and Social Development.* Garden City, N.Y.: Anchor Books.

Mautner, Menachem. 1993. *The Decline of Formalism and the Rise of Values in Israeli Law.* Tel-Aviv: Ma'agalay Da'at, in Hebrew.

_____. 1994. "The Reasonableness of Politics." *Theory and Criticism* 5, pp. 25–53, in Hebrew.

Milgrom, Paul, Douglas North and Barry Weingast. 1990. "The Role of Institutions in the Revival of Trade." *Economics and Politics* 2, pp. 1–25.

North, Douglas and Barry Weingast. 1989. "Constitutions and Commitment: The Evolution of Institutions Governing Public Choice in Seventeenth-Century England." *The Journal of Economic History* 49, pp. 803–833.

Nottage L. and C. Wollschlager. 1996. "What Do Courts Do?" *New Zealand Law Journal.* pp. 369–372.

Nozick, Robert. 1974. *Anarchy, State and Utopia.* New York: Basic Books.

Offe, Claus. 1984. *Contradictions of the Welfare State.* London: Hutchinson.

Olsen, Frances E. 1983. "The Family and the Market: A Study of Ideology and Legal Reform." *Harvard Law Review* 96, pp. 1497–1579.

Olson, Mancur. 1993. "Dictatorship, Democracy, and Development." *American Political Science Review* 87, pp. 567–576.

Peled, Yoav. 1992. "Ethnic Democracy and the Legal Construction of Citizenship: Arab Citizens of the Jewish State." *American Political Science Review* 86, pp. 432–444.

Peled, Yoav and Gershon Shafir. 1996. "The Roots of Peacemaking: The Dynamics of Citizenship in Israel, 1948–1993." *International Journal of Middle Eastern Studies* 28, pp. 391–413.

Peleg, Dov. 1994. "Compulsory Insurance Law for Health." *Social Security* 40, pp. 119–129, in Hebrew.

Peleg, Ilan. 1995. *Human Rights in the West Bank and Gaza: Legacy and Politics.* Syracuse: Syracuse University Press.

Plessner, Yakir. 1994. *The Political Economy of Israel: From Ideology to Stagnation*. Albany: State University of New York Press.

Posner, A. 1997. "The Gal Law as a Parable—The Protection of Property Rights." *Mishpatim* 28, pp. 581–619, in Hebrew.

Raday, Frances. 1987. "Pragmatism versus Principles." In *Bar-Niv Book—Collection of Essays on Labor Law*. Tel-Aviv: Ramot, pp. 110–130, in Hebrew.

Raday, Frances. 1994a. "The Constitutionalization of Labor Law in Israel." In Ruth Ben-Israel, ed. *Labor Law Yearbook 1994*. Tel-Aviv: The Israel Association for Labor Law and Social Security, pp.153–176, in Hebrew.

Raday, Frances. 1994b. "Privatization of Human Rights and the Malevolent Use of Power." *Mishpatim* 23, pp. 21–53, in Hebrew.

_____. 1995. "Freedom of Strike, Third Parties' Suits, and Obligatory Arbitration." *Labor Law Yearbook*. Tel-Aviv: Israel Association of Labor Law and Social Security, Vol. 5, pp.143–152, in Hebrew.

_____. 1996. "An Anatomy of Unionism." *Mishpatim* 26, pp. 585–614, in Hebrew.

Rubinstein, Amnon. 1996. *The Constitutional Law of Israel*. Tel-Aviv: Shoken, in Hebrew.

Scheingold, Stuart. 1974. *The Politics of Rights*. New Haven: Yale University Press.

Schreiber, Herbert. 1993. "The Development of Judicial Sanctions Against Strikers in Israel: The Labour Court's General Theory (1970–1985)." In Roger Blanpain and Manfred Weiss, eds. *The Changing Face of Labour Law and Industrial Relations*. Baden-Baden: Nomos Verlagsgesellschaft.

Segal, Ze'ev. 1997. "Judicial Review of Statutes—Who has the Authority to Declare a Law Unconstitutional?" *Mishpatim* 28, pp. 239–256, in Hebrew.

Shafir, Gershon. 1989. *Land, Labor and the Origins of the Israeli-Palestinian Conflict 1882–1914*. Cambridge: Cambridge University Press.

_____. 1996. "Zionism and Colonialism: A Comparative Approach." In Michael Barnett, ed. *Israel in Comparative Perspective: Challenging the Conventional Wisdom*. Albany: State University of New York Press.

Shalev, Michael. 1989. "Jewish Organized Labor and the Palestinians: A Study of State/Society Relations in Israel." In Baruch Kimmerling, ed. *The Israeli State: Boundaries and Frontiers*. Albany: State University of New York Press.

_____. 1992. *Labor and the Political Economy in Israel*. Oxford: Oxford University Press.

Shamir, Ronen. 1990. "Landmark Cases and the Reproduction of Legitimacy: The Case of Israel's High Court of Justice." *Law and Society Review* 24, pp. 781–804.

_____. 1996. "Suspended in Space: Bedouins Under the Law of Israel." *Law and Society Review* 30, pp. 231–257.

Shapiro, Yonathan. 1977. *Democracy in Israel*. Ramat Gan: Masada, in Hebrew.

_____. 1993. "The Historical Origins of Israeli Democracy." In Ehud Sprinzak and Larry Diamond, eds. *Israeli Democracy Under Stress*. Boulder: Lynne Rienner Publishers, pp. 65–80.

Sharkansky, Ira. 1987. *The Political Economy of Israel*. New Brunswick, N.J.: Transaction Books.

Sheleff, Leon. 1996. *The Rule of Law and the Nature of Politics*. Tel-Aviv: Papyrus, in Hebrew.

Shimshoni, Daniel. 1982. *Israeli Democracy: The Middle of the Journey*. New York: Free Press.

Strum, Philippa. 1995. "The Road not Taken: Constitutional Non-Decision Making in 1948–1950 and its Impact on Civil Liberties in the Israeli Political Culture." In Ilan Troen and Noah Lucas, eds. *Israel: The First Decade of Independence*. Albany: *State University of New York Press*.

Vogel, David. 1978. "Why Businessmen Distrust Their State?" *British Journal of Political Science* 8, pp. 45–78.

Weber, Max. 1978. *Economy and Society: An Outline of Interpretive Sociology*. Berkeley: University of California Press.

Weingast, Barry. 1993. "Constitutions as Governance Structures: The Political Foundations of Secure Markets." *Journal of Institutional and Theoretical Economics* 149, pp. 286–311.

Yoran, Aharon. 1994. "The Constitutional Revolution in Taxation in Israel." *Mishpatim* 23, pp. 55–68, in Hebrew.

_____. 1997. "The Constitutional Protection to Property and Judicial Review of Fiscal Legislation." *Mishpatim* 28, pp. 443–459, in Hebrew.

Zalmanovitch, Yair. 1997. "Some Antecedents to Healthcare Reforms: Israel and the United States." *Policy and Politics* 25, pp. 251–268.

Zamir, Yitzhak. 1992. "Political Contracts." *Israel Law Review* 26, pp. 461–498.

Notes

1. In the years before 1992, the Knesset passed nine basic laws, primarily covering the powers invested in the various branches of government. None of these laws, however, provided any sort of constitutional protection for human rights or civil liberties.

2. The conception of Israel as a Jewish state defies, *prima facie*, a meaningful protection of minority rights (e.g., Arab-Israelis) by a constitutional bill of rights.

3. The dominant members of this group were law professor A. Rubinstein, A. Poraz, U. Linn, S. Aloni, and law professor D. Libai, and then the Minister of Justice D. Meridor, all of whom have high legal education. The dominant figures in Israel's legal academy took a strong positive position in the debate over the enactment of the new laws and supported the political attempt to finally enact major civil liberty legislation in Israel.

4. Basic Law: Freedom of Occupation (S.H. 1994, No. 1454, p. 90) repeals and replaces the former Basic Law on Freedom of Occupation enacted in 1992 (S.H. 1992, No. 1387, p. 114). Basic Law: Human Dignity and Liberty (S.H. 1992, No. 1391, p. 150). The full text of this law is reprinted in *Israel Law Review* 31, pp.21–25 (1997).

5. The first significant economic measure taken by the new Netanyahu government was a deep and immediate cut of more than 3 percent in the national budget, including the abolition of various welfare benefits to the poor and the elderly, and a decrease in government subsidies for public health and public transportation. A second deep cut of about 2.5 percent in the national budget was approved by the Netanyahu government in September 1997.

6. According to Offe, 1984, advanced capitalist states "have the responsibility of compensating for the processes of socialization triggered by capital in such a way that neither a self-obstruction of market-regulated accumulation nor an abolition of the relationships of private appropriation of socialized production results" (p. 49). In order to achieve this balance, mechanisms of decommodification have been developed in capitalist states. Decommodification is a state-controlled process of excluding specific services from the market, and of assigning these services "use" values instead of market values. According to Offe,

due to inherent contradictions embedded in the welfare state, the recommodification of "decommodified" basic welfare services is inevitable.

7. Although the judicalization of everyday life in Israel has not yet reached the U.S. level, the recent constitutional entrenchment of some basic human rights in Israel established the genesis of what Stuart Scheingold has called "the myth of rights," or what Mary Ann Glendon has called "rights-talk." See Scheingold, 1974; Glendon, 1991.

8. Recent studies show that Israeli society has in fact become the most litigious society in the west with over 100 new civil complaints per 1000 residents per year (Nottage and Wollschlager, 1996)

9. The Israeli Supreme Court is the highest judicial authority in Israel. It has jurisdiction as appellate court over appeals from the District Courts in all matters, both civil and criminal (sitting as a Court of Civil Appeal or as a Court of Criminal Appeal). In addition, it is a Court of First Instance on which there is no appeal (sitting as a High Court of Justice) in actions against governmental authorities, and in matters in which it considers it necessary to grant relief in the interests of justice and which are not within the jurisdiction of any other court or tribunal. In its capacity as High Court of Justice, the Supreme Court holds exclusive power to review the legality of and redress grievances against acts of administrative authorities of all kinds and religious tribunals. In the last decade, the Israeli Supreme Court, has become one of the busiest courts in the world. According to the Israel Statistical Abstract 1996 (No. 47, p.462), the Court heard a total of 4741 cases in 1988, 6007 cases in 1991, 6965 in 1994, and 10529 cases in 1996 (an increase of more than 120 percent in the total number of cases brought before the Court from 1988).

10. See also C.A. 6821/93 *United Mizrahi Bank v. Migdal Cooperative Village,* 49(4) *Piskey Din* (Supreme Court Decisions 1995) 195, in Hebrew), and by an extensive judicalization of politics. (Barzilai, 1997; Rubinstein, 1996, ch. 16; Edelman, 1994; Kretzmer, 1992b; Zamir,1992. See also H.C. 3434/96 *Hofnung et al v. Speaker of the Knesset,* 50(3) *Piskey Din* (Supreme Court Decisions 1996) 58, in Hebrew; H.C. 5364/94 *Velner et al v. Rabin et al,* 49(1) *Piskey Din* (Supreme Court Decisions 1995) 758, in Hebrew; H.C. 6163/92 *Eisenberg v. Minister of Housing,* 47(2) *Piskey Din* (Supreme Court Decisions 1993) 299, in Hebrew; H.C. 3094/93 *Movement for Government Quality v. Prime Minister,* 47(5) *Piskey Din* (Supreme Court Decisions 1993) 404, in Hebrew; H.C. 4267/93 *Amitai v. Prime Minister* 47(5) *Piskey Din* (Supreme Court Decisions 1993) 441, in Hebrew.

11. For up-to-date figures and discussion of the "foreign workers" phenomenon in Israel see the 46th Annual Report of the State's Comptroller (Government Printer: Jerusalem, 1996), pp.475–496, in Hebrew. Note that the number of foreign workers now employed in Israel exceeds (by more than 100,000) the estimated number of Palestinians who worked in Israel before the Intifada.

12. Social security laws have never been rigorously enforced with regard to Palestinian workers in the Israeli market. However, the general "by-pass" of mandatory social security laws has become widespread in recent years. For a thorough discussion of the gradual erosion of the social-democratic values of Israeli welfare policy, see Doron & Karger, 1993; Gal, 1994.

13. In June 1998, the unemployment rate was more than 9.3 percent, and in some peripheral development towns it reached 16 percent and more. During the January–December 1997 period alone, the number of unemployed has risen sharply from 119,000 to 157,000, an increase of 30 percent. In June 1998, the number of unemployed reached 210,700.

14. Shapiro, 1977, 1993. Note that the "collectivist spirit" has never been shared with non-Jewish unorganized workers. Since 1967 a dual labor market has emerged in Israel in which applicable labor laws and other legal protections (national insurance, health insurance, and so forth) have never been seriously enforced by state authorities and the Histadrut with regard to the rights of Palestinian workers from the occupied territories who work as day laborers.

15. For a detailed survey of the development of labor law in Israel up until the early 1980s, see Raday, 1987. See also Ben-Israel, 1994b. For a recent call to expand the scope and content of issues adjudicated by labor courts, see Chermesh, 1995.

16. For a review of the status of Israeli strike law before the establishment of the labor court and the deteriorating labor relations scene in the 1970s and the early 1980s, see Schreiber, 1993.

17. The extension order was officially meant to be a tool available for the government to intervene in the labor relations sphere, and to enable non-unionized workers to enjoy the fruits of collective bargaining. In practice, however, the close cooperation between the relevant Mapai ministers and the Histadrut enabled both parties to use the extension order mechanism in order to maintain their control of the labor market.

18. According to the 1997 Annual Report of the UN International Labor Organization, the number of Histadrut members dropped by 75.7 percent from 1985 to 1995—the sharpest drop in labor union membership in the world over this period.

19. In practice, even in those rare cases where the Court has been willing to intervene in contractual relations between an employee and employer, as for example, in a contract which banned an employee from working in her field of expertise for five years after leaving an employer's plant, the court justified its intervention on the basis of the "freedom of occupation" principle, rather than on an examination of the inequalities existing between the parties to the contract. See, for example, Haifa District Court 1605/90 *Kibbutz Gan Shemuel v. Orna Golan*, 51(1) *Psakim Mekhoziyim* (District Courts Decisions 1992) 45, in Hebrew.

20. On balancing as a method of constitutional interpretation see Aleinikoff, 1987.

21. This immunity for strikers was established by the Knesset in 1965, following Supreme Court Appeal 167/62 *Leo Beck High School v. The Organization of High School Teachers*, 16 *Piskey Din* (Supreme Court Decisions 1963), 2205, in Hebrew. The immunity of strikers in torts is protected under the Israeli law of torts (article 62b).

22. See, for example, Tel-Aviv District Court 2233/89 Barclays Discount Bank Ltd. v. Discount Bank Employees Union (Unpublished, 1989), in Hebrew; Haifa District Court 1380/93 National Coal Company Ltd. v. Markowitz (Unpublished, 1994), in Hebrew. Although this notion may be logical in other spheres, it is not logical in the context of labor disputes. In most industrial actions, the predominant intention is to further workers' interests, but this can never be achieved without intentionally damaging employers' interests, including their relations with third parties.

23. National Labor Court 45/3–264 Keisy—Ormoza Garage Ltd. (unpublished). The decision was based also on the employers' property rights as anchored in Basic Law: Human Dignity and Liberty. A prior verdict of the Supreme Court, in the first case to deal with Basic Law: Freedom of Occupation, emphasized that freedom of occupation is not an absolute right but a relative one. Thus, it was argued, freedom of occupation needs to be balanced against other basic interests, such as employers' property rights and their right to privacy. See H.C. 1683/93 Yavinplast v. National Labor Court, 47(4) *Piskey Din* (Supreme Court Deci-

sions 1993), 702, in Hebrew; C.A. 2600/90 *Elite Ltd. et al. v. Saranga et al.*, 49(5) *Piskey Din* (Supreme Court Decisions 1995), 796, in Hebrew.

24. This raises the problem of the "individualization" of human rights and the rejection of social-group or class-based claims for the application of human rights. See Raday, 1994b.

25. See, for example, the recent cases of Uman (textile industries) in the southern development town of Ofakim; several textile, engine assembly, and food processing factories in the northern development town of Beit She'an; the disputes in the 1980s over the shutdown of the Atta textile factory (in the small town of Kiryat-Atta); and the Kittan textile factory (in the development town of Dimona).

26. H.C. 1715/97 *Association of Investment Management in Israel v. Minister of Finance et al.*, decision given on September 25, 1997 (not yet published). An important issue in this regard is the freedom of a person to select a job and the legal status of various professional guilds in view of the new Basic Law. In a recent decision the Supreme Court abolished an official ethical rule of the Israeli Chambers of Advocates which limited the free competition among lawyers (H.C. 4330/93 *Gannem v. The Israeli Bar Association*, 50(4) *Piskey Din* (Supreme Court Decisions 1996), 221, in Hebrew. The constitutionality of regulation of specific occupations by professional guilds was challenged in a series of recent cases by job seekers and trainees who failed to meet the conditions for membership set by such guilds. See H.C. 3930/94 *Gezmawy et al. v. Ministry of Health*, 48(4) *Piskey Din* (Supreme Court Decisions 1994), 778, in Hebrew; H.C. 6290/93 *Zilka v. Ministry of Health*, 48(4) *Piskey Din* (Supreme Court Decisions 1994), 631, in Hebrew; H.C. 3081/95 *Romeo v. Israel's Medical Association*, 50(2) *Piskey Din* (Supreme Court Decisions 1996), 177, in Hebrew; H.C. 4360/94 *Tatur v. Ministry of Police*, 50(2) *Piskey Din* (Supreme Court Decisions 1996), 560, in Hebrew; H.C. 2594/96 *The College of Management v. The Israeli Bar Association*, 50(5) *Piskey Din* (Supreme Court Decisions 1996), 166, in Hebrew.

27. A legally-regulated system of collective bargaining under the control of a specialist labor court is often viewed by mainstream scholars of labor law as a guarantee against the erosion of legal protection of workers' rights. As the Israeli case reveals, however, this assertion is not always accurate. This is not to say, however, that both the de jure and de facto status of workers would have been better without the labor court apparatus.

28. *Associated Newspapers Ltd v. Wilson* and *Associated British Ports v. Palmer and Others* [1995] 2 W.L.R. 354. The House of Lords held that withholding a benefit from an employee who refuses to sign a "personal contract" in place of collectively agreed terms does not infringe the employee's trade union rights under TULRCA section 146(1).

29. National Labor Court 45/4-30 "Amit"—Maccabi Labor Union—Local Government Administration et al. The decision of the National Labor Court was reversed by the Supreme Court on February 27, 1997, following an appeal of the Histadrut. For an analysis of the National Labor Court's decision and its implications upon legal protection of unionism and collective bargaining, see Raday, 1996; Ben-Israel, 1996.

30. Given Barak's central position in shaping the constitutional revolution, it is reasonable to assume that his view will have a substantial impact. For a comprehensive discussion of the Israeli Supreme Court's status, as it has been conceived by the Israeli public, see Barzilai et al., 1994a. The main findings of the book were published by the same authors in Barzilai et al., 1994b.

31. On the Israeli Supreme Court's record in protecting rights of Arab-Israeli citizens and Arab residents of the Occupied Territories, see Sheleff, 1996, ch. 4; Peleg, 1995; Hofnung, 1996b; Shamir, 1990; Kretzmer, 1990.

32. It is interesting to note that the Supreme Court recently ruled (C.A. 1684/96 *"Tnua La'khayot Likhyot"* (Let the Animals Live) v. Hamat Gader Vacation Industries Ltd., decision given in February 1997, not yet published), that based on Basic Law: Human Dignity and Liberty, alligators in a zoo have the right to be kept and removed under "humane" conditions. No one doubts, of course, the great importance of this decision and its positive implications on the general attitude toward animals. It is somewhat odd, however, that alligators, with all due respect, enjoy the constitutional right to basic "humane" conditions while human beings are not constitutionally entitled to this basic right.

33. H.C. 2678/91 *Al Zana et al v. Israel Land Administration,* 46(3) *Piskey Din* (Supreme Court Decisions 1992), 709, in Hebrew. For a comprehensive survey and analysis of the Court's adjudication in cases involving Bedouin claimants, see Shamir, 1996.

34. Article 3 of the new Basic Law states: "A human being's property must not be harmed." Article 8 of the new law states: "Rights under this Basic Law must not be infringed, except by a Law appropriate to the values of the State of Israel which has a valid purpose, and then to an extent that does not exceed necessity."

35. C.A. 6821/93 *United Mizrahi Bank v. Migdal Cooperative Village,* 49(4) *Piskey Din* (Supreme Court Decisions 1995), 195, in Hebrew. See also Yoran, 1997 in Hebrew; Dotan, 1997 in Hebrew; Posner, 1996 in Hebrew; Dagan, 1997 in Hebrew; C.A. 5209/91 *State of Israel v. Ramid Ltd.,* 49(4), *Piskey Din* (Supreme Court Decisions 1995) 830, in Hebrew. Note, however, that in two recent decisions, the Supreme Court rejected claims of Arab residents in Eastern Jerusalem who argued that the seizure of their land by the Government in 1968 for "national security needs," violated their constitutional right to property protected by Article 4 of Basic Law: Human Dignity and Liberty (Further Hearing 4466/94 *Nusseiba et al. v. Minister of Finance et al.* 49(4) *Piskey Din* (Supreme Court Decisions 1995) 68, in Hebrew; H.C. 2739/95 Makhul v. Minister of Finance, 50(1) *Piskey Din* (Supreme Court Decisions 1996) 309, in Hebrew.

36. Bickel, 1962, p.26. Protecting "the enduring values of society" is Alexander Bickel's main justification for judicial review. In Bickel's words, "It is crucial to sort out the enduring values of a society, and it is not something that institutions can do well occasionally, while operating for the most part with a different set of gears. It calls for a habit of mind, and for undeviating institutional customs." Judicial review is thus justified by Bickel as "the principled process of enunciating and applying certain enduring values." (p. 55).

37. Of course, this reasoning raises the problem of short-term versus long-term interests of the capitalist market. See Vogel, 1978.

38. See, for example, H.C. 721/94 *El Al Airlines Ltd. v. Danilowitch et al.* 48(5) *Piskey Din* (Supreme Court Decisions 1994) 749, in Hebrew. It was held that the spouse of a homosexual steward at El Al Airlines was entitled to the same benefits that the spouse of a heterosexual steward would be entitled to. See, also, the decisions in C.M. 537/95 *Gnimmat v. State of Israel,* 48(3) *Piskey Din* (Supreme Court Decisions 1994) 355, in Hebrew, and C.A.H. 2316/95 *Gnimmat v. State of Israel,* 49(4) *Piskey Din* (Supreme Court Decisions 1995) 589, in Hebrew, that, based on suspects' right to human dignity, limited the potential use of detention, arrest, and search on private premises or body of a person by state authorities. In the same spirit, the Court protected the private sphere and put strict limitations on the use of secret listening by the police in C.A. 1302/92 *State of Israel v. Nahamias,* 49(3) *Piskey Din* (Supreme Court Decisions 1995), 309, in Hebrew. In another recent development (May 1997) in the same spirit and following the enactment of Basic Law: Human Dignity

and Liberty, a new law came into force that requires a common criminal defendant to be allowed to meet with a lawyer "without delay." According to this new law, a police officer may prevent a meeting for up to forty-eight hours, but may exercise this power only to save lives or to prevent the commission of time. On the impact of Basic Law: Human Dignity and Liberty on the protection of the human body by criminal due process rights in Israel, see Aharon Barak, 1997; Gross, 1996.

9

"The Promised Land of Business Opportunities:" Liberal Post-Zionism in the Glocal Age

URI RAM

On November 4, 1995, the prime minister of Israel, Yitzhak Rabin, was shot three times in the back. His assassination consummated two decades of growing malevolence between the two new political-cultural tendencies that had emerged in Israel since the 1970s: neo-Zionism and post-Zionism. Toward the century's end, Israel's founding Jewish-nationalist ethos, Zionism, is undergoing a crisis, and two emerging antagonistic foci of identity are struggling to reshape a new ethos for Israel: hyper-nationalist neo-Zionism and civic-liberal post-Zionism. Yitzhak Rabin, "Mr. Security" of Zionism, had fallen victim to a tag of war he facilitated setting in motion, but never really comprehended.

Neo-Zionism and post-Zionism are not majoritarian tendencies. Almost the entire population of Jewish descent in Israel still confesses allegiance to Zionism; yet between the 1970s and the 1990s the boundaries of Zionist discourse have been significantly transgressed from both right and left. "Neo-Zionism" and "post-Zionism" signify, respectively, the right-wing and left-wing transgressions of classical Zionism respectively. Arguably, while neither one is a majoritarian trend, both redefine the contours of Israeli collective identity.

In the present study, an analysis of the "new Israel" is offered along the lines sketched above. The first section discusses the process of globalization-localization, namely, glocalization, and its effects on the spheres of nationality, democracy and welfare. The second section turns the limelight on Israel, offering an initial explo-

217

ration of the effects of glocalization on Israeli society, and introducing the concept of post-Zionism. The following three sections deal with the new political economy of Israel: the emergence of post-industrial economic structure; the integration of Israel in the global market and the neo-liberal policy turnabout; and the evolvement of a new material culture of consumerism. The final three sections deal with the links between glocalization, the peace process and the class structure of Israel. The implications of the glocalization process on three classes are examined: the middle class, capital and labor. Finally, the study concludes with analyzing the major political implications of glocalization on Israel: the decline of statist nationalism, and with it of the welfare state, the globalization of Israeli capital, and, as an opposing trend, the "localization" of the Israeli lower classes, and their adherence to ethno-nationalism.

Globalization and the Nation-State: Glocalization

The current crisis and transformation of Israel may be thought of in terms of the glocal dialectics of the current postmodern era, when global and local trends, in their negating yet complementary reciprocation, erode the major institutional and cultural framework of the nation-state. Global forces— technological, financial, commercial— erode the nation state from above, while simultaneously local forces— ethnic, religious, regional communities—erode it from below. Today, it is no longer permissible to conflate the concept of "society" with that of the "nation-state." Not only are "state" and "nation" eroded, but also, and perhaps above all, the hyphen in-between them, which is supposed to validate their strong tie, is questionable. The unified and homogenized nation-state is thus today torn between the supra-national tendencies which merge it with the larger surrounding environment, and the infra-national tendencies, which fragment it into smaller internal parts. Although the end of the century witnesses vicious outbursts of ethno-nationalism, these may turn out to be , in historical perspective, the death throes of a phenomenon that has lost its historical impetus (which is no consolation, of course, to its current victims). (Hobsbawm, 1990)

Benjamin Barber has described the global and local tendencies as McWorld versus Jihad: "Jihad forges communities of blood rooted in exclusion and hatred" and "McWorld forges global markets rooted in consumption and profit." (Barber, 1995, pp.6–7) The two do not relate to each other in a zero sum game, but rather in a negating-complementary manner, where: "In history's twisting maze, Jihad not only revolts against but abets McWorld, while McWorld not only imperils but re-creates and reinforces Jihad. They produce their contraries and need one another." (Barber, 1995, p.5) What is common to both, according to Barber, is that they undermine the sovereign state and with it the democratic institutions attached to it: "Each eschews civil society and belittles democratic citizenship, neither seeks alternative democratic institutions. Their common threat is to civil liberty." (Barber, 1995, p. 6)

Undermining democracy is just one possible implication, though, of the glocal, Jihad–McWorld dialectics. In fact, glocalization is storming the globe, leaving behind a trail of mixed aftereffects. It is true that hitherto democratic rights and institutions, such as sovereignty, citizenship, representation, elections, political parties, trade unions, and so forth have developed only, or mostly, within the framework of the nation-state. In this sense, any weakening of this framework is tantamount to the weakening of democracy. Yet, nation-states have their oppressive facet, both as institutions and as identities, and in fact most of them are not even democratic. In this sense, then, the creation of a universal and cosmopolitan public sphere only enhances democracy world-wide. (Held, 1995) Yet, the current spread of democracy is confined—and even confining—to the sphere of politics, while social rights are neglected, or even impaired. (Robinson 1996b)

As for Jihad, this is a quintessentially oppressive tendency, which binds people to reified "communities," "identities" and "traditions," which are oppressive by definition. Yet, even in this case, from a post-colonial perspective, "other" identities (other then the dominant white, male, liberal, middle class) may contribute to democratic empowerment and mobilization, as they provide a "localist" voice for subjugated and subaltern groups, who are demolished by the forces of globalization, be it ethnic minorities or immigrant workers or others. (Ashcroft, 1995; Soysal, 1994)

One effect of globalization mentioned only briefly above must be re-emphasized. In addition to destabilizing national cultures, and changing democratic frameworks, globalization has far reaching socio-economic implications. In the developed industrial zones of the West, the period following World War II saw the consolidation of welfare state regimes as a standard neo-corporatist compromise between capital and labor, with the mediation of the state. The welfare state guaranteed full employment (or allowances for the temporarily unemployed), fair level of wages, a social security net, and industrial stability and economic growth. (Cawson, 1986) As is well known, the 1980s witnessed the crisis of welfare states and their undermining by neo-liberal regimes. (Offe, 1984; King, 1989; Pierson, 1991)

Globalization has augmented the recess of the welfare state. The foremost reason for this is the unification of world markets, so that capital can easily flee toward the sites of cheap labor and comfortable taxation, that is, southward and eastward, metaphorically and literally. This has amassed enormous pressure on states where there is a high "social cost" to labor. The defense comes in the form of neo-liberalism, that is, wage contraction, budget constriction, de-regulation and fiscal liberalization. Social structures of accumulation have transmuted from Fordism to post-Fordism (Harvey, 1989), and states have transmuted from the Keynesian welfarism to Schumpeterian workfarism. (Jessop, 1994; Waters, 1995, pp. 65–95) The bottom line is a radical change in class relations both inside states and in the world arena; workers are less organized, less mobilized and less protected, and social gaps are mounting. (Thomas, 1997)

All in all, the effects of globalization on politics, culture and society are mixed: while globalization widens the circle of civic participation, it simultaneously dismantles the scope of social responsibility. It generates the contradictory effects of universal commodification, on the one hand, and of xenophobic reaction, on the other. At the end of the twentieth century, democracy expands and retracts in the same gasp. Let me now turn to the case of Israel.

Globalization and the Nation-State:
Post-Zionism

The current crisis and transformation of Israeli society can be interpreted within the global-local, or "glocalization," perspective outlined above. In a very schematic way, one may divide the history of Israel into two periods: the *modernization* period, which reached completion by the 1970s, and the *globalization* period, since the 1970s. Each of the periods may be characterized by a distinct "pivot" of social relations and social change. The two poles of the pivot of modernization are the pre-modern (traditional-religious) and modern (colonial-national). The two poles of the pivot of globalization are the local (neo-national) and the global (post-national). Table 1 below depicts this schematization:

TABLE 9.1   **Modernization and Globalization Pivots in Israeli History**

The Modernization Pivot until the 1970s:

Traditional -Modern	
Religious	National
Communities	Colony
Diaspora	State

The Globalization Pivot; since the 1970s:

Local -Global	
Neo-National	Post-National
Jihad	McWorld
Jewish People	Israeli Citizenship

The complexity of the crisis in Israel can be deciphered when understood as resulting, first, from a transition from the pivot of modernization to the pivot of globalization, and, second, from the dialectical struggle between the two poles of the globalization pivot: the local and the global. David Gurevitz, a student of Israeli culture, has described this state of affairs as "schizophrenic": "Israeli culture of the 1990s is an awkward mix of an 'ideological society' on the one hand, and of a society starting to be ironic towards its own constituting myth, on the other hand. In one respect, this is still a tribal collective society, a society immersed in a conflict, and hence having low tolerance for heterogeneity. In another respect, this is a culture immersed in a cultural reality which J.P. Lyotard labels 'post-industrial,' 'information society,' which has reached a high level of knowledge. This schizophrenic position of Israeli culture generates an ambiguity towards the 'post-modern condition.'" (Gurevitz, 1997)

The case of Jewish-Israeli nationhood is one of a hundred years of a nationalist movement and a national ideology, and fifty years of an independent nation-state. Jewish-Israeli nationalism emerged in the context of East European nationalism, it materialized in a West European colonization context in the Middle East, and it continued in the framework of a modern independent state. Broadly speaking, in the past Israeli collective-identity emerged along the pivot of "modernization"— that is, it moved in the direction leading from pre-national local and religious communities to a secular nation-state, with all the tensions and conflicts involved (colonialism, etatism, capitalism and the rest.) This stage reached its peak around the 1970s. Since then new vectors had been added to the old scene of collective identities, which is engaged with the tensions and conflicts along the pivot of globalization. The new vectors are post-national civic liberalism, and neo-national ethno-religious fundamentalism.

In the balance of this study I will focus upon one facet of the "new(ly emerging) Israel," a sub-category of the post-Zionist tendency; namely, post-Zionist liberalism. Post-Zionism may be divided into two sub-categories: radical and liberal. *Radical post-Zionism* is associated with the new multi-vocality which emerges from "minority" voices, voices of groups marginalized or repressed by the Israeli national mainstream: women, Palestininan Arabs, mizrachi (Middle Eastern and North African) Jews, religious Jews, and more. (Pappe, 1997; Ram, 1998) *Liberal post-Zionism* is associated with the new integration of Israel in the global capitalist market, and it emerges out of the new life-styles and cultural preferences of the Israeli (Jewish) upper classes. It is this latter tendency on which the present study focuses. An examination of the economic basis, cultural implications and class effects of liberal post-Zionism follows.

Glocalization and Political-Economy: Toward a Post-Industrial Economy

The substructure on which post-Zionist liberalism emerges is the growth of the Israeli economy and its structural transformation. Between the 1970s and the 1990s Israel joined the category of the world industrialized developed societies. Gross domestic product per capi ta reached in the mid-1990s came close to $17,000. (BoI, 1998, Tab. A1) In terms of purchase power the GDP per capita in Israel equals 65 percent of that in the United States. (CBS, 1998a, pp. 11–12) Such indicators, in addition to their economic significance, play an important role in Israeli public consciousness, as testimony to the achievements of Israel as well as to its belonging to the club of the advanced western world.

The distribution in the 1990s of employment by economic sector in Israel is characteristic of post-industrial societies: 2.4 percent agriculture; 20.6 percent industry; 7.2 percent construction; and 69.7 percent services, of which 38.1 percent are in the private sector and 36.1 percent in the public sector. (CBS, 1998b, Tab.12.9)

The Israeli manufacturing core has been transformed from a labor-intensive industry in the 1950s, through a technology-intensive military industry in the 1970s, into a knowledge-intensive high-tech industry in the 1990s. Close to half the industrial product is directed to export. Commerce is done mostly with the developed societies of Western Europe and North America (80 percent of import and 74 percent of export (CBS, 1996a, pp. 222–225, Tab.8.5), mostly with European Union countries and the United States.

As said, the lead economic branches of the 1990s are the information-intensive high-tech industries. (BoI, 1995, pp. 113–115; BoI, 1998, pp. 165–172) In the mid-1970s the labor- and information-intensive industries were of equal proportion in export. By the mid-1990s the part of traditional branches in export had decreased to 10 percent, while that of the information-based industries has risen to almost two-thirds. (BoI, 1998, pp.170–172) Overall, the traditional branches of industry employ some 160,000 employees, and the advanced branches some 95,000, whereas 117,000 are employed in what is defined as mixed branches. (Dori, 1998, pp.12–13, Tab. A2)

Electronic and computer technologies are strong links of Israel to global networks, both as items of production and of consumption, and both as material and cultural artifacts. Stories of small "start-up" partnerships which are assembled by bright young men (always men so far) and are sold to giant American firms for hundreds of millions of dollars make frequent appearance in the headlines and have become the model of high success in Israel. The new year eve issue of the daily *Ha'aretz* inaugurated a series on "virtual Israel," in which high-tech industry was depicted not only as the leading export industry, but also as a "dreamland." (Green, 1998, September 20) Tel Aviv is recognized as one of the ten high-tech centers of the world. (*Newsweek*, 1998) As for users of high-tech networks, it is estimated that 360,000 Israelis are connected to the internet, and numbers rise in ten percents yearly. (Goldman, 1998, September 25)

Globalization and Economic Policy:
Neo-Liberalism

The new economic structure of Israel has evolved together with a profound—even revolutionary—transformation of the relations between state and market. All in all, this transformation may be characterized as a transition from a government-public led economic environment to a private-business led one. Until the 1970s, the government was massively involved in the economy, be that as investor in, or as owner of, economic projects, or as planner and regulator of both production and circulation. In addition, the Federation of Labor (the Histadrut) was one of the largest economic operators in the country (by means of the Workers Corporation). The government and the Histadrut were dominated by the same political party, Mapai, and in fact ruled by a common elite. (Maman, 1997) The magnitude of the public sector, including government and Histadrut, was more than half of the country's GDP. (Aharoni, 1976)

Since the 1980s, this trend has turned; the proportional part of the public sector has decreased while that of the private sector has increased. From 1985 to 1993, the division of employees between the private and public sectors changed from 67/33 percent to 76/24 percent respectively; and the division of product between the two sectors changed from 47/53 percent to 62/38 percent. (BoI, 1995, p.117 Tab. B41) Sharper changes have occurred in the capital market, where, of all investment, the share of government supported finance has fallen from 85 percent to 15 percent only. (Aharoni, 1998, p.138)

This overall change in state-market relations is represented by the term "privatization," (*hafrata*) which entered the Hebrew language in the 1980s. . (Katz, 1997) Since the 1970s a policy of privatization of state owned corporations has been widely implemented. Government revenue from sale of corporations rose from $453 million between 1977 and 1990 to $2.8 billion in the years 1991 and 1995. (Eckstein, 1998, p.192 Tab. Chet 3) The scope of privatization between the years 1986 and 1997 reached more then $4.4 billion. (SoI, 1997, pp. 25, 47) Privatization in its strict sense is accompanied by de-regulation, liberalization—all expressions of the creed of contracting the economic role of government.

Yet beyond liberal economic policies, Israeli society is undergoing a wholesale process of "privatization,", shedding its collectivist past and dressing up in a new possessive individualist future. Selling public corporations is just the spearhead of a sweeping societal privatization, and of the simultaneous crumbling of the collectivist-nationalist (once called socialist-Zionist) world, with its institutions and beliefs. Privatization has meant the shrinking of the trade union federation and the bankruptcy of its economy; constitutional discourse and active judiciary, which strengthen individual human rights and separation of powers; decline of the institutional political parties and rise of a populist televised politics; privatization of communication services and of radio and television broadcasts; sliding privatization of health and education facilities and services; separation between community and management in the kibbutzim ; marketing of formerly nationalized lands; privatization of transportation and roads; privatization of culture, language and sports and much more. Correspondents of both the daily *Ha'aretz* have debated whether all this means the "end of socialism" in Israel, or rather the "end of Zionism" in Israel. Both sides may have been correct.

Globalization and Material Culture

In the everyday life of Israelis the transformation of the socio-economic structure is expressed in the spread of a consumerist culture, which has intensified in the last two decades. Between 1950 and 1996 private consumption per capita rose by an average of 4 percent yearly, and by the end of the period it was 5.5 times higher than at the beginning. Until the 1970s the rise of private consumption was usually lower than the rise of production, but since then, the former has been higher than the latter by 1 or 2 percent yearly. The composition of private consumption is also changing. In the 1950s elementary articles (clothes, foodstuff and so forth) made up 51percent of the "basket," whereas in 1996 such articles made up only 29 percent of it. The proportion of expenses on housing, electricity, gasoline and various services, including travel abroad, has been constantly rising. (CBS, 1998a, pp.11–12)

Traveling abroad is a major indicator of welfare and affluence, especially in a society with no friendly territorial borders. In 1995, 2.5 million exits abroad were recorded in the air and naval ports of Israel. This number equals 40% percent of the population (although some of the exits are of the same persons repeatedly). For the sake of comparison, in 1970 the number of exits was 154,000, which equaled only 5 percent of the population. (CBS, 1997a, p. 49 Tab. 2.1) As an indicator of both business connections and cultural orientation, it is significant that more than 77 percent of the registered exists were to Europe and the United Sates (57 percent and 20 percent respectively). (CBS, 1997b, p.31 Tab. 15)

The globalization of interaction of Israelis is manifested also in the scope of international phone calls made from Israel. With 39 telephone lines for every 100 persons, Israel is fourteenth in the world in this index. (Bezek, 1996, p.117 Tab. Vav1) More than a third of the population (35 percent) makes at least one international telephone call per month, and more than a quarter of the population (28 percent) makes up to four international calls per month (the number of international calls rises with income and education). (Sigan, 1998)

The destination of travelers, of commodities, and probably of telephone calls is by and large the same: Europe and the United States Even those who don't travel, sell or call abroad are subject to influences from abroad. Israelis are exposed today more than in any time in the past to television, and especially to series from America , or Israeli imitations of those. Watching TV and video is the most widespread leisure time habit in Israel, and 95 percent of the population partake in it, each person averaging more than two hours a day. (CBS, 1996c, p.21.)

Television broadcasts started in Israel in 1967. For a long time only one public (state) channel operated, and it— especially its 9 p.m. news broadcast—served as a unifying medium, exposing the whole population simultaneously to its exclusive messages. (Katz, 1995) The situation changed radically in the 1990s, when a second, commercial channel was inaugurated, as well as cable TV. In 1998 satellite transmission was charted, and soon there will be "open skies." A similar process of pluralization and commercialization occurred in radio channels, starting with the official "Voice of Israel," and culminating in a scene of about 150 radio stations, including regional stations and "pirated" ones. Likewise, the printed mass media has been transformed from a prevalence of party daily newspapers, with a handful of privately owned but nationally committed newspapers, to a prevalence of commercial and professional media. Publishing houses as well have made the transition from a prevalence of ideological presses (*Workers Library; Working People; United Kibbutz* and so forth) to the current prevalence of commercial presses. All in all, the cultural and mass media are no longer committed ideologically or nationally, but rather they cater for the mass market or for special market niches.

This has made "rating" (ranking of TV programs, and by implication any other cultural commodity, by the scope of the body of its customers-viewers) into a central concept in Israeli culture. (Bernheimer, 1998, September 18) "Rating" manifests the dependence of mass media on commercial advertisement. Numbers of readers or of viewers are immediately translated into price per inch or per second, which becomes the sole foundation of the media. The outlay of advertisers per capita has risen from $130 in 1994 to $164 in 1997, and the annual domestic outlay on advertisement reaches almost 1 percent of the GDP. (AAI, 1997) As in other places so in Israel the advertising sector plays a leading role in economic and cultural globalization. Fifteen global advertisement firms are already represented in Israel by local firms.

From a society of austerity in the 1950s, Israel has turned into an affluent society in the 1990s. The pulse of the consumption movement has become evident in the so-called "Subaru syndrome," after the brand of Japanese motor vehicles that have swamped Israel since the 1970s. (Melman,1993, pp. 243–258) In the three decades of 1966–1996 the number of motor vehicles in Israel increased four times, from 68 to 268 to every 1000 persons. The largest increase has been in private cars, the proportion of which rose from 33 to 204 for every 1000 persons. (CBS, 1996b, p.23 Tab. 5) The private car is just the forefront of the overall consumerist revolution. Israel is ranked high in the world tables of appliances per capita in items such as video installations, personal computers, Internet subscriptions and mobile phones. In this last item Israel is among the world leaders, with almost every third person in the population having a mobile phone. (Greenwood, 1998, p.239) Seventy-two percent of households own a credit card. (Greenwood, 1998, p.173)

Retail trade has moved more and more from small traders to large retail-chains, and from the street to the shopping mall. The first American-style mall opened in Israel in 1985, and since then, dozens of malls have opened and dozens more are planned, that is, in addition to open-air shopping centers. The malls and other shopping centers offer to customers leading Israeli and international brand names, in all walks of trade, such as fast-food (McDonald's; Burger King); home appliances (ACE; Home Store); toys (Toys 'R' Us); office equipment (Office Depot); fashion (Zara); and more. In many cases, if not all, store names appear in English; in most cases English names are spelled in Hebrew letters. A large mall that opened recently in Tel Aviv advertised itself as "a city within a mall," the ultimate expression of commercial simulation, where a "public arena" is privately owned and guarded. The malls have emptied city centers and have become the preferred pastime of middle class families. They offer sterile zones, isolated from the humid and belligerent Middle Eastern environment. They create the illusion of being "here" and feeling "there"—as any proper globalist simulation should.

What are the political and cultural implications of the transition from a state economic environment to a market economic environment? There is no reason to expect that post-Fordist, privatized and consumptive capitalism will not instigate in Israel political and cultural effects of the kind called "post-material" and later "post-modern," a culture of fragmented individualism and personal realization, a culture alienated from bureaucratic machineries and from collectivist mobilizations. (Inglehart, 1997) A somewhat similar phenomenon took place in South-East Asia, where a growing class of professionals and consumers started demanding an expansion of civic society and civic liberalism. (Robinson, 1996a) The link between capitalism and democracy is not as straightforward as Francis Fukuyama (1992) claims, nor as ineffective as Samuel Huntington (1996) claims. It seems that Daniel Bell hit the right cord when arguing that the Protestant industrious-ascetic ethic may, if successful, lead toward a lavish-hedonistic ethic (Bell, 1976); this argument may be valid for a collectivist no less then for a capitalist society, and in the case of Israel one may say that the successes of the warfare-welfare state may be leading today toward its mutation into a "peacefare-marketfare" state.

Globalization, Peace, and the Middle Classes

In the cultural sphere post-Zionism expresses the diffusion of collective cohesiveness, of the sense of historical continuity and of the belief in a transcendental national significance. These exalted feelings are replaced by identities which are individualistic, presentistic, and pragmatic. Many researches of the Israeli cultural scene find the same: Since the 1970s a culture of hedonistic individualism has emerged in Israel. A few examples will suffice here. Cigarette advertisements from this period onwards appeal to the individual and to his personal gratification, with no reference to national or collective goals. (Orieli, 1989; and see also Kimmerling, 1993; and Whitman, 1988) In Israeli literature the "Other Wave," which emerged in the 1980s, manifests the fragmentation of meaning and a centrifugal sense of reality. Its authors "do not seek a lost wholeness [as former generations of authors did] because they simply do not believe in it." (Balaban, 1995, p.71; see also Gurevitz, 1997; and Taub, 1997) One protagonist from this literature sharply expresses the "worldview," or rather lack thereof, of the post-Zionist culture: "First, I believe there is no God. Second, I believe history has no meaning. No meaning. Third, I believe in the end humanity will achieve no victory of the enlightened over the ignorant and no utopia of any kind." (from Hefner, cited in Balaban, 1995, p.43) There are many examples of this sense of meaninglessness in other cultural artifacts, such as in the works of photographer Tiranit Barzily, who presents Zionist collectivism as a barren ceremony (Katz-Freiman, 1996), or in the everyday idiom of "not being a *frier* (sucker)," which expresses the escape of Israelis from the Zionist collectivist hug. (Roniger, 1993)

Even that ultimate expression of the Israeli nation-state, the military, can no longer operate under the old assumptions of the "people's army" or the "nation in arms." Observers believe that it may end up being transformed from the citizens' conscription model of its early days into the career professional model familiar in the West. (Cohen, 1996) Already today the proportion of conscripts from each annual cohort does not exceed 55 percent, and a fifth to a quarter of conscripts do not complete the standard period of service. (Harel, 1998, September 7) A military committee which examined the "motivation" problems of the youth concluded that the "traditional values" of settlement, Jewish immigration and security, have lost their appeal, and the youth are much more interested in personal fulfillment than in societal contribution. This was particularly noticeable with regard to the group which in the past symbolized the fighting spirit of Israelis: the kibbutz youth (Rabin 1996). Some members of the kibbutz movements are cited to have said after the Likud rise to power in 1977: "We have done our share; let's see them [Likud followers] doing theirs."

The middle class which was made by the state and for the state is now turning away from the service of all to the service of the few (on the creation of this class see Ben-Eliezer, 1995; Rosenfeld, 1976; Shapiro, 1984). The middle-class successors of the older state and military elite are withdrawing from the older career-path and turning to the more attractive and rewarding trajectories offered by civil society and the burgeoning market. (Levy, 1997, pp.176–180) The historic recognition of the Palestinian Liberation Organization by the Rabin-Peres government was facilitated by this change of atmosphere in the Israeli elite. It seems that the election of Netanyahu in 1996 (right after Rabin's assassination) and the halt to the peace process augmented in this social sector the sense of alienation not only from collectivism but also from the collectivity itself. One of the leading newspapers reported that "young couples, educated, secular, economically secure, decide to stop complaining and simply leave the country. Reasons abound: Rabin's assassination, the ultra-Orthodox, the settlers, Bibi (Netanyahu), the occupation, the threat to the rule of law; and more then anything else, a sharp and heavy sense of not belonging." (Capra, 1998)

In Israel, as in other post-industrial societies, a new middle class has emerged— which includes a third of the work force (see CBS, 1998b, Tab. 12:14; Ben-Porat, 1993, pp.152–158)—and which bases its legitimation on professional and rational codes. This strata strives to release Israeli culture from old nationalism and from new tribalism, and to usher it into modernist, Western, or globalist culture. It provides the professional cadres and the intellectual support for liberal post-Zionism, both in its economic and its foreign policy aspects. (Keren, 1996)

However influential in their preferred fields of activities, be it high-tech, business, journalism, law, civil service or others, the new middle classes are weak economically and electorally. The next sections will deal, in order, with capital and with labor in the "new Israel."

Globalization, Peace, and Capital

The fusion between changes in the foreign and defense policies and structural socio-economic changes in Israel was accurately captured by authors Peled and Shafir's equation of "Peace and Privatization" (1996), or what may be also termed "Peace and Profits," or "Peace and Prosperity" (in any event, "the two P's"). They have identified the intimate connection between the two wings of the equation in contemporary Israel. The turn to the Peace Process by the Rabin and Peres duo was generated by an array of circumstances, including the Palestinian *Intifada*, the withdrawal of the Soviet Union from active involvement in the Middle East (as a supporter of the Arab cause) and more. Chief among the considerations leading to the Oslo process was the desire to remove obstacles to the further integration of the Israeli economy into the global market arena. This required international acceptance of Israel as a legitimate business partner, and a national stabilization which will facilitate the flow of foreign investment. (Nitzan, 1996)

A pamphlet of the Peace Now movement from the Oslo Accord period exposes explicitly the link between peace and prosperity. "From the seed of peace your economic growth will flourish" declares the pamphlet. The pamphlet is decorated with a figure of a flower cut from an American dollar bill. The flower symbolizes locality and life, the dollar globality and wealth. The pamphlet details the ways in which peace will contribute to economic growth: it will enable channeling of resources from warfare to welfare; it will open new markets hitherto closed to Israel; it will create stability which will encourage investment; and it will enable a regional cooperation for a more efficient use of common natural resources. (Peace Now, 1993, #1478)

The peace turn has indeed borne the expected economic fruits. The two years following the signature of the Oslo Accord in 1993 were the peak years of the Israeli economy. Overall economic growth (GDP) had reached 6.8 percent in 1994 and 7.1 percent in 1995. On the other hand, the two following years, 1996 and 1997, after Rabin's assassination and Netanyahu rise to power, were years of a downturn (which still continues). Overall economic growth (GDP) dropped to 4.4 percent in 1996 and to 1.9 percent in 1997. (BoI, 1998, p.134 Tab. 2) The flow of foreign investment to Israel in the 1990s reached unprecedented magnitude, with a rebound in 1995. (BoI, 1998, p.178) In 1997 the flow of foreign investment reached an all time peak of $3.7 billion, which equals 3.8 percent of the GDP. Foreign investment is one third of all capital import to Israel. Forty-five percent of it is in direct investment (of which more then 80 percent is in the high-tech industry) and the rest a "fluid" investment in the stock exchange. (Manor, 1999, January 27)

The inflow of investment is also evident in the unprecedented presence of giant international or transnational corporations in Israel (in most cases they are in fact American firms). Table 2 below shows the extension of foreign ownership of Israeli firms by foreign firms in the 1990s. Today about 110 Israeli firms with an overall worth of $30 billion operate in the Wall Street stock exchange.

TABLE 9.2   Foreign Ownership of Israeli Firms, 1998

Foreign Investor	Value (billion $)	Israeli Firms and Share of Ownership	Investment Value (million $)
Bronfmam-Kolber	3.5	Kur (35%); Shikun U'Pituach (25%)	562
Ted Erison	7	Bank H'Poalim (18%); Shikun U'Binui (15%)	512
Safra Brothers	6	PIBI (70%); Selcom (34%)	500
Bellsouth	53	Orek (50%); Selcom (34%)	475
Johnson & Johnson	87	Biosense (100%)	400
Generali	20	Migdal (60%)	350
Applied Materials	12	Opal (100%); Orbot Michshur (100%)	250
Cable and Wireless	7	Bezek (10%)	170
Nestle	60	Osem (40%)	125
Volkswagen	20	Kifal Hamagnesium (33%)	125
L. Abramsohn		Bank Ha'Poalim (4.4%)	112
M. Steinhart		Bank Ha'Poalim (3.9%)	100
C. Schusterman		Bank Ha'Poalim (3.9%)	100
H. Schneider		Teva (3.5%)	96
C.P.C.	15	Tami (75%)	90
Boston Scientific	9	Medinol (30–40%)	87
T.C.A.		Tevel (50%)	87
D. Lewis		Yisrotel (82%)	79
L. Renieri		Bank Ha'Poalim (2.9%)	72
Scilink	.3 ($million)		
		Mechkar Alegorthmim (100%)	72
U.S. Robotics		Scorpio (100%)	70
Siemenns	35	Armon (100%); Rednet (100%)	65
International Paper	15	Scitex (13%)	60
B. Sterns	5	Kalkalit Jerusalem (26%); Alliance (12%)	52
Danone	12	Strauss (20%)	50
Northern Telecom	25	Telrad (20%)	50
Kimberly Clark	30	Hogla (50%)	44
Uniliver	38	Vitco (100%); Strauss (50%)	37
Sara Lee	25	Delta (22%)	19
The Limited	7	Macpel (41%)	16

SOURCE: Lipson 1998, January 21

The overall policy change of the Rabin-Peres government can be conceived of as a transition from a national colonization project to an economic globalization project. The conceptualization of this transformation was provided by Shimon Peres under the heading of "The New Middle East." Peres preaches a comprehensive regional cooperation which will attract foreign investment, lead to economic development, improve welfare and quality of life and even democratize political life. In his view the vigor of nations depends no longer on "quantities," such as territory, natural resources, demography, or geography, but rather on "qualities," such as science, education, technology, and stability. He thus considers economic performance as being today more weighty for national vigor than military might. (Peres, 1993)

Peres expresses the current perspective of the Israeli economic and political elite, the discourse of which is threaded with issues of globalization, intimately interwoven with neo-liberal messages of privatization, competition, efficiency, deregulation, flexibility and so forth. The recent "Prime Minister Economic Conference" which took place in Jerusalem as part of the Jubilee celebration of Israel (in the English language) was titled: "Israel: The Promised Land of Business Opportunities." Sessions topics included: "The Israeli Consumer as a Citizen of the Global Village," "Privatization: the Next Chapter," "Telecommunications and the Media: The Internet as a Tool for a New 21ˢᵗ Century Telecommunications Paradigm" and so forth. (Conference, 1998b) Likewise, in the "Annual Conference of Executives in Israel, 1998," organized by the Israel Center for Management (MIL), a major topic was "management with no borders" (ICM, 1998a), a joint project of the ICM and the Manufacturers' Association offered a workshop on "Globalization and Multi-National Business Management" (ICM, 1998b), and a conference organized by the Ministry for Industry and Commerce dealt with "High-Tech in the Age of Globalization." (Conference, 1998a)

Although the business sector is the big winner in the globalization process and welcomes it enthusiastically, the implications of globalization for labor are much more problematic.

Globalization, Peace, and Labor

The peace and privatization project contains a contradiction. While global capitalism contributes to the development of peace in the Middle East, it simultaneously carries within it the seeds of obstruction to this process. In a nutshell, while the middle and upper classes in Israel are zestfully attracted by the Peace Process and by the globalist logic of "McWorld," the lower classes remain behind as social victims of globalization, and they react by identifying the Peace Process with their societal adversaries, and by adherence to "localist," ultra-nationalistic and fundamentalist "Jihad" orientations.

The new wealth which globalization pours in is not distributed equally, but, on the contrary, it augments economic inequality and social desperation.

One of the factors contributing to the unequal redistribution of wealth in Israel is the privatization of public wealth. Some contend that a small number of families harvested the fruits of privatization and concentrated a large part of the country's wealth: "After fifty years of government and public involvement and ownership, the Israeli economy is knocked into a new shape, with the encouragement of the government: domination in the economy is transferred into the hands of twenty families, Israelis and foreign, which own, directly or indirectly, no less than two-thirds of the private sector." Of $50 billion traded in the stock-exchange, the value of stocks held by the government is about $5 billion, and that of stocks held by the big corporations is about $30 billion. Only $15 billion are publicly held, but only 8 percent of the public are stock owners. (Pluzker, 1998, June 13, pp.20–21)

Moreover, as the cost of labor in the private sector is about one third of that in the public sector, privatization and the decrease of the size of the public sector pulls down the overall level of earnings of the population (in 1992 the cost of labor in the private sector was NIS 44,000, compared to 65,000 in the Histadrut sector and 115,000 in the government sector (BoI, 1995, 117 Tab. B-41.) Integration in the global market also contributes to the lowering of wages, and in some cases to the abolition of waged work altogether, especially in the labor intensive "traditional" industries. The peace process is an important promoter of this trend.

A case in point is the textile industry. Some 25 Israeli textile manufacturers, among them leading firms, have removed their production to areas where the cost of labor is lower: Egypt, Jordan, the Palestinian Authority, Turkey and others. It is estimated that so far 10 percent of textile production has been transferred to countries where labor is cheap. Here is a quintessential case of the peace-profit nexus: The Manufacturers' Association under its president Dov Lautman, the owner of Delta Galil Industries, one of the leading textile firms in Israel, was a strong supporter of the Oslo Accord. Despite the general decline of traditional industries, Delta has gained in 1998 the highest net profit in its history (NIS 60 million) and the highest rise in the value of its stocks (241 percent). The secret of its success is cheap labor; about 50 percent of the firm's production has been transferred to Jordan and Egypt. (Rolnik, 1998, 1999; Gavison, 1998, November 16)

One way to the demolition of Israeli labor then is the "export" of production sites; another way is the "import" of cheap foreign labor. In the 1980s almost 10 percent of the labor force was composed of Palestinian laborers. In the branches of agriculture and construction they reached almost half of the labor force. (Kondor, 1997, p.47, Tab.1) In the 1990s', as a result of security constraints this source of cheap labor was blocked, and in its place labor began being imported from East-Asia, Eastern Europe and South America. The share of these foreign workers today also equals close to 10 percent of the labor force. (BoI, 1997, p.246) The scope of foreign labor in Israel by the end of the 1990s equals more or less the number of unemployed Israelis. Being paid about two-fifths of the average wages in Israel, foreign labor—or, more accurately, any unorganized cheap labor, "foreign" or not—is yet another factor in the downsizing of labor's wages in general in Israel. (Kondor, 1997, p.51)

Inequality in Israel is high. The upper tenth of the population receives one- third of the domestic income, and the upper two-tenths receive two-thirds of it. The share of income of the lower three-tenths is less then 5 percent. After taxation and allowances, the three upper tenths end up with 53 percent of net income, and the three lower tenths end up with less then 13 percent of net income. (Yaniv, 1997, p.87, Tab. 26) In the wage earners category the gross income of a household in the upper tenth is 11.6 percent higher than that of the lower one. (CBS, 1996a, p. 266. Tab. 11.3)

In the 1980s and 1990s a new stratum of "senior" wage earners emerged in Israel, consisting of about 2300 high ranking officials in government and government-sub-sidized organizations. Although the average monthly salary in 1998 was about NIS 6000 (about $1500), senior officials earned five digit salaries, as illustrated in Table 3 below.

TABLE 9.3.   **High Earnings in the Public Sector**

Institution	Number of Senior Executives	Cost of Monthly Salary (NIS)
Electricity Corp.	10	54,564
General Sick Fund	26	51,105
Bank of Israel	10	51,358
Aviation Industry	14	41,203
Bezek	13	42,013
Ports and Trains Authority	13	42,895
Elta	3	37,926
Refineries	33	41,101
Mekorot (Water Authority)	12	38,526
Tel Aviv University	21	39,828

SOURCE: MoF 1999, February 1

Compared to the private sector, even high public income is low. The average cost of monthly income of executives in 520 companies traded in the stock ex-change in 1997 was NIS 96,000. In 54 cases it was higher then NIS 200,000 (not including options, many times valued more then NIS one million.) Tables 4 and 5 show the income of bank directors and of the top ten wage earners in Israel, re-spectively. Such wages are not typical, of course, but their importance is both in setting the parameters and illustrating the models for the Israeli economy as well as culture. In the 1980s and 1990s, simultaneously with the decline in prestige of the army, the business sector started to gain prestige. While in the past military battles and war heroes used to fill the pages of popular books and weekend mag-azines, the popular stories of today deal with business leaders and corporate wars. (for example, Perl, 1997; December 15, 1997; Chen, April 14, 1998, April 14; Petersburg, 1998)

On the other hand, the population living below the poverty line, or slightly above it, is also growing apace, translating into hundreds of thousands of persons. In 1997, 16.2 percent of the population, that is, 210,000 families subsisted underneath the

TABLE 9.4   The Cost of Income of Bank Executives, 1997*

Institution	Executive	Cost of Income (Yearly: NIS millions)
Leumi Bank	Galiya Maor	2.23
Hapoalim Bank	Amiram Sivan	2.29
Discount Bank	Avraham Ashri	1.53
Hamizrahi Bank	Victor Medina	6.4
International Bank	Shlomo Pyoterkowski	5.03
Mercantil Bank	Moshe Gavish	1.56
Igud Bank	David Granot	2.5
Klali Bank	Eli Yonas	1.9
Industry Development Bank	Yehoshua Ichilov	0.82
Commercial Bank	Eli Unger	1.0
Sapanut Bank	David Levinson	1.5

SOURCE: Nachshon 1998, April 1
*The average exchange rate in 1997 was $1=NIS 3.45

TABLE 9.5   Top-Ten Paid Executives in Israel, 1997*

Firm	Executive	Cost of Income (Gross, Yearly; NIS millions)	(Stock options; NIS millions)
Kur	Beni Gaon	2.64	52
International Bank	Shlomo Pyoterkowski	3.61	50
Teva	Eli Horowitz	1.68	20–30
Shikun Ubinui	Uzi Verizer	1.56	20
Hamizrachi Bank	Victor Medina	3.00	15
Agan	Ilan Levita	1.62	10–15
Shikun Ubinui	Ephrayim Zedaka	0.98	10
Poalim Investments	Uri Levit	0.91	8
Discount Investments	Dov Tadmor	2.35	5
IDB Holdings	Eli Cohen	2.04	5

SOURCE: Rolnik and Simpson 1997, December 15
*Due to different sources and methods of calculations there are variations between data reported in Tables 9.4 and 9.5.

official poverty line (defined as half of the net median income). Poverty is expanding and deepening; the average income of a poor family in 1997 was 24.2 percent below the poverty line, compared to 23 percent in 1996. (Saar, 1998a, 1998b)

The high level of inequality in Israel is facilitated by two additional intersecting factors: low social expenditure and low tax burden. The ratio of social services in the government budget is 49.1 percent (in 1997). In this regard Israel ranks behind 15 states belonging to a category of high GDP per capita. For the sake of comparison, in Austria, Holland, New Zealand and France the ratio is around the 70 percent; in Finland, Japan, Australia, Ireland, Sweden and Norway the ratio is 55–60 percent; and in Denmark,

Britain, United States and Canada between 51 percent and 54 percent. It should be emphasized that social expenditures in Israel are even lower then those of the United States and Britain, which have experienced a sharp neo-liberal turn in the 1980s. (Swirski, 1997, p. 9)

The "pocket" from which social expenditure can be paid is the state's tax revenue. Tax burden is defined as the total revenue from taxation as portion of gross domestic product. In Israel the tax burden is 39.3 percent. This tax burden is significantly high compared to Japan, Britain and the United States (average 30.5 percent); but a little low compared to Germany, France, Italy and Austria (42.6 percent); and significantly lower compared to Denmark, Sweden and Holland (49.9 percent). While in many of the states mentioned above, the tax burden has increased in the 1980s and 1990s, in Britain, Denmark and Israel it has decreased in this period. Between 1980 and 1996 the tax burden in Israel fell from 42.3 percent to 37.3 percent. (ASI, 1997, p. 414, Tab. Kaf–3) The rate of one kind of tax has dropped excessively: the tax on corporate revenues, which contracted from 61 percent in 1984 to 36 percent in 1996. (ASI, 1997, p.429, Tab. Kaf–12)

An indicator of the progressiveness of taxation is the ratio between state income from direct taxation on revenues (which "progresses" proportionally with the rise of income) and indirect taxation on goods (which is fixed for the items.) The indirect Israeli tax burden is 20.7 percent, compared to an average of only 13.3 percent in 14 other states in the category of high GDP per capita (ASI, 1997, p. 417) while the direct tax burden is only 18.6 percent, compared to an average of 27.1 percent in these states. (ASI, 1997, p. 415) Yet another indicator of the progressiveness of taxation is the marginal rate of taxation, that is, tax paid on high income. The marginal rate of taxation in Israel (since 1994) is 50 percent ranking Israel in twelfth place among 19 states whose average rate is 56.7 percent (ASI 1997): 428 tab. Kaf–28.)

The growing socio-economic gap, connected, as we saw, to the process of globalization and, in turn, to the peace process, reinforces the already existing overlap between political preference and social status in Israel. The upper social echelons identify globalization and its consequences (foreign investment, individualism, consumerism, professionalism and so forth) as beneficial to themselves, and they identify with the tie between Israeli economic growth and peaceful co-existence in the Middle-East. The translation between their status and their politics is evident, and finds expression both in political behavior and in public opinion polls. In the elections for the fourteenth Knesset (1996), in the wealthy neighborhoods and well established locations, Labor won 60 percent of the votes and Likud won only 27 percent, whereas in development and immigrant towns, Labor won only 26 percent and Likud won 57 percent. (Weiss, 1997) Such results systematically repeat themselves. (Diskin, 1988, 1993) Likewise, a recent conclusion from public opinion studies confirms that two characteristics have positive impact on support for the peace process and for civil rights: middle or high social class and secularism. (Peres, 1998, p.77) Thus sociologists Peres and Yaar-Yuchtman aptly propose to characterize upper class Labor supporters as "capitalist left." Capitalist leftism is the seedbed of post-Zionist liberalism.

Conclusion:
McWorld with and Against Jihad

As the twentieth century comes to its close and the twenty-first century begins, Israeli society is undergoing a fundamental transformation. The Israel of the next century will be very different from the one that has existed up until now. With the decline of the older structures of dominance and foci of identity—pre-modern communalism and modern nationalism—a battle is being fiercely waged between two emergent alternatives: a globalist, civic, post-Zionist agenda, objectively advanced by the logic of "McWorld," and a localist, ethnic, neo-Zionist agenda, subjectively advanced by the logic of "Jihad." McWorld with and against Jihad.

This glocalization of Israel challenges both left and right. Everybody is looking forward to it, but nobody welcomes it in its entirety. The left faces the following contradiction: glocalization advances democracy in Israel, that is, civic equality. Yet, simultaneously it advances liberalization in Israel, that is, social inequality. Furthermore, while globalization is today the major force advancing peaceful coexistence in the Middle East, it is also the major instigator of social instability and reactive localist fundamentalism. The right faces a parallel perplexity: glocalization advances economic liberalization in Israel, and prepares the ground for foreign investment, that is, it advances "free market." Yet, simultaneously, glocalization advances the Americanization of Israeli culture, and the pluralization of cultures and life styles in Israel, which are the main enemies of nationalism. The left may end up with more political democracy but with less social equality, and the right may end up with more capitalism but with less national identification. Each may gain something but is also likely to lose something.

Thus, in the face of the challenges of globalization, the old left, the new right and the center in between them, lack a coherent satisfactory perspective. The movements and parties of yesterday have turned into mere electoral actors, and into the social and cultural void created have burst the two tendencies which determined Israeli political culture in the 1990s: McWorld and Jihad, the business market and the rabbinical community, or, perhaps, the rabbinical market and the business community, and in between them, as mediators, the retired generals.

The data compiled and the analysis conducted above show that with glocalization Israel moves in two contradictory directions simultaneously: it progresses in the scale of income per capita and other indicators of development, while it regresses in the scale of social disparity and inequality. Here is concealed the seed of the political instability sensed in Israel and manifested in the assassination of a prime minister. The results of post-Zionist McWorld—low education, poverty, discrimination and a sense of deprivation, make the lower classes an easy prey for the chauvinist and populist politics of the neo-Zionist Jihad. The civic and reconciliatory policies of the post-Zionist left are then isolated and perceived as an upper-class interest. As all societies are drawn into the global orbit (and there is no other choice, unless for a dear price closure and regression), Israel is undergoing sharp social polarization which is self-injurious.

This is the great challenge to post-Zionism: on the one hand, in a nationalist and collectivist society as Israel used to be, globalization is a quintessential force of democratization. Yet the reach of the universalistic aspects of globalization is limited to the economic and cultural elites. The lower classes identify this process as a threat to their status and identity that a "strong" nation-state could have provided. Although part of the Israeli upper classes have already started their move toward post-Zionist globalization and democratization, they find themselves blocked by the electoral strength of the lower classes, which are mobilized under the banner of localist neo-Zionist ethno-nationalism.

Thus, the major players in the socio-political drama taking place in Israel today are of the right: the socio-economic liberal right of the capitalist upper classes— called in Israel "the left"— and the ethno-religious fundamentalist right of the laboring lower classes—called in Israel "the people." In the midst of the general crisis, in the sound and fury of capitalist globalization and nationalist localization, other voices are struggling to be heard, voices demanding civic equality, social democracy and cultural plurality, but, as yet, the new agenda they propose has not been absorbed by the larger society.

References

Aharoni, Yair. 1976. *Structure and Performance in the Israeli Economy.* Tel Aviv: Tcherikover, in Hebrew.

———— 1998. "The Changing Political Economy of Israel." *Annals of the American Academy for Political and Social Sciences* 555, pp. 127–146.

Ashcroft, Bill, Griffiths Gareth and Hellen Toffin, eds. 1995. *The Post-Colonial Studies Reader.* London: Routledge.

Association of Advertisers in Israel [AAI]. 1997. "More Is Invested in Advertising." Tel Aviv: *Otot*, pp. 6–8, in Hebrew.

Authority of State Income [ASI]. 1997. *Annual Report 1996.* Jerusalem: Authority of State Income, in Hebrew.

Balaban, Avraham. 1995. *A Different Wave in Israeli Fiction.* Jerusalem: Keter, in Hebrew.

Bank of Israel[BoI]. 1995. "Report: 1994." Jerusalem: Bank of Israel, in Hebrew.

———— 1997. "Report : 1996." Jerusalem: Bank of Israel, in Hebrew.

———— 1998. "Report: 1997." Jerusalem: Bank of Israel, in Hebrew.

Barber, Benjamin R. 1995. *Jihad vs. McWorld: How Globalism and Tribalism are Shaping the World.* New York: Times Books.

Bell, Daniel. 1976. *The Cultural Contradictions of Capitalism.* New York: Basic Books.

Ben-Eliezer, Uri. 1995. *The Emergence of Israeli Militarism, 1936–1956.* Tel Aviv: Dvir, in Hebrew.

Ben-Porat, Amir. 1993. *The State and Capitalism in Israel.* Westport, Conn.: Greenwood Press.

Bernheimer, Avner and Biranit Golan. 1998. "Five Years to the Turnabout: How Channel 2 has made Rating into the New Code of Israeli Society." *Yediot Acharonot—Seven Days*, September 10, in Hebrew.

Bezek, Israel's Communication Corporation. 1996. *Statistical Yearbook 1995.* Jerusalem: Israel's Communication Corporation, in Hebrew.

Capra, Michal and Ofer Shelach. 1998. "Yordim 98." *Maariv—Musaf Shabat*, pp. 2–4, 8, in Hebrew.

Cawson, Alan. 1986. *Corporatism and Political Theory.* Oxford: Basil Blackwell.

Central Bureau of Statistics [CBS].1996a. "Statistical Abstract of Israel 1996." Jerusalem: Central Bureau of Statistics.

_____. 1996b. "Motor Vehicles 31–7–1996." Jerusalem: Central Bureau of Statistics.

_____. 1996c. "Time Use in Israel—1991/2." Jerusalem: Central Bureau of Statistics.

_____. 1997a. "Statistical Annual of Israel." Jerusalem: Central Bureau of Statistics.

_____. 1997b. "Tourism 1996." Jerusalem: Central Bureau of Statistics.

_____. 1998a. "National Accounts (Jubilee Publications)." Jerusalem: Central Bureau of Statistics.

_____. 1998b. "Statistical Abstract of Israel." Jerusalem: Central Bureau of Statistics.

Chen, Shoshana. 1998. "And Since They Live Wealthy and Wealthy." In *Yediot Acharonot Seven Days*, April 14, pp. 48, 50, 52, 54, in Hebrew.

Cohen, Stuart. 1996. "Israel Defence Force and Israeli Society: Towards a Contraction of the Roles of the Military?" In Moshe Lissak and Baruch Knei-Paz, eds. *Israel Towards the Year 2000: Society, Politics and Culture.* Jerusalem: Magnes, pp. 215–232, in Hebrew.

Conference. 1998a. "High-Tech Companies in the Global Age [Conference Program]." *Ha'aretz*, November 8, p. 8, in Hebrew.

_____ 1998b. "Israel: The Promised Land of Business Opportunities [Conference Program]." *Ha'aretz*, September 23, p. 8, in Hebrew.

"Decade of Growth 88–97." 1997. *Ha'aretz—Economy* (Special Supplement), December 15.

Diskin, Avraham. 1988. *Elections and Voters in Israel.* Tel Aviv: Am Oved, in Hebrew.

_____ 1993. *The Elections to the 13th Knesset.* Jerusalem: The Jerusalem Institute for Israel Studies.

Dori, Zviya. 1998. *Industry in Israel 1997.* Jerusalem: State of Israel, Ministry of Industry and Commerce.

Eckstein, Shlomo, Shimon Rozevich and Ben Zion Zilberfab. 1998. *Privatization of Public Enterprises in Israel and Abroad.* Ramat Gan: Bar Ilan University, in Hebrew.

Fukuyama, Francis. 1992. *The End of History and the Last Man.* Tel Aviv: Or Am, in Hebrew.

Gavison, Yoram. 1998. "Delta – Major Customer is in Trouble." *Ha'aretz*, November 16, p. 9, in Hebrew.

Goldman, Dudi. 1998 "360 Thousand Israelis Serf the Internet." *Yediot Acharonot, September 25*, p. 6, in Hebrew.

Green, Sagi. 1998. "Virtual Israel: Sand, Plastics and Brain." *Ha'aretz*, September 20, p. D1, in Hebrew.

Greenwood, Naftali. 1998. *Israel Yearbook and Almanach Jubilee Edition.* Jerusalem: IBRT Translation/Documentation Ltd.

Gurevitz, David. 1997. *Postmodernism: Culture and Literature at the End of the 20th Century.* Tel Aviv: Dvir, in Hebrew.

Harel, Amos. 1998. "AKA's Head: 45% of the Yearly Cohort Are Not Drafted." *Ha'aretz*, September 7, in Hebrew.

Harvey, David. 1989. *The Condition of Postmodernity.* Oxford: Blackwell.

Held, David. 1995. *Democracy and the Global Order.*

Hobsbawm, Eric. 1990. *Nations and Nationalism Since 1780.* Cambridge: Cambridge University Press.

Huntington, P. Samuel. 1996. *The Clash of Civilizations: Remaking of World Order.* New York: Simon and Schuster.

Israeli Center of Management [ICM]. 1998a. "The Challenges of the Economy in a Borderless Economy [Advertisement: Conference Program]." *Ha'aretz,* October 9, p. 9, in Hebrew.

Israeli Center of Management [ICM] and AII, Association of Industrialists in Israel. 1998b. "Globalization and Multi-National Business Management (Advertisement)." *Ha'artez,* February 20, p. 8, in Hebrew.

Inglehart, Roland. 1997. *Modernization and Postmodernization.* Princeton: Princeton University Press.

Jessop, Bob. 1994. "The Transition to Post-Fordism and the Schumpeterian Workfare State." In Roger Burrows and Brian Loader, eds. *Towards a Post-Fordist Welfare State.* London: Routledge, pp. 13–37.

Katz, Elihu and Hadassah Hass. 1995. "Twenty Years of Television in Israel: Are There Long Term Effects?" *Zmanim* 52, pp. 80–91, in Hebrew.

Katz, Yizhak. 1997. *Privatization in Israel and in the World.* Tel Aviv: Pecker, in Hebrew.

Katz-Freiman, Tami. 1996. "The Artists: Catalogue." In Tami and Amy Cappellazzo Katz-Freiman, eds. *Deset Clishe: Israel Now—Local Images.* Miami Beach, Fl.: The Israeli Forum of Art Museums and the Bass Museum of Art, pp. 94–110.

Keren, Michael. 1996. *Professionals Against Populism: The Peres Government and Democracy.* Tel Aviv: Ramot, in Hebrew.

Kimmerling, Baruch. 1993. "Yes, A Return to the Family." *Politica* 48, pp. 40–45, in Hebrew.

King, Desmond. 1989. "Economic Crisis and Welfare State Recommodification: A Comparative Analysis of the United States and Britain." In M. Gottdiener and Nikos Komninos, eds. *Capitalist Development and Crisis Theory.* New York: St. Martin's Press, pp. 237–260.

Kondor, Yaakov. 1997. *Foreign Workers in Israel.* Jerusalem: The Social Security Institute, in Hebrew.

Levy, Yagil. 1997. *Trial and Error: Israel's Route from War to De-Escalation.* Albany, N.Y.: State University of New York Press.

Lipson, Nathan. 1998 "Foreign Investments Reached Their Peak. . . ."*Ha'aretz,* January 21, p. 8, in Hebrew.

Maman, Daniel. 1997. "The Elite Structure in Israel: A Socio-Historical Analysis." *Journal of Political and Military Sociology* 25, pp. 25–46.

Manor, Hadas. 1999. "Decrease of 25% in Foreign Investment." *Maariv, January 27,* p. 3, in Hebrew.

Melman, Yossi. 1993. *The New Israelis.* Tel Aviv: Schoken, in Hebrew.

Ministry of Finance [MoF]. 1999. "Report on Wages in the Public Sector." *Ha'aretz,* February 1, p. 1, in Hebrew.

Nachshon, Udi. 1998. "The Profits of the Banks in '97." *Yediot Achronot – Mamon,* April 1, pp. 2–3, in Hebrew.

"New Wage Norms." 1997. *Ha'aretz—Economy (Special Issue).* December 15b, p. 54.

Nitzan, Jonathan and Shimshon Bichler. 1996. "From War Profits to Peace Dividends: The New Political Economy of Israel." *Capital and Class* 60, pp. 61–94.

Offe, Claus. 1984. *Contradictions of the Welfare State.* London: Hutchinson.

Orieli, Nati. 1989. "The Cultural Aspect of Cigarette Advertising in Israel." In *Faculty of Social Sciences.* Tel Aviv: Tel Aviv University, in Hebrew.

Pappe, Ilan. 1997. "Post-Zionist Critique on Israel and the Palestinians." (Three parts). *Journal of Palestinian Studies* 26, pp. 29–41, 37–43, 60–69.

Peled, Yoav and Gershon Shafir. 1996. "The Roots of Peacemaking: The Dynamics of Citizenship in Israel, 1948–1993." *International Journal of Middle East Studies* 28, pp. 391–413.

Peres, Shimon. 1993. *The New Middle East.* Bnei Brak: Steimatzki, in Hebrew.

Peres, Yohanan and Ephraim Yuchtman-Yaar. 1998. *Between Consent and Dissent: Democracy and Peace in the Israeli Mind.* Jerusalem: The Israel Democracy Institute, in Hebrew.

Perl, Moshe. 1997. "The 10 Best Managers in Israel." Tel Aviv: *Maariv*, April 21, in Hebrew.

Petersburg, Ofer. 1998. "Happy in the Penthouses." *Seven Days—Yediot Acharonot,* March 27, in Hebrew.

Pierson, Christopher. 1991. *Beyond the Welfare State?* Cambridge: Polity Press.

Pluzker, Sever. 1998. "They Buy and Sell the State Over Lunch." In *Yediot Aharonot, June 13, in Hebrew.*

Rabin, Eitan. 1996. "A Committee on the Motivation for Service in the IDF." In *Ha'aretz,* November 10, in Hebrew.

Ram, Uri. 1998. "Post-Nationalist Pasts: the Case of Israel." *Social Science History* 24, pp. 513–545.

Robinson, Richard. 1996 *The New Rich in Asia.* London: Routledge.

Robinson, William L. 1996 "A Contribution to the Debate on Globalization: Nine Theses of Our Epoch." *Race and Class* 38, pp. 13–31.

Rolnik, Guy. 1998. "The Peace Process is Halted But Dov Lautman Continues Fast Ahead." in *Ha'aretz,* in Hebrew.

Rolnik, Guy. 1999. "Dov Lautman: Person of the Year." in *Ha'artez,* April 7, p. 7, in Hebrew.

Rolnik, Guy and Nathan Lipson. 1997a. "The Decade of Growth 86-97." *Ha'aretz-Economy* (Special Supplement), December 15, in Hebrew.

Rolnik, Guy and Nathan Lipson. 1997b. "New Wage Norms." pp. 54 in *Ha'aretz-Economy* (Special Supplement), December 15, in Hebrew.

Roniger, Louis and Michael Fiege. 1993. "The Culture of 'Frier' and Israeli Identity." *Alpayim* 7, pp. 119–137, in Hebrew.

Rosenfeld, Henry and Shulamit Carmi. 1976. "The Privatization of Public Means, the State Made Middle Class, and the Realization of Family Values in Israel." In J.G. Peristiany, ed. *Kinship and Modernization in Mediterranean Society.* Rome: The Center of Mediterranean Studies, American University Field Staff.

Saar, Reli. 1998a. "The Poverty Report." In *Ha'aretz,* December 1, p. 1, 11, in Hebrew.

——— 1998b. "The Real Cause for the Deepening of Poverty." In *Ha'aretz,* December 1, p. 5, in Hebrew.

Shapiro, Yonathan. 1984. *An Elite Without Successors.* Tel Aviv: Sifriyat Poalim, in Hebrew.

Sigan, Lilach. 1998. "TGI: 38% of the Population Made at Least One International Phone Call . . ." In *Ha' aretz,* August 3, in Hebrew.

(SoI). 1997. "Report on the Government Companies." Jerusalem: State of Israel, Office of the Prime Minister, Government Companies Authority, in Hebrew.

Soysal, Yasmin Nuhoglu. 1994. *Limits of Citizenship: Migrants and Postnational Membership in Europe*. Chicago: The University of Chicago Press.

Swirski, Shlomo, Meirav Sanzangi, Ethi Konor, Barbara Swirski. 1997. *A View on the Budjet 1998*. Tel Aviv: Adva Center.

Taub, Gadi. 1997. *A Dispirited Rebellion: Essays on Contemporary Israeli Culture*. Tel Aviv: Hakibbutz Hameuchad, in Hebrew.

Thomas, Caroline. 1997. "Poverty, Development and Hunger." In John Baylis and Steve Smith, eds. *The Globalization of World Politics*. Oxford: Oxford University Press, pp. 449–467.

"Trend of the Globalization of Advertisers Continues." 1998. *Ha'aretz*, December 14, p. 5.

Waters, Malcolm. 1995. *Globalization*. London: Routledge.

Weiss, Shevach. 1997. *14,729 Missing Votes: An Analysis of the 1996 Elections in Israel*. Tel Aviv: Hakkibutz Hameuhad, in Hebrew.

"Where Wired is a Way of Life." 1998. *Newsweek*, pp. 38–43.

Whitman, Sasha. 1988. "Surnames as Cultural Indicators: Trends in the National Identity of the Israelis, 1882–1990." In Nurith Graetz, ed. *Nekudat Tatzpit*. Tel Aviv: Open University, in Hebrew.

Yaniv, Gideon, ed. 1997. *Annual Survey 1996/7*. Jerusalem: National Insurance Institute.

PART THREE

The Peace Process

10

Peace and Profits:
The Globalization of
Israeli Business and the Peace Process

GERSHON SHAFIR AND YOAV PELED

Globalization and Decolonization

Israeli moderation toward the Palestinians, the recognition of the PLO, and the decolonization of the Gaza Strip and cities of the West Bank, under the Rabin-Peres governments, should be understood as part and parcel of a broader process of liberalization in Israeli society which continues to sustain the peace making drive in spite of its many setbacks. The process of liberalization consists of replacing a heavily subsidized, inefficient, idiosyncratic, and outmoded if not counterproductive and heavily contested network of political institutions built up to facilitate the colonization and state building project of Zionism with market-based economic incentives and a liberal legal framework at a time when global changes made such transformations possible and beneficial. Both globalization and decolonization may, then, be viewed as sharing the goal of replacing political mechanisms and forces, identified with the nation and the nation-state, with financial and commercial ties which, on their part, are global forces.

The decline and rapid fall of the USSR and its Eastern European satellites, the end of the Cold War, and the rise of U.S. hegemony, so convincingly demonstrated in its ability to put together a wide coalition and defeat Iraq in the Persian Gulf War, were described by President Bush as giving rise to a "New World Order." His U.S.-centric diagnosis was both overconfident and boastful: "Old" forces of nationalism, ethnic exclusion and cleansing, and economic protectionism continue to contest many facets of the alleged new order. Nevertheless, in liberal industrialized countries and the countries and regions under their hegemony, and under the pressure of multinational corporations and international economic institutions, a shift has taken place in the relative weight of social resources, most specifically from political (and related cultural legitimations) to economic factors. This is not to contend that politics are irrelevant or that political aspirations and concerns cannot override economic interests; far from it. It is, however, becoming costlier to assert the primacy of political, and attendant legitimational, concerns, and the effort of putting together a coalition to oppose global economic and cultural forces becomes more difficult and harder to sustain. It becomes, therefore, ever more important to examine simultaneously global, national, and local forces in their multifarious interactions. In this paper we are suggesting the growing importance of the global forces, institutions, and those groups or elites most able to take advantage of the shift in this amalgam.

Global organizations that operate in the interstices of nation-states and are not fully answerable to any of them usually operate though governments and globally-oriented elites or strata within states. The authority wielded by global elites that operate within nation-states is rooted in their relative autonomy from national and local constrains. Such autonomy can derive from various sources. Elite theory, for example, holds that elites are shielded from social influences due to their superior organization, control over central resources, the unique characteristics of the individuals who compose them, and the apathy of the masses or some combination thereof. In the case of globally-oriented elites, autonomy usually stems from their privileged access to global resources and allies. Among these, we would list export revenues, access to international credit, assistance by international organizations, and so on.

If we examine the unfolding of the global processes from within society—that is, the way they work their way through Israeli society and its institutions—we will notice the growing importance of relatively autonomous economic elites, tied with export-oriented high-tech industries and their allies, at the expense of elites, in most part connected with the Histadrut, which were accustomed to employ political means to ensure their position and their followers' interests. The crisis of the Histadrut's extra-market mechanisms in the 1980s made them vulnerable to claims that they were representing particular and outdated interests, whereas the growth of export oriented industries allowed the Israeli business community to demonstrate that there is a working alternative and to enhance its own standing as representing the forces of the future. Although an autonomous business community is relatively new in Israel, its weight is considerable. Global frameworks also continue to provide the incentives for trying, and the penalties for failing, to undertake the peaceful resolution of the, once thought, "intractable" Israeli/Palestinian conflict. With this framework in mind, we decided to focus on the evolution of the positions taken by the globalizing elites: political leaders, professionals, economists, and especially the business community in Israel toward the process of making peace with an age-old adversary.

In this paper we will focus on the new role played by a partially autonomous business community and those political, professional, and civil service elites with whom it shared the vision of a liberalized economy tied into the global market place. The key to such development, the political elites and business leaders agreed, was an end to the Israeli-Palestinian conflict and with it, to the economic boycott and Israel's partial economic isolation. This vision was not only a domestic Israeli one, global allies shared and propagated it as part of their ambition to integrate the Middle East as a whole into the global economy.

The Labor Movement and the
Developmentalist State

Whereas Zionist attempts to colonize economically unattractive Palestine by reliance on private initiative usually ended in failure, the predominant Zionist method of colonization—evolved by the Zionist Labor Settlement Movement [LSM]was founded on the imposition of non-market mechanisms in land acquisition and labor regulation. Simultaneously, this method made possible the provision of "civilized wages" to Jewish workers, who otherwise might have emigrated to more developed countries (making Zionism synonymous in popular parlance with "subsidy").

The Zionist LSM form of colonization required a massive institutional network to ensure, on the one hand, continuous fund-raising abroad and, on the other hand, controlled commitment of funds in Palestine to ensure that this unusual incentive system remained relatively effective. Among the main institutions were the World Zionist Organization's Jewish National Fund and the Jewish LSM's trade union— the Histadrut. Jointly they constituted a separate, co-operative, and socialist Jewish economic sector. These massive, but ultimately inefficient and costly mechanisms and institutions that were created to bypass the market mechanisms, and give Zionist colonization its particular cast, provided Jewish settler-immigrants and their descendants with a "European standard of living." They also gave Israel the largest public sector employment outside the communist countries, and represented the idiosyncrasies of its socio-economic organization. Under conditions of global competitiveness such idiosyncrasies became too burdensome and counterproductive. The impact of global economic forces on the Israeli economy made less viable the unique extra-market features that were the result of their establishment and reproduction as colonial societies

Until the 1970s, these institutions were tied in with a developmentalist state, operating through the Histadrut, its own enterprises, or the private sector. State-driven, or dirigiste, economic growth, typical of "developmentalist states" exhibited an unparalleled financial dependence on non-investment type foreign capital, preferably in the form of unilateral transfers. Developmentalism and unilateral capital imports became more strongly interconnected after the establishment of Israel in 1948 when the state became the main conduit of capital influx and, consequently, maintained and enhanced its control, conjointly with the Histadrut, over the economy.

Domestic capital formation in Israel became a circular affair: The Histadrut's provident funds were made available to the government to finance public and private investments approved by the government itself. The economy's chief source of investment credit remained under effective government control, regardless of whether the investment was effected in the public, Histadrut, or the private sector. As long as the private sector remained dependent on government-allocated credit, it remained for all practical purposes another branch of government and could not attain autonomy. What seemed a private sector was, in fact, tied to the state's apron strings. No autonomous business sector could emerge, and business decisions were made in response to or as part of political decisions.

This arrangement in effect expressed and ensured the identity of the political and economic elites in Israel. (Interview with Efraim Reiner, past Director General of Bank Hapoalim and Secretary of Hevrat Haovdim, December 24, 1995) The members of the elite, recruited from within the second generation of the Labor movement's institutions, many of them from the kibbutzim, by virtue of their personal preferences specialized in the political, military, or economic branches of the elite. Although the members of the elite's "economic wing" sought to employ an economic rationale to establish their autonomy, whereas the political wing was afraid of such autonomy and sought to curtail it, the two wings always remained tied to each other within the given set of institutional arrangements and, in effect, their struggles took place within the same elite. (Reiner: interview) But the same logic operated within the private sector as well. Capital markets remained under effective government control, regardless of whether the investment was effected in the public, Histadrut, or private sector. What seemed a private sector was, in fact, tied to the state's apron strings.

Although the autonomy of the business community attained in Israel came late, it was attained rapidly. Its origins are found in some of the reforms that began with the July 1985 "Emergency Economic Stabilization Plan" (EESP) undertaken by Shimon Peres' National Unity Government with the intention of reducing the 466 percent annual inflation. The EESP tilted the balance from public to private interests and concerns and from workers organizations to capital and employers' bodies. Israel has seen the shrinkage of its welfare, health, and educational system, or social citizenship rights. The 1985 Stabilization Plan led to the liberalization of the capital market by gradually abolishing its most thoroughly interventionist, and inflationary, instrument: the fixed interest non-tradable public bonds issued to provident funds. "The private sector's sources of finance changed radically after the July 1985 stabilization program." (Razin and Sadka, 1993, p.191)

The reduction of government intervention in the disposition of savings in the private sector led private enterprises, for the first time, to raise capital by issuing securities through the stock exchange free from government control. An even more important role in liberating the capital markets was the relaxation in borrowing foreign capital. Israeli corporations began floating their securities on the New York Stock Exchange; these added up to 36 percent of the total market value of publicly held Israeli nonfinancial corporations as of January 1992. Firms received permission to invest up to 40 percent of their equity abroad. Consequently, between 1985 and 1990 the share of government securities held by the public fell from 83 to 65 percent of the stock of financial assets. Similarly, the share of direct or indirect government loans to the private sector fell from 57.6 to 29.7 percent in just three years, from 1987 to 1990. (Razin and Sadka, pp.191–195) The autonomy of the Israeli business community, indeed, the first time the term "business community" entered the Israeli lexicon, dates from its ability to finance itself independently of the government through the Tel Aviv or New York Stock Exchanges.

This new found autonomy was slowly translated into political terms and expressed in the role played by the Israel business community in the peace process with the PLO. The public campaign of the Israeli business community on behalf of peacemaking was unprecedented: This was the first time that its leaders came out in support of a political issue, indeed, the most contentious one in the country. At first this independence manifested itself in regard to the safer question of the absorption of the masses of Jewish immigrants who began arriving in 1989 from the ex-USSR. In his survey of December 4, 1989, John Rossant of *Business Week* pointed out:

> To make Israel more attractive to the immigrants, many Israeli businessmen insist that peace is needed. The pragmatic Israeli business community is putting behind-the-scene pressure on the Shamir government to negotiate with the Palestinians. (Rossant, "Israel Has Everything It Needs – Except Peace," *Business Week*, p.58.)

Rossant continued: Israeli businessmen know that without peace with the Arabs there is little chance of the country building a stable civilian economy." It is against this conviction at a time when the economy has already been restructured into "Israel Inc.," much to the delight of business, and is slated for a take-off that "many Israeli businessmen are joining the Bush Administration in leaning on Prime Minister Yitzhak Shamir to become more flexible in his approach to negotiations." Eli Hurvitz, the Director of Teva Pharmaceuticals and Israel's largest drug company and past president of the MAI [Manufacturers Association of Israel], expressed this consensus by stating that from this economic perspective "the future is problematic without peace." (Rossant, p.54.)

The influence of business community was compounded by its alliance with global institutions which sought out local allies.

Global Allies

Economic boycotts and counter-boycotts have characterized the Israeli-Arab conflict for a long time. The Israeli economy itself was fashioned through "close shop" practices, such as "Hebrew labor" campaigns, from 1905 on. Already in the 1940s the Arab League imposed a primary boycott on Israel, prohibiting Arab countries from trading with her directly, as well as a secondary boycott which forbade Arab countries and companies to do business with foreign companies that maintained business relations with Israel. As a consequence, direct foreign investment in Israel always remained scanty, and it is possible to count on one hand the number of multinational corporations that set up offices in Israel. Although the boycott cut Israel off from its neighbors, it also led Israel to seek affiliation with Western economies. To become an integral part of the world economy, both South Africa and Israel could not just undertake economic reforms, dramatic political actions were required to reverse or erode the political boycotts imposed on them as well.

Against this background, international and private bodies with global economic perspectives played a crucial role in placing on the agenda the convergence of economic development with peace making, in the context of emerging U.S. hegemony. Among these bodies were the World Bank, the European Union, the Council on Foreign Relations and the Davos-based World Economic Forum (which co-convened the first Middle East/North Africa (MENA) Economic Summit in Casablanca), and Harvard University's Institute for Social and Economic Policy in the Middle East. The broad framework for global involvement in the Middle East was laid out in the novel approach taken by the Bush administration to advance the peace process after the Gulf War: the simultaneous conduct of bilateral and multilateral talks. The bilateral talks between Israelis and Palestinians, and between Israel and Syria, covered the political issues such as borders, sovereignty, and recognition, while the multilateral talks involved international and wider regional participation and focused on economic and security issues such as water resources, refugees, arms control, and regional security, environment, and regional economic development. The combination of simultaneous bilateral and multilateral talks highlighted the global dimension of Middle Eastern peace and assumed that a measure of economic cooperation could spur the peace process.

The World Bank played an especially important role by emphasizing the place and contribution of economic development in the larger picture of peacemaking through special studies. In September 1993, the World Bank published its five volume report on "Developing the Occupied Territories: An Investment in Peace." The report made clear that it "would be particularly prudent" to rely on the already existing dynamic and capable private sector (WB: September 1993, Vol.1:13) to attain sustainable growth by opening up foreign markets inter alia by shifting "the external economic relations. . . from almost complete dependence on Israel. . . to interdependence with a range of economies, including Israel." (WB, September 1993, Vol.1:13; Vol.2:55)

Although the World Bank's reports clearly favored a development model consistent with the requirement of a global economy as it was evolving currently, they also served to advance some of the PLO's views and positions. In fact, in the case of the PLO, their legitimizing function went far by extending it into the political sphere. The World Bank is mandated to work only with sovereign states, which the PLO clearly was not, and, therefore, confirmed at least partial recognition of the PLO as a state-in-the-making. (Interviews: Ehud Kofman, Director of Department Foreign Trade, Ministry of Finance, December 30, 1994; Ariyeh Arnon, Research Department, Bank of Israel, January 17, 1995)

In September 1989, a series of conferences and seminars, a private initiative, was undertaken by the Institute for Social and Economic Policy in the Middle East at the John F. Kennedy School of Government at Harvard University. . Out of these came the publication *Securing Peace in the Middle East: Project on Economic Transition*, prepared by Israeli, Jordanian, and Palestinian economists, in June 1993. It concludes that one, Palestinians would benefit from a free, open, market economy, and two, all three parties will only grow rapidly if they are export-oriented. The report was presented to Shimon Peres, Crown Prince Hassan, and Yasir Arafat, and to representatives of business groups in the region. The novelty of the cooperation between Jordanian, Palestinian, and Israeli economists, backed by their political leaders, created a great impression (Institute for Social and Economic Policy in the Middle East, 1993) as did the fact that while the political talks were dragging, consensus was reached in regard to economic issues. (See, for example, David Lipkin, "Economics and Peace," *Ma'ariv*, June 24, 1993.)

Finally, the World Economic Forum that once a year organizes a conference in Davos, Switzerland, to arrange for regional meetings of economic and political leaders played a facilitating role in an informal way. The 1993 Davos conference served as a meeting place for Israeli and Arab business leaders and government economic representatives in 1992 and 1993. Not surprisingly, in 1994 a large part of the WEF's annual conference was devoted to the discussion of the peace economy of the new Middle East.

Political Parties and Liberalization

The same explicit support for combining peacemaking and the liberalization of the economy within moderate social-democratic limits was propagated in the political arena for over a decade by the Meretz party and within the Labor Party, at the time in opposition, by the Chug Mashov (Feedback Circle) and Hakfar Hayarok factions. Chug Mashov was established in 1982 by the younger generation in the party leadership and led by Yossi Beilin, one of the most original minds in Israeli politics.

Mashov's "founding charter," a one-page, typewritten document, calls for a re-examination of the Labor ideology "formulated at the time of the Yishuv," and a clarification of "the meaning of the socialist message" in contemporary Israel. It declares the group's intention to present the party with new ideas in the social sphere, concentrating on issues relating to the party itself and to the Histadrut (Mashov, 1981). Mashov's first conference did not take place until April, 1983. The conference adopted resolutions calling for transforming the character of Hevrat Haovdim, taking a bold initiative for resolving the conflict with the Palestinians, and holding primary elections within the party. (Mashov, 1983). Through the decade of its existence prior to Labor's return to power in 1992, the rhetoric used by Mashov continued to employ the key social-democratic terms of the ethno-republican discourse, while gradually subverting their meaning. Thus "socialism" became "socialism of choice"; "equality" was redefined as "equality of opportunity"; workers, it was argued, need to be regarded as "consumers and citizens," as well; "public companies" were redefined as companies traded publicly on the stock exchange; using unemployment to fight inflation was opposed, "except in rare cases"; and the public healthcare system had an interest, it was claimed, that "the rich turn to real private medicine" so as not to burden the system (Mashov, 1985; 1986; 1987; 1989; 1991a; 1991b).

The liberal character of its program had become crystal clear by the time of Mashov's May 1991 conference. In his keynote address, Mashov's founder and leader, Yossi Beilin, surveyed the failings of the planned socialist economy, and after decorously praising the Histadrut for its illustrious past, proceeded to offer a list of concrete reforms that would essentially gut that historic institution. Among the draft resolutions considered by that conference, were the transfer of control over Hevrat Haovdim enterprises to a variety of owners, including the enterprises' own workers (only in cases of "small companies and/or those with a simple hierarchical structure"), and the separation of Kupat Holim from the Histadrut through the institution of national health insurance (Mashov, 1989; 1991a; 1991b).

Mashov's 1991 conference also adopted positions on the peace process which, while never adopted by Labor as part of its own platform in 1992, turned out to be very influential in laying out the groundwork for the Oslo accords. Thus the conference called upon the government to recognize the Palestinians' right of self-determination and negotiate with whomever they designated as their authorized representatives, provided those representatives would meet certain preconditions. (These preconditions had already been met by the PLO and, in effect, this was a call for negotiating with the PLO.) It also discussed the possibility of setting up a common political framework for Gaza and the West Bank (in effect, a Palestinian state), and instituting a "Gaza first" interim withdrawal plan with full autonomy for the Palestinians in Gaza. (Mashov 1991a, 1991b).

The most innovative aspect of Mashov's 1991 programme, however, was the express linkage it made between the economic and political dimensions of peacemaking. Mashov's resolutions stated: "The chance to successfully address the challenges of the Israeli economy, and especially mass immigration and the necessity of growth, depends on our ability to take the path of peace." Peacemaking, it was argued, will enhance Israel's "ability to transfer resources towards these tasks and mobilize external economic assistance which is contingent on our international standing." A closely related demand was that:

> To advance the peace process an economic program will be undertaken to ensure the development of sources of livelihood and economic infrastructure for the Palestinian community and to simultaneously foster Israeli-Arab economic cooperation (Mashov, 1991b; Interview: Yossi Beilin, Deputy Foreign Minister, July 11, 1995).

The platform of the Meretz Party was even more explicit on the broader issue of linkage between peace and economic development:

Peace agreement with our neighbors and a policy consistent with the values and interests of the democratic world will enable Israel to integrate into the world economy and into a stronger and expanding European Community, to become the recipient of investments and credit and to possess a progressive and exporting economy. (Meretz, 1992, Chapter on "Economy and Society.")

While peace promises to increase Israel's access to Western and international resources, Palestinian economic development itself is further seen a paramount tool of peacemaking. Hence Israel's integration into the regional economy through the conduit of participation in the development of the economy of the West Bank and Gaza was advocated as a related economic goal by both Chug Mashov and Meretz. (Mashov, 1991b, p.7, Meretz, 1992) Finally, reaching peace is described by Meretz as imperative not only for gaining security but also for realizing a larger socio-economic vision: the attainment by Israel of the European Community's standard of living by the year 2000.

Posing so clearly and dramatically the relationship between peace and economic prosperity was yet another manifestation of the desire, shared by liberal reformers within and without the Labor Party, to redefine the Israeli-Palestinian conflict in such a way that its economic dimensions would appear paramount. By redefining the conflict in essentially economic, rather than geo-strategic terms, and advocating its resolution as one element in a package of economic and social reforms, these young liberals succeeded in articulating the concerns of a large and important segment of Israeli society and turning them into a coherent program of social transformation. (Interview: Beilin)

Once Labor and Meretz formed a government, after the 1992 elections, the reformers turned immediately to execute their program. In the Labor-Meretz government constituted in 1992, Yossi Beilin became Deputy Foreign Minister, Chayim Ramon, leader of Chug Hakfar Hayarok, became Minister of Health, and Dedi Zucker of Meretz became Chair of the all-important Constitution, Law and Justice Committee of the Knesset. A division of labor thus developed between the three bodies, with Beilin and Mashov working on the issue of peace, Ramon with some of his political allies working on a national health insurance plan that would remove Kupat Cholim from the control of the Histadrut, and Meretz dealing with constitutional issues.

Paramount place was given to economic cooperation between Israel and the Palestinian Authority and between them and regional bodies in the Declaration of Principles (DOP) reached in the secret talks in Oslo. This is not at all surprising in view of the fact that this document was the fruit of negotiations undertaken at the behest of Beilin between a member of Chug Mashov, Yair Hirschfeld, the author of a study on Israeli-Palestinian economic relations titled *From Dependency to Interdependence*, and his assistant Ron Pundik, and Abu Alla, the director of Tsumud, the PLO's management company of its economic assets and enterprises in Lebanon and elsewhere. Appendixes III and IV of the Oslo Agreement, were already part of the earliest summary of shared views prepared by Hirschfeld for the second round of talks in February 1993 were among the least revised sections when the agreement's parts were renegotiated by the representatives of the Foreign Ministry, Uri Savir and Joel Singer. (Interview: Ron Pundik, Director, Economic Cooperation Foundation and negotiator with PLO delegation in secret Oslo talks, March 30, 1995, and Beilin)

Even more sanguine for regional economic integration and cooperation, in fact, for reversing the historical process of separation of the Israeli and Arab economies by knitting into a common market the Israeli, Palestinian and Jordanian economies, is Shimon Peres. Peres's general outlook, according to his biographer Michael Keren, is geared toward the technocratic and professional stratum in Israeli society, and consequently places major emphasis on "industrialization, modernization, economic productivity, national planning, encouragement of higher education and extended use of science as technology" which he views as antidotes to the populism of both Israel's right wing and Middle Eastern fundamentalism. (Keren, 1994, pp.152, 156) Peres's book, *The New Middle East*, which appeared a few months after the signing of the Oslo DOP, presented a complex three-tiered program of regional cooperation. On top of binational or multinational projects geared toward specific topics such as water desalination or desert management, he expected international consortiums to undertake projects that require massive capital investment, such as the Red Sea-Dead Sea Canal, to be capped by regional cooperation leading to the evolution of official regional institutions. (Peres, 1993) In Keren's summary the main features of this plan are "the precedence of economics over politics, and the formation of partnerships which can be instituted before borders are drawn and peace treaties signed." In short, in Peres's new Middle East "business precedes politics and hence allows cooperation between peoples set apart by political differences." (Keren, 1994, p.157)

The Privatization of Koor

An overview of the transformation of the Koor corporation, from being the Histadrut's, indeed Israel's, largest industrial conglomerate, to Israel's first multinational holding company, will illustrate the multiple, interconnected dimensions of the liberal turn in the Israeli economy. The history of Koor is the history of the Israeli economy in microcosm. Reviewing it will thus open a window on the growing role of foreign capital in the economy, as well as on the business community's newly found and vigorously pursued emphasis on Israeli-Palestinian peace as a necessary step along the road to integration into the global economy.

Koor was established in the late 1940s with the intention of building labor-intensive factories to provide employment to Jewish immigrants, in the time-honored fashion of the Histadrut. With privileged access to labor, land, and capital, it emerged already in the mid-1950's as a major conglomerate. Its role as provider of jobs, rather than growth or profits, was illustrated, for example, in its purchase in 1983 of Alliance, a tire manufacturer that had been threatened with liquidation by its creditors. Koor's subsidiaries mutually guaranteed each other's debts and through an internal clearing-house in effect subsidized the loss-making ones and ensured that wages remained roughly equal among their workers (Interview with Menachem Geller, New Histadrut Trade Union Department, March 26, 1998). The salaried and hourly-paid workers at each plant elected representatives to workers' committees. These formed a central committee to represent all Koor workers that had no management responsibility but played an important role in negotiating the workers' benefits. The central workers' committee nominated six rank-and-file workers to serve four year terms on Koor's 21-person board of directors, and one worker to its six-person executive (*International Management* 1974, p.19).

Without any strategic plan or vision, Koor entered into many unrelated fields, but assigned an especially important role to its military industries. Already in its early years, by setting up Soltam for producing artillery and ammunition and Telrad for the production of telecommunication equipment (adding Tadiran in the early 1960s), Koor became a mainstay of the Israeli arms industry (Asa-El, 1997).

In the 1970s, under the management of Meir Amit, Koor began to emphasize profits, seeking, in Amit's words, to balance profit and the company's social mission by experimenting with profit-sharing, for example. On one occasion, the Histadrut consented to the closing of an unprofitable plant and the firing of its 100 workers and thus of transferring more power to the management. But, in fact, these were piecemeal changes and the "most important matters [were] cleared with the union," which was the company's legal owner (*International Management* 1974, p.18).

Koor relied on bank loans to raise capital throughout its existence, with the exception of two periods. In the early 1960s, it issued securities through the Tel Aviv Stock Exchange [TASE] which, since they were non-voting stocks, in fact resembled bonds. TASE repeatedly demanded the transformation of these into regular stocks, but the Histadrut's Hevrat Haovdim was determined to keep complete control over Koor and refused all such initiatives. In 1986 Koor turned for the first time to the U.S. markets and raised $105 million in the junk bond market through Drexel Burnham Lambert's Michael Milken at a very high 12 percent interest. Shortly afterwards the Bank of Israel [BOI] forbade Israeli companies to raise capital at such high prices. These two ventures indicated that, even when turning to security markets, Koor was not yet willing, or able, to be a full and regular participant.

Until 1987 Koor reported profits. Its 1987 sales of $2.7 billion represented more than 10 percent of Israel's gross national product, while its employees accounted for nearly 11 percent of the country's labor force. But already in 1986 it had a loss of $100 million, which climbed, in 1987, to $188 million and in 1988 to $369 million. In October, 1988, Koor defaulted on its loans, and its ratio of debt to equity was 72:1. Koor's future became doubtful when the financial reports of 1987 revealed a debt of $1.4 billion, and one of its American debtors asked for its liquidation (*Multinational Business* 1989, pp.28–29; Asa-El, 1997). In 1988, 126 out of Koor's 130 subsidiaries were losing money and were bailed out by the four profit-making ones, most of them in military production.

Benny Gaon, who in 1976 set up Koor's foreign trade division, the largest Israeli company in Europe with 15 branch offices and $100 million in yearly sales, and later helped restructure the Histadrut's Co-op—Israel's largest supermarket chain— was appointed Koor's CEO in 1987. Between May, 1988, and September 27, 1991, nerve-wracking negotiations were conducted with 32 Israeli and foreign banks. In what seemed like the last possible moment, these negotiations led to a comprehensive agreement with Koor's debtors, who wrote off a large share of its bad debt ($330 million), and with the Israeli Government and the Histadrut which, reluctantly and after much foot dragging, agreed to provide small new loans (NIS 175 million) for the duration of the reorganization period (Asa-El, 1997). Even so, during the big crisis it became obvious that, in spite of the expectation that Koor's size would leave the Israeli government no choice but to come to its aid, "Big Brother [was] not going to support us anymore" (Waldman 1991). Though some government support was forthcoming, it was relatively small and was offered in the context of changing Koor's ownership structure.

Under Gaon's management Koor was radically and brutally transformed. The mutual guarantee and the internal clearing arrangement among Koor's subsidiaries, which ensured the employment and relative wage equality of its workers, was abolished. The Histadrut conceded that profitability must be viewed as the top priority and, consequently, consented to the sale of assets, the shutting down of loss makers, and the largest ever lay-off in Israeli history, which led to the firing of 40 percent of Koor's workers, or 4 percent of Israel's civilian labor force. Even the *Wall Street Journal* compared the effect of the newfound "capitalist creed" on Koor, which saved the company by shedding so much of its labor force, to that of a "neutron bomb" (Waldman, 1991). And the *New York Times* quipped that Koor turned into a "lean-and-mean conglomerate that sheds money-losing businesses faster than you can say 'Charles Darwin'" (Passell, 1992a, 1992b). Although the layoffs were accompanied by worker demonstrations and protests, the repudiation of worker control, the firing of the very workers who under Hevrat Haovdim's constitution were Koor's putative owners, and the company's transfer, in the words of the *Jerusalem Post*, to "the unabashedly greedy ownership of Wall Street financiers—hardly [caused] anyone to raise an eyebrow" (Asa-El, 1997).

Hevrat Haovdim's 97 percent stake in Koor, already reduced to 71 percent in the reorganization's wake, was dramatically truncated by selling close to 60 percent to the public and to the Shamrock Group of the Shamrock Holdings investment company, wholly owned by the Disney family. In March 1995, Shamrock purchased Hevrat Haovdim's remaining shares, thus ending Koor's close to 50 year association with the Histadrut. The new Koor was no longer a management company but was structured as a holding company in which the management of the individual firms was left to their managers, who were told they would be measured by their ability to maintain profitability. The sale of many of Koor's subsidiaries, and the very reorganization of Koor itself, though termed in Hebrew *havr'aa*, or "nourishing back to health," was in effect a process of privatization, a fact sometimes obscured by the customary use of "privatization" in Israel for the sale of government assets only.

In 1991 Koor reported a net profit for the first time in five years and began a process of financial restructuring (Waldman, 1991; Carnegy. 1991; Passell. 1992). The restructuring turned into a financial success story: The new holding company, consisting of 30 individual firms, remained Israel's largest and became its most profitable industrial conglomerate, led by its electronic and high-tech subsidiary, Tadiran. It was Koor's ability to tap the international financial market directly that was "the turning point of its reorganization" and the key to its success and, concomitantly, to its independence (Gross, 1994, p.13). By late 1992 Koor had raised about $220 million through stock issues in the United States and Israel, and another $120 million in late 1995 in the United States Benny Gaon pointed to the "discovery of the capital market by the Israeli business sector," starting in 1988–90, as the beginning of the economic transformation that has led to the transition to a market-based economy and signaled the shift of the center of gravity from banks to corporations, both holding and investment companies. Gaining access to the capital market demonstrated the dramatic change in the character of the Israeli economy and allowed Israeli corporations, says Gaon, to tell the banks: "Don't call us, we'll call you." (Interview with Benjamin Gaon, CEO Koor, July 7, 1995) "Israel's business community," Gaon summed up, "has discovered the capital market. . . gradually disengaging. . . from a traditional dependency on the banks in favor of the stock market" (Gaon, "Remarks at the Washington Institute's October Policy Conference's session on 'Beyond Politics: The Potential for Economic Cooperation.'" Washington, D.C., October 15–17, 1993)

Both Gaon and Ben-Ami argue that Israeli companies were able to raise great sums of money through the Israeli and U.S. stock exchanges, and were awash with funds (Interview: Gaon). It is this capital abundance, without the mediation and control of the government, which has played a crucial role in the growing weight of the business community and the growing influence of business interests on public decision making in Israel (see Lane, 1998). It is also the basis on which a new collective identity—the Israeli business community—was formed. This identity was partially borrowed; Israeli business people have undergone a process of Americanization. (Interview: Professor Shlomo Ben-Ami, Chairman of the Board of Directors of Koor's Peace Projects, January 25, 1995)

The conceptualization which accompanied, justified, and was used to reflect upon Koor's restructuring, sheds critical light on its broader significance. "Within the 1985 conceptual and operational framework," Gaon argued, "no hope was left for Koor or for Israeli industry in general." The Histadrut itself was not able to help since many of its companies were simultaneously in crisis, and in 1986 it chose to invest its capital reserves in Solel Boneh. Under Koor's new management, reform was not effected in a patchwork form but was "a true, comprehensive, turnaround program" (Koor, 1992). "Koor," stated the *Wall Street Journal* during the restructuring, "adopted a new approach to doing business: the profit motive." It wrote Koor, "got into trouble in the same way socialist enterprises have foundered elsewhere: it tried to create jobs instead of profits" (Waldman, 1991). As we have shown throughout this book, Israeli socialism was above all a form of nationalism which sought to provide employment for nationalist reasons and, hence, enjoyed government support. Gaon is correct, then, in arguing that political considerations had historically overriden economic calculations. (Interview: Gaon) Consequently, "a revolution in corporate culture had to be achieved" (Carnegy, 1991).

In a speech in Washington, to celebrate the end of one stage of Koor's restructuring in April 1994, Gaon claimed that "the restructuring of Koor signaled the end of the concept of social welfare overriding profits and the establishment of a market driven economy." These sober reflections are combined with a different tone, one more typical of the new found self-confidence and bravado of the Israeli business community's leaders. Gaon thus stated that "we have been in the forefront of Israel's turning away from a socialistic approach to our economy to one which rewards enterprise and hard work." (Benjamin D. Gaon, Drafts for remarks at a reception in Washington and at the Waldorf Astoria in New York City to celebrate "The Conclusion of the International Banking Chapter in the Story of Koor's Restructuring," April 20, 1994) Even the boastful and crude character of this statement should be seen as indicative in equal shares of a desire to impress the U.S. businesspeople in the audience and of the triumphant mood of the new Israeli economic elites. Given the centrality of Koor to the Histadrut, Gaon's observations on its pivotal role in Israel's socio-economic transformation are not too far-fetched.

As a "key part" of its recovery plan, Koor Industries under Gaon further emphasized an export oriented approach by seeking out "new markets for our goods and joint ventures with new partners." Its "capitalistic profit-oriented" approach was the basis for Koor's aim "to ensure itself a competitive place in the world's markets as they open up in the West and East alike," that is, to partake in the process most commonly referred to as "globalization" (Koor 1992). In reporting the results of 1993, Gaon singled out for praise the telecommunications and electronics high-tech, construction materials, and agro-chemical companies, whose successful performance in the export market demonstrated the competitive character of Koor products at a time the company "accelerate[s its] efforts to enter new growth businesses serving emerging markets in Israel and around the world." ("Koor Industries 1993 Profits Rose 43% to $124 Million," News Release, mimeo, March 30, 1994) The "future of the company," argued Gaon, "lies in globalization."

By 1995 Koor was in the process of "turning itself into a multinational concern and forging strategic partnerships with international companies" (Ozanne 1995). In 1993, for example, Koor's exports rose by 13 percent, most of the growth coming from the markets recently opened in India, China, Vietnam, and the Commonwealth of Independent Nations. In 1996 Koor made an international stock offering, "thus becoming the first Israeli multinational company to be traded worldwide." This was done as part of an overall plan: "the integration of Koor Industries into the global business community will form the essence of our strategy over the forthcoming years." (Gaon, Hilton, Tel Aviv, June 22, 1995)

Summing up the situation of the Israeli economy and capital market in 1994, Gaon repeated over and over that

There is no doubt that the continued expansion of the economy depends on the significant widening of the Israeli market to foreign investment and in furnishing opportunities and assistance for the strategic investment of Israeli corporations abroad. (For example Gaon, Israel Management Center, May 24, 1994)

Foreign investment in Israel provides strong financial backing as well as new management experience and links to international marketing and data bases, whereas Israeli investment in foreign subsidiaries or in purchasing equity in foreign companies provides a stepping stone for increasing technological know-how and penetration into new markets. (Gaon, Jerusalem Business Conference, November 1994)

The achievement of both of these goals—opening new markets for Israeli industry and attracting foreign capital—required that a solution be found to the Israeli-Palestinian conflict. Many Israeli business leaders realized that the Arab boycott was an obstacle on the road to integrating the Israeli economy into the world market; that while it was in effect all efforts in this direction would yield only limited results. Similarly, only the stability ensured by peace could bring foreign investment and foreign corporations into Israel in significant numbers. For although Israeli companies had been launched in the American stock market, international capital still remained aloof from Israel, due to the political instability in the Middle East. Economic liberalization thus provided an impetus for peace by mobilizing strategic sectors of the emerging Israeli business community, Gaon of Koor most prominent among them, in support of achieving a breakthrough in Israeli-Palestinian relations. The politicization of the business community around this issue was thus, simultaneously, an indication of its newfound autonomy and a major contribution to breaking the stalemate between Israel and the Palestinians.

Peace and Profits

Koor was better equipped to turn to Arab and Middle Eastern markets because, unlike most other Israeli companies, it had some limited experience in this area. As head of Koor's foreign trade operations, Gaon had set up a Koor office in Egypt after the Camp David accord, the first Israeli company to do so. Due to Egyptian reluctance, hopes for expanding trade relations were quickly shattered, however. Still, while until 1994 there were no open trade relations between Israel and the Arab world, it is estimated that in the 1980s about half of the approximately one billion dollars that appear annually in the unclassified category of Israeli exports in Israel's Foreign Trade Statistical Quarterly were destined for Arab countries. For example, in the 1980s Iraq imported hydraulic lifts and agricultural inputs, as well as pharmaceutical products. (Interview: Professor Gideon Fishelson, Associate of the Armand Hammer Fund for Economic Cooperation in the Middle East, January 31, 1995) Morocco has purchased fertilizers, agricultural implements, seeds, and air-conditioners to the tune of $80 million per year. (Interview: Mandi Barak, Head of the Desk of Islamic Countries, Federated Chamber of Commerce, January 13, 1995) Many of these products were supplied by Koor subsidiaries.

Koor's Peace Project was launched shortly after the signing of the DOP in Oslo in September, 1993, and it simultaneously launched its first project for regional co-operation, Salam–2000, in cooperation with Omnium Nord Africa (ONA), Morocco's largest private concern, and a group of Palestinian businessmen (Interview: Ben-Ami). Another effort was to form Jordanian-Palestinian-Israeli partnerships to invest mostly in West Bank and Gaza infrastructure and in the Arab world, in both trade and industry. One of the areas Koor entered in anticipation of a breakthrough in the peace process was tourism, through its new branch "Koor Tourism Enterprises." Koor is also the main company to have established ongoing economic relations with the Palestinian National Authority, exporting cement, construction iron, and telecommunications equipment, worth $80 million in 1994 (Interviews: Gaon and Ben-Ami)

According to Gaon, in a country with a small number of industrial concerns, such as Israel, "it is the responsibility of companies such as Koor. . . to forge new joint projects, to divert funds from war to peace, to deepen the economic bonds between regional economies and the western world and to develop a regional economy of peace." He called on "the leading industrial concerns," that is, IDB, Israel Corp., Israel Chemicals, Clal, and Koor itself, "to take the lead, to take the risk, and invite foreign capital for joint investment projects in Israel as well as in the region." (Gaon, Jerusalem Business Conference, November 1994)

For Israeli companies, the Arab economies held promise as potential markets, suppliers of cheap labor, sub-contractors, business partners, and objects or targets of investment. Low-tech producers, among them food manufacturers, such as Elite and Osem, that occupied semi-monopolistic status in the Israeli economy, anticipated being hurt by the reduction of tariff barriers as part of trade liberalization and were eager to enter into markets of non-industrial societies. Producers of luxury goods recognized the Arab market as stratified and aimed their products at the affluent stratum as well as the more affluent Arab states in the Gulf region. (Interview: Nurith Nachum, General Director, Yaad Business Development of Kesselman and Kesselman, Public Accountants, a subsidiary of Coopers and Lybrand, February 3, 1995)

The abundance of investment capital Israeli companies could raise after the liberalization of the capital market could not find outlets in Israel and led to a search for appropriate markets for investment abroad. Gaon summed up the attractions of the Middle East for Israeli investors:

> Israel's technological and financial know-how, coupled to the financial resources of the Gulf states and to the inexpensive labor available in the area, offers investors a combination of commercial attributes that is probably unique in the world. (Gaon 1993)

Alternatively, Israel could serve "as an important bridge" between the countries of the region and the rest of the world. In the vision of the over-confident business leaders, Israel appeared as the hub and coordinator of a new regional economic grouping without any consideration of the potential conflicts between countries with widely disparate resources. It is hard to escape the conclusion that in peacemaking, as in conflict, the Israeli approach of qualitative superiority continued to prevail. In fact, no such regional economic order has developed yet, although a small number of Israeli companies, mostly in textiles, transferred their plants from development and citizen Palestinian towns and even from the Gaza Strip to Jordan and Egypt. (*Mitzad Sheni,* January/February 1997, pp.16–19)

But benefits were expected not only from the opening of the Arab markets, closed by the primary Arab boycott, but even more so of other markets, closed as part of the secondary boycott (in which third parties doing business with Israel were penalized). In a speech Gaon delivered at the annual conference of the Israel Management Center (MIL), in May 1994, the subject of his comments was "Israel toward an Open Global Economy," and he reiterated them to the Jerusalem Business Conference in November 1994. The peace process, Gaon pointed out, "has opened additional avenues of growth for the Israeli economy." In addition to the immediate circle of Palestinians, Jordan and Syria, he listed the outer circle of the North African and Gulf countries and Turkey, as well the Asian countries of Indonesia, Malaysia, India, Vietnam, Japan, and Korea as potential commercial targets. Economic relations with Arab countries "represent only a fraction of the benefits that Israel stands to gain from peace in the Middle East," and the other, more lucrative, possibilities "would not have been likely before the peace process began."

This multiple set of interests, animated in 1993 many of the meetings of the regional and topical forums of the dense business network operating under the aegis of MIL. Haim Kamenitz, the MIL's Director, recalls that the gatherings of its tourism, marketing, senior managers, and many other groups, were dissatisfied with the pace of the peace process. The hope repeatedly expressed in these meetings was that managers might be able to advance what politicians could not, and that economic ties would provide a good foundation for political arrangements. (Interview: Haim Kamenitz, Director, Israeli Management Center, February 27, 1995) These sentiments were shared by other key leaders of the Israeli business community. Most outspoken was Dov Lautman, President of the Israeli Manufacturers' Association (MA) from June 1987 to June 1993 and, as such, also Chair of the Coordinating Bureau of the Economic Organizations, the broad-based association of Israeli business organizations that includes, in addition to the MA, also the Federation of Chambers of Commerce, and the umbrella organizations of building contractors, banks, private farmers, life insurance companies, the self-employed, diamond manufacturers, hotels, and so forth.

In the early 1990s, the last years of Shamir's government, Lautman was a major critic of government economic policies which, in his view, did not create the conditions for the absorption of the masses of Soviet Jewish immigrants, namely, increased productivity and exports. The pressing need to absorb the immigrants served as a shield behind which it was possible to criticize the government's lack of proper economic policies, and, indirectly, its lack of enthusiasm for the peace process. In the yearly Jerusalem Business Conference, held one week before the crucial 1992 elections, Lautman issued his first open linkage of the peace talks (that had been going on in Madrid, with no apparent progress, since October 1991) with economic growth, and issued an indirect call to advance the negotiations. In his words, the major obstacle to foreign investment in the Israeli economy was regional instability, and only the combination of a proper economic policy with progress in the peace talks could make Israel attractive to foreign investors. (*Ha'aretz*, June 17, 1992; Interview: Dov Lautman, President of the Israeli Manufacturers' Association and CEO, Delta textiles, February 16, 1995)

In November 1992, Lautman added the Arab boycott to his list of conditions that hurt Israel economically, and in this context argued that the business community had made a mistake in the past decade by not placing the linkage between peace and growth at the top of its priorities. (*Ha'aretz*, November 17, 1992) He was seconded in this opinion by Danny Gillerman, President of the Israeli Chambers of Commerce who, relying on a study conducted by his organization, alleged that Israel had lost $44 billion as a result of the Arab boycott. Gillerman called on Rabin, the new Prime Minister, to consider the abolition of the boycott a top priority. (*Ha'aretz*, August 7, 1992) Finally, in January, 1993, Lautman threw in the trump card by promising that a breakthrough in the peace "talks in 1993 will serve as a tremendous turning point *(mifne adir)* in the fortunes of the Israeli economy in general and of industry in particular, by 1994." (*Ha'aretz*, January 1, 1993)

As soon as the news of the pending, but yet unfinished and still potentially collapsible, accord between Israel and the PLO leaked to the public, the *crème de la crème* of Israeli business leaders called on Rabin and Peres, in a paid advertisement, "to bring peace for the sake of good years." (*Ha'aretz*, September 2, 1993) As a sequel, some of the signatories established a committee to support the government's peace policy for example, by plastering billboards with the slogan "Israel awaits peace." (*Ha'aretz*, September 5, 1993) When Rabin and Peres returned from Washington, after signing of the DOP, some of the same individuals were invited to the welcoming ceremony, in order to underline the centrality of the economic dimension of the agreement. (*Ha'aretz*, September 19, 1993) Lautman was mentioned as a possible chair of the Israeli delegation to the economic talks with the Palestinians that followed the DOP, and Eli Horowitz, CEO of the large pharmaceutical concern, Teva, was actually offered that job, but declined due to the extensive time commitment it required. (*Ha'aretz*, October 11, 1993; November 16, 1993; Interview: Eli Horowitz, CEO, Teva, July 9, 1995)

Support for the peace process, and implicitly for recognition of Palestinian national rights, was by no means unanimous among Israeli businesspeople, however. The self-selected business leaders, who expressed their vigorous support and sought to rally others, due to the opening to the world economy peace was expected to yield, were drawn from industries which could benefit from export-oriented growth. They were stubbornly opposed by executives from labor-intensive industries, whose purview was more domestic. This division was clearly revealed in the differing attitudes of the two groups toward the new economic possibilities an autonomous Palestinian authority would present.

In mid-1992 Lautman set up a committee of the Coordinating Bureau of the Economic Organizations, chaired by Dan Gillerman of the FCC, to study the "Economic Implications of the Establishment of Autonomy in the Territories and Ways for Its Integration with the Israeli Economy." (Coordinating Bureau of the Economic Organizations, 1992; 1993) Although the leadership of the Coordinating Bureau and the MAI was clearly supportive of such autonomy, many in the rank and file were fearful of its impact on their particular sectors and expressed their reservations. Both a survey conducted by the MAI (MAI, 1994) and a special issue of its quarterly, devoted to the "autonomy," reveal that textiles, food, wood, leather and plastic products were seen as vulnerable to competition from Palestinian workers, whose wages were only a fraction of the wages of Israeli workers in these fields. Ironically, building contractors, the biggest employers of Palestinian workers, were concerned about losing their workers to what, they expected, would become a booming Palestinian economy, while private and collective farmers thought they might both lose workers and be exposed to cheaper agricultural imports. (Dan Proper; Efraim Kleiman; Dov Kali, 1993)

Summing up the demands that were included in the Gillerman Report and expressing these concerns (that were largely incorporated into the Israeli position at the Paris economic talks in 1994), industrialist Mozi Wertheimer concluded that their acceptance would replace autonomy with Israeli economic domination over the Palestinians. (Wertheimer, 1993; Ben-Shahar, 1995; *Protocol on Economic Relations*. 1995; Savir, 1998) Although the vocal supporters of the peace process were drawn from the very apex of the business community, a considerable part of their efforts was spent in seeking to reduce the anxiety of other industrialists, farmers, and merchants, fearful of the potentially adverse economic effects of a peace accord on their branches of the economy. (Interview: Uri Menashe, CEO Kargal (March 29, 1995) The complaints and fears of the opponents from within the MA were played down, however, by Lautman, who led the MA toward a policy "of free trade and open markets" with the Palestinians. (Interview: Lautman)

Parallel with the public opinion campaign, the MAI, under Lautman and others, and the MIL sought to commence talks with Palestinian businesspeople in order to facilitate economic cooperation and, through it, advance the political talks as well. (Interviews: Lautman and Kamenitz) Some thought that voluntary assistance for a Palestinian organization for export, for a clearinghouse for Israeli-Palestinian trade, or for setting up a Palestinian stock exchange, would serve as proofs that progress could be attained. "Palestinian industrialists," argued Yoram Blizovsky, Director General of the MA, "view us, industrialists, as a more credible partner than the government, since we are perceived as a more neutral factor." (Interview: Yoram Blizovsky, General Director of Manufacturers' Association, January 19, 1995) This sentiment was shared by other Israeli business leaders, who believed that business ties and cooperation between individuals and enterprises would make it possible to bypass political problems. In the words of Uri Menashe, who was in charge of these talks, it was expected that the changing economic reality could marginalize political problems and have politicians follow the lead of economic cooperation. (Interview: Uri Menashe)

Soon after Labor won the 1992 elections, Lautman called for adopting an economic policy toward the Palestinian autonomy in negotiations with its economic leadership in order to ensure that the two economies would be coordinated. (Reiner, 1992). For the first time the grand vision of economic growth in the context of Middle East peace and the immediate reality of Israeli-Palestinian conflict were linked in a single strategic framework. The eventual talks between the two economic elites remained sporadic and inconclusive, however, due to the inability of the Palestinian side, still under Israeli military occupation, to separate its economic from its political concerns, and due to restrictions imposed by their political leadership. (Interview: Uri Menashe; *Ha'aretz*, December 18, 1992) In addition, Palestinian businesspeople were well aware of the past opposition of Israeli industrialists to the establishment of industrial enterprises in the West Bank and were less than keen on an open border policy. Under these conditions, two separate decisions to established a permanent forum for the two elites did not take effect. (*Ha'aretz*, February 17, 1993)

It was in the immediate aftermath of the DOP that the voice of business support for peace economics grew loudest. The Jewish New Year and the Jerusalem Business Conference of November 1993 issues of *Globes*, the main Israeli business daily, were full of glorious and euphoric predictions of the economic benefits of the peace process, propagated, this time, by a broad cross-section of businesspeople and government officials. (*Globes*, September 15 and November 2, 1993) There was a veritable stampede of lesser business leaders and economists rushing in the footsteps of the trailblazers. "The sky is the limit" of the peace economy was their approach, and the economic benefits of peace served as its main selling point. One of the most telling examples of the euphoria was a brochure prepared by MIL for its annual meeting in December 1993, in which the keynote speaker was Rabin, and the other speakers the President of Israel, the Minister of Finance, the President of the MA, and the Chairman of MIL. The brochure was decorated with the picture of the famous Rabin-Arafat handshake on the White House lawn, with President Clinton looking on, under the logo "The Economic Turn Begins." Not the political turn, mind you, but the economic turn! The extensive participation of government representatives demonstrated the extent to which this approach and this sentiment were shared by the government. The government mobilized the industrialists to sell the peace, after the industrialists had identified themselves with the process of peacemaking.

Conclusion

The Israeli-Palestinian conflict had remained at an impasse as long as it was viewed solely as a security matter. It became "solvable" when it was reconceptualized as an obstacle to the integration of Israeli business into the global economy, at a moment of acute consciousness of the difference between "winning" and "losing" countries in the world economic arena. Within this new framework the old issues of the colonial era became secondary to questions of economic growth and development. This created the potential for replacing the traditional, zero-sum game, in which one side's gain was the other side's loss, with a more open-ended game, in which both sides could be winners. This process of redefinition was greatly aided by the outward-looking sectors of the business community, in league with the professional and technocratic elites of the civil service (especially its legal and economic sectors) and the political leadership, after Labor's election victory in 1992. It involved an attempt to extend the boundaries of the "economic" at the expense of the "political," and of the "civic" and "individualistic" at the expense of the "pioneering" and "collective." This approach dovetailed with the experience of financial, trade, legal, and cultural globalization that has pointed up, for most countries of the world, the limits of nation-state autonomy.

References

Asa-El, Amotz. 1997. "Koor Grabs the Future." *Jerusalem Post*, February 19.

Ben-Shahar, Hayim.1995. "Highlights of the Report of the Economic Advisory Team to the Political Negotiations, July 1993." *Rivon Lekalkala* 42, pp.135–54, in Hebrew.

Carnegy, Hugh. 1991. "Koor Optimistic after Struggle for Survival." *Financial Times*, October 1.

Coordinating Bureau of the Economic Organizations, The Committee for Studying the Economic Implications of the Autonomy and the Peace Process. 1992. "Autonomy in the Territories—Economic Implications: Interim Report." Coordinating Bureau of the Economic Organizations, October 29, in Hebrew.

Coordinating Bureau of the Economic Organizations, Report of the Special Committee Chaired by Dan Gillerman of the FCC. 1993. "Economic Implications of the Establishment of Autonomy in the Territories and Ways for Its Integration with the Israeli Economy." Coordinating Bureau of the Economic Organizations, February, in Hebrew.

Gross, Joseph. 1994. *Koor Industries Inc.: The Reorganization Process and the Capital Market.* Tel Aviv: Tel Aviv University, School of Management, in Hebrew.

Institute for Social and Economic Policy in the Middle East, John F. Kennedy School of Government, Harvard University. 1993. *Pressing Peace: The Institute in the News: June-September.*

Kali, Dov. 1993. "Don't Establish in the Territories a Paradise for Industry." *Hata'asiyanim,* No.25, April.

Keren, Michael. 1994. "Israeli Professionals and the Peace Process." *Israel Affairs* 1.

Kleiman, Efraim. 1993. "The Economic Welfare of the Territories is an Israeli Interest." *Hata'asiyanim,* No.25, April.

Koor. 1992. The Making of the New Koor. Tel Aviv: Koor President's Office (mimeo).

"Koor Industries: Israel's Conglomerate Restructured." 1989. Multinational Business 1, pp.28–29.

Lein, Yechezkel. 1998. "The State, the Business Elite and Coalitions: the Stock Exchange Tax as a Parable." Masters thesis, Department of Political Science, The Hebrew University, Jerusalem.

Manufacturers' Association of Israel [MAI], Economics and Foreign Trade Department.1994. *Survey of the Implications of Autonomy for Industry (October-November 1993),* in Hebrew.

Mashov. 1981."Mashov"— Founding Charter, December 28 (mimeo), in Hebrew.

_____. 1983. First Mashov Conference, April, various documents (mimeo), in Hebrew.

_____. 1985. Second Mashov Conference, June, various documents (mimeo), in Hebrew.

_____. 1986. Positions for the Third Mashov Conference, February (mimeo), in Hebrew.

_____. 1987. Fourth Mashov Conference, April, various documents (mimeo), in Hebrew.

_____. 1989. Mashov Council on the Histadrut, July (mimeo), in Hebrew.

_____. 1991a. Proposals Submitted to the Fifth Conference of Mashov. (Mimeo) In Hebrew

_____. 1991b. Resolutions of the Fifth Conference of Mashov, May (mimeo), in Hebrew.

Meretz.1992. Platform for the 1992 Elections, in Hebrew.

Ozanne, Julian.1995. "Koor Raises Almost $120m in Successful IPO." *Financial Times,* November 14.

Passell, Peter. 1992a. "Zionist Dreams, Capitalist Reality." *New York Times,* January 1.

_____. 1992b. "Need Zionism Equal Socialism?" *New York Times,* July 2.

Peres, Shimon. 1993. *The New Middle East.* New York : Henry Holt.

Proper, Dan. 1993. "The Autonomy—Implications for the Israeli Economy." *Hata'asiyanim,* No.25, April.

Protocol on Economic Relations between the Government of Israel and the PLO, Representing the Palestinian People. 1995. *Rivon Lekalkala* 42, pp.160–179, in Hebrew.

Razin, Assaf and Efraim Sadka.1993. *The Economy of Modern Israel: Malaise and Promise.* Chicago: University of Chicago Press.

Savir, Uri. 1998. *The Process: 1,1000 Days that Changed the Middle East* New York: Random House.

"Union-Owned Firm Stresses Profits."1974. International Management, February.

Waldman, Peter. 1991 "Big Brother Is Shown the Door at Koor, Giving Israel's Largest Company a Boost." *Wall Street Journal,* July 3.

Wertheimer, Mozi 1993. "Don't Err with Too Rosy Dreams" *Hataasiyanim* 25 April, in Hebrew.

World Bank. 1993. *Developing the Occupied Territories: An Investment in Peace,* Vol. 2, *The Economy.* Washington: World Bank.

11

Regional Cooperation and the MENA Economic Summits

JONATHAN PARIS

Introduction

The last decade of the twentieth century has been dominated by two themes: the globalization of the economic system as free trade and free market ideas became more widely accepted, and the efforts of the world's only remaining superpower, the United States, to bring the 50-year-old Arab-Israeli conflict to closure and to contain America's number one nemesis of the decade, Saddam Hussein of Iraq.

The Arab-Israeli peace process had started long before the 1990s; the consensus view is that it began in the aftermath of the October 1973 war with the disengagement agreements brokered by U.S. Secretary of State Henry Kissinger. But the peace process became the object of global attention only in the 90s because of the extraordinary confluence of a number of events. The seating of Arab and Israeli belligerents in the same room at the Madrid Conference in 1991, and the secret negotiations between the PLO and Israel in Oslo, Norway, in 1993 represented qualitative changes in Arab-Israeli relations. Apart from Israel, Arab rulers were barraged with rapid fire changes: the breakup of the Soviet Union and downfall of socialist dictators like Ceacaescu of Romania, the threat of Islamic radicals, and the U.S.-led coalition's defeat of Iraq following Iraq's invasion of a fellow Arab country, Kuwait, all of which suggested the status quo could no longer hold.

Arab countries watched uneasily as their neighbor, Israel, shed its socialist baggage and became an international technological and scientific hothouse with the influx of educated Russian immigrants. Madrid and Oslo had internationalized the peace process as multinational corporate investments from the United States, Europe, and Asia began to accelerate with the erosion of the secondary and tertiary Arab boycott. The Arab private sector, together with reformers in Arab governments, realized that they had to shed the relics of Nasserite state-socialism leftover from the 60s and integrate into the global economy if they were to avoid the fate of East European communists.

By 1994, conditions were ripe for a number of international institutions and governments to contribute not only to the successful implementation of the Oslo Declaration of Principles between Israel and the Palestinians, but to the general amelioration of the Middle East/North Africa. James Wolfensohn, before he became president of the World Bank, told a consultation of American and Middle East/North African business and political leaders in Aspen, that less than 1 percent of world capital flows went to the Middle East/North Africa. This had to change if the region was not going to be left out entirely from the new alliance between global capital and emerging markets. Finally, multinationals, especially from Europe, saw the peace process as an opportunity to view the region as a single market comprised of Israel and the Arab countries. With the support of the United States government, international institutions like the World Bank and prestigious non-profit organizations like the Council on Foreign Relations of New York and the Davos-based World Economic Forum, worked to transform the incipient bilateral peace accords into broader regional cooperation and development.

The MENA Summits

Every autumn since the Oslo Accord was signed in 1993, multinational corporations, governments and businesses from the Middle East/North Africa [MENA] region gathered in a major city in the region. The inaugural Summit took place with great fanfare in Casablanca, Morocco, just days after the signing of the peace treaty between Jordan and Israel at the end of October, 1994. The second Summit took place in Amman, Jordan, in 1995, followed by Cairo, Egypt, in 1996 and Doha, capital of the Gulf Emirate of Qatar, in 1997.

The New York-based Council on Foreign Relations and the Davos-based World Economic Forum organized and convened the inaugural Casablanca Summit. Casablanca was the first of the four MENA Economic Summits launched under government co-sponsorship of the United States and Russia to provide an economic track parallel to the political track of the Middle East Peace Process. King Hassan of Morocco pulled out all of the stops to make Casablanca a success following the positive winds of change from the signing of the Oslo Peace Accord in September 1993 between the PLO and Israel. Further momentum was provided only two months before Casablanca, when Jordan and Israel signed a comprehensive peace treaty on October 26, 1994.

The basic programmatic structure of the MENA summit includes plenary sessions and concurrent thematic sessions, to provide interaction between the private sector and the public sector, and country luncheons to highlight that country's comparative advantages for business investment. The Middle East Economic Strategy Group presented its report in a larger thematic session. In 1995, Paul Volcker, the group's chair, presented its report on the proposed new regional bank; in 1996, a panel with Stu Eizenstat, then with the U.S. Department of Commerce, Dan Gillerman of the Israel Chamber of Commerce, Samir Huleileh, then with the

Palestinian Authority Ministry of Trade and Industry, and Ahemed Goweily, the Egyptian Trade and Supplies Minister, discussed the group's report on "Trade Arrangements in the Middle East and North Africa"; and in 1997, Stanley Fischer of the IMF, John Page of the World Bank and two Gulf experts discussed the group's report on "Development in the Gulf Countries."[1]

I became deeply involved with the planning of each of the four Summits as well as three pre-Summit conferences held at the Council on Foreign Relations in New York in the spring of 1994. Many of the same individuals across the region, Europe, and the United States would get together bi-annually and develop personal friendships. But in the autumn of 1998, there was no Summit. What happened?

. In May 1998, the Council on Foreign Relations took advantage of the hiatus in regional economic cooperation to bring together a group of public and private sector participants in previous MENA Economic Summits to step back and evaluate the four Summits[2]. The purpose of this exercise was to examine the value and effectiveness of these annual convocations of government officials and businesspeople. What were the assumptions and goals of the MENA Summits? What did they accomplish?

The Premise

The MENA Summit was designed to reinforce the peace process and Israel's normalization of relations with its Arab neighbors by building a kind of economic scaffolding.[3] Given the reluctance of Arabs and Israelis to commingle in political and cultural venues, an economic summit provided the opportunity to bring together a large number of Arab, Israeli, and other business executives to pursue common economic interests, that is, to "make a buck." By creating at Casablanca a large public-private sector arena for business and economic policy discourse, the architects of the MENA Summits, namely the U.S. government with prodding from then Israeli Foreign Minister, Shimon Peres, hoped to achieve the integration of Israel into the region—an Israel *in* the Middle East, not merely *of* the Middle East.[4] This goal was reflected in the very title of the Summit. MENA stands for Middle East/North Africa, which includes Israel. There has been a plethora of regional trading and political blocs in the Middle East/North Africa, but none had included Israel.[5] The MENA Summit was a novelty because it included Israel and offered the promise that effective regional institutions might result. But its continued success depended on progress on the peace process. That linkage was frequently expressed in the Arab world, which viewed the MENA Summits as a reward to Israel for progress on the political tracks. When the peace process stalled in 1996 under the Netanyahu government, the Arabs sought to slow, and ultimately end, the MENA economic summit process.

The architects of Casablanca hoped that the peace made between Arab and Israeli leaders would be transformed into a peace between Arab and Israeli peoples. Economic dividends from regional economic development and cross-border joint ventures would raise the standard of living of the average Arab and thereby make peace with Israel widely accepted. Shimon Peres echoed this view when he said that "it is not in Israel's interest to have poor economies next to its rich economy."6

A Report Card

Barriers were broken at Casablanca where the Israeli political and business elite mingled for three days with their Arab counterparts with hundreds of European and American business and government leaders, providing a supportive environment. The breakthrough was largely at a psychological level. Few concrete deals were formulated in the euphoria of the conference, although many business cards were exchanged. Dan Gillerman, President of the Israel Chamber of Commerce, spoke about how contacts with Arab businessmen expose Israelis not only to business possibilities, but also to qualitatively better interaction on a human level. "They meet with us as equals," he said, in contrast to the more common Israeli interaction with economically unequal Palestinian workers in Israel.7

As gloomy as prospects for the peace process are today, the breakthrough at Casablanca cannot be completely undone. Even Saudi Arabia sent a minister to the second Summit in Amman. Crown Prince Abdullah, current day-to-day ruler of Saudi Arabia, has told more than one American delegation that despite the political stalemate in the Arab-Israeli peace process, the Saudis would not return to the past when Israel was taboo.8

The first two MENA Economic Summits in Casablanca and Amman were widely viewed as successful. Those Summits highlighted investment opportunities in the region. International investors and multinationals that did not have the Middle East on their screen were drawn to these annual gatherings in significant numbers, and contacts made with government officials and the private sector in the region resulted in some bilateral and multilateral projects and investments. As long as the peace process was on track, this economic activity advanced the intended purpose of reinforcing political efforts and even keeping hope alive when the peace process stalled. However, when the political track became impassible, continued economic cooperation could not by itself restore the political track, or even sustain the economic summit event.9

Before talking about prospects for regional economic cooperation, it is useful to examine closely the important economic and political elements of the summits.

Private Sector Joint Ventures

The MENA summits helped business leaders meet partners and potential partners in the region. An executive of a bottled water company noted that the summits provided "a positive ambiance validating their decision" to invest in the Middle East.10 An executive of a New York money management firm noted that they offered "excellent venues to announce agreements that were concluded in advance."11

Israeli textile companies like Delta Galil Industries, led by Dov Lautman, met their Jordanian and Egyptian partners and were soon setting up manufacturing facilities in those low-wage neighboring countries. In one creative transaction, Lautman, chairman of Delta Galil, set up a garment assembly plant in an empty building in Irbid provided by Omar Salah of the Century Group, his Jordanian partner.[12] Multinationals began to look seriously at Israel as a hub for distribution in the wider MENA region. Asian tourist companies started combining tours of Israel with tours of Arab countries.[13]

Gil Feiler, Director of Info-Prod Research in Israel, provides an account of the mixed prospects for trade and joint ventures between Israel and its immediate neighbors. He writes: "Regarding trade, in 1993, the total merchandise trade output between Egypt and Israel was approximately $20 million. That amount rose to $40 million in 1994, $60 million in 1995, $82 million in 1996, $82.5 million in 1997, but decreased slightly in 1998. Most of the trade between Egypt and Israel is via the land borders at Rafah and Nitzana. In 1997, more than 398,000 people, 2,105 private vehicles and 165,304 tons of commercial cargo, on 6,427 trucks (exports and imports) passed through the Rafah and Nitzana borders. Furthermore, in 1997, Israel imported $375 million worth of Egyptian oil, making it one of the three largest customers for Egyptian oil. In 1998, however, Egyptian oil exports to Israel declined significantly."

Levels of trade between Israel and Jordan have doubled since the signing of the peace treaty. In 1997, Israeli exported $20.1 million worth of goods to Jordan, and imports totaled $12.7 million. In any case, trade potential between the two countries is not large.

Regarding joint ventures, there are some between Israel and the Palestinian Authority, even some large investments, but unfortunately most are structured around Palestinian monopolies. In addition, the Palestinian Authority discourages joint ventures with Israelis. Egyptian authorities also discourage commercial relations with Israel. There are several exceptions to this rule, such as the successful joint venture set up by Delta Galil.

Feiler sees much more success and potential with respect to joint ventures with Jordan. Total investment in the major joint projects, involving Delta, Readymix, Tadiran and Camiel, did not exceed $30 million. These joint ventures have been responsible for creating employment for roughly 200 workers in Jordan.[14]

Clearly, joint ventures offer greater prospects to Israeli companies than trade, but even here, the magnitude is paltry when compared with Israeli trade and joint ventures outside the region.

Regional Infrastructure Projects

The program at the MENA Summit most directly connected to the peace process was a plenary session on regional infrastructure projects. The presenters in this plenary sessions were key ministers from the Core Parties (Egypt, Israel, Jordan, and

the Palestinian Authority), and a senior U.S. official. Started in Amman and continued in the Summits at Cairo and Doha, this council-organized plenary highlighted fast-track regional projects, which were being coordinated with the Core
Parties on a day-to-day level by the Regional Economic Development Working
Group Secretariat based in Amman. REDWG, as this group was called, was one of
the multilateral governmental groups that emerged from the Madrid Conference of
1991.

In the 1996 Cairo Summit, the Council, with the assistance of REDWG, prepared a 55-page booklet detailing the joint projects presented in Cairo by ministers
from the four Core Parties. Egypt presented the interconnection of electricity grids
and the Peace Pipeline, the Palestinians presented the South East Mediterranean
Riviera Project (including the East Mediterranean coastal road from North Sinai
through Gaza into Israel), and the Gaza Industrial Estate at Karni. Jordan presented
several bridge crossing projects and Gulf of Aqaba tourism, and Israel presented the
Dead Sea Theme Park.

Up to the Cairo Summit in 1996, the Council and REDWG were able to facilitate coordination among the Core Parties on regional projects for water conserva-
tion, connecting electricity grids, pollution control, and transportation. The Gaza
Industrial Estate at Karni along the border with Israel, which finally opened in late
1998, was identified in August 1995 as a fast-track project in a preparatory meeting
convened to prepare projects involving the Palestinians for investor consideration at
the Amman Summit.

With the exception of Karni and a few other projects,[15] however, few projects
have been implemented because of the current freeze in the peace process. REDWG
effectively disbanded at the end of 1996. Only where the parties are interested in cooperation (such as between Jordan and Israel), have they undertaken joint regional
projects like the Qualifying Industrial Zone (QIZ) in northern Jordan, and the
Aqaba-Eilat airport.

New Regional Institutions

The political situation has prevented the establishment and functioning of new regional institutions created by the MENA economic summits. This is unfortunate
because each of these institutions serves an important purpose. The failure of these
institutions to materialize undermines Israel's political objective of becoming integrated institutionally into the region via regional business councils, a regional travel
and tourist association, and the development bank.[16]

The Middle East Bank for Development and Cooperation (MENA Bank) is a
particularly interesting example in which the State Department pushed very hard
to get the European and Gulf countries to financially back the Bank. The Department of Treasury helped formulate the Bank's Charter, emphasizing the bank's role
as a catalyst for private sector financing. The Middle East Economic Strategy
Group, chaired by Paul Volcker and comprised of former heads of central banks

and economic officials from Europe, Japan, and the Middle East,[17] met in London in July of 1995 to consider whether such a bank was necessary. The Americans, strongly urged by Stanley Fischer of the IMF and the U.S. Government, supported the bank, whereas the Europeans proposed to fund specific infrastructure projects without setting up the permanent apparatus of a bank. In the region, Egypt supported the bank, in no small part because it would be based in Cairo, and the Palestinians saw it as a means of concessionary-financing.[18] Jordan and Israel both saw the bank as a step forward in spurring regional economic development. The Gulf countries demurred, however, seeing the bank as another opportunity to extract more money from the Gulf countries, already struggling with deficits caused by low oil prices. The Report of the Middle East Economic Strategy Group supported the bank, but felt it should await more support from the region, meaning Saudi Arabia and the GCC.[19]

A bank charter was ratified and shares subscribed by a wide number of countries. However, the U.S. Congress failed to appropriate funds for the U.S. portion (21 percent) of startup capital. The Gulf countries never subscribed, and in December 1998, the nascent MENA Bank "which was supposed to be one of the proud pillars of grand regional projects, closed down, a victim of the impasse in the peace process and the refusal of the US Congress to finance the institution."[20]

Palestinian Economic Development

The Palestinians have not benefited from the MENA summits even though it was their agreement with Israel at Oslo in 1993 that made the summits possible. In a perverse way, the summits may have helped the Palestinians by highlighting the lack of economic development in the West Bank and Gaza. A focus on the Palestinian economy at the MENA summits made sense because Palestinian economic development supports political progress, which in turn is a prerequisite to lasting regional economic cooperation. Here is one area where economic cooperation could have helped the political track. In fact, the Palestinian economy received scant notice at Casablanca. The focus on the Palestinians in the next three Summits was limited to the plenary on Regional Infrastructure Projects, described earlier, the thematic discussion of the Middle East Economic Strategy Group Reports, and, except for the last summit in Doha (which the Palestinians officially boycotted), the country lunch for the Palestinians.

The MENA Summits were designed to expose private sector investors to opportunities in the region. The Palestinian Authority, in particular, wanted to see private sector investors from abroad, including wealthy and talented diaspora Palestinian entrepreneurs, begin investing in the West Bank and Gaza.

Political instability, especially Israeli border closures caused by terrorist bombings, have hindered investors. Even without closures, a businessperson with a plant in the West Bank and Gaza could not easily travel back and forth.[21] But Israeli closures and other security-driven actions do not explain the failure to attract investment. The lack of transparency and accountability in the Palestinian Authority's Ministries, the absence of a coherent and tested commerce law, arbitrary judicial procedures, and a non-business-friendly ethos within the Palestinian Authority explains much of the reticence. As important as attaining private sector investment is for the Palestinians, the building of institutions of self-government is a higher priority.[22]

The strategy for Palestinian economic development continues to rely on public sector donor support, illustrated most recently in the post-Wye Accord donor conference in Washington, D.C., on November 30, 1998. The United States, European Union, Japan, and other countries pledged an aggregate of $3.2 billion for the 1998–2003 period to develop the Palestinian economy. The United States doubled its previous commitment made at the original donor conference in October 1993. With that kind of international governmental support, there is less urgency on the part of the Palestinians to seek out private sector investors at MENA summits.

Host Country Reform

One of the positive benefits of the MENA summits, particularly in Amman and Cairo, is the way reform-minded ministers and private sector leaders used the international spotlight on the host country provided by the summits to push through regulatory reforms, privatization measures, and trade liberalization policies to facilitate greater foreign investment. While it may be true that Egypt and Jordan would have adopted the reforms without having hosted the MENA Summit, the international attention and desire of the host countries to make the summits succeed *accelerated* the enactment of those reforms. Host country reforms were contagious, generating consideration of economic reform in other countries of the region that attended the summits.

Host country reform has a political benefit to Israel as well. The private sectors in Jordan and Egypt represent a constituency for peace. They draw power away from the military and government bureaucracies, and from the intelligentsia (which is the group that is least pro-Israeli). This pro-peace constituency depends on national economic growth made possible by reform.[23] The summits put the spotlight on the private sector and the need for the public sector to listen to and work in partnership with the private sector. The expanding influence of the private sector, and its supporters among reform-minded ministers, spurs greater global and regional economic integration which, in turn, helps their national economies grow. [24]

Political Issues

The role of heads of state and foreign ministers at the Summit plenary sessions has always been controversial. On the one hand, King Hassan, Shimon Peres, Tancu Ciller (Turkey's Prime Minister at the time of Casablanca), Madeleine Albright and other political leaders add star quality to the Summit, giving Casablanca an aura not conveyed at the Abu Dhabi Air Show. Yet, the plenary speeches by Arab and Israeli leaders have politicized the Summit and diverted attention from economic issues. In Casablanca, Rabin took umbrage after Arafat declared in the opening plenary that East Jerusalem was Palestinian. Rabin's brusque words in reaction to Arafat's speech soured the mood of many Arab business participants. In Amman, Foreign Minister Amre Moussa of Egypt publicly accused Jordan of chasing after Israel. Even though the political track of the peace process was going relatively well at that time, those verbal jousts cast a pall on the proceedings.

At the same time, the participation of trade, industry, and finance ministers was an important asset. Their presence facilitated critical dialogue with the private sector on economic policy and reforms relating to investments, regulatory procedures, and tariff-reduction. The presence of government officials also helped attract executives from major multinational corporations. Business leaders want to meet government officials "in order to get first-hand information on the actual situation and more particularly to assess the 'political risk' associated with their economic decisions."[25]

Business Community's Desire for Further Economic Conferences

The business community in the region, together with their supporters within governments, are the constituents for continuing regional economic conferences. International business executives find MENA regional economic conferences to be a useful vehicle for developing contacts with regional companies. Conferences provide an opportunity not only to cement existing relationships, but also to expand the pool of investors who might decide to join those already investing in the region.

Conversely, business leaders worry that the absence of *any* regional economic gathering would send a message to the international and regional business community that the Middle East and North Africa are once again "closed for business."[26]

Private sector leaders will seek some way to hold conferences to promote regional economic development in the absence of a MENA Summit. They can count on the support of reform-oriented ministers who want to accelerate the pace of structural reform. Reformers believe that the region's integration into the global economy would be unnecessarily delayed if regional economic reform were held hostage to the political fortunes of the peace process.

A View from Jordan

For Jordan, regional cooperation is an economic imperative to provide markets for its exports. Jordan has a population of only four million, and its trade with Iraq is limited by UN sanctions. Jordan needs incremental trade with Israeli, West Bank and Gulf markets.[27] The MENA Summit legitimizes Jordanian trade with Israel in the context of wider regional economic development, and exposes foreign investors to opportunities in Jordan.

A View from Egypt

For Egypt, its much larger population makes regional trade less critical. In the first two summits, Israel was seen in the words of Ephraim Sneh, as "a linchpin to regional integration."[28] In the 1996 Cairo Summit, however, Israeli integration into the region was downplayed in an effort by Egypt to emphasize foreign investment into Egypt. Held shortly after Netanyahu's election, the Egyptian government showed that it could achieve economic reform and open up to the world, while largely ignoring Israel.

Egyptian and Israeli business leaders attempted to fill the vacuum created by the absence of any Israeli minister at the Cairo Summit with the exception of then-Minster of Economy, Dan Meridor. The business leaders attending the Summit formed a joint business council, in part, to lobby their respective governments to get the peace process back on track. Most of the Israeli business leaders serving on those councils, however, come from the Labor Party and had minimal influence on Netanyahu.[29]

For the Egyptians and most Arabs, the MENA Summit was viewed as a necessary reward to Israel. Absent the huge effort by the U.S. government to include Israel, most Arab states prefer to pursue regional mechanisms that exclude Israel. They perceive Israel as both intransigent in the political track and a potential economic heavyweight or hegemonic power in any regional mechanism.[30] They see no point in holding a proxy or mini-MENA economic summit until the political situation will have improved sufficiently to allow broad Arab participation, including Syria and Lebanon, the two countries bordering Israel that have boycotted all of the MENA Summits.

In the meantime, the Egyptian government will discourage its business leaders from participating in any interim conference that can be seen as a backdoor to a MENA Summit. Egypt has less objection to a smaller meeting, independent of government sponsorship, to focus on economic issues. Such a gathering would not be seen as a subterfuge for a MENA Summit. The rationale for the meeting is not to cement the integration of Israel into the region but to foster much-needed foreign investment into the region.

The View from Israel

It is not only Egypt and other Arab governments that oppose the MENA summits. Prime Minister Netanyahu is less sanguine than his predecessor, Shimon Peres, about the political value of regional economic cooperation. In Netanyahu's view, real peace and security with Israel's Arab neighbors will come only after they mature politically into democracies.[31] Although the Netanyahu government did not oppose the MENA Summit, they pursued it less avidly than their predecessor, Shimon Peres, who was one of MENA's chief architects.

Many in the Israel electorate, particularly the mizrachim, react negatively to Shimon Peres's vision of a New Middle East based on Jewish brains, Gulf capital, and

Arab labor. This backlash is part of a fear among many Israelis about normalizing, integrating, and entering the post-Zionist era. A significant part of that fear, I believe, is the prospect of living next to a State of Palestine.

Conclusion

The reality is that the stalled peace process makes impossible a MENA Summit in the region. Egypt and other Arab governments are determined to prevent Israel's economic integration into the region from getting ahead of political normalization.

What happens to regional cooperation in the meantime? Arguably, a postponement of all regional economic meetings might somehow induce the governments to restore momentum on the political track. But this argument assumes that regional economic cooperation and integration is a high priority in the Israel and the Arab world. The foregoing analysis suggests that it is not.

The spirit of Casablanca that celebrated the integration of Israel into the Middle East and North Africa region has withered since the change of government in Israel in May 1996. This is not to say that Israel gains nothing from the MENA Economic Summits or regional economic cooperation. Peace or no peace, regional economic development makes possible structural reform within individual Arab countries. Israel becomes more secure as its poorer neighbors are able to develop the necessary infrastructure and competitiveness to connect into the global marketplace.

The attraction of foreign investment into the Arab world and the economic transformation of Arab countries from state-dominated to export-oriented economies will make the region more secure if only because the new Arab business class and their allies in government will lobby harder against waging any conflict that would jeopardize their newly-created economic assets.

Israel is also more attractive to multinational corporations and other foreign investors if it can serve as a hub for wider trade in the region. In the uncertain hiatus after four reasonably successful regional economic summits, these companies are less likely to invest in Israel if the Middle East and North Africa region appears closed down for business.

Notes

1. See note 17 for list of members of the group. All three reports were issued by the Council on Foreign Relations. The Middle East Economic Strategy Group was meeting to discuss regional trade on September 27, 1996, when Palestinian riots broke out over the opening of the tunnel in Jerusalem. The group decided to incorporate its discussion of the Palestinian dimension in an Addendum to the 1996 Report entitled, "Recommendations on the Palestinian economy."

2. The Council on Foreign Relations U.S./Middle East Project, directed by Henry Siegman, convened the meeting on May 15, 1998, at the request of the International Steering Committee of the MENA Summit, chaired by the U.S. Department of State. The Evaluation Meeting included senior officials from Israel, Jordan, Egypt, and other countries in the region.

3. This phrase was used in Henry Siegman's address at the closing plenary of the Doha Economic Summit in November 1997.

4. Gershon Shafir made the distinction in a conversation with me in September 1997.

5. Ablatif Al Hamad, director of the Kuwait-based Arab Fund for Economic and Social Development, pointed out in a meeting of the Council's Middle East Economic Strategy Group in New York on March 15, 1995, that none of the existing Arab regional mechanisms were particularly successful at reducing high intra-regional tariffs, convoluted customs laws, and bureaucratic red tape which, in his view, caused the region to lag behind other emerging markets in the world.

6. Meeting with Council on Foreign Relations mission in Jerusalem, May 3, 1998.

7. Meeting with Dan Gillerman in Tel Aviv, May 2, 1998. Gillerman made the important point that stereotypes of Arabs held by Israeli businessmen were broken by the personal contact.

8. He stated this in his meeting with the Council on Foreign Relations Mission in Jeddah, April 29, 1998. He is reported to have made the same point in a meeting with an ADL delegation in the fall of 1998, as reported in *Jewish Week*, December 1998.

9. See unpublished Report on Evaluation of MENA Economic Summits, Council on Foreign Relations, May 1998 (hereafter "Report on MENA Evaluation").

10. Ibid.

11. Ibid.

12. Salah was only in his twenties at the time he became the first Jordanian to form joint ventures with Israeli companies. He was criticized heavily by other Jordanians, particularly in the press and professional unions, for getting ahead of the political track. Conversely, he was lionized by the pro-MENA Summit constituency, and even hosted by President Clinton in Washington.

13. One Israeli tourist operator introduced to me by Omar Salah proposed to transport by bus Muslim Indonesians on Haj from Amman to Jerusalem for Umra (pilgrimage) to Muslim holy sites. Royal Jordanian Airlines would fly the pilgrims from Jeddah to Amman. At the end of the Umra, upon returning by bus to Amman from Jerusalem, Royal Jordanian would fly the pilgrims to Jakarta, Indonesia, via Kuala Lumpur, Malaysia.

14. From Feiler to the author dated January 3, 1999.

15. The largest joint venture between Israel and an Arab country is the Merhav Group's venture with Egypt in Midor, an oil refinery in Alexandria.

16. The travel association, known as MEMMTA and based in Tunis, is one of the regional institutions to survive. The chamber of regional business councils was supposed to be based in Israel, but never got off the ground. The MENA Executive Secretariat, based in Rabat, Morocco, and designed to provide a database on regional projects and to be a resource base in between summits, effectively closed down after the Doha Summit. The International Steering Committee for the MENA Summits was the official multilateral entity for deciding on the location of the summits and reviewing the Summit Declaration issued at the end of each summit. Gaining consensus for the Doha Declaration was especially arduous in light of the Qatari desire to show the Arab world that its hosting of the summit did not represent acquiescence in Israeli policies.

17. Members of the Council on Foreign Relations Middle East Economic Strategy Group, chaired by Paul A. Volcker, included Jawad Anani, Jordan, Prof. Haim Ben-Shahar, Israel, Richard A. Debs, United States, Attila Karaosmanoglu, Turkey, Yoh Kurosawa, Japan, Prof.

Manfred Lahnstein,Germany, Said El-Naggar and Taher Helmy, Egypt, Abdulaziz O'Hali, Saudi Arabia, Francois Xavier Ortoli, France, Franco Reviglio, Italy, Felix Rohatyn, United States, William Ryrie, United Kingdom. Prominent public sector leaders served on the Group's Advisory Board, comprising Andre Azoulay and Mustapha Terrab, Morocco, Caio Koch-Weser and Kemal Dervis, World Bank, Stanley Fischer, IMF, Jacob Frenkel, Governor of Central Bank of Israel, and Abdlatif Al-Hamad, Director of the Arab Fund for Economic and Social Development, Kuwait. The Council on Foreign Relations Staff of the Middle East Economic Strategy Group comprised Henry Siegman, Director, Jonathan Paris, Project Co-ordinator, and Albert Fishlow, Economist. The full Group met three times in 1995, once in 1996, and once in 1997.

18. Such below-market rate financing is available through World Bank subsidiaries. The charter of the MENA Bank did provide for concessionary financing, but it was not the central thrust of the MENA Bank, which the U.S. Treasury designed to be like a lean and mean merchant bank with relatively low paid-in capital. The designers sought to avoid the heavily bureaucratic and public sector oriented ERBD based in Europe.

19. The Report on New Financing Institutions for the MENA Region was presented by Paul Volcker, former Chairman of the U.S. Federal Reserve Bank and Chair of the Middle East Economic Strategy Group, at the Amman Economic Summit in November 1995.

20. Agence France Presse, reprinted in *Ha'aretz* English edition, December 17, 1998.

21. This problem will be ameliorated with the opening of a safe passage road connecting Gaza and the West Bank. Safe passage was one of the key concessions that Israel made, in addition to permitting the opening of the Gaza airport, at the Wye River negotiations in November, 1998.

22. This point is more fully developed in the Report of the Council-sponsored Independent Task Force on Strengthening Palestinian Institutions (1999), which offers practical recommendations for improving Palestinian public institutions.

23. Ehud Yaari developed this theme of the New Arab Class in an address to Tel Aviv University in 1997.

24. This was the core premise of the Middle East Economic Strategy Group Report on "Trade Arrangements in the Middle East and North Africa" (Council on Foreign Relations 1996). The greater the trade among countries in the MENA region, the greater the impetus to both lower tariffs and undertake economic restructuring. The other conclusion of the report is that regional integration, when non-discriminatory and positive (i.e. reducing tariffs), reinforces trade with the wider world and encourages integration of individual MENA countries into the global economy.

25. See Report on MENA Evaluation, infra.

26. See Report on MENA Evaluation, infra.

27. Economists refer to Jordan, Israel, and the Palestinian Authority as forming an economic triad. Nadav Halevi of Hebrew University presented a paper on this topic, entitled "Trade Prospects in the Triad" for the Middle East Economic Strategy Group meeting on September 28, 1996.

28. Conversation at the Council on Foreign Relations in 1997.

*economic hegemony. If peace breaks out in the region, Egypt wants to slow regional cooperation for fear that Israeli companies will run roughshod over their less competitive Arab counterparts. If the political stalemate continues, economic normalization cannot get ahead of political normalization.

31. Martin Kramer, director of the Dayan Center of Tel Aviv University, made this point in a presentation to the Council on Foreign Relations Mission in Tel Aviv on May 2, 1998.

Index